Web-Based Intelligent E-Learning Systems:
Technologies and Applications

Table of Contents

Web-Based Intelligent E-Learning Systems:
Technologies and Applications

Zongmin Ma
Northeastern University, China

MA, ZONGMIN

Web-based Intelligent E-learning Systems

London: Information Science   1591407303

 Information Science Publishing

Hershey • London • Melbourne • Singapore

Acquisitions Editor: Michelle Potter
Development Editor: Kristin Roth
Senior Managing Editor: Amanda Appicello
Managing Editor: Jennifer Neidig
Copy Editor: Jane Conley
Typesetter: Cindy Consonery
Cover Design: Lisa Tosheff
Printed at: Integrated Book Technology

Published in the United States of America by
    Information Science Publishing (an imprint of Idea Group Inc.)
    701 E. Chocolate Avenue
    Hershey PA 17033
    Tel: 717-533-8845
    Fax: 717-533-8661
    E-mail: cust@idea-group.com
    Web site: http://www.idea-group.com

and in the United Kingdom by
    Information Science Publishing (an imprint of Idea Group Inc.)
    3 Henrietta Street
    Covent Garden
    London WC2E 8LU
    Tel: 44 20 7240 0856
    Fax: 44 20 7379 0609
    Web site: http://www.eurospanonline.com

Library of Congress Cataloging-in-Publication Data

Web-based intelligent e-learning systems : technologies and applications / Zongmin Ma, editor.
    p. cm.
  Summary: "This book offers a complete understanding of the notions, techniques, and methods related to the research and developments of web-based e-learning systems"--Provided by publisher.
  Includes bibliographical references and index.
  ISBN 1-59140-729-X (hardcover) -- ISBN 1-59140-730-3 (soft cover) -- ISBN 1-59140-731-1 (ebook)
  1. Web-based instruction--Design. 2. Education--Computer network resources. 3. Educational technology. I. Ma, Zongmin, 1965-
  LB1044.87.W434 2006
  371.33'44678--dc22
                 2005020187

British Cataloguing in Publication Data
A Cataloguing in Publication record for this book is available from the British Library.

All work contributed to this book is new, previously-unpublished material. The views expressed in this book are those of the authors, but not necessarily of the publisher.

Section II

Preface

Many organizations, private companies, and academic and education institutions currently devote a substantial part of their capital to employee or student training. Computer-based training/learning tools offer a cost-effective solution. Advances in information and communication technologies and, specifically, in Multimedia, Networking and Software Engineering allow the apparition of a new generation of computer-based training systems. Intelligent Tutoring Systems (ITSs) form an advanced generation of Computer-Aided Instruction (CAI) systems. Their key feature is their ability to provide a user-adapted presentation of the teaching material. ITSs have been developed and evaluated for many years in the field of artificial intelligence in education. The emergence of the World Wide Web increased the usefulness of such systems.

Internet is today the ubiquitous supporting environment for virtual and distributed learning environments. As a consequence, many institutions, both public and private, take advantage of new technologies to offer training products and services at all levels. Compared with the classical educational methods, learning over the Internet, that is, Web-based learning/training, has some advantages. First, the individual who wants to learn is not restricted by his/her geographical location or time limitation. Second, a person who can quickly grasp the subject matter need not wait for others to understand too, which is not possible in a typical classroom environment. At the same time, a person who is a little slow may take the course at his or her own pace. Third, courses developed for the Web may prove cheaper than hiring a qualified teacher each time the course is administered.

However, just putting a tutorial online does not provide education in the real sense. There is always a need for communication between the tutor and the students as well as among students. Therefore, facilities such conferencing, mailing, bulletin boards, and so forth need to be sensibly applied and integrated with the course material. The course conducted may also be a combination of classroom sessions and the Internet. More important, the Web-based learning/training systems should be very similar to human tutor. So such systems should be more intelligent through the adoption of artificial intelligence and cognitive science techniques. The Web-based intelligent e-learning systems are interdisciplinary in nature, related closely to such fields as artificial intelligence (decision making, machine learning, planning, and scheduling), cognitive science, software engineering, Web-based information systems, and education.

On the other hand, with the increasing popularity of e-learning systems, the proliferation of interoperability e-learning specifications raises the need to extend existing e-learning platforms so that they can be used efficiently in a distributed environment where material producers, service providers, and users (either learners or teachers) exchange information using standard models. The interoperability consequence of the proliferation of Web-based e-learning systems is being considered by key standardization institutions and the most relevant educational software consumers worldwide. Up to this date, proposals are available for the standardization of information models, such as educational metadata or course structures. Specifications and standards serve to build standard-driven distributed and interoperable learning systems.

This book focuses on the technologies and applications of Web-based intelligent e-learning systems and presents the latest research, development, and application results in Web-based intelligent e-learning systems. In addition to the architecture of systems, interface design, teaching and learning strategies, some major issues on the theories, key techniques, design, implementation, and applications of Web-based intelligent e-learning systems are investigated in the book. The different chapters in the book have been contributed by different authors and provide possible solutions for the different types of technological problems concerning Web-based intelligent e-learning. Each of the contributors to the book is a leading researcher in the field of Web-based intelligent e-learning who has made numerous contributions to Web-based e-learning.

Introduction

This book consists of 17 chapters organized into two major sections. The first section discusses the issues of the theories, key technologies, and designs of Web-based intelligent e-learning systems in the first thirteen chapters. The next four chapters covering the development, implementation, and application issues in Web-based intelligent e-learning systems comprise the second section.

First of all, we take a look at the problems of the theories, key technologies, and designs of Web-based intelligent e-learning systems.

Inductive reasoning ability is one of most important mental abilities that give rise to human intelligence and is regarded as the best predictor for academic performance. However, most of the adaptive virtual learning environments tailor the learning material adaptively according to only learners' domain performance thus leaving learner's cognitive capacity, such as inductive reasoning ability, unsupported. In Chapter I, Kinshuk, Lin, and McNab present a framework of adaptive support for inductive reasoning ability in virtual learning environment based on researches in cognitive science. The authors discuss the use of the adaptive theory, Exploration Space Control, and adaptive techniques to achieve the adaptivity required in detail.

Focusing on Adaptive Educational Hypermedia (AEH) authoring, in Chapter II, Cristea and Stewart describe advances in *intra*-system automation using the LAOS framework, whereby an author is only required to create a small amount of educational material which then automatically propagates throughout the system. The authors also describe advances in *inter*-system conversions; the aim is to move away from a "create once, use once" authoring paradigm, currently in force with most AEH systems, towards a "create once, use many" paradigm. The goal is to allow authors to use their content in the AEH delivery system of their choice, irrespective of the original authoring environment. As a step along this road, the authors describe the usage of a single authoring environment (MOT) to deliver content in three independently designed Educational Hypermedia systems (AHA!, WHURLE, and SCORM-compliant Blackboard).

Automatic courseware authoring is recognized as among the most interesting research questions in intelligent Web-based education. Automatic courseware authoring is the process of automatic learning object selection and sequencing. In most intelligent learning systems that incorporate course sequencing techniques, learning object selection and sequencing is based on a set of teaching rules according to the cognitive style or learning preferences of the learners. In spite of the fact that most of these rules are generic (i.e., domain independent), there are no well-defined and commonly accepted rules on how the learning objects should be selected and how they should be sequenced to make "instructional sense." Moreover, in order to design adaptive learning systems, a huge set of rules is required, since dependencies between educational characteristics of learning objects and learners are rather complex. Karampiperis and Sampson address the learning object selection and sequencing problem in intelligent learning systems in Chapter III, proposing a methodology that—instead of forcing an instructional designer to manually define the set of selection and sequencing rules—produces a decision model that mimics the way the designer decides, based on the observation of the designer's reaction over a small-scale learning object selection case.

Augar, Raitman, Lanham, and Zhou introduce the concept of virtual learning communities in Chapter IV and discuss and further enhance the theory and definitions presented in related literature. A model comprising four criteria essential to virtual learning communities is presented and discussed in detail. Theory and case studies relating to the impact of virtual learning communities on distance education and students from diverse cultural groups are also examined. In addition, the authors investigate the enabling technologies and facilitation that is required to build virtual learning communities. Other case studies are used to illustrate the process of building virtual learning communities. Emerging technologies such as wikis and video lectures are also analyzed to determine the effects they have on building and sustaining effective virtual learning communities.

Learning is more than knowledge acquisition; it often involves the active participation of the learner in a variety of knowledge- and skills-based learning and training activities. Interactive multimedia technology can support the variety of interaction channels and languages required to facilitate interactive learning and teaching. A conceptual architecture for interactive educational multimedia can support the development of such multimedia systems. Such an architecture needs to embed multimedia technology into a coherent educational context. Pahl investigates the development of interactive educational multimedia as a platform to implement activity-based learning and training through a conceptual architecture in Chapter V. This architecture is open to further extensions, integration with other frameworks and standards, and adaptations to particular needs.

Jaques and Viccari put their focus on the current state of the art of the e-learning systems that consider the student's affect in Chapter VI. The authors present the perspectives adopted by the researchers for the solution of the problems (for example, which kind of tools we might use to recognize users' emotions) and also some better-known works in order to exemplify. It also describes the necessary background to understand these studies that involves some concepts on Artificial Intelligence, Computer in Education, and Human-Computer Interaction research fields, as well as a brief introduction on the main theories about emotion. The authors also present challenges and the main difficulties of the research in affectivity in e-learning systems and ideas on some new work on the matter.

In Chapter VII, Carbonaro introduces how to use a Web-based hybrid recommender system developed with a collaborative bookmark management system approach. The system combines content analysis and the development of virtual clusters of students and of educational sources. It provides facilitation in the use of huge amount of digital information stored in a distributed learning environment on the basis of the student's personal requirements and interests. By adopting a hybrid approach, the system is able to effectively filter relevant resources from a wide heterogeneous environment like the Web, taking advantage of the common interests of the users and also maintaining the benefits provided by content analysis.

MetaLinks is a domain-independent authoring tool and Web server for adaptive textbooks ("hyperbooks") that supports active reading. Murray shows how cognitive and educational research and theory from the areas of text comprehension and active reading strategies can be applied to hyperbooks in Chapter VIII. Adaptivity and other MetaLinks features allow us to create a single hyperbook that serves multiple purposes. A MetaLinks hyperbook can serve as textbook and reference book, can be equally appropriate for novice and advanced readers, and can be coherently read from a number of thematic perspectives. "Active reading/learning" refers to a set of high-level reading, searching, problem-solving, and metacognitive skills. The author describes the MetaLinks system and how its features support a number of behavioral, cognitive, and metacognitive active reading skills.

Hatzilygeroudis and Prentzas deal with knowledge representation in intelligent educational systems (IESs) in Chapter IX. The authors make an effort to define requirements for knowledge representation (KR) in an IES. The requirements concern all stages of an IES's life cycle (construction, operation, and maintenance), all types of users (experts, engineers, and learners) and all its modules (domain knowledge, user model, and pedagogical model). The authors also briefly present and compare various KR schemes as far as the specified KR requirements are concerned. It appears that various hybrid approaches to knowledge representation can satisfy the requirements in a greater degree than that of single representations. Another finding is that there is not a hybrid scheme that can satisfy the requirements of all the modules of an IES. So, multiple representations or a multi-paradigm representation environment could provide a solution to requirements satisfaction.

Combining methods of Artificial Intelligence and Cognitive Science led to the development of ITSs more than 30 years ago. In contrast to the common agreement about the ITSs' architecture, components of ITSs are rarely reusable. Reusability in ITSs is intimately connected with the application domain, that is, with the contents that should be learned and with the teaching and learning strategy. An example of a learning strategy is case-based learning, where the adaptation of the learning material to the learner plays a major role. Adaptation should take place automatically at run-time, and thus should be part of the ITS's functionality. To support the development of ITS with reusable components and the communication about and the evaluation of similar ITS, a formal approach is chosen. This approach is called the tutoring process model. In Chapter X, Martens describes a formal, adaptive tutoring process model for case-based ITSs.

Current standardized e-learning systems are centred on the concept of learning object. Unfortunately, specifications and standards in the field do not provide details about the use of well-known knowledge representations for the sake of automating some processes, like selection and composition of learning objects or adaptation to the user or platform. Precise usage specifications for ontologies in e-learning would foster automation in learning systems, but this requires concrete, machine-oriented interpretations for metadata elements. In Chapter XI, Sánchez-Alonso, Sicilia, and García put their focus on ontologies as shared knowledge representations that can be used to obtain enhanced learning object metadata records in order to enable automated or semi-automated consistent processes inside Learning Management Systems. In particular, the authors present two efforts towards enhancing automation: a contractual approach based on pre- and post-conditions, and the so-called process conformance profiles.

The fast development of technologies requires specialized and complex skills that need to be renewed frequently. Thus, the role of continuing education and lifelong learning is becoming still more important. E-learning adapts well for continued education as it can be done in parallel to other work. This in turn sets new requirements for universities: they have to build e-learning infrastructures, and course material has to be in digital form. Moreover, the e-learning systems should be designed in a way that they provide easy access to courses and course material. A cornerstone of easy access is the metadata attached to courses and other relevant elements. However, the mere metadata itself is not very useful without the ontology that gives the semantics for the metadata. Puustjärvi gives an overview of the role of metadata and ontologies in e-learning systems in Chapter XII. The author also considers the standards of educational metadata and the utilization of metadata and ontologies in three e-learning systems.

As e-Learning gets more widespread, its definition is becoming more distinctive, implying the use of the Web for learning. The Web's original functionality was to provide access to materials located in servers. This has been the core strategy for e-Learning. However, the Web is becoming more versatile. The new interactive Web functionalities are organized in services offered to users. The content-based Learning Management Systems are evolving into more interactive systems providing agent-like learning services rather than only learning content. By designing an interactive environment with a learning objective, we can develop an effective e-Learning appliance: the application of strategic Web functionalities on a technologically enhanced learning environment. Ortega and Sánchez-Villalón present AWLA in Chapter XIII. Designed under the constructivist perspective, AWLA is an organized set of interactive Web-based utilities that—when applied in a technologically enhanced learning environment—allow learners to develop their writing skill in language learning and fulfill writing activities in any other discipline, both individually and in collaboration.

In the second section, we see some development, implementation, and application issues of Web-based intelligent e-learning systems.

The North Dakota State University (NDSU) World Wide Web Instructional Committee (WWWIC) is an inter-disciplinary research team that since the 1990s has developed multi-user, interactive virtual environments (IVEs) to teach the structure and process of various branches of science. The most developed of these include the "Geology Explorer" and the "Virtual Cell," (VCell). In Chapter XIV, Daniels et al. describe the key features the Virtual Cell and the Geology Explorer, the underlying philosophy and educational theory guiding their development, and results of large controlled experiments that investigate their effectiveness on student learning. Additionally, ongoing projects and experiments of the team relevant to the development and dissemination of these software programs are explored.

In Chapter XV, Bouras, Nani, Panagopoulos, and Tsiatsos present the design and implementation of an integrated platform for Educational Virtual Environments. This platform aims to support an educational community, synchronous online courses in multi-user three-dimensional (3D) environments, and the creation and access of asynchronous courses through a learning content management system. In order to offer synchronous courses, the authors have implemented a system called EVE-II, which supports stable event sharing for multi-user 3D places, easy creation of multi-user 3D places, H.323-based voice-over IP services fully integrated in a 3D space and as many concurrent 3D multi-user spaces.

Woolf and Stern describe Web-based instructional tutors that support active and engaging learning in Chapter XVI. Towards that end, a theoretical foundation for designing such tutors is proposed and two Web-based tutors described. The tutors reason about a student's knowledge and their own teaching strategies while taking advantage of the possibilities of the Web by being open to other resources (Web sites) and other people (online communities). One tutor, Rashi, provides problem-based activities and tracks a student's critical thinking in biology and geology, and the second, iMANIC, uses hypermedia to customize online lectures for individual students based on learning need. This work provides promising data points for the development of authentic and effective learning that can take advantage of the possibilities of the Web, without being rooted in extensions of what already exists in the classroom, such as lectures or bulletin boards.

Kordaki presents the concept of Special Purpose E-Learning Environments (SPELEs) in Chapter XVII. The main aim of these environments is to meet the learners' individual learning differences related to a specific learning subject. The author presents an architecture of the design of SPELEs. The background of this design, which is based on interpretations of modern constructivist and social views of learning in the Internet context, is also presented. Based on this architecture, a specific SPELE, designed to the learning of concepts related to Files and Peripheral Storage Devices (F.P.S.D.), is demonstrated and its pilot evaluation study with real students is reported. The analysis of the data verifies the theoretical design of SPELEs, which consists of five parts: (a) organization of the content of a specific learning subject, (b) learning activities, (c) learner activity space, (d) learner assessment, and (e) learner communication. The analysis of the data also gives evidence for future improvements of the specific SPELE mentioned above.

Acknowledgments

The editor would like to acknowledge the help of all involved in the collation and review process of the book, without whose support the project could not have been satisfactorily completed. A further special note of thanks goes also to all the staff at Idea Group Publishing, whose contributions throughout the whole process—from inception of the initial idea to final publication—have been invaluable.

Most of the authors of chapters included in this book also served as referees for papers written by other authors. Thanks go to all those who provided constructive and comprehensive reviews.

Special thanks also go to the publishing team at Idea Group Publishing and, in particular, to Mehdi Khosrow-Pour, whose enthusiasm initially motivated me to accept his invitation for taking on this project, and to Michele Rossi, who continuously prodded via e-mail to keep the project on schedule.

In closing, I wish to thank all of the authors for their insights and excellent contributions to this book. I also want to thank all of the people who assisted in the reviewing process. In particular, I'd like to thank Taiyu Lin, Ali Fawaz Shareef, and Michael Verhaart from Massey University, New Zealand, and Jarkko Suhonen from University of Joenssu, Finland. In addition, this book would not have been possible without the ongoing professional support from Mehdi Khosrow-Pour and Jan Travers at Idea Group Publishing.

Zongmin Ma, PhD
Shenyang, China
February 2005

Section I

Chapter I

Adaptive Support for Inductive Reasoning Ability

Kinshuk
Massey University, New Zealand

Taiyu Lin
Massey University, New Zealand

Paul McNab
Online Learning System Ltd, New Zealand

Abstract

Inductive reasoning ability is one of most important mental abilities that give rise to human intelligence and is regarded as the best predictor for academic performance. However, most adaptive virtual learning environments tailor the learning material adaptively according to the learner's domain performance only, thus leaving the learner's cognitive capacity, such as inductive reasoning ability, unsupported. This chapter presents a framework of adaptive support for inductive reasoning ability in a virtual learning environment based on researches in cognitive science. The use of the adaptive theory, Exploration Space Control, and adaptive techniques to achieve the adaptivity required is discussed in detail. A summarising discussion points out future research possibilities and concludes the chapter.

Introduction

Adaptive virtual learning environments, such as adaptive hypermedia systems (e.g., AST by Specht, Weber, Heitmeyer, & Schoch, 1997; and InterSim by Kinshuk, Oppermann, Patel, & Kashihara, 1999) and intelligent tutoring systems (e.g., WBITS by Yang, Kinshuk, and Patel, 2002; and ISIS-Tutor by Brusilovsky and Pesin, 1998), tailor the learning material adaptively according to learners' needs and characteristics. Most of the research on adaptivity emphasises only the issue of how adaptivity should be provided according to the domain performance of the learner. A learner's cognitive skills, such as inductive reasoning ability and working memory capacity, are of great importance to the learning process but are often overlooked and unsupported in most learning systems (Lin, Kinshuk, & Patel, 2003).

In student-centred learning environments, learners are expected to take the initiatives in learning and construct their own knowledge with facilitation from teachers, peers, and/ or with the help of computer-based learning systems. In these environments, the learner's inductive reasoning ability acts as a cognitive tool used for the construction of knowledge, thus bearing great influence on the learning experience and the outcomes. Adaptive support for inductive reasoning ability is therefore a very important facility for the learners. Research on cognitive trait model (Lin, Kinshuk, & Patel, 2003) has attempted to profile the learner's cognitive attributes, such as inductive reasoning ability and working memory capacity, in order to allow virtual learning environments to provide learning materials adapted to an individual learner's cognitive capacity.

Inductive reasoning is one of the important characteristics of human intelligence. Researchers have regarded inductive reasoning as one of the seven primary mental abilities that account for intelligent behaviours (Selst, 2003). Pallegrino and Glaster noted that the inductive reasoning ability can be extracted in most aptitude and intelligent tests and is the best predictor for academic performance (Harverty, Koedinger, Klahr, & Alibali, 2000). Harverty et al. (2000) cited several other research works that viewed inductive reasoning as a significant factor for problem solving, concept learning, mathematics learning, and development of expertise. Heller, Heller, Henderson, Kuo, and Yerushalmi's (2001) research showed that inductive reasoning is a necessary ability for extracting the knowledge of problem solving in physics.

Despite the recognised importance of inductive reasoning underlying the learning process of human beings, there is very little research available on how to support the inductive reasoning process in virtual learning environments (Lin, Kinshuk, & Patel, 2003). Existing methods for providing adaptivity in learning systems do not consider the individual differences in learners' inductive reasoning ability. This chapter aims to address this issue and attempts to fill the gap between research on advanced adaptive techniques and research of human induction in cognitive psychology. The chapter will: (1) examine closely the characteristics of inductive reasoning ability, (2) enumerate a list of patterns of activities that could be used to find out a student's inductive reasoning ability, and (3) propose a framework of adaptivity to support inductive reasoning ability.

In order to find out the characteristics of inductive reasoning ability, research in many fields, including cognitive science, psychometrics, and machine learning, is examined. Working memory capacity (Holland, Holyoak, Nisbett, & Thagard, 1987; Lin, Kinshuk,

& Patel, 2003), the ability to learn from analogy (Holland et al., 1987), hypothesis generation, and domain knowledge (Harverty et al., 2000; SGW, 1996) have all been found to bear direct influence on human inductive reasoning process, and exhibition of these attributes during the learner's interaction with the virtual learning environments can be a source for inferring and modelling the inductive reasoning ability of the learner.

Once a model of inductive reasoning ability of the learner is developed, it is then possible to raise the question of how the learning environment should respond and adapt to suit the needs of the learners with regard to their individual inductive reasoning abilities. The rest of the chapter aims to address this question. Derived from the work of Exploration Space Control (Kashihara, Kinshuk, Oppermann, Rashev, & Simm, 2000) and Multiple Representation Approach (Kinshuk et al., 1999), a set of parameters, including number of paths, relevance of paths, amount of content, concreteness of content, structureness of content, and number of information resources, is obtained. This set of parameters can be used to adapt both the presentation and navigation of the learning material. A framework is proposed providing a prescription on how these parameters should be adjusted based on the level of inductive reasoning ability of the learner. The discussion will also include how different adaptive techniques are suitable and can be used to support inductive reasoning.

Characteristics of Inductive Reasoning

Harverty et al.'s (2000) study in the domain of mathematics proposed that there are three main activities in inductive reasoning process:

- data gathering,

- pattern finding, and

- hypothesis generation.

Data gathering refers to the pre-inductive preparatory activities that, if properly carried out, can optimise the inductive reasoning. Research has confirmed that external organisation of data can indeed affect the result of internal inductive reasoning (Wexler, 1999). Pattern finding is, according to Holland et al. (1987), detection of co-variation from a stack of samples (or past experiences). In the research done by Heller et al. (2001), the instructors believed that the attainment of problem-solving skills in physics comes from reflective practices to extract knowledge from previous experiences of working on other problems or from sample problem solutions. Both data gathering and pattern finding are the preliminary steps for hypothesis generation.

Harverty et al. (2000) observed the behaviours of the subjects in their experiment of mathematical function finding and noted that subjects who successfully completed the task employed common solution strategies. In the experiment, subjects were asked to find the mathematical formula (in terms of y and x) given the data of the formula. One solution strategy is local hypothesis strategy, in which subjects formed a local hypothesis from a single instance of data and tested whether the local hypothesis works for other data instances as well. The subjects may have to generate and test many local hypothesises before they can find one that works. However, this strategy is useful in finding the elements of the global hypothesis (solution), and combination of the elements could lead to greater chance of successfully finding the formula. The action of finding one local hypothesis and testing if it works for other data instances is in fact a process of pattern finding. A mathematical formula is constructed by its elements, which are algebraic expressions translated from observed patterns, and a certain pattern of behaviour of the formula can be defined by an element of the formula; for example, $(x-3)$ is an element of the formula $y = (x-3)(x/2)$. Finding both the elements and the relationship of the elements is sufficient to find the formula.

Another strategy that the subjects employed to successfully solve the problem was called the pursuit strategy (Harverty et al., 2000). In pursuit strategy, subjects found a pattern expressed in quantity(ies), Q, in addition to the original quantities (x and y). The subjects then tried to understand the formula using Q, and decided whether Q is worthy to pursue or not. In this process, there could be more than one q in Q. If the formula could be understood in Q, then the subject tried to translate Q in terms of x and perform the test on the global hypothesis to see if the corresponding y value could be found correctly for each x value. Harverty et al. (2000) found that the pursuit strategy is the most popular one, and that it worked by finding intermediate quantity(ies), Q, so that the behaviour of the formula could be understood in an easier way than its original quantities, and then by trying to understand the Q in terms of the original quantities. Q is supposed to be easier to understand than y, and hence it transforms a complex process into many simpler ones. By finding the right q(s) and combining them correctly, an algebraic equivalent expression of the formula can be achieved. The q(s) are analogous to the puzzle pieces for the formula (Harverty et al, 2000).

Klauer (Harverty et al., 2000, p. 251) summarised and classified the tasks of inductive reasoning that the participants were required to do in psychometric tests (including series-completion problems, Raven matrices, classification problem, and analogy problems, for inductive reasoning ability) and proposed a system for classifying inductive reasoning tasks. Klauer's system is listed below:

- **Generalisation:** Detect similarity of attributes
- **Discrimination:** Detect differences of attributes
- **Cross classify:** Detect similarity and differences in attributes
- **Recognise relationships:** Detect similarity of relationships
- **Differentiate relationships:** Detect differences in relationships
- **System construction:** Detect similarity and differences in relationships

In Klauer's system, there is a corresponding cognitive operation (e.g., detect similarity of attributes) for each of the task (e.g., generalisation). The system excludes the task related to data gathering, probably due to its pre-inductive nature, and places much more emphasis on pattern finding. The tasks of generalisation, discrimination, and cross classify are for the detection of patterns in attributes, whereas the tasks of recognise and differentiate relationships aim for the recognition of reoccurring patterns in relationships.

Thus far, characteristics of inductive reasoning had been studied in its own nature. Further in this chapter, characteristics of inductive reasoning will be examined in relation to prior domain knowledge, human-learning process, working-memory capacity, use of analogy, and hypothesis generation. The aim is to find out manifestations of inductive reasoning ability that demonstrate the level of learner's inductive reasoning ability. The manifestations can then be translated into learner behaviours that are observable using browsing pattern-analysis methods.

Knowledge Background and Induction

SGW (1996) noted that the prior domain knowledge influences the inductive behaviour of the learner in addition to the general intellectual ability to make induction. The latter is referred as generic knowledge that is domain independent. SGW (1996, ¶ 8) cited Klahr and Dunbar's Scientific Discovery as Dual Search (SDDS) theory, which postulated that discovery activities can be located in either of the two spaces: hypothesis space (HS) and experiment space (ES). They used these two spaces to analyse the discovery behaviours of the learner. SGW further correlated the predicted behaviours of the learners with different level of generic knowledge and domain knowledge, both in terms of high and low, to the two spaces stated in the SDDS theory. The categorisation is shown in Table 1.

In a discovery task aimed at a problem solution, High Generic Knowledge/High Domain Knowledge (HGK/LDK) learners will typically start by searching hypothesis space because they would already have an understanding of the variables in the problem domain. Their focus would be on the selection or creation of a hypothesis that could be applied to the problem at hand, and they would go to the experiment space only to validate their hypothesis. Learning effect is best for this kind of learners.

Low Generic Knowledge/High Domain Knowledge (LGK/HDK) learners may start by searching the hypothesis space because of the high stack of relevant domain knowledge. However, due to the lack of a systematic approach, they would fail to discover the right relationship among the objects, hence they would fail to select or create the right hypothesis to apply. They would be forced to search in the experiment space and would go back and forth between the two spaces until they found the solution.

High Generic Knowledge/Low Domain Knowledge (HGK/LDK) learners will typically start with experiment space due to their lack of understanding of the domain variables. However, they will gradually discover the working patterns of the variables and start to work in the hypothesis space and gradually become learners of HGK/HDK.

Low Generic Knowledge/Low Domain Knowledge learners would probably start with experiment space. Due to their lack of understanding about the domain and the inability to discover/induce new knowledge from systematic patterns, they will struggle and

Table 1. Learner categorisation (SGW, 1996)

Domain Knowledge \ Generic Knowledge	High (HGK)	Low (LGK)
High (HDK)	Start with Hypothesis Space, only goes into Experiment Space to test the validity of hypothesis.	Constant switching between Hypothesis Space and Experiment Space
Low (LDK)	Start with Experiment Space and gradually into Hypothesis space	Stay and Struggle in the Experiment Space

remain in the experiment space. Learning effect of the discovery task aimed at a problem solution is therefore the worst for learners of this kind. Learning efficiency decreases from HGK/HDK to HGK/LDK to LGK/HDK to LGK/LDK (SGW, 1996).

In additional to the finding of SGW (1996), other research has also demonstrated the link between inductive reasoning ability and domain knowledge. Heit (2000) showed that one form of inductive reasoning—the diversity-based reasoning—is demonstrated less by children than by adults, but further comparison of American adults and Itzaj adults (who resided in Guatemala, Central America, and had no formal education) showed that diversity-based reasoning depends not only on cognitive processing capacity but on learned knowledge as well.

Human Learning and Induction

The term induction is derived from the Latin rendering of Aristotle's *epagoge* that is the process of moving to a generalisation from its specific instances (Rescher, 1980). Bransford, Brown, Cocking, Donovan, and Pellegrino (2000) pointed out that generalisations aimed at increasing transferability of learning can result in (mathematical) models or global hypothesis that, in Harverty et al.'s (2000) term, can be applied to a variety of contexts in an efficient manner.

Zhu and Simon pointed out that the learner has to induce how and when to apply the problem-solving method from worked-out examples to novel problem situations (Harverty et al., 2000). In addition, the learner also needs to induce where to apply the learned knowledge in order to apply the knowledge successfully or creatively. It thus follows that induction happens to a number of aspects of learning: from the more superficial learning (the know-how), to the contextually aware and deeper learning (the know-when and know-where) where reasoned mental models are formed.

Transferability of learning is regarded as an important part on how people develop competencies (Bransford et al., 2000). Transferability refers to the ability to apply the problem-solving skill, which can contain only conceptual knowledge obtained from case studies or procedural knowledge obtained from previous hands-on exercise in the lab, in a novel context. Previous procedural knowledge does not guarantee the ability to solve a problem in a novel context, nor does mere understanding of concepts. Thus curriculum with focus on transferability tries to provide as much context of the problem/case studies as possible to increase the success rate of transferring problem-solving knowledge to new contexts. The student creates a set of different mental models all related to the concept under scrutiny from the set of different contexts. Context variables are encoded to differentiate one mental model from another.

Often, transferability is used as a measure of the quality of learning (Bransford et al., 2000). For the assessment of the transferability to be fair, a "new" context must differ from any previously experienced contexts, but the differences can neither be 0% nor 100%— there must be similarities between the contexts. And it is up to the learner to induce which learned mental model to apply to current task at hand. Selecting an appropriate mental model to apply requires pattern matching. Pattern matching will be discussed in further detail later in the chapter, however, it is important to note that the individual difference in the performance of pattern matching can be explained in Holland, Holyoak, Nisbett, and Thagard's (1987) "adaptive default hierarchy" of mental models.

Holland et al. (1987) proposed a rule-based mental model as a framework for explaining human induction behaviour. They postulated that there is a general default set of rules for every mental model, such as a permission mental model has the following rule: "If X is true then Y is allowed." For example, a Chocolate-Permission mental model for a child could be like this: "If Mom says I cannot have chocolate, then I am not allowed to have the chocolate." Their framework is adaptive because it allows exceptions to exist within a mental model to form a sub-level mental model. A sub-mental model could be created under the Chocolate-Permission mental model, for example, "If Mom says I cannot have chocolate, and Dad is present and does not confirm her, then I am allowed to have the chocolate." The sub mental model can have further sub-mental models and thus forms a hierarchy of mental models. The mental models in the higher level of the hierarchy are usually more general mental models, and in the lower levels more specific. The number of rules in the higher level is less than the ones in the lower level.

Induction to search for which mental model is applicable in a given situation requires the comparison of the rules in a mental model to the variables observed in the environments. In Holland et al.'s (1987) point of view, a match during the comparison indicates a successful induction, whereas no match means the desired result could not be induced. Comparison speed is highly related to working memory capacity and will be discussed next.

Working Memory Capacity and Induction

Salthouse et al. (1989) proposed that working memory consist of (1) a storage capacity sensitive to the number of items presented, and (2) an operational capacity sensitive to the number of operations performed on items. Salthouse et al. (1989) found that young adults have higher operational capacity than older adults especially among the highly capable participants. Little or no difference was reported on the storage capacity across the age differences. Therefore, they concluded, at that time, that it was the operational capacity that causes age-related working memory decline. A further study of the operational efficiency of working memory showed, however, that it was not the operational capacity (number of operations allowed) that contributed most to the efficiency of working memory, but it actually was the speed of execution, such as comparison speed, that determined the performance of the overall system of working memory (Salthouse & Babcock, 1991). It thus logically follows that that higher working memory capacity lays the foundation to higher inductive reasoning ability.

Other evidence suggesting that the relation of inductive reasoning ability to working memory capacity is the fact that external representation (what a learner sees) can indeed influence one's internal cognitive processes. Wexler (1999) gave the example of how rearranging a card in one's hand to reduce the load of working memory renders the relation of the cards more perceptually salient and hence aids induction. It brings up the point that a human being's cognitive capacity is limited in nature. One important factor to be able to perform generalization, as a form of induction, is to remember the particulars and their attributes. This remembering certainly has to take up the available working memory capacity if external representation in any form is not available. Therefore, it is plausible to postulate that the efficiency of inductive reasoning depends also on working memory capacity.

Analogy and Induction

Use of analogy also plays an important role for inductive reasoning. Researchers of instructional technology had long recognised the important value of using analogies or parallel concepts to support understanding of important concepts. Kinshuk, Oppermann, Patel, and Kashihara (1999) identified the parallel concept link as one of the major six types of navigational links in Web-based educational systems.

Holland et al. (1987) pointed out that analogous thinking enables one to view a novel situation using familiar concepts, and showed that many great scientific discoveries could be attributed to the use of analogy as a basis for induction. The wave nature of light was discovered by drawing an analogy to the wave of liquid for observed properties such as reflection and diffraction. Analogy, in their view, provides an already-structured framework for the information available in the new context to fill in. Structural information and the information on how operations can change the problem state are readily available from the analogy and thus greatly facilitate the learning process. Metaphors, according to their perspective, serve a similar role.

Hypothesis and Induction

Hypothesis formation is an essential step for induction, whether the hypothesis is local or global. A hypothesis, once formed, can then be proved to become part of legitimate knowledge or disapproved to allow identification of wrong path. Either way, it contributes, directly or indirectly, to overall knowledge building in the learning process.

However, an hypothesis primarily exists only as a mental construct for students when they are reading or exploring to learn. This then poses a great problem for any online learning system to detect the formation of hypothesis since there is no explicit way to examine what is happening in the learner's mind. However, once the learner has constructed an hypothesis, he or she will need to confirm it, whether the result of confirmation is positive or negative. According to Popper (cited by Holland et al. 1987, p. 328), a philosopher of science, the primary function of scientific laws and theories is prediction. "The process of inductive reasoning which moves from an observed uniformity across the examined cases of a certain sort to the conclusion that all cases of this sort have the feature in question" (Rescher, 1980, p. 39).

The rationale of an hypothesis is primarily based on the observed pattern from the data gathered. Without the activity to confirm an hypothesis, it can never be proved or disproved. As a result, these loose cognitive structures are deemed as the source of fundamental attribution error, by which "people's judgment strategies in the social domain, like their empirical rules in the physical domain, are defective" (Holland et al., 1987, p. 222). The loose cognitive structures are accountable for wrong judgements and predictions at later time when this cognitive structure is used as a basis of induction. Thus, it follows that, in the case of learner's online learning experience, the lack of the action to confirm an hypothesis is functionally equivalent to no hypothesis at all.

Manifestations of Inductive Reasoning Ability

Based on the previous discussion, certain behaviours of learners, called the manifestations, can be used to approximate the level of their inductive reasoning abilities. The manifestations of inductive reasoning are summarised as follows:

1. Higher generalisation ability manifests higher inductive reasoning ability.

2. Inability to learn from analogy manifests lower inductive reasoning ability.

3. Activities to confirm hypothesises indicate the formation of hypotheses and therefore manifest higher inductive reasoning ability.

4. Higher domain knowledge manifests higher inductive reasoning ability.

5. Higher working memory capacity manifests higher inductive reasoning ability.

Manifestations listed are made detectable by a technique called relation-based browsing pattern analysis (Kinshuk, Lin, & Patel, 2003), which can perform domain-independent browsing pattern analysis based on the relations of learning objects defined in the Learning Object Model (LTSC, 2002). Manifestations 1, 2, and 3 will be translated into patterns defined by learning object relations, whereas manifestations 4 and 5 can be retrieved from the student models in the virtual learning environment. Each of the manifestations of inductive reasoning ability will be discussed in more detail next.

Generalisation Skill as a Manifestation of Inductive Reasoning Ability

Generalisation skill denotes the ability to abstract consistent patterns from row phenomena. The generalised pattern is assumed to be applicable to other similar situations by a human's intuitive assumption about the regularity of the world. The assumption of nature's regularity may be erroneous, as some have argued, but it obviously contributed to the survival of the fox in the *Aesop's Fable*, "The Sick Lion." When the fox sees only the footprints of other animals *entering* the old Lion's den, supposedly to pay their respects to the dying lion, but none *returning*, he wisely elects not to go in, thereby avoiding the trap set by the Lion—namely, being devoured. For positivists, "scientists were supposed to closely observe nature, looking for regular occurrences and reliable correlations" (Leahey, 1997, p.6).

The observed row phenomena are often examples or case studies trying to demonstrate underlying principles in a more memorable manner, namely, in adequate context. The measure of this skill is determined by whether the learner can generalise the principles correctly from the presented examples or not. The relations of learning object required are the HasExample, and IsExampleOf. Therefore, the statement of "higher generalisation ability manifests higher inductive reasoning ability" can be translated to:

HasExample (O) $\rightarrow$ ... $\rightarrow$ **Pass (O)**

Where   **O** is a learning object,

$\rightarrow$ means followed by,

HasExample (O) is the activation of the HasExample relation of **O**,

Pass (O) is the function to determine whether **O** is passed after the evaluation,

... indicates other relations that are not take into account for this manifest.

The function Pass(O) evaluates whether the student has correctly answered the questions in the evaluation unit that contains learning object O. If Pass(O) is true, it indicates that the learner has successful generalised, and hence has higher inductive reasoning ability, whereas the opposite (i.e., Pass(O) is false) is the manifestation of lower inductive reasoning ability.

Analogy as a Manifestation of Inductive Reasoning Ability

Inducing and hence understanding the theories could be facilitated by use of analogies. Analogy presents the learner an alternative perspective to look at current concepts. This alternative point of view provides a certain degree of familiarity from already learned knowledge to make solving the present problem or learning the present concept earlier. Concepts analogous to the current concept at hand are implemented by parallel concept links that lead to "the analogous domain unit for comparative learning or to the unit related to another aspect of the currently being learnt domain content" (Kinshuk et al., 1999.

An example of a parallel concept to the concept of how sound waves travel in air could link to an explanation of how waves travel in a pond. By first seeing the already familiar analogy of a pond wave and then presented with the new concept of a sound wave, the student certainly has a higher possibility to induce the properties of sound wave. Therefore, the statement of "inability to learn from analogy manifests low inductive reasoning ability" can be translated, in terms of learning object relations, into:

Parallel (O) $\rightarrow$ ... $\rightarrow$ Fail (O)

Where   **O** is an learning object,

$\rightarrow$ means followed by,

Parallel (O) is the activation of an parallel concept link of **O**,

Fail (O) is the function to determine whether **O** is failed after the evaluation

... indicates other relations that is not take into account for this manifest.

The function Fail(O) evaluates whether the learner has failed in the evaluation unit that contains learning object O. If Fail(O) is true, it indicates that the learner is unable to induce from analogy, and hence has lower inductive reasoning ability, and the opposite (i.e., Fail(O) is false) is the manifestation of high inductive reasoning ability.

Hypothesis Generation as a Manifestation of Inductive Reasoning Ability

In online learning systems, learners can view an example of a concept by using a link with a HasExample relation that brings the learner to the example of that concept. The reverse of a HasExample relation is the IsExampleOf relation. If any of the hypothesis is formed during the viewing of the example learning object, the best way to confirm it is to follow the IsExampleOf relation back to the original theoretical learning object. Thus, this navigational pattern can be used to detect the existence of this manifestation.

The statement of "activities to confirm hypotheses indicate the formation of hypotheses and therefore manifest higher inductive reasoning ability" can be translated into:

HasExample(O) → IsExampleOf (O')

Where   **O** is a learning object,

        O' is the example that the **HasExample(O)** links to,

        → means followed by,

        HasExample(O) is the activation of an HasExample relation of **O,**

        IsExampleOf(O') is the activation of an IsExampleOf relation of **O'.**

The above navigational pattern can be interpreted as the learner ability to navigate to the theoretical explanation in order to confirm hypothesis, thus demonstrating the act of hypothesis generation.

Domain Knowledge as a Manifestation of Inductive Reasoning Ability

Domain knowledge is confirmed to bear influence over the inductive reason process (Heit, 2000; SGW, 1996). Domain knowledge—though beyond the scope of this discussion—is available in many learning systems in the form of performance-based models (Martin, 1999; Staff, 2001). The representational value of the domain competence can be retrieved from the performance-based model of the learning environment and used as a factor to determine how well the learner can perform induction in this domain. It would be an interface problem rather than a theoretical problem, and hence not addressed in this article.

Working Memory Capacity as a Manifestation of Inductive Reasoning Ability

Working memory capacity had been identified as an influential factor to the inductive reasoning process in the previous discussion. Working memory capacity is anther cognitive trait that had been modelled by cognitive trait model (Lin, Kinshuk, Patel, 2003), and the value of the learner's working memory capacity is readily available as part of cognitive trait model.

Adaptive Framework for Induction

The discussion above focused on how to determine the inductive reasoning ability of the learners. The purpose for the elaborate research and technique to estimate the learner's inductive reasoning ability is to allow learning systems to be able to adapt the learning material to suit the particular learner based on inductive reasoning ability. Existing research results are already available for the information structure of hypermedia-based virtual learning environments, and can be used as a foundation by which the information structure can be manipulated and tailored to the learner's inductive reasoning ability. Kashihara, Kinshuk, Oppermann, Rashev, and Simm (2000) proposed such a theory, called exploration space control (ESC), in order to support exploratory learning in multimedia-based educational systems. Exploration space control will be discussed, followed by the proposed adaptive framework for supporting inductive reasoning.

Exploration Space Control

Exploration is a self-directed process and is an effective way of learning (Carroll, Mack, Lewis, Grischkowsky, & Robertson, 1985). Exploratory learning, which involves searching the information, navigation through the learning space, understanding domain-related conceptual knowledge, and acquiring skills, often requires a high cognitive effort on the part of the learner.

Exploration space control (ESC) attempts to limit the learning space, called exploration space, to control the students' cognitive load at an adequate level, depending on their learning approaches. ESC tries to facilitate adequate learning for a whole spectrum of learning competence by adopting two extreme approaches—active learning support and step-by-step learning support.

Active learning support offers an initial learning space as wide as possible, using only those restrictions that are required to protect the students from cognitive overload, and adding or removing restrictions according to students' progress. This approach fits the students with higher competence levels and greater familiarity and experiences of the domain, for example, those who come back for further education after working in an area related to the domain.

The step-by-step learning support adopts an opposite approach from active learning support by starting with as restricted information space as possible and then gradually enlarging it. This approach provides a sense of comfort and security for those who are completely new to the domain area or do not have active learning styles. By the combination of these two approaches, "ESC can be employed to facilitate proper learning for all types of learners" (Kashihara et al., 2000).

Exploration Space Control Elements

The aim of ESC is to provide guidance to the instructional designers who wish to have their instructional systems equipped with adaptive and customisation functionalities.

Table 1. Exploration space control elements

Category	Element
Path/Links	Number
	Relevance
Content	Amount (detail)
	Concreteness
	Structureness
Info Resource	Number

Table 2. Types of link and their relevance to the domain

Types of link	Relevance to the domain
1. Direct successor link	
2. Fine-grained link	
3. Glossary link	
4. Problem link	
5. Parallel concept link	
6. Excursion link	

Exploration space control elements (ESCEs) are those parameters on both the learning content and navigational paths that could be modified to create different presentations/views of the same materials to suit different needs.

Therefore, the selection of the exploration space control elements (ESCEs) has to cover both the content presentational and navigational aspect of the learning material. Table 1 attempts to list some of these parameters.

There are two elements related to the path—the number of the paths and the relevance of the paths. Relevance of path can be rated using the categorisation of six types of navigational paths identified by Kinshuk et al. (1999) as listed in Table 2.

Links with higher relevancy are those that are closely related to the domain (such as direct successor and fine-grained links), while the links with lower relevancy are to the concepts that are more of a supplementary nature (such as excursion links). The category of path (Table 1) covers both the number of paths and their relevance. The "number of paths" represents the amount of links to be presented to the students, and the "relevance of paths" guides how relevant the linked targets should be and the proportions of various types of links (Table 2).

In Table 1, there are three ESCEs for the category of content: the amount/detail, the concreteness, and structureness. Amount/detail of content decides how detailed the knowledge presentation is. The degree of detail affects the volume of the presentation, therefore, both of them are classified as only one ESCE.

The concreteness determines the abstract level of the information. The more concrete a piece of information is, the more fundamentals and examples it should include. Abstraction refers to the opposite of the concreteness.

The structureness of information indicates the ordering, arrangement, and sequencing of the information presented as a series/set of concepts. Concepts may or may not be directly or indirectly related to each other with certain sequence. The elaboration theory (Reigeluth, 1992) suggested a structured approach by stating that the instruction should be organized in increasing order of complexity for optimal learning. The more structured the information is, the more orderly the fashion in which it can be presented. Structured information helps the learner in building up the mental model, but provides less freedom for free navigation.

Another category in Table 1 is information resource. Information could be presented by different media, such as text, audio, visual, and so on. The effect of each medium for presenting information is different. "Audio is good to stimulate imagination, video clips for action information, text to convey details whereas diagrams are good to convey ideas" (Kinshuk et al., 1999). In addition, each media type has a different impact on each individual's learning. If there is more than one medium (e.g., a textual explanation and a chart), the information will be more impressive and easier to remember. The greater the number of information resources, the more choices the system has for selection to suit the students' characteristics.

The list of exploration space control elements provides a set of parameters that can be used to modify the learning materials. Once the list of elements identified, the question can be asked about how each of the elements should be changed to support students with different abilities of inductive reasoning. A framework is proposed to address this question and is discussed next.

Framework of Adaptive Learning Supporting Inductive Reasoning

Induction is the generation of the rules/theories/principles from observed instances of event. It is a bottom-up approach and has an open-ended and exploratory nature. The research on inductive reasoning skill (Bower & Hilgard, 1981; Heit, 2000) shows that the higher the inductive reasoning ability, the easier it is to build up the mental model of the information perceived.

A mental model is a cognitive structure that "provides meaning and organization to experiences and allows the individual to go beyond the information given" (Kearsley, 1998). From the constructivist's point of view, the learner's selection/transformation of information, construction of hypotheses, and decision-making processes all rely on a mental model (Bruner, 1973). It is easier for learners who possess better inductive reasoning skills to recognize a previously known pattern, generalize higher-order rules and, as a result, the load on working memory is reduced. Consequently, the learning process is more efficient and performance is better.

For educational value, there is a need to specify the means to support learners with lower inductive reasoning skill and to maximize the learning performance for those who are already good at induction. The following sections will address separately how the exploration space control elements should be adjusted for different groups of learners (poor or good inductive reasoning ability).

When the Learner's Inductive Reasoning Skill is Poor

The number of links—in particular, example links and parallel concept links—should be increased to give the learner more opportunity to observe how concepts are applied in examples or are different from similar concepts. More stimulations of difference of contextual variables can promote inductive reasoning and make the learning more transferable to other contexts (Bransford et al., 2000). Following this line of logic, the relevance of links should be decreased and the concreteness of the information should be increased so the learner can have more diverse observations in order to promote induction.

The amount of information should be increased to give detailed and step-by-step explanations to the learners so they can see the occurrences of pattern easier. More detailed explanations also facilitate the build-up of a more robust hierarchy of mental models (Holland et al., 1986) the learners can use to test their understanding (at the stage of local hypothesis) and predict future events (at the stage of global hypothesis). A robust hierarchy of mental models provides higher tolerance to minor exceptions and can only be obtained when the teaching information is understood instead of only memorised.

The structure of the information should be increased so that it is easier for the learner to build up the mental model from the clues given in the structure of the information. Seeing the sequential relationship of the topics and relationships of concepts provides, in a sense, another set of implicit information that could be used to facilitate inductive reasoning about the nature of the domain. Experimentally, Wexler (1999) proved that using external representation (e.g., a visual semantic network of the topic) can indeed assist inductive reasoning.

Research on learning style also confirmed that individuals respond differently to different modes of information (Liu & Ginther, 1999). The number of information resources can be increased to provide a variety of modes of information so that there is a higher possibility that the concept to be learned can be associatively/analogically matched to a previously learned concept, and hence increases the possibility for successful induction (Holland et al., 1987).

When the Learner's Inductive Reasoning Skill is Good

When the inductive reasoning ability of the learner is good, it is not necessary to present too many examples and analogies because they are only going to slow down the learning

Table 3. Adaptive framework addressing different ESCEs to different level of inductive reasoning ability

	Path		Content			Info Resource
Level	Number	Relevance	Amount	Concreteness	Structure	Number
Poor	\+	\-	+	+	+	\+
Good	\-	\	\	\-	\	\

process; the number of paths should therefore be decreased. Some adaptive techniques, such as stretch text (Boyle & Encarnacion, 1994) and link removal (De Bra, Brusilovsky, & Houben, 1999), are designed and have been proven to speed up the learning process for more able learners. The concreteness of the information should be decreased to avoid the learner boredom that can result from too many similar examples, and more abstracted explanation should be supplied.

The amount of the information, the structure of the information, the number of information resources, and the relevance of paths do not need to change, because changing them does not provide any direct support to the learner or can actually cause the reverse effect.

Table 3 summarises the above discussion of inductive reasoning skill and how the ESCE should/could be changed. The meanings of the symbol are: + means should be increased, \+ means could be increased, - means should be decreased, \- means could be decreased, and \ means no change.

Adaptive techniques for both adaptive navigational control and adaptive content presentation can be employed to achieve the effect required by the framework, and will be discussed next.

Adaptive Navigational Techniques and Inductive Reasoning Ability

Adaptive navigation focuses on building a customised navigational path for an individual learner. Adaptive navigation plays a supportive role and provides suggestions on how to go through the learning materials in a way that could suit the learner's needs and characteristics. Adaptive navigation is often presented as visual cues, and can be implemented as annotation, direct guidance, link filtering and re-ordering, link, and map adaptation (Eklund & Zeiliger, 1996).

A simple annotation could be highlighting the previously visited link(s). Annotation is generally used to augment a link with some form of hint/comment that tells about the link's destination. Annotation could be in textual form (Zao, O'Shea, & Fung, 1993) or as visual cues (Brusilovsky, 1994), and both can be used to support inductive reasoning ability: visual annotations can be used to provide suggested guidance to select the learning path that is tailored to the learner's inductive reasoning ability, whereas textual annotation can provide an explanation of why the suggestion is made.

Direct guidance recommends the best next learning unit for the learner on the basis of the information available in the learner model (Specht et al., 1997). It also involves the inference and consultation of the expert model, which contains the pedagogical information and rules, and the learner profile. This technique can help a learner to find an optimal path suitable for his or her inductive reasoning ability by simply clicking the next button.

Link filtering and re-ordering works like a filter. The most relevant link is displayed while the links with lower relevancy are hidden or displayed at the bottom of the page. The hiding removes those links that are less useful and thus reduces the amount and complexity of the information contained on the page. For learners who are good at induction, "the cognitive load of student required for the re-ordered page is less than if it is not, and speed up the learning process" (De Bra et al., 1999). On the contrary, a greater amount of information, such as example or analogy, offers a higher possibility that a previously learned mental model can be used as the basis of induction to the current concept, and thus is appropriate for learners who are not good at inductive reasoning. Less relevant links may be a distraction to some learners, but a great resource to stimulate inductive reasoning for others. Without taking into account a learner's inductive reasoning ability, use of adaptive techniques could render unexpected results.

The structureness of the information space (domain) should become more obvious to the learner through the use of adaptive techniques so that it is easier to build a mental model from the clues given in the structure of the information. Being able to see the semantic relationship of the concepts in the domain gives the learner another set of implicit information that could be use to facilitate inductive reasoning. Wexler (1999) proved that using external representation, such as a semantic network of the topic, can indeed assist inductive reasoning. Some hypermedia systems use graphic representations of the link structure, called a topic map. The whole map shows an overall view of the links/paths and their relationships with each other in a topic, and is a very good tool to facilitate reflection. In the study by Heller et al. (2001), instructors believed that the attainment of problem-solving skills in physics comes from reflective practices to extract knowledge from previous experiences of working on other problems or from sample problem solutions.

Adaptive Presentational Techniques and Inductive Reasoning Ability

"There is considerable evidence that different people learn best in different ways" (Kay & Kummerfeld, 1994, ¶ 2). It is very unlikely that one presentation style would suit all learners. Information can be presented in different abstract levels and has varied effects on a group of learners with diverse characteristics. For example, as described by Kay and Kummerfeld (1994), programmers tend to like very terse and extremely abstract presentations of new information, unlike non-programmers. Adaptive content presentation emphasizes the point that the presented learning content has to be tailored to the learner's needs for the optimal performance to occur.

Adaptive content presentation works at the content level: how the content is presented. The information contained in a Web page can be adapted to various details, difficulty, and media usage, and is aimed to suit learners with different needs, background knowledge, interaction styles, and cognitive characteristics (Recker, Ram, Shikano, Li, & Stasko, 1995).

Adaptive presentation on a page is often the manipulation of text fragments. The manipulation is aimed at "providing prerequisite, additional or comparative explanations" (De Bra et al., 1999). Conditional inclusion is one adaptive presentation technique where additional information is added according to the learner's attributes. The amount of information could be increased using this technique to give a detailed and step-by-step explanation to the learners so that it is easier for them to see the occurrences of pattern. More detailed explanation facilitates the build-up of a more robust hierarchy of mental models, which learners can use to test their understanding and predict future events (Holland et al., 1987).

Hothi and Hall (1998) introduced another technique called explanation variant, by which the level of difficulty, other related concepts, the length of the presentation, and media type can be adjusted according to the learner attributes. For learners who need more support in inductive reasoning, abstract information should be supplemented with concrete examples and case studies. Research on learning style has also confirmed that individuals respond differently to different modes of information (Liu & Ginther, 1999). The number of information resources could be increased to provide a variety of modes of information so that there is a higher possibility that the concept to be learned can be associatively/analogically matched to a previously learned concept and hence the possibility for induction is increased (Holland et al., 1987).

However, the additional inclusion technique can be replaced by another technique called stretch text (De Bra et al., 1999). By stretch text, each information fragment is represented by a short and visible "place holder" that can be stretched (information displayed) or shrunk (information hidden) so that all information is still available to learners who have higher inductive reasoning ability without too much visual distraction.

Summary

This chapter provides a comprehensive discussion on the nature and importance inductive reasoning ability in learner-centred virtual learning environments. The characteristics of inductive reasoning ability are examined along the dimensions of knowledge background, working memory capacity, ability to learn from analogy, hypothesis generation, and generalisation skill. Consequently, a list of manifestations of inductive reasoning ability is developed. The list includes the following:

1. Higher generalisation ability manifests higher inductive reasoning ability.

2. Inability to learn from analogy manifests lower inductive reasoning ability.

3. Activities to confirm hypotheses indicate the formation of hypotheses and therefore manifest higher inductive reasoning ability (Holland et al.,1987).

4. Higher domain knowledge manifests higher inductive reasoning ability.

5. Higher working memory capacity manifests higher inductive reasoning ability.

Each item in the list is then further translated into machine-detectable patterns or values available from student models so that they can be readily adopted in learning environments that aim to profile the learner's inductive reasoning ability.

Once the profile of the learner's inductive reasoning ability is available, the virtual learning environment can, based on the proposed adaptive framework, tailor the course to suit a particular learner's inductive reasoning ability by controlling the number of links, relevance of the links, amount of content, structure of the content, concreteness of the content, and the number of information resources. Adaptive techniques can be used to achieve the tailoring required.

Navigational adaptation provides learning support by manipulating the available links. It could take the form of annotation, direct guidance, link filtering and re-ordering, link, and/or map adaptation. Using adaptive navigation, the amount of links, relevance of the links, and visibility of the course structure can be controlled to suit the learner's inductive reasoning ability.

Adaptive content presentation concerns the adjustment of information content, often by manipulation of information fragments. Techniques used for adaptive content presentation includes conditional inclusion of fragments, stretch text, and explanation variant. Using adaptive content presentation, the amount of information, concreteness of the information, and number of information resources can be adjusted to assist learners with both good and poor inductive reasoning ability. The discussion in this chapter has also shown that the selection of adaptive techniques without consideration of the learner's cognitive capacity, such as inductive reasoning ability, sometimes can have the reverse effect.

More research along this line will be carried out to find out how other cognitive traits, such as associative learning ability and information process speed, can be modelled and how they can be supported using advanced adaptive techniques.

Acknowledgments

This research was supported by Online Learning Systems Ltd. in conjunction with the New Zealand Foundation for Research, Science & Technology.

References

Arthur, B. (1994). Inductive reasoning and bounded rationality. *American Economic Review, 84*, 406-411. Retrieved October 14, 2003, from *http://www.santafe.edu/arthur/Papers/El_Farol.html*

Bower, G. H. & Hilgard, E. R. (1981). *Theories of learning.* Englewood Cliffs, NJ: Prentice Hall.

Boyle, C. & Encarnacion, A. O. (1994). Metadoc: An adaptive hypertext reading system. *User Modeling and User-Adapted Interaction, 4*, 1-19.

Bransford, J. D., Brown, A. L., Cocking, R. R., Donovan, M. S., & Pellegrino, J. W. (2000). *How people learn: Brain, mind, experience, and school.* Washington, DC: National Academy Press.

Bruner, J. (1973). *Going beyond the information given.* New York: Norton.

Brusilovsky, P. (1994). The construction and application of student models in intelligent tutoring systems. *Computer and System Sciences International, 32*(1), 70-89.

Brusilovsky, P. & Pesin, L. (1998). Adaptive navigation support in educational hypermedia: An evaluation of the ISIS-tutor. *Journal of Computing and Information Technology, 6*(1), 27-38.

Carroll, J., Mack, R., Lewis, C., Grischkowsky, N., & Robertson, S. (1985). Exploring a word processor. *Journal of Human-Computer Interaction, 1*, 283-307.

De Bra, P., Brusilovsky, P., & Houben, G. J. (1999). Adaptive hypermedia: From systems to framework. *ACM Computing Surveys, 31*(4). Retrieved November 7, 2003, from *http://www.cs.brown.edu/memex/ACM_HypertextTestbed/papers/25.html*

Eklund, J. & Zeiliger, R. (1996). Navigating the Web: Possibilities and practicalities for adaptive navigational support. Retrieved November 7, 2003, from *http://ausweb.scu.edu.au/aw96/tech/eklund1/*

Harverty, L. A., Koedinger, K. R., Klahr, D., & Alibali, M. W. (2000). Solving inductive reasoning problems in mathematics: No-so-trivial pursuit. *Cognitive Science, 24*(2), 249-298. Retrieved October 14, 2003, from *http://12.238.20.107:5150/yb/cse5393/abstracts/haverty.pdf*

Heit, E. (2000). Properties of inductive reasoning. *Psychonomic Bulletin & Review.* Retrieved May 13, 2004, from *http://www-psych.stanford.edu/~jbt/205/heit.pdf*

Heller, P., Heller, K., Henderson, C., Kuo, V. H., & Yerushalmi, I. (2001). Instructors' beliefs and values about learning problem solving. Retrieved October 15, 2003, from *http://groups.physics.umn.edu/physed/Talks/Heller%20PERC01.pdf*

Holland, J., Holyoak, K. J., Nisbett, R. E., & Thagard, P. R. (1987). *Induction: Processes of inference, learning, and discovery.* London: The MIT Press.

Hothi, J. & Hall, W. (1998). An evaluation of adapted hypermedia techniques using static user modeling. In *Proceedings of the Second Workshop on Adaptive Hypertext and Hypermedia,* Pittsburgh, PA, June 20-24 (pp. 45-50).

Kashihara, A., Kinshuk, Oppermann, R., Rashev, R., & Simm, H. (2000). A cognitive load reduction approach to exploratory learning and its application to an interactive simulation-based learning system. *Journal of Educational Multimedia and Hypermedia, 9*(3), 253-276.

Kay, J. & Kummerfeld, R. J. (1994). An individualised course for the C programming language. Retrieved November 7, 2003, from *http://www.ncsa.uiuc.edu/SDG/IT94/Proceedings/Educ/kummerfeld/kummerfeld.html*

Kearsley, G. (1998). Theory into practice (TIP) database. Retrieved on May 13, 2004, from *http://www.gwu.edu/~tip/index.html*

Kinshuk, L. T. & Patel, A. (2003). User exploration based adaptation in adaptive learning systems. *International Journal of Information Systems in Education, 1*(1), 22-31.

Kinshuk, Oppermann, R., Patel, A., & Kashihara, A. (1999). Multiple representation approach in multimedia based intelligent educational systems. In S. P. Lajpie & M. Vivet (Eds.), *Artificial intelligence in education* (pp. 259-266). Amsterdam: ISO Press.

Leahey, T. H. (1997). *A history of psychology: Main currents in psychological thought* (4th ed.). Englewood Cliffs, NJ: Prentice-Hall.

Lin, T., Kinshuk, & Patel, A. (2003). Cognitive trait model for persistent student modelling. In D. Lassner & C. McNaught (Eds.), *EdMedia 2003 Conference Proceedings,* June 23-28, Honolulu, HA (pp. 2114-2147). Norfolk, VA: AACE.

Liu, Y. & Ginther, D. (1999). Cognitive styles and distance education. *Online Journal of Distance Learning Administration, 2*(3). State University of West Georgia, Distance Education. Retrieved May 14, 2004, from *http://www.westga.edu/~distance/liu23.html*

LTSC (2002). Draft standard for learning object metadata. Retrieved May 5, 2002, from *http://ltsc.ieee.org/doc/wg12/LOM_WD6_4.pdf*

Martin, B. (1999). Constraint-based modeling: Representing student knowledge. *New Zealand Journal of Computing, 7*(2), 30-38. Retrieved November 7, 2003, from *http://www.cosc.canterbury.ac.nz/~bim22/paper_nzjc.pdf*

Recker, M., Ram, A., Shikano, T., Li, G., & Stasko, J. (1995). Cognitive media types for multimedia information access. *Journal of Educational Multimedia and Hypermedia, 4*(2/3), 183-210.

Reigeluth, C. (1992). Elaborating the elaboration theory. *Educational Technology Research & Development, 40*(3), 80-86.

Rescher, N. (1980). *Induction.* Pittsburgh, PA: University of Pittsburgh Press.

Salthouse, T. A. & Babcock, R. (1991). Decomposing adult age differences in working memory. *Developmental Psychology, 27,* 763-776.

Salthouse, T. A., Mitcheel, D. R. D., Skovronek, E., & Babcock, R. L. (1989). Effects of adult age and working memory on reasoning abilities. *Journal of Experimental Psychology: Learning, Memory, and Cognition, 15,* 507-516.

Selst, M. (2003). Intelligence. Retrieved October 14, 2003, from *http://www.psych.sjsu.edu/~mvselst/courses/psyc235/lecture/chapter14intelligence.pdf*

SGW (1996). Inductive learning. Retrieved October 14, 2003, from *http://web.swi.psy.uva.nl/projects/il/NWO-AAN.html*

Specht, M., Weber, G., Heitmeyer, S., & Schöch, V. (1997). AST: Adaptive WWW-courseware for statistics. In P. Brusilovsky, J. Fink, & J. Kay (Eds.), *Proceedings of Workshop "Adaptive Systems and User Modeling on the World Wide Web" at 6th International Conference on User Modeling: UM97,* June 2, Chia Laguna, Sardinia, Italy (pp. 91-95).

Staff, C. (2001). *HyperContext: A framework for adaptive and adaptable hypertext.* PhD thesis, University of Sussex, Brighton, UK.

Wexler, M. (1999). Inductive learning with external representations. In A. Riegler & M. Peschl (Eds.), *Understanding representation*. New York: Plenum Press. Retrieved November 5, 2003, from *http://wexler.free.fr/papers/induction.pdf*

Yang, A., Kinshuk, & Patel, A. (2002). A plug-able Web-based intelligent tutoring system. *Proceedings of the Xth European Conference on Information Systems*, June 6-8, Gdadñsk, Poland (pp. 1422-1429). Gdadñsk, Poland: Wydawnictwo Uniwersytetu Gdanskiego.

Zao, Z., O'Shea, T., & Fung, P. (1993). Visualisation of semantic relations in hypertext systems. In T. Ottman & I. Tomek (Eds.), *Educational multimedia and hypermedia: Proceedings of Ed-Media 93* (pp. 556-564). Norfolk, VA: AACE.

Chapter II

Automatic Authoring of Adaptive Educational Hypermedia

Alexandra I. Cristea
Eindhoven University of Technology, The Netherlands

Craig Stewart
University of Nottingham, UK

Abstract

Adaptive Hypermedia (AH) can be considered the solution to the problems arising from the "one-size-fits-all" approach to information delivery prevalent throughout the WWW today. Adaptive Educational Hypermedia (AEH) aims to deliver educational content appropriate to each learner, adapted to his or her preference and educational background. The development of AEH authoring tools has lagged behind that of delivery systems. Recently, AEH authoring has come to the fore, with the aim of automating the complex task of AEH authoring, not only within a system but also porting material between different AEHs. Advances in intra-*system automation are described using the LAOS framework, whereby an author is only required to create a small amount of educational material that then automatically propagates throughout the system. Advances in* inter-*system conversions are also described; the aim is to move away from a "create once, use once" authoring paradigm currently in force with most AEH systems, towards a "create once, use many" paradigm. The goal is to allow authors to use their content in the AEH delivery system of their choice, irrespective of the original authoring environment. As a step along this road, we describe the usage of a single authoring environment (MOT) to deliver content in three independently-designed Educational Hypermedia systems—AHA!, WHURLE and SCORM-compliant Blackboard. Therefore, this chapter describes advances in automatic authoring and conversion towards a simple and flexible AEH authoring paradigm.*

Introduction to AEH Authoring

Adaptive hypermedia (AH) (Brusilovsky, 2001a) started as a spin-off of hypermedia and Intelligent Tutoring Systems (ITS) (Murray, 1999). Its goal was to bring the user model capacity of ITS into hypermedia. However, due to technical limitations, such as bandwidth and time constraints, AH only implemented simple user models. This simplicity also gave AH its power as, suddenly, there were many new application fields and also implementation was considerably easier. Early AH research concentrated on variations of simple techniques for adaptive response to changes in user model. No wonder that most of AH development was research oriented, applied only to the limited domain of courses the researchers themselves were giving (e.g., AHA!, De Bra & Calvi, 1998; Interbook, Brusilovsky, Eklund, & Schwarz, 1998; TANGOW, Carro, Pudilo, & Rodriguez, 2001) and with very rare commercial applications (e.g., Firefly, developed at MIT Media Lab and acquired by Microsoft).

Recently there has been a shift in attitudes. The development of the Semantic Web (Berners-Lee, 2003) and the ongoing push to develop Ontologies (Gruber, 1992) for knowledge domains has extended the importance of AH. Indeed, AH now appears to be the tool of choice for collating the static information of these new approaches and bringing then to life.

Moreover, AH is spreading from its traditional application domain—education—to others, especially the commercial realm, which is eager to be able to provide personalization for its customers. Indeed, we often see the phenomenon of other communities re-inventing adaptive hypermedia for their own purposes and applications.

Adaptive Educational Hypermedia (AEH) (Brusilovsky, 2001b) is, in principle, superior to regular Educational Hypermedia (EH) as it allows for personalization of the educational experience. Regular EH, such as that delivered by WebCT and Blackboard, is not adaptive—exactly the same lesson is delivered to each student. Pedagogical research has shown that different learners learn in different ways (Coffield, 2004). This is a truth self-evident to most teachers; if a student is having trouble learning a subject, then the teacher will alter the manner in which he or she is teaching it and try a different approach. Traditional EH systems could be compared to inflexible teachers who base their lesson mainly on drilling and repetition. Educational systems (real or virtual) that adapt their presentation to the needs of each learner aim to improve the efficiency and effectiveness of the learning process (Stach, Cristea, & De Bra, 2004). If each learner has his or her own Learning Style (Coffield, 2004) and is given a set of resources specific to that particular style then that learner will not only learn "better," but will be able to more effectively develop the given information into deeper understanding and knowledge. AEH systems seek to address the inflexibility of current EH methods. Systems such as My Online

Teacher (MOT), AHA!, and WHURLE all answer the need for an adaptive and flexible approach to teaching. They allow current online educational systems to break away from the "one-size-fits-all" mentality and move towards having an appropriate lesson for each student.

AEH systems aim to improve upon current static EH systems. This is not to say that AEH is the universal panacea for online education. Education is not undertaken in a vacuum; the social aspect is also vital. It is essential for learners: to be able to build common ground; to ask and answer (negotiate meaning); to argue and debate; to explicate mental models; to share expertise; to collaborate; and to construct novel ideas and understanding. Work on computer-supported cooperative work (CSCW) addresses this side of the educational process, and often AEH systems will fold this research into them (for example, WHURLE can be used in such a social manner). Collaborative work can be encouraged by the use of simple online social tools: e-mail, for asynchronous communications; fora, for persistent asynchronous group discussions; and chat rooms, for synchronous group discussions. The addition of Adaptation to this whole structure is another improvement to the student's personal online educational experience.

However, with increasing numbers of students and the resulting increase in class size of many learning bodies, traditional methods of education (such as the tutorial and the field trip) often become impractical in terms of time and cost. Online education can help to fill this need. EH and AEH were developed to do just this.

Given the qualities of AEH systems, it might be reasonable to expect a much wider uptake than actually is happening. A major hindrance of this is that the creation of good quality AEH is not trivial, often involving a greater expenditure of time and money to produce than standard online educational systems. Creating content within a single AEH system can be a complex and difficult undertaking.

Many issues must be considered, among them:

- What knowledge domain(s) will the lesson partake of?

- Do any previous e-learning materials exist that are both available and re-usable?

- What are the objectives of the lesson and how are they to be achieved for a heterogeneous group of learners?

- Which traits of a learner are to be modelled and how is this user model created?

- How is the data concerning these traits to be gathered, implicitly (without the learner's knowledge) or explicitly (information is requested from the learner)?

- Given that there exists a heterogeneous group of learners, how many versions of the same material need to be created? For example, if a group of learners are to be divided into two sub-groups, one that requires visual materials and the other that requires text-based materials, then it follows that at least two sets of the material will be required to teach that lesson.

- What are the rules for adaptation? Does the author of the lesson have any control over their use or creation?

- How are the various versions to be presented to the learner, and does the learner have any control over this?

Most AEH systems require the author to consider these issues with little or no help. The author is left adrift and often must become an expert in Adaptive Hypertext before creating anything.

It is hardly surprising then, that AEH systems are not used widely outside of their own development circles, as these developers are the only people with the required level of expertise to create content for them! This problem arose while AEH was still a new area of research. A natural "one-to-one" paradigm developed, with developers creating an AEH system that was specific to their desires and insights, along with the necessary authoring tools. Cross-platform considerations were not important; transporting data between systems was generally considered irrelevant.

Nowadays, a lot of research effort concentrates on the "authoring challenge" (Cristea & Cristea, 2004; Murray, 2003; Specht, Kravcik, Pesin, & Klemke, 2001; Wu, Houben, & DeBra, 1998; Cristea & De Bra, 2002) in AEH, with the goal of reducing complexity, thereby delivering the greater flexibility of an AEH for the same cost as current online systems. This chapter approaches this challenge from the point of view of automation, minimizing but not restricting the author's input and reducing overload.

Advances in *inter*-system conversions are also described, the aim being to move away from a "create once, use once" authoring paradigm, as with most AEH systems, towards a "create once, use often" paradigm. The goal is to allow authors to use their content in the AEH system of their choice, irrespective of the original authoring environment. As a step down this road, we describe using a single authoring environment (MOT) to deliver content in three independently designed Educational Hypermedia systems (AHA!, WHURLE, and SCORM-compliant Blackboard).

The remainder of this chapter is organized as follows. First, we present LAOS, a generic AH authoring framework that incorporates several layers of semantics to better express the authored AEH. The major part of this chapter focuses on the two major dimensions of AEH authoring automation that we have identified: automation within an AEH authoring environment, and automation outside it, comprising conversion between AEH systems. Finally, we draw conclusions.

LAOS Layered Model

The Layered AHS Authoring-Model and Operators (LAOS) model (Cristea & De Mooij, 2003b) (Figure 1) addresses the issue of AEH authoring complexity by dividing it into subtasks corresponding to five explicit semantic layers of adaptive hypermedia (authoring) that together act as a framework for designing an AEH.

These five semantic layers of LAOS are:

- **Domain model (DM)**, containing the basic *concepts* of the contents and their representation (such as learning resources).

- **Goal and constraints model (GM)**, a constrained version of the domain model. The constraints are based on educational goals and motivations.

- **User model (UM)**, represents a model of the learner's educational traits.

- **Adaptation model (AM)**, a more complex layer that determines the dynamics of the AH system. Traditionally, this layer is composed of IF-THEN rules and therefore the LAOS version also translates such rules at the lowest level.

- **Presentation model (PM)**, provided to reflect the physical properties and the environment of the presentation; it reflects choices, such as the appropriate background contrast to support a learner with poor eyesight.

Each of these semantic layers is composed of semantic elements. LAOS allows flexible (re-) composition of the defining semantic elements of the layers, according to each learner's personalization requirements. We are not going to go into details about the semantic elements, except for those directly used in internal automatic transformations or external conversion. At this point, it suffices to remark that the LAOS structure simply serves to make explicit the complex layers of an AEH system.

Such a detailed structure requires a lot of time to populate with AEH instances. As an alternative, we discuss semi-automatic authoring techniques (Cristea & De Mooij, 2003a), which populate the whole structure based on a small initial subset that has been authored by a human. Here we analyze two different possible initial subsets:

- **Internal semi-automatic authoring:** the theoretical analysis of the semi-automatic generation of one LAOS layer based on the content and structure of another one. The practical analysis of this is performed in MOT (My Online Teacher) (Cristea & De Mooij, 2003c). MOT can be downloaded from *http://adaptmot.sourceforge.net/* and a comprehensive MOT page (with links to downloads, papers, online trial systems) can be found at *http://www.is.win.tue.nl/~acristea/mot.html.* In short, we see this research line as another step towards adaptive hypermedia that "writes itself."

- **External semi-automatic authoring:** the theoretical and practical analysis of conversions between AEH authoring systems, such as MOT, into AEH delivery systems, such as AHA! and WHURLE (Moore, Brailsford, & Stewart, 2001) or educational systems, such as Blackboard. We examine the structures resulting from using a single authoring system to convert content for use in each system. In effect, we propose a paradigm shift for AEH authoring, away from "write once, use once" (i.e., every AEH has its own authoring systems) towards a middleware system that allows for delivery of the same material to many different AEHs. We describe the current "state of the art" towards this goal—using MOT as an authoring environment to deliver adaptive content to WHURLE and AHA! (also the connection to Blackboard).

Figure 1. LAOS adaptive hypermedia (authoring) framework

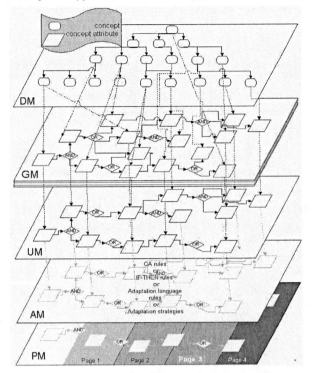

Transformations within an AEH System

Adaptive Educational material is obviously more difficult to create than linear educational material because of the alternative content versions and path descriptions. Therefore, we investigate the possibilities of automatic generation of some of the LAOS layers, using information from other layers. In the following sections, we will sketch some of these transformations, focussing on their semantics. The flexibility of general transformations has been addressed by Cristea (2004).

From Domain Model to Itself (DM→DM)

The DM contains the learning resources of the AEH, such as the actual course materials, figures, graphs, videos, and so forth. These resources are grouped under the domain concept to which they belong, using the established domain semantics. That is, resources are grouped into *attributes* of given (rhetoric or other) *types*, such as "text," "introduction," "conclusion," "figure," and the like. The DM also contains the *links* between the semantic wrappers of the domain resources, such as links between concepts, grouping them into concept *hierarchies* or other *relatedness links*. This section discusses the way in which the DM can be automatically (adaptively, adaptably) enriched by interpreting the semantics of its structure and contents.

New Semantic Links

The easiest way to enrich the domain model is by automatically finding new domain links between existing domain concepts.[1] For instance, new *relatedness relations* can be generated for relations between concepts that share a common topic. This commonality can be computed at concept attribute level and, therefore, can automatically be labelled with a type that corresponds to the type attribute of the connecting attribute. In the following, we illustrate this with the help of an abstract example.

Consider, we have two domain concepts from two possibly different domain concept maps, $c1 \in C1$, $c2 \in C2$ (concept "NN Introduction" and concept "The biological neuron" from the concept maps "Neural Networks I" and "Neural Networks II," respectively[2]). Now consider two respective attributes of these concepts, $a1 \in c1$, $a2 \in c2$; these attributes can be given as pairs of variable names and their respective values: $a1=<var1,val1>$, $a2=<var2,val2>$. If the attributes are of the same type ($var1=var2=var$; for instance, var="keywords"), then a **weighted, typed semantic domain link** can be generated between the two concepts $c1$ and $c2$, with the link type (label) given by the type of the attribute, and the weight defined as the number of common features between the two value fields: $weight=number\_common\_features(val1,val2)$. This link will only make sense if the weight is positive.

This is one semantically explicit, symbolic way of generating new links between domain concepts. Another way is, for instance, to apply an algorithm that checks the domain map for missing link types and prompts the author, asking if new ones should be searched for.

New Semantic Attributes

A different method to enrich the domain model involves link analysis to compare semantically similar concepts (semantically similar can mean similar from a link point of view, such as concepts sharing the same ancestor-concept, for example; concepts at the same level of the hierarchy; or concepts related to each other via some special link (of a given type), etc.) and to determine if some attributes (or even sub-concepts) are missing.

For instance, consider a concept called "Discrete Neuron Perceptrons" from a Neural Networks course that has an attribute of the type "Example." whereas the concept "Continuous Neuron Perceptrons" does not, although they are linked via a relatedness relation as described in the previous subsection. In this case, the system can signal the author concerning the possible "missing" content item, corresponding to the semantics (attribute, sub-concept, etc.). It may even look for possible candidates for the "Example" attribute via other links to this concept. This search space is not limited in scope but can continue "outside" the LAOS model, leading to a transition from a closed space to the Open Adaptive Educational Hypermedia space.

From Domain Model to Goal and Constraints Model (DM→GM)

The Goal and Constraints Model filters, constrains, and restructures the Domain Model, corresponding to a *pedagogic goal*. For instance, a lesson aimed at *beginners* starts by filtering the necessary introductory information from a larger pool defined by one or more appropriate domain maps. Therefore, the *primary content* of the GM is not resources, but copies of (or, rather, to avoid redundancy, pointers to) the resources. The Goal and Constraints Model also contains prerequisite relationships that establish the general recommended order of visiting the course items. Moreover, here the differentiation is made between alternative content (OR relations) and obligatory content (AND relations). Therefore, the GM Model contains mainly structural elements or links. The GM can also contain resources if these are of a pedagogical nature only (such as a text explaining why it is better for beginners to study resources, grouped as attributes, with the type "Introduction").

Automatic (adaptive, adaptable) Goal and Constraints Model enrichment or creation based on the Domain Model can be achieved based on semantic presentation constraints or goals (e.g., envisioned pedagogical strategies or pedagogical techniques). This transformation represents the first step from *information* to *knowledge*, therefore promoting a higher level of semantics.

Semantic Generation of Primary Content

Concept attributes, as has been mentioned, can be grouped into types. A semantically relevant subset of these types can be used to determine a semantic filter for the selection of the items that will appear in the Goal and Constraints Model. The filter represents the constraints in the GM model, while the semantics of the filter represents the goal.

For instance, a lesson dedicated to beginners can form a filter containing domain attributes of types such as: "Introduction" or "Explanation." These attributes can be semantically grouped in the GM as *alternative contents* (OR) and obligatory contents (AND) concepts.

Semantic Generation of Links

Links in the domain layer can be, as previously noted, hierarchical or of another nature. These link types can be used to generate specific links at the level of the GM model.

For instance, the GM model can be generated by filtering only links of a specific semantically relevant type (e.g., only hierarchical links). These links then are semantically interpreted, therefore becoming *prerequisite* relations. In MOT, automatic transformations of hierarchical links are used to create a hierarchical, ordered-link structure; that is, the selected attribute subset will keep the same *hierarchical structure* as its DM source. However, the semantics change from an *inclusion hierarchy* to that of a *prerequisite hierarchy*.

From Domain Model to Adaptation Model (DM→AM)

The role of the adaptation model is to interpret the other models: the domain, goal, and even presentation model. Moreover, it can update these models and generate the presentation. Typical elements of the adaptation model are condition-action (or IF-THEN) rules that change learner model variable values or presentation aspects. LAOS actually uses the Layered Adaptive Granulation (LAG) model (Cristea & Calvi, 2003) to express adaptation with richer semantics. LAG has, at the lowest level, *adaptation assembly rules* such as IF-THEN rules, but wraps them in a second layer of an *adaptation language*, and at the highest level *adaptation strategies*. There are not many semantic descriptions at the lowest LAG level, hence the semantics are built into the other layers. The semantics of the adaptation language correspond to typical educational adaptation constructs that commonly appear during different adaptive interactions with the learner. The highest level, adaptation strategies, corresponds semantically to pedagogic strategies.

Automatic (adaptive, adaptable) adaptation model enrichment based on the Domain Model is also a matter of semantic interpretation, with respect to a goal, for example, a pedagogical strategy.

Automatic Semantic Rule Generation Based on Attribute Types

Attribute types can be used to semantically create rules that control the display of specific types of attributes under specific conditions. These conditions can be automatically deduced by the system (as in adaptivity) or triggered by the AH user (adaptability).

For instance, a generated *specific* automatic adaptive rule can express the fact that we only want to show the domain attribute of type "text" of concept $c1$ after the attributes with types "title" and "introduction" were accessed:

IF(c1.title.access='TRUE' AND c1.introduction.access='TRUE')
THEN c1.text.available='TRUE';

Note that we wrote the condition in this form for simplification purposes, and that attribute states such as "access" and "available" are part of the user model.

In order for this to be a *generic* automatic transformation rule that can be applied to any concept in the domain model, the rule becomes:

IF(concept.title.access='TRUE' AND concept.introduction.access='TRUE') THEN concept.text.available='TRUE';

From Goal and Constraints Model to Adaptation Model (GM→AM)

The Adaptation Model should actually work together with the Goal and Constraints Model, as the latter is the filtered version of the initial information, tailored for the group (stereotype) of learners envisioned. The Adaptation Model fine-tunes this stereotyping, catering to the individual learner's needs as opposed to the group's needs. Enriching or generating the Adaptation Model based on the GM means semantically interpreting the GM according to an adaptation strategy or technique (e.g., based on a pedagogical strategy or technique).

Automatic Semantic Rule Generation Based on Link Type

The GM, as said, contains pre-ordered and pre-selected information from the DM. This structure can already be semantically interpreted in terms of the adaptation that is to be performed on it. For instance, the GM allows "AND" relations between concepts, as well as "OR" relations with some weights.

These can be used to automatically generate rules that express the requirement that all concepts in an "AND" relation must be read:

IF ((c.name.access='TRUE' OR c.contents.access='TRUE')

AND link(c,c2,'AND',*))

THEN { c2.name.accessible='TRUE'; c2.contents.accessible='TRUE';}

In a similar way, an "OR" relationship can be semantically interpreted into inhibition rules:

IF ((c.name.access='TRUE' OR c.contents.access ='TRUE')

AND link(c,c2,'OR',*))

THEN { c2.name.accessible='no'; c2.contents.accessible='no';}

In such a way, various constructs can be automatically added to the generic adaptation rules, directly by interpreting the *goal and constraints model.*

From User Model to Adaptation Model (UM→AM)

The LAOS user model is a *hybrid model* (similar to Zakaria & Brailsford, 2002). This means that the learner model consist of a *stereotype model* and an *overlay model.*

The first consists of *variable-value pairs*, which specify information on a student; for instance:

- interests (e.g., main interests, cross-domain interests, etc.);
- current educational status;
- residential constraints (e.g., preferred cities, maximum distance to travel per day, etc.);
- preferred study duration;
- language (e.g., mother tongue, preferred study language);
- medical status; and
- age.

Such variables can enter conditions in adaptive rules or can be modified by these rules.

The second model specifies not only variable-values but also the relationships between these variables, which can be deduced from the underlying domain model (or goal and constraints model).

Automatic Semantic Rule Generation Based on Attribute Type

To illustrate a semantic interpretation of user model elements to generate an AM rule, we consider the state of "interest" a learner manifests about a concept. A possible semantical interpretation of this state, evaluated via the domain overlay attribute with the same name, is to generate a rule that displays everything in the concept, if this concept is of interest to the user:

IF (concept.interest > threshold)
THEN{concept.name.available='TRUE'; concept.contents.available='TRUE';}

Note that this rule is a generic rule, which can be applied on all concepts in a concept map, drastically reducing the workload.

UM→AM: By Link Type

Link type can only be used when the UM is itself a concept map. Via UM links, we can express, for instance, the fact that two states in the user model are related.

Here, however, we try to look at a different type of link between UM concepts. For this, we will consider the link of type "influence." Such a link can be automatically interpreted into a rule saying that the interest in a subject *c* might decrease if the user is interested in another subject *c2*.

IFLINK(c,c2,'influence',*)
THEN {c.interest= c.interest – c2.interest;}

Conversions between AEH Systems

Paradigm Shift (One-to-One → Many-to-Many)

LAOS addresses many of the issues regarding the complexity of authoring but cannot cover all of them. This is because the problem is compounded when one considers other factors, such as software rot and the multitude of systems available. Software rot occurs over time because software is not maintained or software necessary for the correct workings of a program is altered in such a way that the original code ceases to function correctly. Imagine a situation where an author goes to the not inconsiderable time and trouble to create a lesson in an AEH system, be it based on LAOS or not. What happens if this system ceases to be maintained? As many AEH systems are currently developed by individual research groups around the world, the above situation has occurred many times and will occur again. Before this happens, the author must consider the future. Does he stay with the old system that will slowly rot away? Or does he spend the time and effort to learn how to author in a new AEH system? It is possible that the original content is locked into the previous format, hence he may have to re-create all of his old lessons.

With the ongoing growth and maturation of AEH, these issues are raised. It is more widely recognised as desirable to move away from a "one-to-one" AH authoring paradigm to a general "many-to-many." That is, an author may create a lesson in any system in which he is an expert or wishes to spend the time and effort to learn, and export (or *convert*) this data for use in an other system. It would then be of no concern if an individual system "rotted" or was no longer available; a simple conversion from that system to a new one would solve this problem. This is an extended form of authoring.

What follows is a description of the first steps taken in this direction. However, rather than the ultimate goal of a "many-to-many" system, we describe a half-way point—a "one-to-many" methodology. Using MOT as an authoring tool (as it is based on the powerful and flexible LAOS framework), it is possible to create whatever content is desired. It is then possible to transform the lesson into one of three different formats: AHA!, Blackboard, or WHURLE (actually there are *four* formats, but the original MOT delivery format requires no conversion). The process involved in doing this is described in the following sections.

Existing Multi-System Authoring Environments

In the following sections we will analyze some inter-system authoring experiments. We will discuss how learning material can be created in one system, MOT, and converted into other delivery systems. The conversions described below represent the one-to-many paradigm shift.

MOT→AHA!

My Online Teacher (MOT) is an AEH authoring system based on the LAOS framework. At the time of the writing, MOT implements the:

- domain model, as a *conceptual domain model* for courses,

- goal and constraints model, as a *Lesson map*,

- user model, featuring *stereotypes* and *overlay user model* (Wu, 2002),

- adaptation model (MOT-adapt), in the form of an *(instructional) adaptive strategy* (Cristea, 2004b) creation tool, based on an *adaptive language* (Cristea & Calvi, 2003) that uses as an intermediate representation level of LAG (Layers of Adaptive Granulation) grammar (Cristea & Verschoor, 2004), and

- presentation model is currently being implemented, in the form of a hybrid model, similar to the user model.

AHA! is a general-purpose, adaptive Web-based engine, first created as a simple support engine for adaptive online courses (De Bra & Calvi, 1998). The key features of AHA! (Version 2.0) are:

- Open Source project;

- Web-based adaptive engine;

- built on Java Servlet technology;

- authoring through Java Applets ;

- general-purpose user-model and adaptation rules;

- extensive use of XML; and

- database support using mySQL.

In addition to these, AHA! Version 3.0 contains constructs called "objects." These "objects" allow a complex inclusion structure of elements of a learner presentation, in a more flexible way than in earlier versions.

As MOT's first version implemented only the *domain* and the *lesson* maps, the first MOT to AHA! conversion focussed on the conversion of these maps only.

The version currently under implementation is aiming to make use of the new facilities in AHA! 3.0 and the extensions in MOT.

In the following, these conversions will be sketched separately, from a semantic and implementation point of view.

Semantic Mapping of the Domain Model

The MOT domain model layer contains a hierarchy of domain concepts and their respective domain attributes. Moreover, the DM contains also (typed and weighted) relatedness relations between domain concepts. The conversion from MOT to AHA! was initially performed using AHA! v2.0.

AHA! v2.0 only knew how to handle conditional inclusion of fragments, which are parts of an (xhtml) page. Therefore, the (xhtml) pages had to be generated for the AHA! v2.0 engine.

Note, however, that if a concept attribute appeared in more than one condition, it had to be pasted as a conditional fragment in each of the (xhtml) pages in which it could appear. The object inclusion in AHA! 3.0 solves this redundancy problem. This is the reason why the conversion process only started to function closer to the desired requirements with the advent of AHA! 3.0.

A conversion of MOT domain concept maps into AHA! 3.0 involves the following steps:

1. Creation of an XHTML (basic) resource file for every domain attribute in MOT.[3] This will generate AHA! object concepts[4] for each attribute (Attr 1 to Attr k) in Figure 2.

2. Grouping of domain attributes (representing the different aspects of a concept that should appear when certain instructional strategies are triggered) into XHTML files, containing lists of "objects," pointing to the XHTML files created in Step 1. This will generate AHA! page concepts (as shown in Figure 2).

3. Writing the actual conditions that determine which (or how many) of the alternatives are really shown to the student in AHA! rules during conversion.

Semantically, this means that MOT domain attributes correspond to AHA! resources, whereas MOT domain concepts correspond to a special type of AHA! concept called "page concept."

The actual representation of the domain map conversion in the AHA! implementation is shown in Figure 3. The figure shows how an AHA! page concept can be created by connecting together a list of object concepts. The actual display of the object concepts can be made to depend on some conditions (such as user preferences, state, etc.).

Figure 2. Semantic representation of MOT domain concepts and domain attributes in AHA!

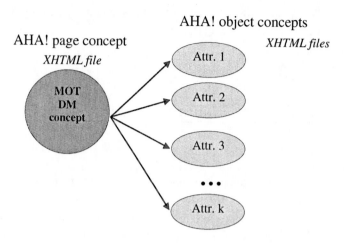

Semantic Mapping of the Lesson Model

The Lesson map has similar elements to the DM (according to the LAOS model), so similar conversions can be expected. One major difference is determined by the (weighted) AND-OR relations, which can be directly interpreted as *prerequisite relations*, allowed by the AHA! engine.

Lesson map conversion into AHA! 3.0 structure is similar to the conversion of domain concept maps. The semantics are represented in Figure 4. The contents of the MOT lesson concepts have previously been created as XHTML basic resources during the domain attribute conversion, therefore this process is not repeated (i.e., the resources that are connected to the attributes Attr. 1 to 3 in Figure 4 are already bound to some AHA! object concepts, as shown in Figure 2. This is due to the LAOS restriction that attributes of the Domain map become concepts in the Lesson map). These MOT lesson concepts are then converted into AHA! page concepts, in a similar way.

To enforce the hierarchy and order relationship, the XHTML files translating lessons contain a separate, ordered list of sub-lesson pointers in addition to the list of object alternatives (as shown in the Figure 4).

The access to sub-lessons might not be always desirable, depending on the instructional strategy. Therefore, the implementation is again via the "object" paradigm in AHA!. Moreover, a small trick is here necessary, as for sub-lessons AHA! should not display the content but the link to the content. This can be realized in AHA! with the help of some extra link concepts containing just a link to the respective sub-lesson (see Figure 5, AHA! concept corresponding to XHTML link).

Figure 3. Implementation of MOT domain concepts and domain attributes in AHA!

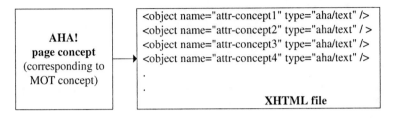

AHA!
page concept
(corresponding to
MOT concept)

```
<object name="attr-concept1" type="aha/text" />
<object name="attr-concept2" type="aha/text" / >
<object name="attr-concept3" type="aha/text" />
<object name="attr-concept4" type="aha/text" />
.
.
```

XHTML file

MOT→WHURLE

Web-based Hierarchical Universal Reactive Learning Environment (WHURLE) is an adaptive learning environment (Brailsford, Stewart, Zakaria, & Moore, 2002; Moore, Brailsford, & Stewart, 2001; Zakaria, Moore, Stewart, & Brailsford, 2003) that stores information as atomic units, called *chunks*. These are the smallest possible, conceptually self-contained units of information that can be used by the system. They may be as small as a captioned image or a paragraph of text, or as large as an entire legal or historical document. Lessons consist of a collection of *chunks*, together with a default pathway, or *lesson plan*, defined by authors. The lesson plan is filtered by an *adaptation filter* that implements the user model based on data stored in the user profile.

WHURLE, however, has no specific authoring system. Both chunks and lesson plans are created using XML editors; anything from a simple text editor to an XML authoring environment may be used. Meanwhile, the user profile has, in part, to be created using

Figure 4. Semantic representation of MOT lesson concepts in AHA!

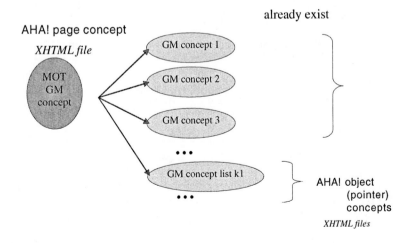

already exist

AHA! page concept

XHTML file

MOT GM concept

GM concept 1

GM concept 2

GM concept 3

•••

GM concept list k1

•••

AHA! object
(pointer)
concepts

XHTML files

Figure 5. Implementation of MOT lesson concepts in AHA!

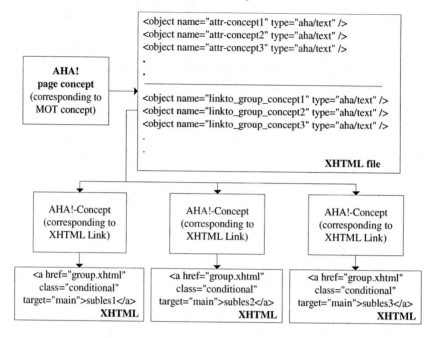

SQL statements that are entered manually into the MySQL database. For a novice author with no expertise in XML or SQL, creating lessons in WHURLE is a time consuming and confusing process.

Using MOT as an authoring tool solves many of the problems that novice, or even experienced, authors have when authoring in WHURLE. Learning to use MOT is a simple feat compared to learning to author in WHURLE, as MOT authors are only required to understand HTML at the outset. There are still design decisions that need to be made, but they are of a pedagogical nature, not a technical one.

Authoring in MOT is a many stage process. Initially, the domain maps are built; then the lesson map is created using the concepts from whichever domain maps are appropriate. The MOT-to-WHURLE conversion focuses on these two steps and therefore has two options: the conversion of domain maps or lesson maps.

Semantic Mapping of the Domain Model

This is a simple method of conversion resulting in a WHURLE lesson plan that has no adaptation built into it. A single MOT concept (Figure 6) is converted into a single WHURLE chunk by gathering all of the attributes for that concept, extracting the title, keywords, and placing the rest of the attribute contents into the body of the chunk.

Figure 6. A MOT Domain Map, Biochemistry, with a single concept

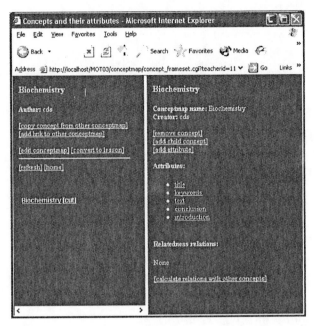

Figure 7. The WHURLE chunk created after conversion of the MOT concept in Figure 6. The original order of the attributes in the concept is maintained, hence "introduction" at the end of the attribute list.

```
<chunk type="" name="MOT-CM71-369.wcml"
           irks="0"
           title="Biochemistry"
           learning="ip"
           bandwidth="low"
           browsercap="low">

<versionlist>
       <version author="XXXXX" date="dddddd" />
</versionlist>

<text><p>

<p>The rest of this lesson is going to go into detail several areas of the
discpline. Areas such as:

<ul>
<li>Cellular chemistry</li>
<li>Macromolecules</li>
<li>Reaction Rates</li>
<li>Novel compunds</li>
</ul>
</p>

<p>By the end of the course you should be able to pass yours exams!</p>

<p>This course is for Degree level undergraduates.</p>
       </p></text>

       <keywords>
       </keywords>
</chunk>
```

Figure 8. A section of a WHURLE lesson plan, produced by transforming the MOT domain map in Figure 6.

```
<level name="zdncrng" title="Biochemistry">
      <page>
            <chunk domain="general" stereotype1="" stereotype2="">MOT-LM71-369-0</chunk>
      </page>
</level>
```

Of course, in addition to chunks, WHURLE requires a lesson plan. This is also a part of the conversion output, and a section of the lesson plan produced from the domain map in Figure 6 is shown in Figure 8.

As a domain map has no adaptation information contained within it, it is not necessary to convert any further information. This can be seen in Figure 8, where the value for the "domain" is "general" and both "stereotype1" and "stereotype2" are left blank. This indicates that there is no adaptation taking place in this lesson plan.

By ignoring adaptation, this simple form of conversion does not take full advantage of the functionality of WHURLE. For that, we must turn to the second method of conversion.

Semantic Mapping of the Lesson Model

Examine Figure 9 and the highlighted areas within it. These mark two of the major differences between a MOT domain map and a lesson map.

Compared to a MOT domain map, the lesson map allows for the possibility of adaptation. It does this by allowing an author to assign an "OR" condition to any particular concept ("AND" is the default). This signifies that all of that concept's children—be they attributes or sub-concepts—can have a "weight" (and a "label," not shown) associated with them.

The MOT-to-WHURLE lesson map conversion has three stages:

1.   **Define structure:** This stage of the conversion trawls through the lesson map and creates the WHURLE lesson plan. Each concept has to be linked to its parent, siblings, and children. As lesson maps can be made up from many domain maps (Figure 10), each concept must also have its parent domain map identified as this will be used as the value for the "domain" section of a lesson plan (Figure 11).

As can be seen from Figure 11, the value of "domain" is a number ("113" or "119"), because WHURLE requires a numeric value here. This is linked to the "real" name ("MOT user guide" and "Biochemistry," respectively) for each domain, in the WHURLE database.

Once the structure has been defined, the final process during this stage is to produce the WHURLE lesson plan. To do this, additional structures (e.g., XML specific data, a title, author information, etc.) are added to the lesson plan.

Figure 9. A MOT lesson map. The highlighted region shows that the attributes for this concept are all part of an "OR" and that each attribute has a "weight"—identified by the percentage (0%, 10% and 90%).

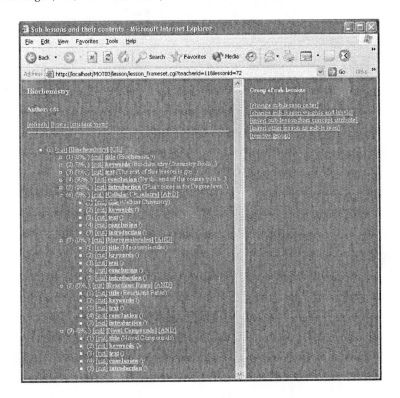

2.   **Associate attributes:** As the first process is ongoing (lesson plan elucidation), this second process, production of the chunks, begins. Whenever a concept is encountered, all of the attributes for that concept are gathered and sorted according to their MOT "weights." Each weight is associated with others of the same weight, except for weight "0." Weight "0" is treated as a special case, as it allows the author to determine which attributes are to be "common," that is, available to all chunks created from that concept.

Table 1 shows which attributes will be associated with which chunks after conversion. The standard, weight "0," attributes are collected together and form chunk *C1*. Chunk *C2* is made up from the standard attributes plus all those with a weight of "'90," while chunk *C3* collects together the attributes of weight "10" and "0."

So far, this is of no obvious use to the author. However, used in conjunction with a table like Table 2, it becomes possible for the author to determine his own weight boundaries when deciding which attributes belong to which WHURLE knowledge level: "beg" (beginner), "int" (intermediate) or "adv"(advanced).

Figure 10. MOT lesson maps can be built from concepts from many domain maps

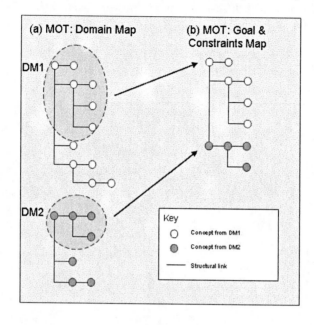

Figure 11. This WHURLE page and its sub-level have been converted from a MOT lesson map using two domain maps, called "119" and "113."

```
<page>
      <chunk domain="general" stereotype1="" stereotype2="">
            MOT-LM72-369-0
      </chunk>
      <chunk domain="119" stereotype1="beg" stereotype2="">
            MOT-LM72-369-10
      </chunk>
      <chunk domain="119" stereotype1="adv" stereotype2="">
            MOT-LM72-369-90
      </chunk>
</page>
<level name="yncioxd" title="Choose sub-topic">
      <page>
            <chunk domain="general" stereotype1="" stereotype2="">
                  MOT-LM72-223-0
            </chunk>
            <chunk domain="113" stereotype1="adv" stereotype2="">
                  MOT-LM72-223-90
            </chunk>
      </page>
</level>
```

Table 1. A simple MOT concept with seven attributes and their associated weights will be converted into three WHURLE chunks, C1-3. Note attributes that are empty are ignored.

MOT attributes		WHURLE chunks		
Attribute	*Weight*	*C1*	*C2*	*C3*
Title	0	✓	✓	✓
Keywords	0	✓	✓	✓
Pattern	90		✓	
Text	10			✓
Explanation	90	No attribute contents		
Conclusion	10	No attribute contents		
Exercise	10			✓
		✓ = included in the chunk		

3. **Update WHURLE database:** The final step in the MOT->WHURLE conversion is to create the SQL commands that will update the WHURLE database. Like MOT, WHURLE uses a MySQL database, which is used to record certain information about each of the WHURLE lessons, for example, the name and unique ID of each lesson, a list of the knowledge domains (appearing as numbers in Figure 11,"<chunk domain= "113" …") used in each lesson, pre-test and post-test to be used when a student first accesses a lesson, and so on.

Therefore, this final step has to initially check the WHURLE database to determine what information already exists; for example, has a lesson of the same name already been created and what Lesson and Domain IDs are available for use? As another example, imagine that a lesson on Chemistry already exists under the name "Chemistry," the lesson ID of "8," and the domain ID of "100." A new author has used MOT to create a second lesson "Biochemistry," using the domains of Chemistry, Biology, and Biochemistry. The conversion system must check the WHURLE database to see if any of the domains used in the new lesson already exists. In our example, Chemistry already does, so WHURLE returns the domain ID (100) and uses this in the creation of the WHURLE Lesson Plan. Domains that are not already extant are then created, given an ID, and then used in the WHURLE Lesson Plan. After this, the database will be updated with all of this new information: the lesson name of "Biochemistry"; the lesson id of "9"; and two additional domain IDs of "101" and "102."

The actual SQL commands are irrelevant here, as the MOT-to-WHURLE conversion program handles all of this transparently. Once the author supplies the location of the WHURLE database, everything else is automatic.

MOT→Blackboard

The "Academic Suite" by Blackboard (http://www.blackboard.com), contains the Blackboard Learning System. This product is not an AEH, as Blackboard has no adaptability

Table 2. An example weight boundary table. All MOT lesson attribute weights from 1-49 will be assigned to the WHURLE stereotype of "beg," with 50-89 as "int" and 90-99 as "adv." These boundaries are set by the author. These weight boundaries establish the WHURLE stereotype. Along with the domain for that concept, they form the complete definition of the lesson plan chunk. With this done, the attributes are all associated and used to produce the chunk. Note that the "title" and "keywords" attributes are always of weight "0" as they are required in every chunk. The chunk structure itself is similar to that displayed in Figure 2.

Weight	Stereotype
1 - 49	beg
50 – 89	int
90 - 99	adv

functionality built into it. Blackboard does, however, use an open architecture, which means that it is possible to extend its functionality by designing and building a Blackboard plug-in.

Even with no adaptation plug-in currently available for Blackboard, there are ways to simulate adaptation with the use of "adapted" lessons. Blackboard supports the IMS Simple Sequencing Specification (SSS) (http://www.imsglobal.org), which can be used to describe how learning materials can be sequenced into a specific lesson. Thus, it is possible to produced "pre-adapted" lessons, one for each type of user, giving the learner the illusion of adaptation.

Work has recently begun at the University of Southampton on this innovative method for delivering adapted content in a non-adaptive system, using MOT as the authoring tool to describe the lesson before adaptation. The MOT to Blackboard conversion uses only the MOT lesson map and, like the MOT-to-WHURLE conversion, it uses MOT weights to determine which attributes are delivered to which adapted Blackboard lesson. Figure 12 shows a MOT lesson map, similar to that depicted in Figure 9, with weights ascribed to all of the attributes.

The weights are used to determine which attributes are gathered together in to a single Blackboard lesson. Table 3 gives some example boundaries.

Unlike the MOT-to-WHURLE weight boundaries where the aim to is split the content up into ability levels (so that, for example, a beginner will only get material appropriate to a beginner's ability), the MOT to Blackboard weight boundaries are designed to create lessons appropriate to the established *goal* of an individual learner. For example, a learner can state that he or she only wants to pass a specific subject and, therefore, will only be presented with a lesson designed for "Pass only" learners—with MOT attributes of a weight of less than 50. Figure 13 shows how a single MOT lesson can produce all of the relevant Blackboard lessons.

Blackboard is not an adaptive system. However, it *is* in widespread use, and along with WebCT, it is one of the most popular Learning Systems in use. This widespread usage, along with its open architecture, means that designing any form of adaptation for users

Figure 12. A MOT lesson map with each attribute given a weight

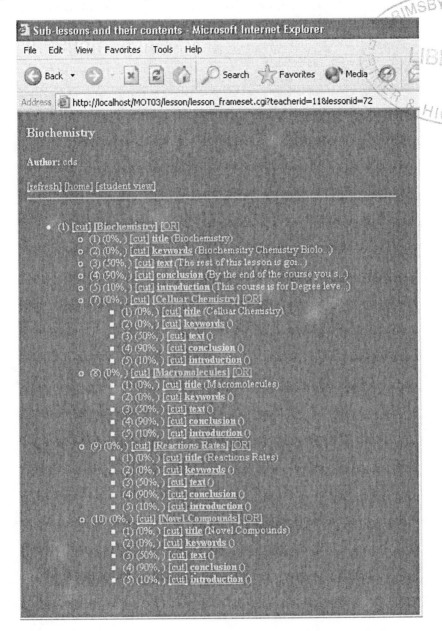

Table 3. Some example boundaries for MOT weights, associated with a specific passing grade that a learner is aiming to achieve

Weight	Learner's goal
90 +	Top of the class
70 - 90	'A' grade
60 - 70	'B' grade
50 – 60	'C' grade
Less than 50	Pass only

Figure 13. A single MOT lesson map (a) (goal & constraints map) would be converted to three (b) Blackboard lessons. The weights are associated into different lessons according to the weight boundaries set in Table 3.

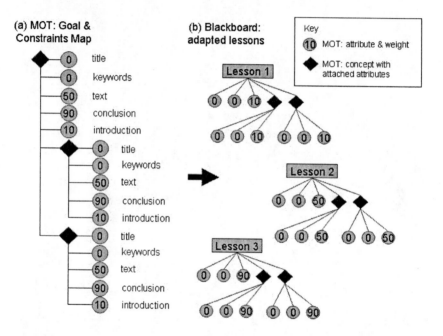

of Blackboard (be it illusory, via "adapted" lessons or by creating an adaptation plug-in) will be an important tool to advance the use and awareness of AEH outside of the discipline.

The Future: Middleware

All three example conversion systems are limited in scope to the initial use of a single authoring system, MOT. No matter how good MOT is as an authoring system, this is still a far step from our stated goal of a "many-to-many" paradigm for both authoring and delivery. However, these first steps in that direction are vital. A modular approach to authoring is important to encourage other AEH systems to use MOT as an authoring system; this content can be subsequently used in other systems, via conversion. Even more useful is the experience and insight that writing these modules gives to the developers. It is from these insights that a more powerful system will emerge. That system is for the future, but a brief outline of it can now be envisioned.

LAOS—LAG

As described in the LAOS Layered Model, the methodology includes an Adaptation Model layer. This layer is actually a more complex layer, as it is the one that determines the whole dynamics of the adaptive hypermedia system. Traditionally, this layer is composed of IF-THEN rules. Layered Adaptive Granulation (LAG) is, as said, an extension of the Adaptation Model, and its implementation is MOT-adapt.

In MOT-adapt, by using the general rule set of IF-THEN rules, it is possible for authors to write their own adaptation rules. While at first glance this may sound rather complex and daunting, the LAG structure itself offers the solution to this. LAG, as previously discussed, has itself three layers of rule definition. To recapitulate, they are as follows: the first, and most basic, is the aforementioned "IF-THEN rules"; the second is that of an "adaptation language," made up of more complex programming procedures; and the third layer is that of broad "adaptation strategies." These are pre-written strategies that an author can use, for example, to automatically adapt all of a lesson's content depending on whether the learner is "textual" based or "visual/image" based.

By using LAG structure to define the conversion of adaptive behaviour of courseware, it is possible to perform flexible interpretations of the semantics of the adaptation conversion, instead of using fixed semantics.

As the model includes high-level strategies, it is possible to see the real benefits in using LAG to guide a generic authoring system. Pedagogic experts can write MOT-adapt strategies, which can then be shared with all MOT users. The author is not required to develop strategies of his own, but can always alter a pre-written strategy to suit his own specific requirements. Therefore, building LAG into any future conversion system is vital.

Middleware

What is "middleware"? Consider a heterogeneous world of AEH systems. There will be entrenched, fully developed systems that are in use in many locations with many lessons. Then there will be new systems, still under development, informed by current research. And, of course, there will be many systems between these two extremes. To have a *true* "many-to-many" paradigm, it should be possible to use any system to author for any other system. To put it another way, it should be possible to convert between any two systems of choice. MOT would no longer be the only inter-system authoring tool, and lessons written in WHURLE using an XML editor could be converted to a format that MOT could use.

How is this conversion performed? Through a piece of software that sits between each system—in the "middle." This middleware would accept all conversion calls from a system and output the desired lesson(s) to the specific target system. Obviously, for such a system to function, all AEHs would have to know how to communicate with it. All data would have to have certain semantics attached to them; that is, each would have to have some "meaning" defined. Also, each AEH would have to declare to the middleware what sort of data it can accept. For example, it may be that WHURLE will be offered content from another AEH that will adapt around both a learner's knowledge level (stereotype) and his or her language preference – WHURLE would have to declare that it would accept adaptation based on knowledge level but reject the adaptation based on language as it could not use that.

Using a middleware system that implemented LAG would offer a great deal of power and flexibility, both to the authors of a lesson and to the learners themselves. Authors would still have to learn how to use a system, but they would then be able to chose the simplest system appropriate to their needs and have the content delivered to any AEH anywhere in the world.

Discussion and Conclusion

Adaptive Educational Hypermedia (AEH) aims to deliver flexible and appropriate educational materials to each student. This is in response to the inflexible and inappropriate use of learning resources in many static online Educational Hypermedia systems.

Authoring adaptive materials is no simple matter. An author must determine which of a multitude of AEH systems best suit his desires and requirements; this can involve a great deal of research. Even once a specific AEH is chosen, it may not be the correct one—it may no longer be supported, or it may lock down the content in a format that the author does not wish.

Moving on from these initial problems an author comes face-to-face with the many difficulties involved in actually producing adaptive content, for example, the multiple versions of information required for each type of learner, each possible adaptation of the content. With each problem, the author has to develop a new solution, but a solution that is limited to that specific AEH. While some of the expertise gained in writing lessons can be applied to multiple AEH systems, if an author wishes to move onto a new system then much of the hard-earned expertise becomes worthless.

After outlining the difficulty of the authoring task for Adaptive Hypermedia, we proposed solutions in the form of automatic authoring techniques, achieved by semantic interpretation of partial content of AH, as in internal transformations, or in semantic interpretation of integral AH content, as in the external conversions into several AH delivery platforms.

Internal transformations within an AEH authoring system allow the *author to write only a minimal amount of material*, which will be exploited and semantically interpreted automatically by the system into a complete AEH.

Moreover, this chapter has introduced a solution to this perennial authoring problem— that of an *author creating educational content once* (in a generic authoring environment, such as MOT) and subsequently being able to view it in multiple AEH delivery environments. This "write once, use many" approach is, of course, only an intermediate step towards a middleware system that will allow a dynamic interchange of information between all AEHs.

This "inter-operability" between AEH systems has recently been identified by the community as being important. For example, AHA! (De Bra & Calvi, 1998), a well-known AEH system in academic circles, has also experimented with conversion, notably, authoring with Interbook for AHA! (De Bra, Santic, & Brusilovsky, 2003), and using AHA! as the user model server for Claroline (Arteaga, Fabregat, Eyzaguirre, & Merida, 2004). Both of these developments represent a step in the right direction, and demonstrate the fundamental principle of AEHs being able to interchange data. However, they both lack the coordination represented by the three examples given in this chapter, as they are both separate developments that do not reference a common interface system, such as LAOS. Due to the fact that these conversions were both uniquely designed to interface with AHA! and no other AEH, they do not really move closer to a "many-to-many" approach.

By examining the conversion between MOT and WHURLE in detail, we can perceive a great many conceptual similarities. WHURLE is organised by lesson plans and the pages within them, which are clearly equivalent to MOT lesson maps and concepts, respectively. As the two systems developed independently, this similarity probably grew out of the comparable aims of each system, a case of parallel evolution.

Even systems that are conceptually much more divergent than MOT and WHURLE, such as MOT compared to Blackboard, are nevertheless similar enough to allow for a generic conversion system to deliver an illusion of adaptation.

Generic conclusions drawn from a few test cases such as these should be treated with caution. However, within the discipline of AEH, it could be productive to consider the conclusions that can be drawn from the insights gained during these conversions. The obvious conclusion is that many AEH systems will share a similar semantic structure, or that, at least, there will be enough of an overlap between the semantics of each system to allow for a productive conversion to occur.

This overlap must be made when preparing to convert between two systems, semantic mapping of the educational materials and the system data models is vital. Without such a mapping it is impossible to state that a "title" attribute in MOT is used in the same manner as a "title" section in the target AEH. Without such an assurance, it is impossible to be certain that any conversion system will in fact produce output that retains the same meaning.

Using a layered framework such as LAOS has another advantage for authors in addition to those already discussed, as LAOS has its own semantics that are built into each layer. The author need no longer consider the semantics of the material he is creating, as this will automatically be assigned when he designs the lesson. From the point of view of an AEH developer, we claim that if a target AEH system implements LAOS, then the target semantics are already known and a conversion module is straightforward to create.

Acknowledgments

This research is linked to the European Community Socrates Minerva project ADAPT: "Adaptivity and adaptability in ODL based on ICT" (Project Reference Number 101144-CP-1-2002-NL-MINERVA-MPP; http://wwwis.win.tue.nl/~acristea/HTML/Minerva/index.html).

References

Berners-Lee, T. (2003). Semantic Web status and direction ISWC'03. Keynote, ISWC'03. Retrieved from *http://www.w3.org/2003/Talks/1023-iswc-tbl/slide26-0.html*

Arteaga, C., Fabregat, R., Eyzaguirre, J., & Merida, D. (2004) Adaptive support for collaborative and individual learning (ASCIL): Integrating AHA! and CLAROLINE. In P. DeBra & W. Nejdl (Eds.), *Adaptive hypermedia and adaptive Web-based systems* (pp. 279-282). LNCS 3137. Berlin: Springer-Verlag.

Brailsford, T.J., Stewart, C.D., Zakaria, M.R., & Moore, A. (2002). Autonavigation: Links and narrative in an adaptive Web-based integrated learning environment. *Proceedings of the 11th International World Wide Web Conference (WWW2002)*, alternate track 2002, Honolulu, Hawaii, May 7-11. Retrieved June 27, 2005, from *http://www2002.org/CDROM/alternate/738/*

Brusilovsky, P. (2001a). Adaptive hypermedia. *User Modelling and User Adapted Interaction, 11*(1/2), 87-110.

Brusilovsky, P. (2001b). Adaptive educational hypermedia (invited talk). *The 10th International PEG Conference*, Tampere, Finland, June 23-26 (pp. 8-12).

Brusilovsky, P., Eklund, J., & Schwarz, E. (1998). Web-based education for all: A tool for developing adaptive courseware. *Computer Networks and ISDN Systems, Proceedings of the Seventh International World Wide Web Conference*, April 14-18, *30*(1-7), 291-300.

Carro, R.M., Pulido, E., & Rodríguez, P. (2001). TANGOW: A model for Internet based learning. *International Journal of Continuing Engineering Education and Life-Long Learning, IJCEELL, 11*(1-2). Retrieved June 27, 2005, from *http://www.inderscience.com/ejournal/c/ijceell/ijceell2001/ijceell2001v11n12.html*

Coffield, F. (2004). Learning styles and pedagogy in post-16 learning: A systematic and critical review. Learning & Skills Research Centre. Retrieved June 27, 2005, from *http://www.lsda.org.uk/files/pdf/1543.pdf*

Cristea, A. (2004). Flexibility of automatic authoring for the semantic Web. *WWW'04, Workshop on Application Design, Development and Implementation Issues in the Semantic Web*, May 18. Retrieved from *http://server2.tecweb.inf.puc-rio.br/we-sw-2004/www2004-Cristea-workshop.pdf*

Cristea, A. (2004b). Adaptive course creation for all. In *Proceedings of ITCC'04 (International Conference on Information Technology)*, April, Las Vegas, NV. IEEE.

Cristea, A. & Cristea, P. (2004). Evaluation of adaptive hypermedia authoring patterns during a Socrates programme class. *Advanced Technology for Learning Journal, 1*(2), 115-124. Retrieved from *http://www.actapress.com/journals/onlinejournals.htm*

Cristea, A. & De Mooij, A. (2003a). Designer adaptation in adaptive hypermedia. *ITCC'03*, Las Vegas, April. Los Alamitos, CA: IEEE Computer Society.

Cristea, A. & De Mooij, A. (2003b). LAOS: Layered WWW AHS authoring model and its corresponding algebraic operators. In *Proceedings of WWW'03*, Alternate Education track, Budapest, Hungary, May 20-24. New York: ACM.

Cristea, A. & De Mooij, A. (2003c). Adaptive course authoring: MOT, my online teacher. ICT-2003, *IEEE LTTF International Conference on Telecommunications, "Telecommunications + Education" Workshop*, February 23-March 1, Tahiti Island in Papetee, French Polynesia.

Cristea, A.I. (2003). Automatic authoring in the LAOS AHS authoring model. *Hypertext'03. Workshop on Adaptive Hypermedia and Adaptive Web-Based Systems.*

Cristea, A.I. & Calvi, L. (2003). The three layers of adaptation granularity. *Proceedings of UM'03 (International Conference on User Modelling)*, Pittsburgh, PA. Berlin: Springer Verlag.

Cristea, A.I. & De Bra, P. (2002). Towards adaptable and adaptive ODL environments. In *Proceedings of AACE E-Learn'02*, Montreal, Canada, October (pp. 232-239).

Cristea, A.I. & Kinshuk. (2003). Considerations on LAOS, LAG and their integration in MOT. In D. Lassner & C. McNaught (Eds.), *Ed-Media 2003 Conference Proceedings* (pp. 511-518). Norfolk, VA: AACE.

Cristea, A.I. & Verschoor, M. (2004). The LAG grammar for authoring the adaptive Web. In *Proceedings of ITCC (International Conference on Information Technology)*, April, Las Vegas, NV (Vol. 1, pp. 382-388). IEEE.

De Bra, P. & Calvi, L. (1998). AHA! An open adaptive hypermedia architecture. *The New Review of Hypermedia and Multimedia, 4*, 115-139. London: Taylor Graham Publishers.

De Bra, P., Santic, T., & Brusilovsky, P. (2003). AHA! meets Interbook, and more... *Proceedings of the AACE ELearn 2003 Conference*, Phoenix, AZ, November (pp. 57-64). AACE.

Gruber, T. R. (1995). Towards principles for the design of ontologies used for knowledge sharing. *International Journal of Human-Computer Studies, 43*, 907-928.

Moore, A., Brailsford, T. J., & Stewart, C. D. (2001). Personally tailored teaching in WHURLE using conditional transclusion. *Proceedings of the 12ᵗʰ ACM Conference on Hypertext and Hypermedia*, August 14-18 (pp. 163-164). Arhus, Denmark: ACM Press.

Murray, T. (1999). Authoring intelligent tutoring systems: An analysis of the state of the art. *Journal of Artificial Intelligence in Education (Special Isue on Adaptive and Intelligent Web-Based Systems)*, *13*(10), 98-129. Retrieved from *http://aied.inf.ed.ac.uk/members99/archive/vol_10/murray/paper.pdf*

Murray, T. (2003). MetaLinks: Authoring and affordances for conceptual and narrative flow in adaptive hyperbooks. *Journal of Artificial Intelligence and Education,* (Special Issue on Adaptive and Intelligent Web-Based Systems), *13*.

Specht, M., Kravcik, M., Pesin, L., & Klemke, R. (2001). Authoring adaptive educational hypermedia in WINDS. *Online Proceedings of ABIS Workshop*, (Adaptivität und Benutzermodellierung in Interaktiven Softwaresystemen), Dortmund, Denmark. Retrieved June 27, 2005, from *http://www.kbs.uni-hannover.de/~henze/ABIS_Workshop2001/final/Specht_final.pdf*

Stach, N., Cristea, A.I., & De Bra, P. (2004). Authoring of learning styles in adaptive hypermedia: Problems and solutions. In *Proceedings of WWW'04, 13ᵗʰ International World Wide Web Conference*, May, New York (pp. 104-113).

Wu, H. (2002). *A reference architecture for adaptive hypermedia applications.* PhD thesis, Eindhoven University of Technology, The Netherlands.

Wu., H., Houben, G.J., & De Bra, P. (1998). AHAM: A reference model to support adaptive hypermedia authoring. In *Proceedings of the Zesde Interdisciplinaire Conferentie Informatiewetenschap* (pp. 77-88). Antwerp, Belgium.

Zakaria, M.R. & Brailsford, T.J. (2002). User modelling and adaptive educational hypermedia frameworks for education. *New Review of Hypermedia and Multimedia, 8,* 83-97.

Zakaria, M.R., Moore, A., Stewart, C.D., & Brailsford, T.J. (2003). "Pluggable" user models for adaptive hypermedia in education. In *Proceedings of the Fourteenth ACM Conference on Hypertext and Hypermedia*, August 26-30, Nottingham, UK (pp. 170-171). New York: ACM Press.

Endnotes

[1]   These new links can be between the concepts of the *current content* (concept map: e.g., course), between the current content and some *other content created by the same author*, or, finally, between the current content and some *other content created by a different author*.

[2]   Examples taken from LAOS implementation in MOT.

[3]   This only means adding a header and a footer to the attribute and saving it into a file with unique name, <file-name>.xhtml.

4   AHA! has different types of concepts, such as object concepts, page concepts, etc. The type of the concept specifies how the AHA! delivery engine will render the content of the respective concept.

Chapter III

Automatic Learning Object Selection and Sequencing in Web-Based Intelligent Learning Systems

Pythagoras Karampiperis
Piraeus University and Informatics and Telematics Institute,
Centre for Research and Technology Hellas, Greece

Demetrios Sampson
Piraeus University and Informatics and Telematics Institute,
Centre for Research and Technology Hellas, Greece

Abstract

Automatic courseware authoring is recognized as among the most interesting research questions in intelligent Web-based education. Automatic courseware authoring is the process of automatic learning object selection and sequencing. In most intelligent learning systems that incorporate course sequencing techniques, learning object selection and sequencing are based on a set of teaching rules according to the cognitive style or learning preferences of the learners. In spite of the fact that most of these rules are generic (i.e., domain independent), there are no well-defined and commonly accepted rules on how the learning objects should be selected and how they should be sequenced to make "instructional sense." Moreover, in order to design adaptive learning systems, a huge set of rules is required, since dependencies between educational characteristics of learning objects and learners are rather complex. In this chapter, we address the learning object selection and sequencing problem in intelligent learning systems proposing a methodology that, instead of forcing an instructional designer to manually define the set of selection and sequencing rules, produces a decision model that mimics the way the designer decides, based on the observation of the designer's reaction over a small-scale learning object selection case.

Introduction

The high rate of evolution of e-learning platforms implies that, on the one hand, increasingly complex and dynamic Web-based learning infrastructures need to be managed more efficiently and, on the other hand, new type of learning services and mechanisms need to be developed and provided. To meet the current needs, such services should satisfy a diverse range of requirements, such as *personalization* and *adaptation* (Dolog, Henze, Nejdl, & Sintek, 2004).

Learning object selection is the first step to adaptive navigation and adaptive course sequencing. Adaptive navigation seeks to present the learning objects associated with an online course in an optimized order, where the optimization criteria takes into consideration the learner's background and performance on related learning objects (Brusilovsky, 1999), whereas adaptive course sequencing is defined as the process that selects learning objects from a digital repository and sequences them in a way that is appropriate for the targeted learning community or individuals (Knolmayer, 2003). Learning object selection and sequencing are recognized as among the most interesting research questions in intelligent Web-based education (Devedžić, 2003; Dolog, Nejdl, 2003; McCalla, 2000).

Although many types of intelligent learning systems are available, we can identify five key components that are common in most systems, namely, the student model, the expert model, the pedagogical module, the domain knowledge module, and the communication model. Figure 1 provides a view of the interactions between these modules.

In most intelligent learning systems that incorporate course sequencing techniques, the pedagogical module is responsible for setting the principles of content selection and instructional planning. The selection of content (in our case, learning objects) is based on a set of teaching rules according to the cognitive style or learning preferences of the learners (Brusilovsky & Vassileva, 2003; Stash & De Bra, 2004). In spite of the fact that most of these rules are generic (i.e., domain independent), there are no well-defined and commonly accepted rules on how the learning objects should be selected and how they should be sequenced to make "instructional sense" (Knolmayer, 2003; Mohan, Greer, & McGalla, 2003). Moreover, a huge set of rules is required to design adaptive learning systems, since dependencies between educational characteristics of learning objects and learners are rather complex.

In this chapter, we address the learning object selection and sequencing problem in intelligent learning systems proposing a methodology that, instead of forcing an

Figure 1. Main components of intelligent learning systems

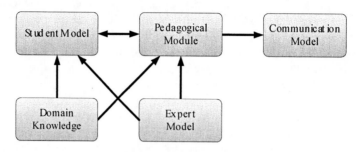

instructional designer to manually define the set of selection rules, produces a decision model that mimics the way the designer decides, based on the observation of the designer's reaction over a small-scale learning object selection problem. In the next section, we discuss the learning object selection process and the instructional planning process as part of automatic course sequencing. The third section presents a methodology for capturing expert's decision model on learning objects selection. The fourth section presents a methodology for automating instructional planning and constitutes the main contribution of this chapter. Finally, we present experimental results of the proposed methodology by comparing the resulting learning objects selected and sequenced by the proposed method with those selected and sequenced by experts.

Automatic Course Sequencing

In automatic course sequencing, the main idea is to generate a course suited to the needs of the learners. As described in the literature, two main approaches for automatic course sequencing have been identified (Brusilovsky & Vassileva, 2003): *Adaptive Courseware Generation* and *Dynamic Courseware Generation.*

In *Adaptive Courseware Generation,* the goal is to generate an individualized course taking into account specific learning goals, as well as the initial level of the student's knowledge. The entire course is adaptively generated before presenting it to the learner, instead of generating a course incrementally, as in a traditional sequencing context. In *Dynamic Courseware Generation,* on the other hand, the system observes the student's progress during his interaction with the course and dynamically adapts the course according to the specific student needs and requirements. If the student's performance does not meet the expectations, the course is dynamically re-planned. The benefit of this approach is that it applies as much adaptivity to an individual student as possible.

Both the above mentioned techniques employ a pre-filtering mechanism to generate a pool of learning objects that match the general content requirements. The main goal of filtering is the reduction of the searching space. Learning Object Repositories often contain hundreds or thousands of learning objects, thus the selection process may

Figure 2. Generalized framework of automatic course sequencing

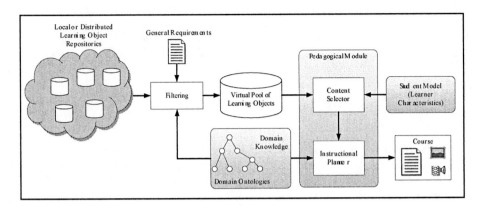

require a significant computational time and effort. In most intelligent learning systems, learning object filtering is based either on the knowledge domain they cover or on the media type characteristics they contain (Kinshuk, Oppermann, Patel & Kashihara, 1999). In the IEEE LOM metadata model (http://ltsc.ieee.org/wg12/, there exist a number of elements covering requirements such as the subject, the language, and the media type of the targeted learning object. Alternatively, filtering can be based on integration of the IEEE LOM metadata model elements and ontologies (Kay & Holden, 2002; Sicilia & Garcia, 2003), but those approaches assume that both the domain model and the learning objects themselves use the same ontology (Mohan, Greer, & McGalla, 2003) and limit the filtering only to knowledge domain filtering. The result of the filtering process falls in a virtual pool of learning objects that will act as an input space for the *content selector*. This pool can be generated from both distributed and local learning object repositories, provided that the appropriate access controls have been granted.

After the creation of the initial pool of learning objects, the *content selection process* is applied based on learner characteristics such as accessibility and competency characteristics or even historical information about related learning activities, included in the Student Model module. Figure 2 presents a generalized framework of the above mentioned course sequencing techniques that utilize filtering, content selection, and instructional planning processes. In the next sections, we will present a methodology for automatic learning object selection and sequencing.

Learning Object Selection

Typically, the design of adaptive learning systems requires a huge set of rules, since dependencies between educational characteristics of learning objects and learners are rather complex. This complexity introduces several problems related to the definition of the rules required (Wu, De Bra, 2001; Calvi & Cristea, 2002), namely:

- **Inconsistency**, when two or more rules are conflicting;

- **Confluence**, when two or more rules are equivalent; and

- **Insufficiency**, when one or more rules required have not been defined.

The proposed methodology is based on an intelligent mechanism that tries to mimic an instructional designer's decision model on the selection of learning objects. To do so, we have designed a framework that attempts to construct a *suitability function* that maps learning object characteristics over learner characteristics and vice versa.

The main advantage of this method is that it requires less effort by the instructional designer, since instead of identifying a huge set of rules, only the designer's selection from a small set of learning objects over a reference set of learners is needed. The machine learning technique will try then to discover the dependence between learning object and learner characteristics that produces the same selection of learning objects per learner, as the instructional designer did.

The proposed methodology does not depend on the characteristics used for learning objects and learner modeling, thus it can be used for extraction of even complex

Figure 3. Selection Model Extraction Framework

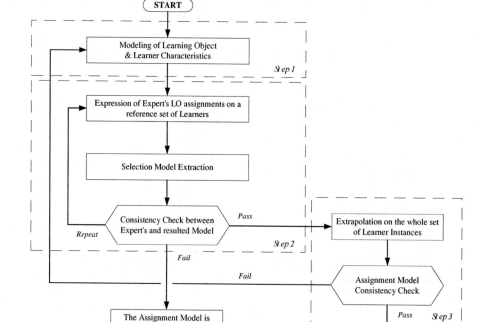

pedagogy-related dependences. It is obvious that since characteristics/requirements like the domain are used for filtering, the dependencies produced are quite generic, depending only on the educational characteristics of the content and the cognitive characteristics of the learner.

Figure 3 presents a graphical representation of the Selection Model Extraction Framework, consisting of three main steps: Modeling and Selection of Criteria, Selection Model Extraction, and Extrapolation.

Step 1: Modeling and Selection of Criteria

The selection methodology is generic, independent of the learning object and the learner characteristics used for the selection. In our experiment, we used learning object characteristics derived from the IEEE Learning Object Metadata (LOM) standard and learner characteristics derived from the IMS Learner Information Package (LIP) specification.

There exist many criteria affecting the decision of learning objects selection. Those criteria that lead to a straightforward exclusion of learning objects, such as the subject, the language, and the media type, are used for filtering. The rest set of criteria, such as the educational characteristics of learning objects, are used for selection model extraction, since the dependencies of those criteria can model the pedagogy applied by the instructional designer when selecting learning objects. Due to the complexity of interdependencies between them, those criteria are the ones that cannot be directly mapped to rules from the instructional designer. Thus, an automatic extraction method, like the proposed one, is needed. In Tables 1 and 2, we have identified the LOM and LIP characteristics, respectively, that can be used as an input space (set of selection criteria) to the learning object selector.

Step 2: Selection Model Extraction

After identifying the set of characteristics/criteria (Step1) that will be used as the input space of the LO Selector, we try to extract for each learning object characteristic the expert's suitability evaluation model over a reference set of LIP-based characterized learners. The input to this phase is the IEEE LOM characteristics of a reference set of learning objects, the IMS LIP characteristics of a reference set of learners, and the suitability preference of an expert for each of the learning objects over the whole reference set of learners. The model extraction methodology has the following formulation: Let us consider a set of learning objects, called A, which is valued by a set of criteria $g = (g_1, g_2, ..., g_n)$. The assessment model of the suitability of each learning object for a specific learner, leads to the aggregation of all criteria into a unique criterion that we call a suitability function: $S(g) = S(g_1, g_2, ..., g_n)$. We define the suitability function as an additive function of the form $S(g) = \sum_{i=1}^{n} s_i(g_i)$ with the following additional notation:

Table 1. LO Selector input space (learning object characteristics)

Selection Criteria	IEEE LOM Path	Explanation
General	LOM/General/Structure	Underlying organizational structure of a LO
	LOM/General/Aggregation Level	The functional granularity (level of aggregation) of a LO
Educational	LOM/Educational/Interactivity Type	Predominant mode of learning supported by a LO
	LOM/Educational/ Interactivity Level	The degree to which a learner can influence the aspect or behavior of a LO
	LOM/Educational/Semantic Density	The degree of conciseness of a LO, estimated in terms of its size, span or duration
	LOM/Educational/Typical Age Range	Age of the typical intended user -- this element refers to developmental age and not chronological age
	LOM/Educational/Difficulty	How hard it is to work with or through a LO for the typical intended target audience
	LOM/Educational/Intended End User Role	Principal user(s) for which a LO was designed, most dominant first
	LOM/Educational/Context	The principal environment within which the learning and use of a LO is intended to take place
	LOM/Educational/Typical Learning Time	Typical time it takes to work with or through a LO for the typical intended target audience
	LOM/Educational/Learning Resource Type	Specific kind of LO -- the most dominant kind shall be first

- $s_i(g_i)$: Marginal suitability of the ith selection criterion valued g_i,
- $S(g)$: Global suitability of a learning object.

The marginal suitability evaluation for the criterion gi is calculated using the formula $s_i(x) = a_i + b_i \exp(-c_i x_2)$, where x is the corresponding value of the gi learning object selection criterion. This formula produces, according to parameters a, b and c as well as the value space of each criterion, the main criteria forms, we have identified:

- **Monotonic form:** when the marginal suitability of a criterion is a monotonic function;
- **Non monotonic form:** when the marginal suitability of a criterion is a non-monotonic function.

The calculation of the optimal values of parameters a, b, and c for each selection criterion is the subject of the Knowledge Model Extraction step. Let us call P the strict preference relation and I the indifference relation. If S_{O_1} is the global suitability of a learning object O_1 and S_{O_2} is the global suitability of a learning object O_2, then the following properties generally hold for the suitability function S:

$$S_{O_1} > S_{O_2} \Leftrightarrow (O_1)P(O_2),$$
$$S_{O_1} = S_{O_2} \Leftrightarrow (O_1)I(O_2)$$

and the relation $R = P \cup I$ is a weak order relation.

Table 2. LO selector input space (learner characteristics)

Selection Criteria	IMS LIP Path	Explanation	Usage Condition
Accessibility	LIP/Accessibility/ Preference/typename	The type of cognitive preference	-
	LIP/Accessibility/ Preference/prefcode	The coding assigned to the preference	-
	LIP/Accessibility/Eligibility /typename	The type of eligibility being defined	-
	LIP/Accessibility/Disability/ typename	The type of disability being defined	-
Qualifications Certifications Licenses	LIP/QCL/Level	The level/grade of the QCL	LIP/QCL/Typename, LIP/QCL/Title and LIP/QCL/Organization should refer to a qualification related with the objectives of the learning goal
			LIP/QCL/date > Threshold
Activity	LIP/Activity/Evaluation/ noofattempts	The number of attempts made on the evaluation.	LIP/Activity/Typename, LIP/Activity/status, LIP/Activity/units and LIP/Activity/Evaluation/ Typename should refer to a qualification related with the objectives of the learning goal
	LIP/Activity/Evaluation/ result/interpretscope	Information that describes the scoring data.	
	LIP/Activity/Evaluation/ result/score	The scoring data itself.	LIP/Activity/date > Threshold
			LIP/Activity/Evaluation/date > Threshold

The expert's requested information then consists of the weak order R defined on A for several learner instances. Using the provided weak order relation R and based on the form definition of each learning object characteristic we can define the suitability differences $\Delta = (\Delta_1, \Delta_2, ..., \Delta_{m-1})$, where m is the number of learning objects in the reference set A and $\Delta_k = S_{O_k} - S_{O_{k+1}} \geq 0$ depending on the suitability relation of (k) and (k+1) preferred learning object for a specific learner of the reference set. We can introduce an error function e for each suitability difference:

$$\Delta_k = S_{O_k} - S_{O_{k+1}} + e_k \geq 0.$$

Using constrained optimization techniques, we can then solve the non-linear problem:

$$\text{Minimize} \sum_{j=1}^{m-1} (e_j)^2$$

Subject to the constraints:

$$\begin{aligned} \Delta_j > 0 \quad &\text{if } O_j P O_{j+1} \\ \Delta_j = 0 \quad &\text{if } O_j I O_{j+1} \end{aligned} \right\} \text{ for each one of the learners of the reference set.}$$

This optimization problem will lead to the calculation of the optimal values of the parameter a, b and c for each learning object selection criteria over the reference set of learners.

Step 3: Extrapolation

The purpose of this phase is to generalize the resulted marginal suitability model from the reference set of learners to all learners, by calculating the corresponding marginal suitability values for every combination of learner characteristics. This calculation is based on the interpolation of the marginal suitability values between the two closest instances of the reference set of learners.

Suppose that we have calculated the marginal suitability $s_i^{L_1}$ and $s_i^{L_2}$ of a criterion c_i matching the characteristics of learners L_1 and L_2 respectively. We can then calculate the corresponding marginal suitability value for another learner L using interpolation if the characteristics of learner L are mapped inside the polyhedron that the characteristics of learners L_1 and L_2 define, using the formula:

$$s_i\left(c_i^L\right) = s_i\left(c_i^{L_1}\right) + \frac{c_i^L - c_i^{L_1}}{c_i^{L_2} - c_i^{L_1}}\left[s_i\left(c_i^{L_2}\right) - s_i\left(c_i^{L_1}\right)\right], \text{ if } s_i\left(c_i^{L_2}\right) > s_i\left(c_i^{L_1}\right)$$

Let $C_i = \left[c_{i^*}, c_i^*\right] i = 1,2,\ldots n$ be the intervals in which the values of each criterion—for both learning object and learners—are found. Then we call global suitability surface the space $C = \times_{i=1}^n C_i$. The calculation of the global suitability over the above mentioned space is the addition of the marginal suitability surfaces for each of the learning object characteristics over the whole combination set of learner characteristics.

Learning Object Sequence Selection

The instructional plan of an intelligent educational system can be considered as two interconnected networks or "spaces": a network of concepts (knowledge space) and a network of educational material (hyperspace or media space).

Accordingly, the instructional planning process involves three key steps (Brusilovsky, 2003)]:

- **Structuring the knowledge:** The heart of the knowledge-based approach to developing intelligent learning management systems is a structured domain model that is composed of a set of small domain knowledge elements (DKE). Each DKE represents an elementary fragment of knowledge for the given domain. Depending on the domain, the application area, and the choice of the designer, concepts can represent bigger or smaller pieces of domain knowledge. The use of ontologies can significantly simplify the task of knowledge structuring by providing a standard-based way for knowledge representation. Ontologies are specifications of the conceptualization and corresponding vocabulary used to describe a domain (Gruber, 1993). Ontologies typically consist of definitions of concepts relevant for the domain, their relations, and axioms about these concepts and relationships. For the instructional planning process, we have identified four classes of concept relationships, namely:

- "Consists of": this class relates a concept with it's sub-concepts';

- "Similar to": this class relates two concepts with the same semantic meaning;

- "Opposite of": this class relates a concept with another concept semantically opposite from the original one; and

- "Related with": this class relates concepts that have a relation different from the above mentioned.

- **Structuring the media space:** Structuring of the media space is based on the use of learning object metadata. More precisely, in the IEEE LOM metadata model, the "Relation" Category defines the relationship between a specific learning object and other learning objects, if any. The kind of relation has been described by the sub-element "Kind" that holds 12 predefined values based on the corresponding element of the Dublin Core Element Set. In our case, we use only four of the predefined relation values, namely:

  - "is part of" / "has part";

  - "references" / "is referenced by";

  - "is based on" / "is basis for"; and

  - "requires" / "is required by."

- **Connecting the knowledge space and the media space:** The connection of the knowledge space with educational material can be based on the use of the "Classification" Category, defined by the IEEE LOM Standard as an element category that describes where a specific learning object falls within a particular classification system. The integration of IEEE LOM "Classification" Category with ontologies provides a simple way of identifying the domains covered by a learning object. Since it is assumed that both the domain model and the learning objects themselves use the same ontology, the connection process is then relatively straightforward. Figure 4 presents an example of the connection of the two spaces.

Figure 4. Knowledge space and media space connection

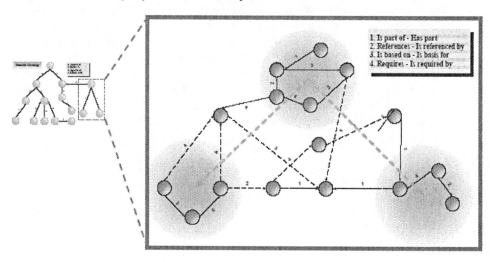

The result of the merging of the knowledge space and the media space is a directed acyclic graph (DAG) of learning objects inheriting relations from both spaces. In order to extract from the resulting graph of learning objects the "optimum" sequence of learning objects, we need to add learner preference information to the DAG. This information has the form of weight on each connection of the DAG. As a weighting function we use the inverse of the suitability function calculated at the content selection phase. This means that the bigger a weight is, the less suitable the target learning object is. After weighting the DAG with the use of the suitability function, we need to find the optimum (shortest) path by the use of a shortest path algorithm.

The result of applying the shortest path algorithm is the optimum sequence of learning objects that covers the desired concepts (thus reach the learning goal) according to cognitive characteristics and preferences of the learner.

Experimental Results and Discussion

In order to evaluate the total efficiency of the proposed methodology both on calculating the suitability on the reference (training) set of learning objects and on estimating the suitability of learning objects external from the reference set, we have designed an evaluation criterion, defined by:

$$Success\,(\%) = 100 * \left(\frac{Correct\ Learning\ Objects\ Selected}{n} \right)$$

where n is the number of the desired learning objects from the virtual pool that will act as input to the instructional planner. We assume that the number of desired learning objects is less than the total number of learning objects in the input space (learning objects pool) and that both the learning object metadata and the learner information metadata have normal distribution over the value space of each criterion.

Additionally, we have classified the learning objects for both sets of learning objects in two classes according to their aggregation level, since granularity is a parameter affecting the capability of an instructional designer to select learning content for a specific learner. The classification is based on the value space of the "General/ Aggregation_Level" element of the IEEE LOM standard. Table 3 presents a description of the two classes used.

We present experimental results of the proposed methodology by comparing the resulting selected learning objects with those selected by experts. We have evaluated the success on both the reference set of learning objects (Training Success) and on the suitability estimation of learning objects external to the reference set (Estimation Success). Figures 5 and 6 present average experimental results for learning objects with aggregation level 1 and 2, respectively.

If we consider that, for one learner instance, the different combinations of learning objects calculated as the multiplication of the value instances of characteristics in the IEEE LOM information model lead to more than one million learning object categories, it is evident that it is almost unrealistic to assume that an instructional designer can manually define the full set of selection rules that correspond to the dependencies extracted by the proposed method and, at the same time, avoid the inconsistencies, confluence and insufficiency of the produced selection rules.

The proposed methodology is capable of effectively extracting dependencies between learning object and learner characteristics affecting the decision of an instructional designer on the learning object selection problem. More analysis on the results, presented in Figures 5 and 6, shows that when the desired number of learning objects (n) is relatively small (less than 100), the selected learning objects by the extracted decision model are almost similar to those the instructional designer would select.

On the other hand, when the desired number of learning objects is relatively large (about 500), the success of the selection is affected but remains at an acceptable level (about 90%).

The granularity of learning objects has proven to be another parameter affecting the selection success. Granularity mainly affects the capability of an instructional designer

Table 3. Learning objects aggregation level according to IEEE LOM standard

IEEE LOM Element	Value Space	Description
General/Aggregation_Level	1	The smallest level of aggregation, e.g., raw media data or fragments
	2	A collection of level 1 learning objects, e.g., a lesson chapter or a full lesson

Figure 5. Average experimental results for learning objects with Aggregation Level 1

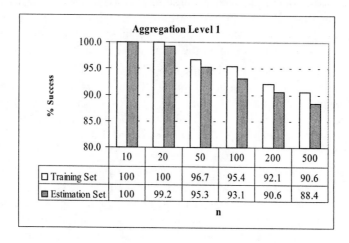

Figure 6. Average experimental results for learning objects with Aggregation Level 2

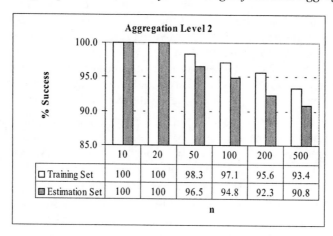

to express selection preferences over learning objects. Learning objects with a small aggregation level have a bigger possibility of producing "gray" decision areas, where the instructional designer cannot decide which learning object best matches the cognitive style or learning preferences of a learner. In our experiments, learning objects with Aggregation Level 2, which can be small, or even bigger collections of learning objects with Aggregation Level 1 appear to have less possibility of producing indifference relations, enabling secure decision making, even for a bigger desired number of learning objects (n=200).

Conclusion

In this chapter we address the learning object selection problem in intelligent learning systems proposing a methodology that, instead of forcing an instructional designer to manually define the set of selection rules, produces a decision model that mimics the way the designer decides, based on the observation of the designer's reaction over a small-scale learning object selection problem.

Since one of the primary design goals of learning objects is reusability in a variety of diverse learning contexts, learning objects are generally designed in a highly de-contextualized manner (South & Monson, 2000). At the same time, it is nearly impossible to define learning characteristics, such as difficulty or semantic density, which affect both selection and sequencing of learning objects.

The proposed content selection methodology can provide the framework for designing highly adaptive learning systems, provided that learning objects are as small as needed - *learning threshold* - in order for a content author to be able to identify the pedagogical features they contain (Gibbons, Nelson, & Richards, 2000). Figure 7 presents the optimum granularity of learning objects as the space in between the learning and the context thresholds.

Future research agenda includes learning object decomposition from existing courses, allowing reuse of the disaggregated learning objects in different educational contexts. The intelligent selection of the disaggregation level and the automatic structuring of the atoms (raw media) inside the disaggregated components in order to preserve the educational characteristics for which they were initially designed, is a key issue in the research agenda for learning objects (Duval, 2003).

Figure 7. The Granularity/Aggregation Spectrum (South & Monson, 2000)

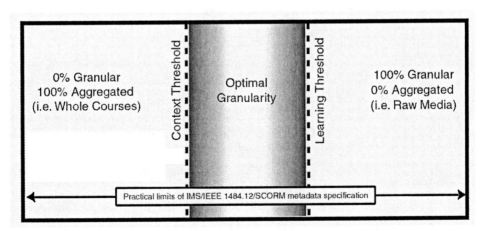

Acknowledgments

The work presented in this paper is partially supported by European Community under the FP6 Information Society Technologies (IST) programme *ICLASS contract IST-507922*, and the Leonardo da Vinci programme *eAccess contract EL/2003/B/F/148233*.

References

Brusilovsky, P. (1999). Adaptive and intelligent technologies for Web-based education. *Künstliche Intelligenz, 4*, 19-25.

Brusilovsky, P. (2003). Developing adaptive educational hypermedia systems: From design models to authoring tools. *Authoring Tools for Advanced Technology Learning Environment.* Dordrecht: Kluwer Academic.

Brusilovsky, P. & Vassileva J. (2003). Course sequencing techniques for large-scale Web-based education. *International Journal of Continuing Engineering Education and Life-long Learning, 13*(1/2), 75-94.

Calvi, L. & Cristea, A. (2002). Towards generic adaptive systems: Analysis of a case study. In *Proceedings of the Second International Conference on Adaptive Hypermedia and Adaptive Web Based Systems,* LNCS 2347, Malaga, Spain (pp. 79-89). Springer.

Devedžić, V.B. (2003). Key issues in next-generation Web-based education. *IEEE Transactions on Systems, Man and Cybernetics Part C, 33*(3), 339-349.

Dolog, P., Henze, N., Nejdl, W., & Sintek M. (2004). Personalization in distributed eLearning environments. In *Proceedings of the 13th International World Wide Web Conference,* May 17-22, New York (pp. 170-179). ACM Press.

Dolog, P. & Nejdl, W. (2003). Challenges and benefits of the Semantic Web for user modelling. *Workshop on Adaptive Hypermedia and Adaptive Web-Based Systems, Proceedings of* the *12th International World Wide Web Conference,* Budapest, Hungary, May (pp. 20-24). ACM Press.

Duval, E. & Hodgins, W. (2003). A LOM research agenda. In *Proceedings of the 12th International World Wide Web Conference,* May 20-24, Budapest, Hungary (pp. 659-671). ACM Press.

Gibbons, A. S., Nelson, J., & Richards, R. (2000). The nature and origin of instructional objects. In D.A. Wiley (Ed.), *The instructional use of learning objects: Online version.* Retrieved from *http://reusability.org/read/chapters/gibbons.doc*

Gruber, T. (1993). A translation approach to portable ontology specifications. *Knowledge Acquisition, 5*, 199-220.

IEEE Learning Object Metadata (IEEE LOM) standard. Retrieved from *http://ltsc.ieee.org/wg12/*

Kay, J. & Holden, S. (2002). Automatic extraction of ontologies from teaching document metadata. In L. Aroyo & D. Dicheva (Eds.), *Proceedings of the ICCE 2002 Workshop on Concepts and Ontologies in Web-based Educational Systems,* December 3-6, Auckland, New Zealand (pp. 25-28).

Kinshuk, Oppermann, R., Patel, A., & Kashihara, A. (1999). Multiple representation approach in multimedia-based intelligent educational systems. *Artificial Intelligence in Education,* 259-266. Amsterdam: IOS Press.

Knolmayer, G.F. (2003). Decision support models for composing and navigating through e-learning objects. In R. H. Sprague (Ed.), *Proceedings of the 36th IEEE Annual Hawaii International Conference on System Sciences*, January 6-9, Hawaii (pp. 31-40). IEEE Computer Society.

McCalla, G. (2000). The fragmentation of culture, learning, teaching and technology: implications for the artificial intelligence in education research agenda in 2010. *International Journal of Artificial Intelligence in Education, 11*, 177-196.

Mohan, P., Greer, J., & McGalla, G. (2003). Instructional planning with learning objects. In P. Baumgartner, P. A. Cairns, M. Kohlhase, & E. Melis (Eds.), *Proceedings of the Workshop on Knowledge Representation and Automated Reasoning for E-Learning Systems, 18th International Joint Conference on Artificial Intelligence*, August 9-15, Acapulco, Mexico (pp. 52-58). Universitat Koblenz-Landau.

South, J. B. & Monson, D. W. (2000). A university-wide system for creating, capturing, and delivering learning objects. In D.A. Wiley (Ed.), *The instructional use of learning objects: Online version.* Retrieved from *http://reusability.org/read/chapters/south.doc*

Stash, N. & De Bra, P. (2004). Incorporating cognitive styles in AHA! *First International Workshop on Adaptable and Adaptive Hypermedia. Proceedings of the IASTED Conference on Web Based Education,* February 16-18, Innsbruck, Austria (pp. 378-383).

Sicilia, M. A. & García, E. (2003). On the integration of IEEE-LOM Metadata Instances and Ontologies. *IEEE Learning Technology Newsletter, 5*(1), 27-30.

Wu, H. & De Bra, P. (2001). Sufficient conditions for well-behaved adaptive hypermedia Systems. *Proceedings of the First Asia-Pacific Conference on Web Intelligence: Research and Development,* October 23-26, Maebashi City, Japan (pp. 148-152). Springer.

Chapter IV

Building Virtual Learning Communities

Naomi Augar
Deakin University, Australia

Ruth Raitman
Deakin University, Australia

Elicia Lanham
Deakin University, Australia

Wanlei Zhou
Deakin University, Australia

Abstract

This chapter introduces the concept of virtual learning communities and discusses and further enhances the theory and definitions presented in related literature. A model comprising four criteria essential to virtual learning communities is presented and discussed in detail. Theory and case studies relating to the impact of virtual learning communities on distance education and students from diverse cultural groups are also examined. In addition, this chapter investigates the enabling technologies and facilitation that is required to build virtual learning communities. Other case studies are used to illustrate the process of building virtual learning communities. Emerging technologies such as wikis and video lectures are also analysed to determine the effects they have on building and sustaining effective virtual learning communities.

Introduction

Virtual communities are created when people form groups online to share a common interest and create a social bond that is nourished with continued interaction over time (Powazek, 2002). Social virtual communities, also known as discourse communities, have existed on the Internet for many years. Communities supported by Internet discussion boards and the like are dedicated to interests as diverse as pop stars and football. All involve the sharing of knowledge, support, and common interests through ongoing social interaction online (Jonassen, Howland, Moore, & Marra, 2003; Rheingold, 1994; Wood & Smith, 2001).

Computer-supported collaborative work has been the subject of research since the 1970s when communications technology evolved to support virtual communities in the work-place (Lewis, 2002). Work-related virtual communities are also known as communities of practice (Wenger, 1998). These communities allowed their workers to share business knowledge and learn from and support one another (Jonassen et al., 2003). Employees at different offices and those working from home can also share a mutual sense of presence provided by such communities (Dourish & Bly, 1992; Schraefel, Ho, Chignell, & Milton, 2000).

The advent of the Internet has had a huge impact on teaching and learning around the world. The Internet and its associated communication media have the potential to revolutionise learning (Lewis, 2002). It is not only a powerful tool for content provision, but it also lends itself to the creation of groups of learners who can support each other in the learning process (Bruckman, 2002).

Traditionally, universities have used classroom-situated tutorials as a means of facilitating discourse among learners so they can construct a solid understanding of course materials through social interaction with their peers and instructors. Virtual learning communities can now provide a classroom online, in which students may interact with each other and their instructors. The virtual nature of the classroom means that students can join in regardless of their location. Consequently, participation in a learning community can be particularly beneficial to those who study entirely online, such as distance learners. It can help learners to overcome their feelings of isolation and enhance their learning experience through interaction with their peers (Blunt, 2001; Haythornthwaite, Kazmer, Robins, & Shoemaker, 2000; Lanham & Zhou, 2002).

The work of Haythornthwaite et al. (2000) describes a virtual learning community that used multiple technologies to connect distance learners. The distance program included some classroom-situated seminars. However, the bulk of the learning experience was conducted online. E-mail and Internet discussion boards were the prime means for communication among students and staff. Internet Relay Chat (IRC), a text-based synchronous discussion program, allowed students to partake in informal social communication known as "whispering" during real-time virtual lectures. IRC was also used by students to ask the instructor questions during the live lectures. The lectures were delivered online using PowerPoint slides accompanied by narration. Interviews conducted throughout the duration of the course showed that students who communicated actively identified themselves as members of a learning community and felt less isolated and less stressed than those who did not participate.

Palaver Tree Online is a virtual learning community that connects students with mentors who help the students build a database of oral history. Students interview elders online using specially developed discussion software that integrates individual profiles of the elders. Students can also create stories that summarise what they have learned in their interviews and publish them within the integrated online environment (Ellis & Bruckman, 2001).

Jonassen et al. (2003) describe several virtual learning community projects such as Knowledge Forum, CaMILE, SWiki, and Shadow netWorkspace. All share discourse as the common method for building communities of learners. The projects use various tailor-made software solutions to create flexible discussion forums and platforms for collaboration on documents and the construction of knowledge by students. Some of these communities also involve mentors interacting with students to share knowledge and achieve learning goals in a manner similar to the Palaver Tree Online project.

These examples illustrate some of the possibilities of virtual learning communities. Subsequently, this chapter defines virtual learning communities and discusses the technologies and facilitation required to build them. It explores the pedagogy of virtual learning communities and presents case studies to illustrate the community building process.

Virtual Learning Communities

The evolution of modern day virtual learning communities can be traced back to the industrial revolution and beyond. People have formed learning communities to share knowledge throughout history. Virtual learning communities facilitated by the Internet are an extension of this trend (Lewis, 2002).

There are varied notions of what constitutes a virtual community (Daniel, McCalla, & Schwier, 2002; Jones, 1997). A learning community is made up of individuals who work together in a shared space to increase their knowledge and understanding of a subject through study and experience (Saragina, 1999). In a virtual learning community, the shared space that the community inhabits is the Internet.

A virtual learning environment is created on the Internet using study materials, discussion boards, and instructors (Augar, Raitman, & Zhou, 2004a; Augar, Raitman, & Zhou, 2005; Oren, Nachmias, Mioduser, & Lahav, 1998).

However, the provision of content in a virtual environment accompanied by a discussion board is not sufficient in and of itself. For virtual communities to exist, they must have a minimum level of interactivity among a variety of communicators in a common public space, with a minimum level of membership sustained over time (Augar et al., 2004a; Jones, 1997; Wood & Smith, 2001).

A virtual learning community is a group of learners that interact in a common online environment to gain understanding of subject matter. Learners build on their knowledge by interacting with each other, their instructors, and learning materials. By sharing a common learning goal and interacting socially over a period of time, learners develop and share a sense of belonging and shared purpose (Augar et al., 2004a; Augar et al., 2005).

E-Learning Environment or Virtual Learning Community?

"Community" is a common word in current e-learning literature. This section compares and contrasts e-learning environments and virtual learning communities to clarify their similarities and differences.

An e-learning environment comprises the tools and content required to facilitate an online learning experience for students. It may comprise threaded discussions, synchronous chat, whiteboard tools, and content such as HTML, PDF files, or even multimedia presentations. Note that this definition implies that providing learning tools and content to students online does not automatically result in the creation of a virtual learning community. Such a view is technologically deterministic (Augar & Zhou, 2003; Jones, 1997). Rather, the provision of learning tools and content online creates an e-learning environment.

In most cases, e-learning environments require facilitation from teaching staff, as is the case for virtual learning communities. Facilitation may take the form of tutors moderating online discussion forums for students. E-learning environments and virtual learning communities are similar because students have a shared learning goal in both settings. However, the outcome of the shared learning goal in an e-learning environment is the successful completion of the subject. As later sections will discuss, virtual learning communities can encourage students to become more active in defining their shared learning goal. Moreover, virtual learning communities allow students to work together as a group to achieve shared learning goals.

Similarities aside, the key point that differentiates a virtual learning community from an e-learning environment is social context. Students develop social presence as a sense of community emerges in an e-learning environment. In developing social context, students feel a shared sense of community with their fellow learners and they identify with the community as a whole.

E-learning environments and virtual learning communities share the following common aspects: tools, content, facilitation, and shared learning goal. However, it is the development of social context among learners that turns an e-learning environment into a virtual learning community. Hence, careful consideration should be given to labelling an e-learning environment a "community." A host can provide the tools and facilitation that lay the foundations, but a community will only emerge if and when the participants choose to identify themselves as members of a community (Haythornthwaite et al., 2000; Powazek, 2002).

While this chapter will outline what the developer can do to increase the chances of building a virtual learning community, it is the users who will determine whether the developer's efforts are a success. As Jonassen et al. (2003) point out, virtual learning communities are an ideal that may not ever be completely attainable. Therefore, the important aspect to note is whether the learning group is moving towards or away from the ideal of a community.

Essential Criteria for Virtual Learning Communities

To further refine the discussion presented in the previous sections, four interrelated criteria are presented that are building blocks for the development of a virtual learning community. These criteria are: social context, facilitation, technology, and a shared learning goal. They are presented in the model depicted in Figure 1 (Augar et al., 2004a).

These four interrelated essential criteria are critical to the process of fostering a sense of community amongst learners. They are themes that will be reiterated throughout this chapter, as they are central to the process of building effective virtual learning communities. The following sections explore these criteria in greater depth.

Technology

For a sense of community to emerge in a virtual setting where people interact with one another in an online environment, there must be a shared space where communication can occur (Augar & Zhou, 2003; Blunt, 2001; Jones, 1997; Wood & Smith, 2001). Technology allows learners to transmit, save, organise and extend the knowledge shared by the community members (Jonassen et al., 2003).

Consequently, technology is fundamental to the development of any virtual learning community. Reliability and ease of use are fundamental requirements for technology that supports e-learning. Students learning online can become alienated when they experience technical difficulties, which can diminish their motivation to participate (Augar et al., 2004a; Hara & Kling, 1999).

One of the most widely used technologies for enabling virtual learning communities is the asynchronous discussion forum. Asynchronous discussion tools and e-mail are used to create lively discourse relating to learning materials. Real-time collaboration tools may also be used, but they may disadvantage distance learners where time

Figure 1. Critical building blocks for a virtual learning community

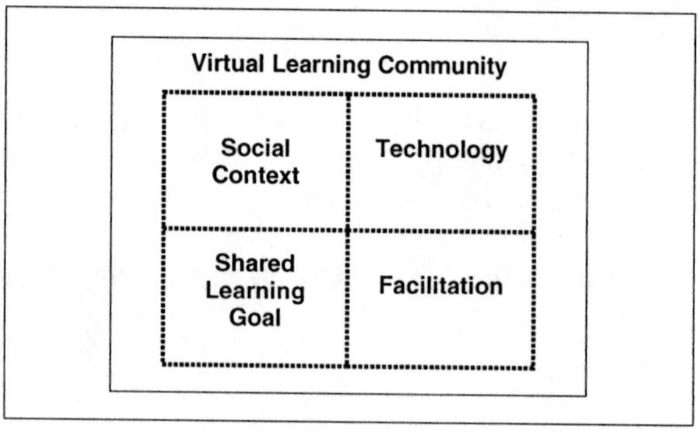

differences are a factor. Learning materials are provided as supplements to the interactive tools that facilitate the virtual learning community. Text-based and multimedia reference materials containing course content such as lecture notes, video lectures, or weekly readings provide resources to support the discourse that is the foundation of the community.

Most virtual learning communities are text-based. Access to these learning communities is gained via a software interface, which runs over the Internet. Students can use their personal computer to type messages and contribute or "post" them to ongoing asynchronous discussions that are maintained on a host server (Augar & Zhou, 2003).

Deakin University runs an e-learning environment called Deakin Studies Online (DSO). DSO uses WebCT Vista software, which has been customized especially for Deakin University. Figure 2 shows a screen shot of the DSO asynchronous discussion tool. This tool is used regularly by students, both to communicate with their peers informally and to participate in structured learning activities, such as online tutorials.

Synchronous text-based chat systems can also facilitate virtual learning communities. IRC, MSN Messenger, and ICQ provide simple examples of software interfaces that allow learners from around the world to participate in real-time discussions. Each user can compose messages, which can be immediately viewed by other participants who in turn have the opportunity to respond. MSN Messenger and ICQ differ from asynchronous technologies in that each "chat" session is initiated by individual users and is not hosted on a designated central server. Unless a participant chooses to "log" a chat session (keep a transcript), there is no ongoing record of discourse between users (Augar & Zhou, 2003).

Deakin University's DSO system has an integrated chat facility for learners. Instructors may add this facility to their subject's learning area for students to access as part of learning activities. The interface of the DSO chat facility is depicted in Figure 3.

Figure 2. DSO's discussion tool

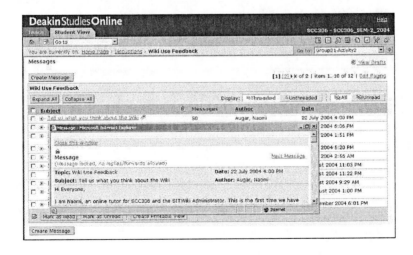

Figure 3. DSO's chat integrated facility

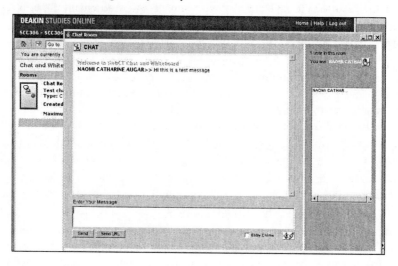

The advent of cheap, accessible multimedia technology has allowed virtual learning communities to evolve and thus include video and audio content. Previously, video conferencing and streamed video placed a huge load on telecommunication networks. Consequently, video was an expensive and cumbersome medium for use in virtual learning communities. However, as the telecommunications network bandwidth has increased and the price of services such as broadband Internet has decreased, video has been adopted by some community builders. This trend has been encouraged further by the reduced cost of audio and video capture devices, and the increased speed and memory of personal computers (Augar & Zhou, 2003).

Computer-mounted video cameras (Web cams) can be used in conjunction with programs that support video such as MSN Messenger or Microsoft NetMeeting to establish video conferences with groups. Shareware such as CU-SeeMe allows larger groups of people to conduct video conferences in video chat rooms that can be supported with text-based chat facilities (Jonassen et al., 2003).

Facilitation

Facilitation plays a key role in the successful development of a virtual learning community (Augar et al., 2004a; Carlsen, 2003; Stacey, 2001). The facilitation of virtual learning communities occurs when instructors begin interacting with learners in the e-learning environment. The process of guiding the learners in their development of social context and shared learning goals is critical to building the virtual learning community.

Salmon (2003) proposes a five-stage model of teaching and learning online that was developed as a result of action research undertaken at Open University in the United Kingdom. The model charts the changing needs of students and the role of the facilitator throughout the online learning process:

1. **Access and motivation:** Students focus on gaining access to and becoming familiar with the system. Facilitation at this stage is based on welcoming students, solving access issues, and encouraging participation.

2. **Online socialisation:** Students develop their online identity and begin to interact with the group. Facilitation focuses on helping individuals create their own social presence and encouraging social interaction amongst the group.

3. **Information exchange:** Participants exchange course-related information. Facilitation at this stage focuses on guiding students through the learning task, helping them to access appropriate learning materials, and guiding them in the process of information exchange. Up to and including this stage, the interaction is cooperative and supports the goals of the individual. At Stage 4, the interaction becomes collaborative.

4. **Knowledge construction:** At this stage, interaction becomes collaborative and communication is based on the common culture of the group. The facilitator adopts a more passive approach to moderation, allowing the students to engage in active discourse and broaden and develop their knowledge. The facilitator may guide the discussion by providing summaries of the group's ideas and relating them back to the central learning goals of the course.

5. **Development:** Individuals look for ways to benefit from the system and achieve their learning goals. The facilitator takes on a supportive role at this stage and responds to queries posed by the group. The learners are active and confident in learning through discourse in the online environment.

This model documents the critical and changing role the facilitator plays in the community-building process. They must teach the students how to interact and learn online, facilitate appropriate social interaction, guide their learning, and be responsive to and supportive of the needs of the learning group.

Participation in a virtual learning community requires students to review and understand the input of others, and formulate and contribute appropriate responses so they can have meaningful participation in online discourse. However, students may be more familiar with memorizing course content than they are with evaluating information and forming their own opinions about it. Consequently, the instructor may need to teach students how to communicate online, and provide ongoing monitoring to support active discourse (Jonassen et al., 2003).

The facilitator plays a critical role in modeling social presence and identity for students. The facilitator can set the tone for the community, and aid the development of trust and social bonds among learners. Building trust among learners is critical. Students can create a shared history and develop a sense of trust by sharing their experiences and knowledge within the virtual environment (Augar et al., 2004a; Daniel et al., 2002; Rovai, 2002).

The instructor needs to encourage the emerging sense of community among students while ensuring that the learning task is being completed (Lewis, 2002; Rovai, 2002). Students can become frustrated when they do not receive timely and clear advice in an online environment. By identifying and being responsive to student needs, facilitators can provide added motivation for students to participate (Augar et al., 2004a; Blunt, 2001; Hara & Kling, 1999). Another important aspect of establishing and facilitating appropriate social interaction in a virtual learning community is the implementation of a set of usage policies that are clearly and simply communicated in the e-learning environment, and enforced when necessary (Augar, Raitman, & Zhou, 2004b; Augar et al., 2005; Powazek, 2002).

Social Context

Social context defines the way social interactions are carried out within a virtual learning community. It is the sum of the identity and behaviour of individual participants and helps to define the communities' social identity (Jonassen et al., 2003). Over time, virtual communities develop unwritten rules on how to behave in the online environment. These rules allow participants to expect a certain standard of behaviour and help to develop a level of trust between community members (Haythornthwaite et al., 2000).

Virtual learning communities require students to develop social bonds in a short period of time so they can interact freely and focus on the course content. The process of developing and sustaining social context depends on the ability of learners to interact socially for enough time to develop a level of trust among the group (Augar et al., 2004a; Daniel et al., 2002).

In virtual learning communities, students are largely restricted to text-based communication, which has inherent limitations. Face-to-face communication is regulated by visual and audible cues that indicate someone has finished speaking and another person may start to talk. These cues include for example, finishing a sentence, body language, and vocalizations. Students new to learning in a virtual environment can be frustrated by their inability to detect these cues (Augar & Zhou, 2003; Hiltz & Turoff, 1993).

The absence of audible and visual cues may result in people being ruder than normal because they cannot see the recipients' reaction or gauge non-verbal cues (Baym, 1995). However, the absence of contextual cues can also be helpful as authors must take more care to ensure they communicate clearly (Jonassen et al., 2003). Consequently, the facilitator's role in modelling appropriate social interactions during the founding stages of a virtual learning community is critical to its ongoing success (Augar & Zhou, 2003; Stacey, 2001).

In a virtual learning community, each student's online identity is based on what he or she tells other community members about him or herself. Tools such as profiles (text-based biographies with an optional photograph posted within the e-learning environment) can help new students introduce themselves to the learning group in a non-threatening way (Augar & Zhou, 2003; Blunt, 2001). An interactive extension of this idea is an icebreaker exercise where groups of learners answer sets of socially oriented questions as a group in a discussion forum, introducing themselves to the other group members in the process. The facilitator can model appropriate social presence by taking part in the icebreaker exercise and constructing a profile of his or her own for the students to mimic (Augar et al., 2004b, 2005).

Shared Learning Goal

Virtual learning communities develop when participants can share knowledge about common interests and work to achieve shared learning goals (Daniel et al., 2002; Jonassen et al., 2003). Students may have their own learning goals, including attaining a degree or passing a subject. However, they may not consider participation in a discussion group or a virtual learning community to be a part of achieving those goals. Consequently, the development of a shared learning goal in a group of online learners can be very difficult to achieve (Augar et al., 2004a; Lewis, 2002).

Students can be motivated to participate through assessment that evaluates whether their contributions to group discussions were on time, relevant, and of a high quality (Rovai, 2002). However, Carlsen (2003) feels that for community to emerge, participation should be at least partially voluntary. A student's motivation for participation plays a critical role in the development of a shared learning goal. If students cannot see the benefits of participating in terms of their own goals, they may have a negative perception of the experience. Encouraging participation through assessment may be effective, but it may not result in an authentic virtual learning community.

Certain student groups may be more predisposed to participating in virtual learning communities. The work of Haythornthwaite et al. (2000) demonstrates the benefits virtual learning communities have for distance learners who experienced a reduced sense of isolation by belonging to the learning community. Reduced isolation and the support offered by the community influence a student's motivation to interact socially with other students, who would otherwise be strangers online.

Finally, the goal of any virtual learning community should always be communicated clearly to students (Blunt, 2001). Simple, unambiguous explanations about the aim of the exercise or discourse can reduce student frustration and help them focus on the learning task, rather than questioning why they have to participate. Continued prompt feedback and guidance from facilitators throughout the learning process can help students move toward the development of a shared learning goal.

The interrelated nature of the four criteria outlined here—technology, facilitation, social context, and shared learning goal—means that while all must be present, aspects of the criteria overlap. For example, by guiding the students in the completion of tasks, the facilitator aids in the process of developing the students' shared learning goal. This process highlights the relationship between effective facilitation and the development of a shared learning goal in the community. Likewise, facilitation is critical in the process of building social context. By modelling appropriate online behaviour, the facilitator helps the student establish an online identity and develop social bonds with other members of the learning group. Finally, effective facilitation can only occur if the enabling technology is usable by both the teacher and the students alike.

The Pedagogy of Virtual Learning Communities

This section looks at the theory of teaching and learning that provides the basis for using virtual learning communities as a teaching tool. Specifically, the areas of computer-supported collaborative learning (CSCL), constructivism, and constructionism are discussed. These areas lay the foundation for the central theme of learning communities: students working together and supporting one another in building knowledge that meets the learning objectives of the group (Jonassen et al., 2003).

Computer-Supported Collaborative Learning

The study of virtual learning communities encompasses the research areas of collaborative learning and CSCL. Collaborative learning can be achieved when students work together and share the responsibility for building on their existing knowledge (Myers, 1991). CSCL is a process where students work together on learning tasks using technology to facilitate their collaboration. CSCL can support and enhance peer interaction while enabling the sharing and distribution of knowledge and expertise among community members (Augar et al., 2004b; Lipponen, 2002; Raitman, Augar, & Zhou, 2004).

Constructivism and Constructionism

Constructivism is a process whereby the learner plays an active role in the learning process. The learner constructs new knowledge by building on his or her past and current experience (Brook & Oliver, 2003). Phillips (2000) identifies two different perceptions of constructivism. The first idea promotes constructivism as the shared body of knowledge built up through history. The second promotes the idea that knowledge is made as a result of learners constructing their own internal meaning and understanding of information (Duffy & Jonassen, 1992; Phillips, 2000).

Social interaction among learners plays a key role in the construction of knowledge. It provides students with a means to explore knowledge and achieve understanding of theory and concepts transmitted in the learning environment (Vygotsky, 1978, as cited by Stacey, 1999, 2001). In virtual learning communities, students can use discussion boards to discuss course content, question each other about subject matter, and through this process enhance their understanding of the material (Augar & Zhou, 2003).

Constructionism is similar to constructivism in that individuals create artefacts and in the process of doing so construct a greater understanding of subject matter (Dougimas & Taylor, 2002; Papert & Harel, 1991). Papert and Harel (1991) differentiate constructionism from constructivism by pointing out that constructionism occurs when learners construct real-world objects and enhance their knowledge in the process.

Bruckman (2002) contends that the true power of learning using the Internet lies not in the delivery of content to students who receive it passively. Rather, students should be active learners, gathering information resources and sharing them with their peers in an online environment supported by innovative collaborative tools. CSCL, constructivism, and constructionism all highlight the importance of learners interacting and collaborating to construct knowledge and artefacts that reflect their understanding of course materials. Research in these areas provides strong support and motivation for building virtual learning communities.

Building Culturally Inclusive Virtual Learning Communities

Over that past five years, the number of international students studying at Deakin University has increased. This trend is predicted to continue over the next five years. These international students are from different cultural backgrounds and therefore have different approaches to learning. This increase is not limited to Deakin University. International student enrolments have also been on the increase over recent years at other Australian tertiary institutions, and this trend is expected to continue.

Dr. Brendan Nelson (2004) stated in a media release that Australia's international student enrolments reached an estimated 303,324 in 2003. This translated to a 17% growth in the higher education sector. The media release also indicated that Asia continues to remain the major source of international students, representing more than three-quarters of Australia's overseas students market (Lanham & Zhou, 2004a, 2004b).

An Australian Trade Commission report (2004) stated that in the year 2000, there were 182,000 international students studying at Australian institutions (150,000 onshore and 32,000 offshore). Fifty-six percent of these figures specifically related to University enrolments. The Australia-wide figures correlate with those collected by Deakin University.

During the period 2000 to 2002, there was an increase in the number of international students from Asian countries enrolling for study at Deakin. A significant increase in the number of students from China and Hong Kong was noted, showing an increase from 154 and 325 respectively in 2001, to 276 and 427 respectively in 2002 (Deakin University, 2003).

It has been indicated in several publications (Chin, Chang, & Bauer, 2000; Conlan, 1996; Lanham & Zhou, 2003a; Munro-Smith, 2002) that students with different cultural background have different learning styles. The figures above represent a diverse student body, with a majority of those international students from the Asian culture. Therefore, issues relating to virtual learning environment design for international audiences need to be addressed. Before a virtual learning community is created, an environment where this diverse student body can feel comfortable must be developed. In order to establish such an environment, the developers must focus on the issues relating to the design of virtual environments for international use.

When dealing with international or culturally diverse audiences, it is important to consider the design and layout of the interface. Nielsen (1996) suggests that the developer should ensure that the interface contains culturally neutral icons that will not cause offence to a culturally diverse audience. Metaphors and visual puns are not universally understood. For example, using a coffee cup as a visual icon representing a cyber café may provide a useful visual cue to some Western computer users. However, the developer should not assume that such an icon will be universally understood by a culturally diverse audience. Finally, where content is translated into multiple languages, developers should ensure that content is translated in its entirety so that all students have access to the same materials (Lanham & Zhou, 2003a, 2003b). Following these guidelines can aid in the construction of a culturally unbiased virtual learning environment.

Developers should also consider the design of learning materials when creating a culturally inclusive virtual learning environment. The following guidelines can aid this process:

- Avoid using colloquial language and cultural slang that can be misinterpreted by an audience from a diverse cultural background.

- Review all content and language to ensure it is not offensive to other cultures.

- Identify how different cultures approach learning, and factor this into the learning outcomes of the subject.

- Try to tailor the learning environment so that all students can understand the content provided (Lanham & Zhou, 2003a, 2003b).

These points are a sample of the techniques that can be employed in an attempt to reduce the barriers between cultures in an online learning environment. Providing a culturally inclusive environment can allow students from diverse backgrounds to feel as though they are valued participants within a virtual learning community.

Using Wikis to Build Virtual Learning Communities

"Wiki" is a Hawaiian word meaning "quick" or "fast" in English. In 1994, Ward Cunningham used the word "wiki" as the name for a fully editable Web site that he invented (Leuf & Cunningham, 2001). In their book *The Wiki Way,* Leuf and Cunningham (2001) present wikis as an ideal technology for building virtual communities. Ongoing research at Deakin University is exploring this contention by attempting to use wikis to build virtual learning communities. This section introduces wikis, explains how they work, and describes a wiki pilot study undertaken at Deakin University.

Figure 4. MediaWiki provides editing toolbar instead of using wiki syntax

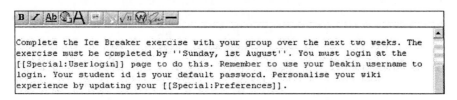

Wikis

Wikis are Web sites that allow users to collaborate to create new documents (Web pages), edit the content of existing Web pages (text and pictures), or edit the structure of the whole site. All a user needs to edit, re-organize and read a wiki is a Web browser. Many wiki clones (versions of wiki scripts written in various programming languages) are available free of charge on the Internet. Most wiki clones are relatively easy to install on a Web server for immediate use. Consequently, wikis have the potential to provide an efficient, flexible, user-friendly, and cost-effective interface for collaboration, knowledge creation and archiving, and student interaction (Augar et al., 2004b; Leuf & Cunningham, 2001).

Wikis can be used in *document mode* or *thread mode*. Wikis that are used in *document mode* act as knowledge repositories. Multiple users update the wiki content and over a period of time the wiki content grows to reflect the shared knowledge of the contributors, who remain anonymous. Wikis can also be used in *thread mode* to facilitate discussion amongst wiki users who each sign their posts (the content or message they added to the wiki) (Augar et al., 2004b, 2005; Leuf & Cunningham, 2001; Raitman et al., 2004).

To edit a wiki, users need to learn a set of basic mark-up rules, known as *wiki syntax,* that format wiki content in a manner similar to HTML. An example of using *wiki syntax* is enclosing a word in double apostrophes to make the word appear as bold text. However, many variations of *wiki syntax* exist. Some wikis provide an editing toolbar so the user can type in his or her content and format it by selecting the required text with a mouse and clicking on the appropriate formatting button in the toolbar. MediaWiki (http://wikipedia.sourceforge.net) has toolbar functionality, which is depicted in Figure 4 (MediaWiki, 2004). Examples of wiki syntax including square brackets and double apostrophes can also be seen in the text area shown in Figure 4 (Augar et al., 2004b, 2005; Leuf & Cunningham, 2001).

Background to the Wiki Pilot Study

Deakin University Australia offers a third-year computing subject "Computers, Society and Professional Ethics" that is taught entirely online. Students use DSO (introduced in the Technology section of this chapter) to participate in online discussion groups of ten students about subject matter over a 13-week semester. In addition to engaging in discourse, students produce collaborative documents that reflect their understanding of the subject matter as a result of their discussions (Augar et al., 2004a; 2004b; 2005). This mode of e-learning reflects the constructivist and constructionist approaches to learning outlined in the Pedagogy section of this chapter.

In the 2003 delivery of this subject, students were encouraged to develop a social presence in the first week of semester by publishing a single-page biography within their designated DSO discussion forum. It was envisaged that group members would read all of the biographies and use them as a means to get to know their fellow group members. However, very little social interaction occurred, and students did not engage in true discussion about the subject matter. Most students simply added their thoughts close to the deadline for contributions and did not comment about the contributions of others (Augar et al., 2004a; 2004b; 2005).

Survey research results indicated that students also experienced technology problems during the semester that impacted negatively upon their motivation to participate. Many students also felt that facilitators did not provide feedback and guidance in a prompt and clear manner. Students expressed general dissatisfaction about participating in the online discussion forums at the end of the semester (Augar et al., 2004a; 2004b; 2005).

Subsequent research has focused on improving the collaborative aspects of the delivery technology by introducing wikis. An icebreaker exercise was developed for use on the wiki that aimed to help learners construct their online identity and enable each learning group to develop social context. Students were surveyed at the end of the 2004 semester to gauge their response to the wiki and the icebreaker exercise.

Which Wiki?

MediaWiki was selected for use in this study because of its toolbar, tracking, and authentication capability. The toolbar functionality was judged to be a critical feature as it meant students would not need to be familiar with *wiki syntax* to use the wiki. Tracking and authentication was required to enable marking of student contributions and to minimise the possibility of intentional misuse of the wiki. Authentication also allowed students to create personal profiles and sign their contributions, contributing to their development of social presence. Finally, MediaWiki is the wiki clone used to power a well-known online collaborative encyclopaedia, Wikipedia (http://en.wikipedia.org/wiki/Main_Page). Consequently, it was judged to be robust enough to support the 450 students who would use it as part of the study. The wiki was known as the Science and Information Technology wiki, SITWiki (Augar et al., 2004b; 2005).

The Wiki Icebreaker Exercise

Each discussion group (comprising 10 students) had its own icebreaker document on the wiki to complete as a group. Eighteen statements were included in the icebreaker exercise. Each statement prompted the students to add their name below the statement if it applied to them. Students could elaborate on the statement and in doing so tell the group a little

Figure 5. SITWiki icebreaker exercise

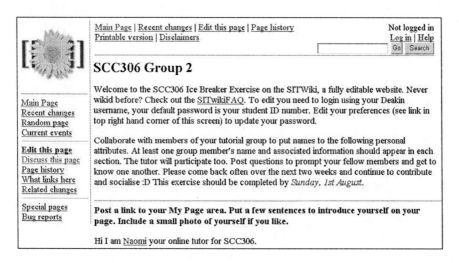

about themselves. An example of a statement is "Members who have lived overseas." This example prompted students who had lived outside of Australia to post a signed message underneath the statement that detailed the country where they had lived.

Each group had two weeks to update the icebreaker document so that every statement had at least one group member's signed response underneath it. A partially completed example is shown in Figure 5.

Prior to commencing the exercise, instructors seeded icebreaker with information about themselves. They did this to introduce themselves to the group whilst modelling appropriate social presence and setting the tone for the exercise. Instructors signed their posts and in doing so created a hyperlink (as shown in Figure 5) to their wiki user page which contained a photo and a brief biography about themselves (Augar et al., 2004b, 2005).

Results

Prior to the icebreaker, many students had not used a wiki before. Some had not even heard of a wiki. The only training students received was in the form of e-mail-based technical support (to respond to specific queries) and an FAQ page provided on the wiki that contained simple instructions on how to edit and perform other required tasks. However, all students who used the wiki were able to satisfactorily complete the icebreaker exercise and introduce themselves to the other students in their discussion group (Augar et al., 2004b; 2005).

A usage policy was developed and displayed on every page of the wiki. The policy consisted of four guidelines that were written in a positive simple manner to encourage a wiki culture of cooperative, respectful usage. Across the 50 groups who used the wiki, there were no incidences of intentional misuse or deletions of wiki content. Sixty-seven percent of students reported that they enjoyed participating in the wiki environment. These positive results were mirrored in the students' overall rating of the wiki experience, as can be seen in Figure 6 (Augar et al., 2004b; 2005).

Technology

MediaWiki proved itself to be a reliable collaboration platform, supporting over 450 users with no system failures during the two-week icebreaker exercise. Students viewed the wiki between one- to two-thousand times per day and, on average, edited the wiki 150 times per day. When the SITWiki was installed and all the exercises and associated pages were uploaded, the wiki contained approximately 100 pages. Throughout the two-week duration of the exercise, the number of pages increased steadily each day to a final tally of over 1000 pages (Augar et al., 2004b).

Seventy-three percent of students surveyed found the wiki easy to use. Part of the survey asked students to identify what they felt were the positive characteristics of the wiki. Many students felt that the ability to interact with the wiki from anywhere at any time was a valuable feature. This response may be due to the fact that 31% of total enrolments for the subject comprised distance education students, for whom time differences and flexibility are key issues. This anywhere-anytime aspect of wiki functionality positions the wiki as an accessible and inclusive platform for building virtual learning communities (Augar et al., 2005).

Some students felt that the user interface lacked simplicity and could benefit from more colour and icons. They indicated that they would appreciate more control in the final presentation of their work via greater support for HTML formatting. However, they did appreciate the fast download speeds that resulted from the basic HTML format of page content (Augar et al., 2005).

Students also recommended a feature they felt would enhance the wiki—a tool that would highlight the modifications that were made since their last access. Some students found it difficult to keep track of what they had or had not read on the wiki due to the unstructured nature of the editing process. Such a feature may include e-mail alerts that may help inspire students to revisit the wiki in order to make further contributions or read and comment on the contributions of others.

The final technical feature that students disliked was the possibility that inconsistencies could occur through simultaneous page editing. For example, if Student A started to edit at 2:00 p.m., Student B started at 2:01 p.m. and finished at 2:03 p.m., when Student A completed his or her editing at 2:06 p.m., this final edition may not contain any of Student B's modifications (MediaWiki does include merge function that can handle this problem in certain situations). Although there was no report of this occurring in this exercise, students felt insecure about losing their wiki additions should this situation arise (Augar et al., 2005).

In fact, it can be noted that the two main concerns of content deletion and simultaneous editing were well highlighted by the students in the feedback, but in reality, there was

Figure 6. Students rate the wiki experience

not one incident that occurred to validate their anxieties. Leuf and Cunningham (2001) call this phenomenon the *open-edit issue*. The fear of losing work or having to create a backup of their input dissuaded students from believing the wiki environment was secure.

Facilitation

The wiki icebreaker exercise had a dual purpose of introducing the students to the other members of their group and to their instructor. Eighty-three percent of students surveyed felt that they got to know their instructor a little better through completing the icebreaker exercise as shown in Figure 7 (Augar et al., 2005).

The icebreaker focused on providing an interactive way of promoting online socialisation, which constitutes the second phase of Salmon's five-stage model of facilitation presented earlier in this chapter (Salmon, 2003). Facilitators not only introduced themselves by participating in the exercise, they modelled appropriate social presence and encouraged group interaction (Augar et al., 2004b; 2005).

Figure 7. Students rate whether the icebreaker helped them get to know their instructor

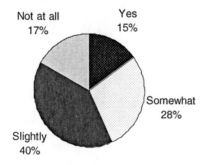

In parallel to this exercise, technical support was provided to students via e-mail and FAQ by wiki administrators. This ensured that students could access the wiki quickly and easily. Student user accounts were created prior to the start of the semester, however, there were ongoing enrolments throughout the duration of the wiki icebreaker exercise. This made quick administrative responses to student requests for account creation imperative to ensuring that phase one of Salmon's (2003) model involving access and motivation was not jeopardised.

Social Context

The goal of the icebreaker exercise was to encourage students to socialise with their online group members. Eighty-seven percent of students surveyed felt that the wiki exercise helped them get to know their group members a little better as shown in Figure 8 (Augar et al., 2005).

Observation indicated that students contributed actively to most questions in the icebreaker exercise. The most popular questions (gaining responses from virtually every group member) were those that asked if students spoke another language and in what suburb or country they resided. In addition, 68% of students placed some text or pictures on their user page to introduce themselves to the group (Augar et al., 2004b; 2005).

All students signed their posts; most used the hyperlinked signature tool supported by the SITWiki toolbar. Over half the students changed their hyperlinked signature to their preferred name; a third left it as their default wiki username; and less than 10% of students chose not to use the signature tool (Augar et al., 2005).

Some interesting trends were observed among the groups of students who did not use the signature tool to sign their posts. One group commenced each individual post by including their preferred name plain text and a colon; their post would follow this signature (this format is common in synchronous chat programs). Another group

Figure 8. Students rate whether the icebreaker helped them get to know other group members

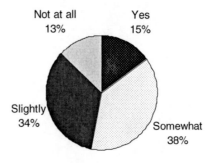

Figure 9. Students rate whether the icebreaker enhanced group communication throughout semester

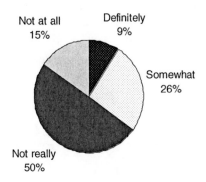

hyperlinked signatures to introduce themselves under the first icebreaker statement and then signed the rest of their posts using plain text. In these instances, it was noted that rather than adopting the format modelled by their instructor, students used the format modelled by the first student to make a post. This trend can be perceived as indicating the emergence of a group culture (Augar et al., 2005).

Shared Learning Goal

The icebreaker exercise focused on online socialisation and introducing students to online learning in a fun and informal manner. Consequently, the development of a shared learning goal relating to the subject matter did not occur. However, some students felt that the socialisation did enhance (if only slightly) their ability to communicate with their group throughout the semester, as shown in Figure 9.

Wikis in Review

The wiki icebreaker exercise showed that MediaWiki is a reliable and usable technology for supporting collaboration among large groups of students. However, research indicates that the SITWiki technology should be improved for future use.

Students were not comfortable with the possibility of losing work. Developing a short-streamed multimedia training video (supported by text- and graphics-based explanations) that explains the backup and security procedures in place may make students feel more secure. Similar training resources about what a wiki is and how to use it effectively may also make the wiki easier to use.

In addition, resolving the possibility of data loss through inadvertent synchronous editing could further enhance the perceived security of the wiki. This issue could be addressed by providing either alerts to the user that a page is being edited, or by locking a page while it is being edited to ensure no data can be lost via synchronous editing.

Future research aims to further explore the community building potential of wikis by using them to facilitate student creation of collaborative knowledge repositories. Research will explore whether using a wiki in document mode empowers students with a sense of ownership that fosters a sense of community in the learning group.

Using Online Lectures to Support Virtual Learning Communities

This section introduces online lectures. It explains how they work and describes a pilot study involving online lectures recently completed at Deakin University. This pilot study explores the use of video and audio lectures to enhance the delivery of distance education. A long-term aim of this ongoing research is to explore whether the inclusion of audio and video lectures enhances the sense of community felt by distance education students (DES). Another goal of this study is to determine whether or not the students' ability to "see" the lecture theatre and lecturer and to "feel" the experience as if they are a part of the lecture enhances the development of a community spirit.

Online Lectures

Video lectures are the display of lecture material in a visual context. Video lectures can be delivered in several different formats, such as recorded video files available for download, broadcast or streamed real-time video lectures, and video conferences. Video lectures can be stand-alone, individual video files, or they can be teamed with other media applications such as PowerPoint presentations.

Audio lectures convey on-campus lectures using text-based lecture materials with the addition of audio files. The audio lectures can consist of purely audio recordings or they can also include other media applications such as PowerPoint presentations or static video. The audio recordings can also be provided in several different formats such as audio cassette tapes, downloadable digital audio recordings (e.g., wave files or mp3 files), and online audio streaming.

Enhancing Distance Education at Deakin University

Distance education students at Deakin University have in the past received a hardcopy of text-based lecture notes, study guides, and readers via the postal service to help them complete their studies. Video and audio lectures have been used on occasion in the delivery of distance education units at Deakin University. However, they were made available to students via video tapes and CD-ROMs. The current pilot study extends this idea by exploring the provision of video and audio lectures online for students to access.

The provision of video and audio lectures can benefit students in many ways. It can allow students to:

- review lecture material they did not understand at the time of the first delivery;
- add to, or amend the notes they had taken in the lecture;
- catch up and take lecture notes from any lectures they had missed;
- revise the lecture at times more suited to their life style; and
- allow DES access to material which was previously unavailable to them (Lanham & Zhou, 2004b; McCrohon, Lo, Dang, & Johnston, 2001).

The learning styles and approaches of individual students can vary widely (McCrohon et al., 2001). The use of video lectures caters to the needs of students with a visual learning style, just as the use of text-based lecture notes caters to students with a preference for learning from text-based materials.

It is apparent that an increase in the use of visual material would be beneficial to English as second language (ESL) students. Studies support this contention and acknowledge that Korean, Chinese, Arab, and Filipino students are more oriented toward visual learning styles than Anglo students (Park, 1997; Reid, 1987) cited in (Park, 2002).

Students from non-English speaking backgrounds may find lectures easier to understand when the visual and verbal cues are combined in video streaming (McCrohon et al., 2001). When static images are used in conjunction with text, it attracts the learner's attention, aids knowledge retention and recall, and acts as a clarification tool when verbal forms are insufficient (Duchastel & Waller, 1979, as cited in Asensio & Young, 2002). These studies all indicate that the inclusion of video and audio lecture materials can enhance the learning experience of ESL and international students.

As discussed in an earlier section of this chapter, Deakin University has a culturally diverse student body with a large number of international students from Asian countries. It is envisaged that providing these students with visual alternatives to text-based learning materials will create a more culturally inclusive learning environment, thus enhancing the delivery of distance education at Deakin University.

The Online Lecture Pilot Study

This pilot study involved the participation of students studying a tertiary subject as part of an Information Technology Master's Degree. Students can study this subject in either on-campus or off-campus study modes. Previously, text-based lectures notes for this subject were provided to all students online using DSO. The goal of introducing online lectures was to provide all students with access to the "physical" lectures via the Internet, and to document their interaction with the lectures provided.

The pilot study was conducted in two stages. The first stage dealt with the creation and implementation of the video and audio lectures and the provision of student access. The lectures were created in both video and audio formats in order to determine which format would suit the students' learning requirements.

The second stage of this pilot study was the completion of an anonymous survey, in which students recorded their experiences and opinions regarding the online lectures. This pilot study was primarily concerned with discovering the most efficient and usable technologies for the delivery of lectures online. Future detailed studies will explore the effects that video and audio lectures have on building culturally inclusive learning environments and supporting virtual learning communities.

Producing Online Lectures

Several lectures were recorded (via audio and video devices) during the second semester in 2004. These recorded lectures were then made available to students in streaming format via the Internet, and the Deakin intranet. Providing the video and audio lectures in streaming format meant that the students did not have to download the files to their personal computers. They could simply view the information as it streamed from the University's server.

The audio lectures were recorded using an audio recording device such as Mini-disk player. The files were then transferred from the audio device to a PC where they were edited and then converted into either a wave or mp3 file. Once transferred, the complete audio files (approximately 45 minutes in length) were edited and then modularized into smaller files (approximately 1 to 5 minutes in length). The modularized files are then linked to their corresponding topics contained in the lecture material (Lanham & Zhou, 2004b). The unit lectures were delivered on-campus by lecturers using a PowerPoint presentation. The synchronized audio files and PowerPoint slides were then transferred to DSO where they could be accessed by students.

Streaming video lectures were also provided in conjunction with a PowerPoint presentation to enhance the delivery and clarity of the lecture content. The video files were captured by using a Mini-DV (digital video) camcorder, and the files were then transferred to a PC via a Firewire cable (IEEE 1394). The files were imported from a camcorder into Microsoft Windows Movie Maker and then encoded into MPEG-2 movie files.

Once the MPEG-2 file was encoded, it was transferred into sofTV© (XStream Software, http://www.softv.net/Public/index.asp) so that the PowerPoint slides could be synchronised with the corresponding video content. This synchronisation process ensured that the slide show could run independently without user involvement, which enabled the students to avoid having to familiarise themselves with the sofTV© program.

Results

Results were gathered immediately after the first online lecture was made public. At that time, a brief survey was conducted focusing on the student's ability to access and interact with the online lectures. The questions covered issues that included accessibility, usability, quality, and usefulness to their studies. The majority of students who responded to the preliminary survey were enrolled in an on-campus mode and were male, international students aged between 20 and 25. There were no female respondents to the survey.

The students were able to access the online lectures at their convenience and as frequently as they required. It is interesting to note that, of the students that responded to the survey, only one student stated that he had not used the online lectures more than once. The other participants indicated that they had used the online lectures on several occasions.

All of the students who completed the survey indicated that they would use the online lectures again, that they found the online lectures helpful in their studies, and that they thought the inclusion of video materials in the future would be worthwhile.

The pilot study indicated that students would appreciate the use of online lectures in the future. The high level of use exhibited by on-campus international students indicates that off-campus, international, and DES might also benefit from the use of online lectures in the future.

Online Lectures in Review

The predominantly text-based existence of DES has often led to feelings of isolation, solitude, and the absence of connection with other students. The use of video can put a face to the name, and give a voice and actions to otherwise static text. These features combine to help create a virtual lecture environment for the DES and off-campus students.

The importance of actually seeing who is responsible for the delivery of the subject content can help to promote a sense of physically being in the lecture. Further exploration into the role that video may play in the support of virtual learning communities is planned for implementation in the first semester 2005. This research will explore the benefits that online lectures provide to students, how they support different learning styles, and their impact on learning for students from diverse cultural backgrounds.

Future Directions for Virtual Learning Communities

The two studies outlined in this chapter use wikis and online lectures to support the creation of virtual learning communities. As technology evolves, many more affordable and accessible means of community building will become available to developers. The focus of future learning communities will be in bringing the community to the student and providing enhanced learning materials that take advantage of the latest technology and support the range of learning styles that exist within the learning community.

The research presented in the wiki case study outlined the possibility of providing e-mail alerts to students to notify them of recent activity and encourage them to return and contribute to the learning exercise. In the future, Short Message Service (SMS) may be the preferred technology. While enthusiastic students may check their e-mail every day to keep abreast of updates, e-mail cannot provide the instantaneous real-time alerts to students that SMS can. SMS can provide students with a sense of connection to their community, reminding them of important deadlines, and studies indicate that students appreciate the use of SMS as a means of communicating with their instructors (Horstmanshof, 2004).

As bandwidth increases and Internet access costs decrease, the provision of multimedia and streamed resources to support diverse learning styles has become a viable option. Virtual learning communities based on discourse about subject matter can be daunting for some students who have difficulty absorbing information provided in a text-based format. The provision of alternatives such as video or audio lectures, animations, and the like can make learning more accessible and enjoyable for students.

Additionally, where time differences are not an issue, some virtual learning communities are already moving away from text-based discussion forums. Real-time video and audio conferences between students and instructors have the potential to further enhance the social presence and sense of belonging felt by community members. Using video and audio in teaching materials and forums provides students with a more personalised and authentic learning experience. Putting a face and a voice to their instructors and peers can help them to feel less isolated and provide a richer learning experience, enhancing the sense of community and inclusion provided by the e-learning environment.

Conclusion

This chapter has introduced virtual learning communities and discussed their key criteria: social context, facilitation, technology, and shared learning goal. Essential theory relating to the pedagogy of virtual learning communities clearly supports the validity of such communities and their benefits to the e-learning arena and to distance education in particular. The focus of the chapter was, however, building virtual learning communities. Research results and case studies, such as DSO and SITWiki, were presented and analysed to show practical examples of how e-learning environments can be developed into virtual learning communities.

Having read this introduction to virtual learning communities, it is now left to the developer to innovate and create the virtual learning communities of the future.

References

Asensio, M. & Young, C. (2002). Section 2 —A learning and teaching perspective. In S. Thornhill, M. Asensio, & C. Young (Eds.), *Video streaming: A guide for educa-*

tional development (Vol. 1, pp. 10-19). Manchester, UK: The JISC Click and Go Video Project.

Augar, N., Raitman, R., & Zhou, W. (2004a). From e-learning to virtual learning community: Bridging the gap. Paper presented at *ICWL '04*, Beijing, China.

Augar, N., Raitman, R., & Zhou, W. (2004b). Teaching and learning online with wikis. Paper presented at *ASCILITE*, Perth, Australia.

Augar, N., Raitman, R., & Zhou, W. (2005). Towards building Web-based learning communities with Wikis. Paper presented at *IADIS International Conference on Web-Based Communities 2005*, February 23-25, Algarve, Portugal (pp. 207-214).

Augar, N., & Zhou, W. (2003). *Virtual communities: Literature survey*. Technical Report No. TRC04/03. Geelong, Australia: Deakin University.

Australian Trade Commission. (2004). *Education capability overview*. Retrieved August 30, 2004, from *http://www.austrade.gov.au/overseas/layout/0,,0_S3-1_3zo-2_-3_PWB1153530-4_-5_-6_0-7_,00.html.1*

Baym, N. K. (1995). The emergence of community in computer-mediated communication. In S.G. Jones (Ed.), *Cybersociety computer-mediated communication and community* (pp. 138-163). Thousand Oaks, CA: Sage Publications.

Blunt, R. (2001). *How to build an e-learning community*. Retrieved January 19, 2004, from *http://www.elearningmag.com/ltimagazine/article/articleDetail.jsp?id=5040*

Brook, C. & Oliver, R. (2003). Online learning communities: Investigating a design framework. *Australian Journal of Educational Technology, 19*(2), 139-160. Retrieved June 28, 2005, from *http://www.ascilite.org.au/ajet/ajet19/brook.html*

Bruckman, A. (2002). The future of e-learning communities: The learning potential of Internet technology can come from the most familiar sources—peers and elders. *Communications of the ACM, 45*(4), 60-63.

Carlsen, R. (2003). Building productive online learning communities: Investigating and interacting with Internet educational genres. Paper presented at *Quality Education @ a Distance*, Geelong, Australia (pp. 137-144). Kluwer.

Chin, K.L., Chang, V., & Bauer, C. (2000). The use of Web-based learning in culturally diverse learning environments. Paper presented at the *Sixth Australian World Wide Web Conference*, Cairns, Australia.

Conlan, F. (1996). Can the different learning expectations of Australian and Asian students be reconciled in one teaching strategy? In J. Abbott & L. Willcoxson (Eds.), *Proceedings of the 5th Annual Teaching and Learning Forum* (pp. 41-45). Perth, Australia: Murdoch University. Retrieved June 28, 2005, from *http://lsn.curtin.edu.au/tlf/tlf1996/conlan.html*

Daniel, B., McCalla, G., & Schwier, R. (2002). A process model for building social capital in virtual learning communities. Paper presented at the *International Conference on Computers in Education*, Aukland, New Zealand (pp. 574-575).

Deakin University. (2003). *FactBook 2002*. Victoria, Australia: Deakin University.

Dougimas, M. & Taylor, P. C. (2002). Interpretive analysis of an Internet-based course constructed using a new courseware tool called Moodle. Paper presented at the

Annual International Conference of the Higher Education Research and Development Society of Australasia (HERDSA), Perth, Australia. Retrieved June 28, 2005, from *http://www.ecu.edu.au/conferences/herdsa/main/papers/nonref/pdf/ MartinDougiamas.pdf*

Dourish, P. & Bly, S. (1992). Portholes: Supporting awareness in a distributed work group. Paper presented at *SIGCHI Conference on Human Factors in Computing Systems*, Monterey, CA. Retrieved June 28, 2005, from *http://pages.cpsc.ucalgary.ca/ ~saul/601.13/readings/portholes.pdf*

Duchastel, P. C. & Waller, R. (1979). Pictorial illustration in instructional texts. *Educational Technology,* (November), 20-25.

Duffy, T. M. & Jonassen, D. H. (1992). Constructivism: New implications for instructional technology. In T. M. Duffy & D. H. Jonassen (Eds.), *Constructivism and the technology of instruction: A conversation* (pp. 1-15). Hillsdale, NJ: Lawrence Erlbaum Associates.

Ellis, J. B. & Bruckman, A. (2001). Designing Palaver Tree online: Supporting social roles in a community of oral history. Paper presented at *CHI01*, Seattle. Retrieved June 28, 2005, from *http://www.cc.gatech.edu/elc/palaver/papers/pt-chi01.pdf*

Hara, N. & Kling, R. (1999). Students' frustrations with a Web-based distance education course. *First Monday, 4*(12). Retrieved June 28, 2005, from *http:// www.firstmonday.dk/issues/issue4_12/hara/*

Haythornthwaite, C., Kazmer, M. M., Robins, J., & Shoemaker, S. (2000). Community development among distance learners: Temporal and technological dimensions. *Journal of Computer-Mediated Communication, 6*(1). Retrieved June 28, 2005, from *http://www.ascusc.org/jcmc/vol6/issue1/haythornthwaite.html*

Hiltz, S. R. & Turoff, M. (1993). *The network nation: Human communication by computer* (revised ed.). Cambridge, MA: MIT Press.

Horstmanshof, L. (2004). Using SMS as a way of providing connection and community for first-year students. Paper presented at *ASCILITE*, Perth, Australia (pp. 432-427).

Jonassen, D. H., Howland, J., Moore, J., & Marra, R. M. (2003). *Learning to solve problems with technology: A constructivist perspective* (2nd ed.). Upper Saddle River, NJ: Pearson Education.

Jones, Q. (1997). Virtual-communities, virtual settlements & cyber-archaeology: A theoretical outline. *Journal of Computer Mediated Communication, 3*(3). Retrieved July 20, 2004, from *http://www.ascusc.org/jcmc/vol3/issue3/jones.html*

Lanham, E. & Zhou, W. (2002). *E-learning: Literature survey.* Technical Report No. TR C 02/20. Geelong, Australia: Deakin University.

Lanham, E. & Zhou, W. (2003a). Cultural issues in online learning: Is blended learning a possible solution. *International Journal of Computer Processing of Oriental Languages, 16*(4), 275-292.

Lanham, E. & Zhou, W. (2003b). Cultural issues relating to teaching IT professional ethics online: Lessons learned. Paper presented at *Advances in Web-Based Learning ICWL 2003*, Melbourne, Australia (pp. 134-144). Springer.

Lanham, E. & Zhou, W. (2004a). Giving lectures a voice for a cross-cultural audience. Paper presented at *ASCILITE*, Perth, Australia. Retrieved June 28, 2005, from *http://www.ASCILITE.org.au/conferences/perth04/procs/lanham-poster.html*

Lanham, E. & Zhou, W. (2004b). Video lectures for cross-cultural use: A three phase model. Paper presented at *World Conference on E-Learning in Corp., Govt., Health., & Higher Ed.*, Washington, DC (pp. 2368-2373). AACE.

Leuf, B. & Cunningham, W. (2001). *The Wiki way: Quick collaboration on the Web.* Upper Saddle River, NJ: Addison Wesley.

Lewis, R. (2002). Learning communities: Old and new. Paper presented at *International conference on Computers in Education*, Auckland, New Zealand (pp. 6-13). IEEE Computer Society.

Lipponen, L. (2002). *Exploring foundations for computer-supported collaborative learning.* Finland: University of Helsinki. Retrieved June 28, 2005, from *http://newmedia.colorado.edu/cscl/31.pdf*

McCrohon, M., Lo, V., Dang, J., & Johnston, C. (2001). Video streaming of lectures via the Internet: An experience. Paper presented at *ASCILITE*, Melbourne, Australia (pp. 397-406).

Munro-Smith, N. (2002). A tale of two cities: Computer-mediated teaching & learning in Melbourne and Singapore. Paper presented at *ASCILITE*, Auckland, New Zealand (pp. 861-864).

Myers, J. (1991). Cooperative learning in heterogeneous classes. *Cooperative Learning, 11*(4).

Nelson, B. (2004). International student numbers. Retrieved August 30, 2004, from *www.dest.gov.au/Ministers/Media/Nelson/2004/03/n638040 304.asp*

Nielsen, J. (1996). International Web usability. Retrieved June 15, 2003, from *http://www.useit.com/alertbox/9608.html*

Oren, A., Nachmias, R., Mioduser, D., & Lahav, O. (1998). *LEARNET: A model for virtual learning communities in the World Wide Web* (Research Report No. 52). Tel-Aviv, Israel: Tel-Aviv University. Retrieved March 15, 2004, from *http://muse.tau.ac.il/publications/learnets.html*

Papert, S. & Harel, I. (1991). *Constructionism.* Norwood, NJ: Ablex Publishing Company. Retrieved June 28, 2005, from *http://www.papert.org/articles/situatingconstructionism.html*

Park, C. C. (1997). Learning style preferences of Asian American (Chinese, Filipino, Korean, and Vietnamese) students in secondary schools. *Equity & Excellence in Education, 30*(2), 68-77.

Park, C. C. (2002). Cross-cultural differences in learning styles of secondary English learners. *Bilingual Research Journal, 26*(2), 213-229.

Phillips, D. C. (2000). An opinionated account of the constructivist landscape. In D. C. Phillips (Ed.), *Constructivism in education.* Chicago, IL: The National Society for the Study of Education.

Powazek, D. M. (2002). *Design for community. The art of connecting real people in virtual places*. Indianapolis, IN: New Riders Publishing.

Raitman, R., Augar, N., & Zhou, W. (2004). Constructing wikis as a platform for online collaboration in an e-learning environment. Paper presented at the *International Conference on Computers in Education*, Melbourne, Australia.

Reid, J. (1987). The learning style preferences of ESL students. *TESOL Quarterly, 21*(1), 87-111.

Rheingold, H. (1994). *The virtual community: Finding connection in a computerized world*. London: Secker & Warbur.

Rovai, A. P. (2002). Building a sense of community at a distance. Retrieved February 19, 2004, from *http://www.irrodl.org/content/v3.1/rovai.html*

Salmon, G. (2003). *E-moderating: The key to teaching and learning online* (2nd ed.). London: RoutledgeFalmer.

Saragina, P. (1999). Creating a virtual learning community. Retrieved March 15, 2004, from *http://leahi.kcc.hawaii.edu/org/tcon99/papers/saragina.html*

Schraefel, M. C., Ho, J., Chignell, M., & Milton, M. (2000). Building virtual communities for research collaboration. Paper presented at *Academia/Industry Working Conference on Research Challenges (AIWORC'00)*, Buffalo, NY (pp. 27-32). Retrieved June 28, 2005, *http://www.dgp.toronto.edu/~mc/papers/virtualOrgPaper.pdf*

Stacey, E. (1999). *Collaborative learning in an online environment, 14*(2), 14-33. Retrieved June 27, 2005, from *http://cade.icaap.org/vol14.2/stacey.html*

Stacey, E. (2001). Social presence online: Networking learners at a distance. Paper presented at the *Seventh IFIP World Conference on Computers in Education*, Copenhagen, Denmark.

Vygotsky, L. S. (1978). Mind in society: The development of higher psychological processes. In M. Cole, V. John-Steiner, S. Scribner, & E. Souberman (Eds.). Cambridge, MA: Harvard University Press.

Wenger, E. (1998). *Communities of practice: Learning, meaning, and identity*. Cambridge, UK: Cambridge University Press.

Wikipedia. (2004). *Wikipedia*. Retrieved August 9, 2004, from *http://en.wikipedia.org/wiki/Main_Page*

Wood, A. F. & Smith, M. J. (2001). *Online communication: Linking technology, identity, and culture*. Hillsdale, NJ: Lawrence Erlbaum Associates, Inc.

Chapter V

A Conceptual Architecture for the Development of Interactive Educational Multimedia

Claus Pahl, Dublin City University, Ireland

Abstract

Learning is more than knowledge acquisition; it often involves the active participation of the learner in a variety of knowledge- and skills-based learning and training activities. Interactive multimedia technology can support the variety of interaction channels and languages required to facilitate interactive learning and teaching. A conceptual architecture for interactive educational multimedia can support the development of such multimedia systems. Such an architecture needs to embed multimedia technology into a coherent educational context. A framework based on an integrated interaction model is needed to capture learning and training activities in an online setting from an educational perspective, to describe them in the human-computer context, and to integrate them with mechanisms and principles of multimedia interaction.

Introduction

Interactivity is central for teaching and learning (Moore, 1992; Ohl, 2001)—the active involvement of learners is of paramount importance for a successful learning experience (Sims, 1997). This importance is reflected recently by more interactive resources provided for e-learning environments (Northrup, 2001). Platforms such as the World Wide Web are ideal for making learning resources in various forms accessible without any restrictions in time or location. The current predominant focus on knowledge-based learning using Web-based e-learning environments is partly a result of a lack of interactive multimedia technologies. With the recognition of skills training as being equally important to knowledge acquisition, more work has recently been done on *activity-based learning and training* supported by *interactive multimedia* technology.

Multimedia technology has been widely used in computer-based teaching and learning (Okamoto, Cristea, & Kayama, 2001; Trikic, 2001). Central to a learner's interaction with the environment is the interaction with learning content. In particular in e-learning environments, the learner-content interaction is often more central than the learner's interaction with instructors and peers (Ohl, 2001). Our focus here is on the development of *interactive educational multimedia*. A variety of learning and training activities can be supported by a variety of multimedia interaction channels and languages (Elsom-Cook, 2001). The acquisition of, firstly, declarative knowledge and, secondly, of procedural knowledge and skills-based experience and expertise through learning and training needs to be integrated through a coherent multimedia channel and language design.

Support frameworks for multimedia *development* for e-learning environments exist (Heller, Martin, Haneef, & Gievska-Krliu, 2001). However, the focus of these frameworks is mainly on knowledge acquisition-oriented environments. Our objective is to introduce a *conceptual development architecture* for *interactive educational multimedia* supporting *activity-based learning and training*. Our aim is to support the development of *educational multimedia content,* including development activities such as description, classification, and comparison. The development of e-learning technology is a *participative* effort, requiring collaboration and cooperation among those involved. Instructors, instructional designers, and software developers shall benefit from such an architecture.

The proposed architecture is based on three layers, integrating three perspectives of interaction ranging from the educational context to the human-computer interface to the multimedia implementation. An activity model reflects the importance of learning and training activities. Development of educational multimedia content is usually a complex process – the three layers address the needs of three different stages in the development process. The purpose of the architecture is to provide a standardised description notation for various aspects and a guideline for a multi-stage development process. A database learning environment called the Interactive Database Learning Environment (IDLE) (Murray, Ryan, & Pahl., 2003; Pahl, Barrett, & Kenny, 2004) will illustrate the concepts and terminology of our architecture. Making knowledge about interaction that is inherent in the design explicit is our objective. *Explicit knowledge* is a prerequisite for evaluation and comparison, and also the deployment of content elements in *intelli-*

gent educational systems. Domain and instruction-related knowledge shall be our primary focus.

Interaction in E-Learning and Training Systems

We can distinguish three central aspects of activity-based e-learning and training systems: knowledge and skills learning and training, human-computer interaction, and multimedia implementation (see Figure 1).

Knowledge and Skills

Pedagogical theories determine the learning process design. The individual learning activities in this process—the learner interaction with content—are often subject-specific. In general, we can distinguish various *types* of *learner activities*. Learning is about the acquisition of knowledge or skills. The *purpose* of acquiring knowledge on the one hand and skills on the other differs:

• **Knowledge:** We refer here to what is often called *declarative knowledge*, namely, facts. The objective of the learner is to be able to *reason* about knowledge. The style of learning is usually classical studying. We use the term *learning* to refer to this activity.

Figure 1. Learner-content interactions: A layered view

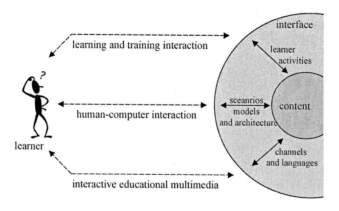

- **Skills:** This shall denote here what is sometimes called *procedural knowledge*, namely, instructions. The objective of the learner is the ability to *perform* instructions and procedures—in this case, we speak about skills. The style of learning is *training*.

The basis for this distinction is the *meaning of the interaction* for the learner in terms of her/his *goals* and *tasks*.

- **Knowledge-level interaction:** This is interaction in terms of concepts and relationships of the subject domain. Meaningful communication with these elements is essential for declarative knowledge acquisition and knowledge production.
- **Activity-level interaction:** This is interaction in terms of subject-specific procedures and activities. Meaningful activities are important for the acquisition and execution of skills, namely, procedural knowledge and experience.

This distinction is necessary to reflect the different cognitive processes of knowledge and skills acquisition.

Human-Computer Interaction

Languages and processes at the interface of a human-computer environment need particular attention in order to meet the requirements of the human user (Dix, Finlay, Abowd, & Beale, 1993). Three models are central:

- **Cognitive models and architectures** represent the user's knowledge, intentions, and abilities. Acquisition and production of plans of activities are central.
- A hierarchical **task and goal model** structures the user goals and the corresponding tasks that have to be executed to accomplish the goals.
- **Linguistic models** introduce a vocabulary and constrain the interaction through a user-system grammar.

Multimedia

Multimedia systems (Elsom-Cook, 2001) are characterised by the channels provided to access and communicate knowledge and to enable activities.

- A **channel** is considered as an abstraction of a connection device used to communicate encoded information. Examples are text or audio.

- Specific **languages** are used to communicate information along the channels between the user and the multimedia system. For instance, English is a language that can be communicated along a text channel.

A *medium* is a set of coordinated channels. *Communication* using these media needs to be *meaningful*, that is, it should allow users to determine their behaviour based on communicated information. In this case, we call a communication an *interaction*. The user interacts with the system in the form of *dialogues* to access knowledge and to engage in activities.

State-of-the-Art

In recent years, the focus of research in e-learning technologies has been on the provision of knowledge learning through suitable technologies—work on knowledge media (Ravenscroft, Tait, & Hughes, 1998) addressing adequate media representation and access for learning technology is an example. However, with a change of focus moving towards skills and activities, other types of interactions need to be supported. Ravenscroft et al. (1998) acknowledged that the style and level of interaction is central— a result that needs to be applied to this new context.

Development of E-Learning and Training Systems

The Development Context

The development of e-learning and training systems is a challenging task. These systems are complex, consisting of a number of different components (learning objects and supporting infrastructure). Consequently, their design and implementation involves several activities:

- The development of individual learning objects from scratch is often the central activity. As content can vary from static to interactive or from textual to multimedia-based, it is difficult to provide a universal approach here. We will focus on supporting interactive multimedia content here.

- With increasing complexity of these systems, reusing components is gaining importance. A number of metadata and annotation standards—such as the IEEE Learning Object Metadata standard LOM (IEEE LTSC, 2002)—have been developed that allow providers to describe and publish their learning objects and potential users to discover suitable resources.

- The assembly of components (e.g., sequencing of learning objects) is another important task. The Learning Technology Standard Architecture LTSA (IEEE LTSC, 2002) is a reference architecture onto which learning objects and other infrastructure components can be mapped. The logical assembly of learning objects or units of learning can be expressed in terms of the SCORM Sequencing and Navigation (SN) standard (ADL, 2004).

- The final step that follows the design activities in the system implementation. The SCORM Run-Time Environment (RTE) standard (ADL, 2004) addresses the delivery of learning content, possibly based on assemblies expressed using SCORM SN.

Our focus will be on the first aspect even though the context is important, as our approach will need to be embedded into a more comprehensive framework.

Knowledge and Intelligent Systems

An intelligent e-learning and training system is based on three knowledge components: domain, learner, and instructional knowledge (Burns & Capps, 1988). While we do not address the implementation of an intelligent learning or tutoring system here, our aim is to address knowledge aspects that arise during development—in particular with respect to domain and instructional knowledge and their explicit representation.

State-of-the-Art

Recent work addressing the development of educational multimedia (Okamoto et al., 2001; Pahl, 2003; Trikic, 2001) does not provide an adequate conceptual framework that can form an underpinning for the development of these systems. A coherent architecture integrating the different notions of interactivity is, however, necessary to support the seamless implementation of educational concepts in multimedia technology.

A Conceptual Architecture

Interaction is central in the development and implementation of learning activity. An *interaction model* focussing on learner-content interaction forms the core of our *conceptual development architecture*. It shall capture and relate meaningful activities and interactions with educational multimedia. This will seamlessly embed interactive multimedia into the educational context.

The Architecture

The notion of interaction has a meaning in different contexts. Clarifying these meanings in a terminological framework is important. We can distinguish *three perspectives* on interaction—presented in *three layers* of the architecture: learning and training interaction, human-computer interaction, and interactive educational multimedia. Overall, the *conceptual architecture* (see Figure 2) is a combination of:

- a **taxonomy:** a structured terminology that allows the description, classification, and comparison of interaction-related knowledge of educational technology systems;

- a **conceptual model:** an integrated model that captures the various perspectives on activities and interaction in the three layers; and

- a **process model:** a development framework that guides instructors, instructional designers, and software developers through the stages of educational multimedia development based on the layered model.

Figure 2. A conceptual architecture for interactive educational multimedia

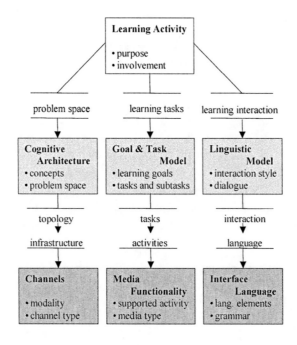

The Case Study

Our case study—the Interactive Databases Learning Environment (IDLE)—is a Web-based e-learning and training system providing an online undergraduate introduction to databases (Murray et al., 2003; Pahl et al., 2004). It supports learning and training activities such as design, implementation, and analysis of database applications, enabled by a variety of media features including interactive applets for graphical modelling, audio-supported lectures, simulations and other animation types to explain the behaviour of a database system, and a variety of text-based submission, execution, and feedback features. We describe the development of IDLE in stages that follow the layers of the conceptual architecture.

Learning and Training Interaction

Learning should be an active process in which interactivity is central (Northrup, 2001). The aim of an *interaction model* at this level is to support the *design of learning activity*. Moore (1992) distinguishes three types of interactions— learner-learner, learner-instructor, and learner-content. It is often argued (Ohl, 2001; Sims, 1997) that *content* has a more *central function* in computer-based education than interaction with peers or instructors. Ohl defines interaction as an internal dialogue of reflective thought that occurs between learner and the content.

Activity Model

The learning and training activities facilitated by educational multimedia interactions between learner and content shall be captured in the form of an *activity model*. We distinguish two aspects:

- We can define *activity types* based on the *purpose of the learning process*. We introduce three types (see Table 1). The second category is particularly important in the sciences and engineering domain where an understanding of the subject activities is required for a learner.

- The *style of the activity execution* can be based on the *degree of involvement and influence* of the learner on the environment, see Table 2. We can distinguish environment types ranging from system-controlled to learner-controlled.

Often the two aspects are related. Declarative knowledge is often acquired through observation, procedural knowledge for reasoning purposes through controlled animations, and skills through artefact creation and processing. The individual types for each

Table 1. Activity types based on learning purpose

Activity Type	Description
declarative knowledge acquisition activities	the aim is the acquisition of declarative knowledge in order to reason about it
procedural knowledge acquisition activities	the aim is the acquisition of procedural knowledge in order to reason about it
skills acquisition activities	the aim is the acquisition of procedural knowledge and experience in order to perform the instructions

Table 2. Activity types based on degree of involvement

Activity Type	Description
observation	a form of knowledge acquisition with no influence on the environment activities by a passive learner
controlling	a form of knowledge acquisition mixed with knowledge production, based on observational elements, but allowing the learner to influence the environment activities to control their ordering
creation	a form of activity where knowledge or skills are created by producing some form of artefact that can be processed by the learning environment

of the categories are not meant to be exclusive—a more fine-granular classification can replace our types if needed.

Learning and Training Interaction: The Case Study

The learning-by-doing idea is part of the active learning approach. It captures the interplay of knowledge acquisition and knowledge creation in an interactive process with the learning environment. We have widened this focus in IDLE by considering *knowledge acquisition* on the one hand and *skills and experience acquisition* on the other hand as dual sides of learning and training.

The *virtual apprenticeship model* (Murray et al., 2003) is a pedagogical theory—based on terminology defined in the activity model—that defines an activity-based and skills-oriented learning and training framework for the IDLE system. An apprentice is a learner who is coached by a master to perform a specific task. In an e-learning and training environment, the master's role is often replaced by an intelligent software tool such as IDLE. Tools reflect the experience that people, such as the apprentice's master or the instructor, have had in trying to solve a particular problem. The apprenticeship model determines a number of aspects including the activity purpose and the degree of involvement, interaction styles (e.g., the organisation of learning into sessions and cycles), and the interconnectedness of activities and features. The virtual apprenticeship model puts an emphasis on skills-oriented activities with a high degree of involve-

Table 3. IDLE activities and their types based on learning purpose and degree of involvement

Activity	Activity Type (Purpose)	Activity Type (Involvement)
lecture participation	declarative knowledge acquisition	observation
tutorial participation	procedural knowledge acquisition	controlling
lab participation	skills acquisition	creation

ment of the learner. The main activity categories are summarised in Table 3. Further categorisation is, however, necessary for a detailed design. For instance, the lab activity could be refined into specific activities such as graphical design, programming, or optimisation.

One of the skills acquisition activities in the IDLE system is SQL (i.e., database) programming. Integrated with a database system, the student—a virtual apprentice—works through guided material covering a range of individual problems. Each problem is based on a submission- and execution-cycle with a high degree of involvement of the learner through knowledge creation. Each solution—content-specific knowledge that is created by the learner—is analysed and, based on an individual activity history and integrated assessments, personalised feedback is given by the virtual master. At this level, the concern is the abstract classification of learner activities in the context of the pedagogical model. For the database course IDLE, the central design decision at this level is to focus on an integrated approach with a strong support of skills training activities.

Human-Computer Interaction

Architectures and Models

The notion of learning as a dialogue between learner and content (Ohl, 2001) needs to be adapted to the human-computer environment (Dix et al., 1993). Models for this context formulate these interactive dialogues as cycles consisting of computer-based executions and human evaluations (Norman, 1998). Three models are essential for human-computer interaction:

- A **cognitive architecture** for the educational context addresses cognitive learning processes as interactions in the human-computer environment. The architecture provided by a computer-supported learning and training system defines a problem space based on the central concepts of the subject domain in which a learner should be able to accomplish a learning goal. The architecture is defined by the actions that allow the learner to traverse the space, namely, to learn and train, and by the desirable states that represent the successful accomplishment of the goal, namely, to find a solution for the learning goal.

- The **task and goal model** is based on learner goals and activities. A task is an operation to manipulate concepts of the subject domain, that is, a goal is the desired output from a task. A hierarchy is defined by dividing goals into subgoals and tasks to accomplish these subgoals. A learning strategy defines how learning goals on the same level are connected. The tasks have to be mapped onto the actions supported by the multimedia infrastructure.

- Different interaction styles and learning activity dialogues, for example, different pedagogical activities, are captured in a **linguistic model** through basic vocabularies and user-system grammars. Style examples include commands, direct manipulation, menus, or form fill. The purpose of a language capturing the interaction processes is the specification of learner dialogues, including the sentence elements, the legal user actions, and the system responses.

Scenarios

A representational form to express learning activities at the human-computer interface are *scenarios* (Bødker, 2000). Scenarios are brief descriptions of interactions of a user with a system. We use a scenario language that is close to the SCORM sequencing and navigation standard (SN). We use sequencing operators such as *choice* and *flow*. We also use rules that constrain behaviour. SCORM SN, however, is a declarative format, whereas we prefer here an operational format. It suits the design view for individual content components better, since SCORM SN assumes a navigation approach between components, while we focus on internal behaviour not restricted to navigation.

Scenarios can be used to refine the learning activities from the first stage. Scenarios relate to different models on the human-computer interaction layer of our conceptual architecture:

- The cognitive architecture defines the basis including concepts and procedures on which scenarios can be expressed.

- The possibility to refine abstract activities allows tasks and subtasks to be defined.

- Scenarios formulate the grammar of a linguistic model.

A scenario language based on the problem space combines two aspects. Firstly, knowledge and content creation and processing aspects are covered. Secondly, dialogue activities and interaction patterns can be described.

Human-Computer Interaction: The Case Study

The interface between learner and multimedia system is defined by three models:

- **Cognitive architecture:** The IDLE learning and problem space is based on subject-specific concepts such as data models and implementation languages, as well as subject-specific activities. An example is presented in Figure 3 that classifies queries in the database language SQL.

- **Task and goal model:** Learners will traverse the problem space in order to accomplish learning goals. To develop a database application using IDLE is one of the central course goals; it involves tasks such as modelling, implementation, and optimisation. These tasks have to be mapped onto activities that are supported by the educational multimedia environment.

- **Linguistic model:** The linguistic model has to enable and structure activities. Different linguistic styles can be deployed; for example, direct manipulation for the data modelling tasks or a forms-based input facility to submit SQL database programs for execution.

The *problem space* defined by the *cognitive architecture* resembles a domain ontology for the subject domain—it identifies the central concepts and their properties. Figure 3 is an example. This complements other explicit knowledge, for example, on learning and interaction, that is made explicit. For the database context, the cognitive architecture is defined by concepts such as database table or query statement. Dependencies between the concepts define the problem space topology. For instance, the table concept is more basic than an SQL query (which is an operation on tables).

An example shall illustrate the *scenario language* to support the *task/goal model* and the *linguistic model* (see Figure 4), which is based on an underlying cognitive architecture for SQL organised in form of an activity tree (see Figure 3). The scenario specifies

Figure 3. Conceptual architecture in form of an activity tree

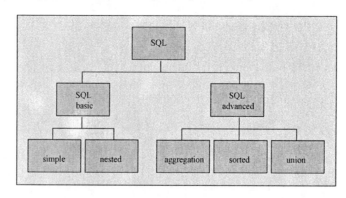

exercise activities for SQL queries that define the user-system dialogue—it combines the tutorial navigation with lab programming activities.

Interactive Educational Multimedia

Learner-content interaction in computer-supported learning and training actually occurs as interaction between the interactive multimedia features that implement the cognitive architecture and the linguistic model, and that enable the tasks to be executed and the learning goals to be accomplished. Multimedia systems for education are usually hypermedia systems providing structure through hierarchy and guidance for learning tasks through navigation topologies (Jonassen & Mandl, 1990). Different media supporting different activities are connected through hypermedia structures. Crucial for educational multimedia are the multimedia interface and the interaction dialogues a multimedia system allows through channels (text, mouse, etc.) and languages (natural, formal, etc.).

Interactive multimedia for activity-based learning and training can be distinguished into interaction with knowledge media and with activity media. Activity-based training focuses on skills-oriented activities, but needs to be integrated with knowledge learning aspects. *Knowledge media* focus on knowledge information to be communicated. *Activity media* focus on artefacts that are produced and processed in activities. The purpose of interactive educational multimedia is twofold:

*   In addition to knowledge-level interaction, domain-specific activities need to be facilitated, that is, activity-level interaction with the educational multimedia feature through artefacts and instructions has to be enabled.

*   The instructor can be replaced by a virtual form of an intelligent educational multimedia feature that provides advice and feedback, thus adding more meaning to the interaction.

Figure 4. Scenario SQL training

```
Scenario SQL training
SQL : flow
        basic     : flow
                simple_query(table)
                nested_query(tables)
            if completed then continue
        advanced : choice
                aggregation(table)
                sorted_output(table)
                union(tables)
            if completed then exit
```

Educational Media Taxonomy

We can classify educational multimedia through different *metadata facets* (see Table 4) —essentially, different dimensions that allow us to describe educational media. We distinguish two *facet types*:

- **General multimedia facets** cover multimedia aspects such as channel and language. These facets together describe a medium as a coordinated set of channels and their languages. It is important, however, to develop an education-specific view on multimedia.

- **Education-specific facets** cover aspects specific to learning and training such as the activity purpose, the activity style, and the content topic.

The *range* in Table 4 refers to the possible set of values of each facet. The aim of this *taxonomy* is to describe, distinguish, and classify educational multimedia. It supports the development and the comparison of educational media objects. This aims at an abstract description of multimedia from an educational perspective. Strict adherence to description standards is not the primary concern here, since design is our focus.

The two general facets of multimedia—channel and language—shall be revisited in the context of education. In comparison with classical uses of multimedia for knowledge-oriented learning (Heller et al., 2001), here the interaction between learner and content, determined by the channels and their languages, is more central.

Educational Multimedia Channels

Multimedia is about channels and meaningful communication along these channels. Often, a natural language such as English is used over a text channel (written English)

Table 4. Educational multimedia facets

Facet	Type	Range	Description
channel	general	common range	the abstraction of a communication device, characterised by modality
language	general	not restricted but can be categorised	information is encoded in common language for communication over a channel
activity purpose	education	predefined	distinguishes whether declarative knowledge reasoning, procedural knowledge reasoning, or skills acquisition is aimed at
activity style	education	predefined	classification of activities into observation, controlling, and creation that describes the degree of influence of a learner on the environment
content topic	education	no restriction	topic or domain within which activities or knowledge-level access is provided

or over an audio channel (spoken English). For our context, we will identify a number of specific *educational channels*—supporting partly more formal languages, partly languages specific to the subject or instruction context (see Table 5). We distinguish two types of channels—those that support *core* content-oriented learning activities and those that are part of the *meta*-context of instruction; the latter including instruction-related learner actions and coaching actions by a master or instructor.

Educational Multimedia Interface Language

Multimedia interface languages capture and constrain the channel communications. A language defines the interaction dialogues; it describes the legal actions, how a learner can engage in an activity, or how a learner can perform a task towards a learning goal. These interaction languages detail dialogue structure captured in the scenario language. The difficulty in defining an adequate language is to capture all three interaction model layers. The learning and training interaction model provides the conceptual model in which the language semantics is to be defined.

We can classify languages for the educational context based on *content-related aspects*:

- Natural languages—in text or audio form—are often the basis of content.

- Formal languages—in text form—are often involved if some sort of mechanical processing is part of the subject domain.

- Simulations—automated processing of some real-world activities—are based on objects and procedures from the subject domain.

In addition to the content aspect, *dialogue* and *interaction patterns* form the instructional aspect addressed by interface languages. On the most basic level, the learner interacts with multimedia—usually through keyboard- and mouse-based input; output can be static visual (text, graphics), dynamic visual (animations, video), or involve other modalities such as audio. The basic inputs are part of low-level activities such as

Table 5. Educational channels

Channel	Type	Description
declarative knowledge	core	declarative knowledge usually communicated in a domain-specific natural or formal language
procedural knowledge	core	procedural knowledge usually communicated in a domain-specific natural or formal language
skills	core	artefacts to be processed in form of activities are communicated with corresponding execution instructions
actions	meta	instruction-related actions executed by the learner (navigation or location of learning units)
feedback	meta	response of the system for each core activity
coaching	meta	meta-level information capturing an instructor's advice and guidance

navigation (knowledge acquisition request) or text input/submission (knowledge generation). A learning activity can be composed of more basic activities. The *dialogue and interaction part* of the language consists of:

- **basic activities:** select (knowledge acquisition by learner), submit (knowledge generation by learner), reply (response to knowledge acquisition/generation) ;

- **activity combinators:** ; (sequence), ! (iteration), | (choice) ;

- **system components:** learner and multimedia system in a simple e-learning architecture.

Interactive Educational Multimedia: The Case Study

Activities are supported by multimedia features. IDLE supports three classical forms of third-level teaching—lectures, tutorials, and labs—in a virtual form. These three forms can be described using the educational multimedia classification scheme (see Table 6), which describes how some selected learning activity styles for particular topics are mapped onto multimedia features. For example, a simulation can be a subcategory of a moving pictures/images language. However, the elements of simulations can be identified and have meaning in the context of content (e.g., tables or records in the database context). Equally, operations (simulation activities) are represented in the procedural knowledge.

The channel and language characterisation using the taxonomy in Table 6 is high-level. These two aspects can be described in more detail. Table 7 provides a channel-oriented view on IDLE; it lists the educational channel types and some sample features that are based on these channels.

Table 6. Sample IDLE media classification

Facet Activity	Channel	Language	Purpose	Type	Topic
lecture	text and audio	natural language	declarative knowledge	observation	introduction to databases
tutorial	dynamic animation	simulation	procedural knowledge	controlling	relational algebra
lab	text	formal language	skills-oriented activities	creation	SQL

Table 7. Sample IDLE media channels

Channel	Feature	Activity	Language
declarative knowledge	database introduction lecture	HMTL and audio-based synchronised virtual lecture	natural language (written and spoken)
procedural knowledge	relational algebra animation	interactive simulation of algebra operator execution	formal language (interaction – animation control)
skills	SQL programming lab	submission of query solutions and dynamic page update by system	formal language – SQL (solution and result)
action	SQL tutorial navigation	guided tour through a series of connected exercises	formal language (interaction – navigation)
feedback	SQL programming lab	correction and provision of partial solutions for SQL exercises	semi-formal language (text and error classification)
coaching	self-assessment	multiple choice questions and virtual master's feedback	natural language (written)

The interaction language is based on the scenario language. The expression

!(LR.select(exercise); LR.submit(solution); MM.reply(result))

is the interaction specification of an exercise activity scenario. A language needs to facilitate declarative and procedural knowledge communication, skills-oriented activity execution, learner actions, and meta-level pedagogical interactions (coaching). *select* denotes a learner action; *submit* and *reply* support skills-oriented activities; and *reply* could, in addition to conveying, for example, SQL submission results, also convey meta-level feedback and coaching. In contrast to scenarios, we distinguish here between learner (*LR*) and multimedia system (*MM*) components. For instance, the SQL multimedia lab system (*MM*) replies with a result that includes the result of the solution execution and feedback.

Future Trends

Developments on both the educational and the technological side will influence educational multimedia design and implementation in the future.

- The importance of learner involvement and activity has long been recognised (Northrup, 2001). In the corporate sector, activity- and skills-based learning and training is becoming increasingly essential.

- A number of issues will impact multimedia technology development (Elsom-Cook, 2001). The fact that knowledge is becoming central in our societies will be reflected in multimedia through the integration of knowledge management and the support of processes of communications.

The development of e-learning technology moves closer to systems where multimedia technology excels. On the other hand, multimedia also moves towards knowledge, languages, and the Web—which are all central aspects of computer-supported learning and training technology. Knowledge management is central for intelligent e-learning systems, both for content and learner modelling. Practically, knowledge representation frameworks such as ontologies and other metadata languages and standards will impact the area.

Development of interactive educational multimedia is the context of the presented conceptual architecture. Other uses of the architecture can, however, be considered:

- **Standardisation and metadata:** There is a similarity between the taxonomy we introduced and metadata frameworks, such as the IEEE Learning Object Metadata (LOM) standard. Our focus here is on multimedia, interactivity, and the process of development. An integration with LOM is nonetheless possible. Multimedia development is expensive; therefore, sharing and reuse is desirable and, consequently, annotations are needed to facilitate this.

- **Multimedia integration and assembly:** Multimedia features can be combined with complex systems through channel assembly and language integration. This type of context would form part of a development framework for multimedia architectures.

The process of educational multimedia development and management needs to be supported by a coherent engineering framework, integrating different development activities.

Conclusion

Activity-based learning and training based on interactive educational multimedia can provide an answer for the current need to support not only knowledge acquisition, but also skills and experience acquisition in computer-supported educational environments.

In this chapter, we have investigated the development of interactive educational multimedia as a platform to implement activity-based learning and training through a conceptual architecture.

- A taxonomy based on the conceptual models allows us to describe activities, interactions, and multimedia objects and their channels and languages and compare different systems.

- Detailed technical descriptions allow the implementation and integration of educational technology components. An intricate understanding of the interaction characteristics of each of these components on all three layers is essential.

This architecture provides support for instructors, instructional designers, and software developers in a participative, multi-stage development environment. It is meant as an open architecture, that is, open to further extensions, integration with other frameworks and standards, and adaptations to particular needs.

One of the central lessons we have learned over the years of developing, managing, and maintaining educational multimedia systems is that there are a number of reasons for a domain-specific, systematic, and co-operative approach to activity-based learning and training systems development:

1. Interactivity is central and especially complex in the educational domain. The learning and training activities need to be embedded into a pedagogical framework in order to achieve a high-quality learning experience. A domain-specific approach is therefore needed.

2. The need for activity-based education is increasing. Consequently, the integration and maintenance of educational multimedia is becoming increasingly a problem. Only a systematic approach to development and maintenance can provide a solution.

3. Learning and training are multi-channel and multi-language activities. Seamlessly integrated interactive multimedia is therefore an ideal support technology.

4. Instructors, instructional designers, and software developers need to co-operate in the development of these systems that are characterised by complex learning and instruction processes on the one hand and advanced multimedia technology on the other.

One of our objectives was to provide a central element for such a development approach and to guide educational system design through our architecture. Interactive multimedia has the potential to support innovative approaches of teaching and learning, but in order to be successful, it needs to be embedded into a systematic and comprehensive framework for development and management.

References

ADL. (2004). Sharable Content Object Reference Model (SCORM)—Content Aggregation Model (CAM), Run-Time Environment (RTE), Sequencing and Navigation (SN). Retrieved June 12, 2004, from *http://www.adlnet.org/index.cfm?fuseaction=scormabt*

Bødker, S. (2000). Scenarios in user-centred design: Setting the stage for reflection and action. *Interacting with Computers, 13*(1), 61-75.

Burns, H.L. & Capps, C.G. (1988). Foundations of intelligent tutoring systems: An introduction. In M.C. Polson & J. J. Richardson (Eds.), *Foundations of intelligent tutoring systems*. Hillsdale, NJ: Lawrence Erlbaum Associates.

Dix, A., Finlay, J., Abowd, G., & Beale, R. (1993). *Human-computer interaction*. London: Prentice Hall.

Elsom-Cook, M. (2001). *Principles of interactive multimedia*. London: McGraw-Hill.

Heller, R.A., Martin, C.D., Haneef, N., & Gievska-Krliu, S. (2001). Using a theoretical multimedia taxonomy framework. *Journal of Educational Resources in Computing, 1*(1). Retrieved June 21, 2005, from *http://portal.acm.org/citation.cfm?id=376701*

IEEE LTSC (Learning Technology Standards Committee) (2002). Learning Object Metadata (LOM) (1484.12.1) and Learning Technology Standard Architecture (LTSA). Retrieved June 12, 2004, from *http://ltsc.ieee.org/*

Jonassen, D.H. & Mandl, H. (Eds.) (1990). *Designing hypermedia for learning*. Berlin: Springer-Verlag.

Moore, M.G. (1992). Three types of interaction. *The American Journal of Distance Education, 3*(2), 1-6.

Murray, S., Ryan, J., & Pahl, C. (2003). A tool-mediated cognitive apprenticeship approach for a computer engineering course. In *Proceedings of IEEE International Conference on Advanced Learning Technologies ICALT'03,* Athens, Greece, June 9-11 (pp. 2-6). IEEE Press.

Norman, K.L. (1998). Collaborative interactions in support of learning: Models, metaphors, and management. In R. Hazemi, S. Wilbur, & S. Hailes (Eds.), *The digital university: Reinventing the academy* (pp. 39-53). London: Springer-Verlag.

Northrup, P. (2001). A framework for designing interactivity into Web-based instruction. *Educational Technology, 41*(2), 31-39.

Ohl, T.M. (2001). An interaction-centric learning model. *Journal of Educational Multimedia and Hypermedia, 10*(4), 311-332.

Okamoto, T., Cristea, A., & Kayama, M. (2001). Future integrated learning environments with multimedia. *Journal of Computer Assisted Learning, 17*, 4-12.

Pahl, C. (2003). Evolution and change in Web-based teaching and learning environments. *Computers & Education, 40*(1), 99-114.

Pahl, C., Barrett, R., &. Kenny, C. (2004). Supporting active database learning and training through interactive multimedia. In *Proceedings of International Conference on Innovation and Technology in Computer Science Education ITiCSE'04,* Leeds, UK, June 28-30 (pp. 27-31). New York: ACM Press.

Ravenscroft, A., Tait, K., & Hughes, I. (1998). Beyond the media: Knowledge level interaction and guided integration for CBL systems. *Computers & Education, 30*(1/2), 49-56.

Sims, R. (1997). Interactive learning as "emerging" technology: A reassessment of interactive and instructional design strategies. *Australian Journal of Educational Technology, 13*(1), 68-84.

Trikic, A. (2001). Evolving open learning environments using hypermedia technology. *Journal of Computer Assisted Learning, 17,* 186-199.

Chapter VI

Considering Students' Emotions in Computer-Mediated Learning Environments

Patrícia Augustin Jaques
Universidade Federal do Rio Grande do Sul, Brazil

Rosa Maria Viccari
Universidade Federal do Rio Grande do Sul, Brazil

Abstract

This text aims to present the current state of the art of the e-learning systems that consider the student's affect. It presents the perspectives adopted by researchers for the solution of problems (for example, which kind of tools we might use to recognize users' emotions) and also some better-known works in order to exemplify. It also describes the necessary background to understand these studies, including some concepts in the fields of Artificial Intelligence, Computers in Education, and Human-Computer Interaction, and a brief introduction on the main theories about emotion. The authors conclude the chapter by presenting challenges and the main difficulties of research in affectivity in e-learning systems and ideas on some new work on the matter.

Introduction

Due to the traditional dichotomy in Western society between reason and emotion, which was inherited from Descartes' dualist vision of the mind and body, little attention has been paid to the role of the affectivity in cognition and learning. As it occurred in a real class, educational computing environments considered only the cognitive capacities of the student and his knowledge in order to make the system more customized to him.

Recent works of psychologists and neurologists have been pointing out the important role of the motivation and of the affectivity in cognitive activities, such as learning (Damasio, 1994; Izard, 1984). Psychologists and pedagogues point out the way that the emotions affect learning (Goleman, 1995; Piaget, 1989; Vygotsky, 1994).

Due to the important role of the affectivity in learning, researchers of the Computer in Education field have studied techniques of Artificial Intelligence in order to make the educational systems more customized to the affective states of the student.

The field of Artificial Intelligence that researches about emotion in computers is called "Affective Computing." Picard (1997) defines Affective Computing as "computing that relates to, arises from, or deliberately influences emotions." According to Picard (1997), an affective (computational) system must have some of the following capacities: (1) to recognize, (2) to express, or (3) to possess emotions.

In order to adapt the system to the student's affectivity, the system should *recognize* the student's *emotions*. For example, if a student is disappointed with his performance, he will probably abandon the task. The system needs to know when the student is disappointed in order to encourage him to continue studying and accomplish the task at hand. This way, it is necessary for the system to have not only a cognitive model of the student, but also an emotional one that takes into account the affective history of the student—all the emotions that he felt while using the educational system.

The educational system may *express emotions* as empathic teachers do in a real class. When they are able to show emotions, they can motivate and engage the student in the learning process, become amusing, and promote positive emotions in the student, which is an upswing for more effective learning (Coles, 1998; Izard, 1984). In order to transmit emotions, generally, the educational systems are represented by a lifelike character.

Several researchers believe that for a computational system to exhibit affective behavior in a coherent manner, they should also be constituted of models of emotions, which Picard (1997) referred to as *Emotion Synthesis*. The system has a computational architecture that allows it to analyze situations and events of the environment with some heuristics that are based on a human model of emotions. But the inclusion of an architecture of emotions must be well justified, since the process of emotion synthesis makes the system substantially more complex.

In the next sections, we first present an introduction to emotions and affectivity. In order to implement e-learning systems that are able to recognize, express, and simulate emotions, we need to know the main theories about emotion, what an emotion is, and also know the main psychological models of emotions that are used by the works on affective computing.

Next, we begin the presentation of the current state of the art in affectivity in e-learning systems. This section is divided into three sub-sections that represent the main research interest of the scientific community: (1) inference of student's affective states, (2) expression of emotion by machine, and (3) simulation of emotion in machine. In each sub-section, we will present the perspectives adopted by different researchers for the solution of the problems (for example, which kind of tools they use to recognize user's emotions) and will describe some works that are best known to exemplify and clarify explanations. We will also present the background to understand these works that involves some concepts from the fields of Artificial Intelligence, Computer in Education, and Human-Computer Interaction.

In the conclusion, we present some considerations about the current state of the art, challenges, and the main difficulties of the research in affectivity in e-learning systems. We end the chapter with the presentation of some ideas of new work on the matter.

Understanding Emotions

In order to better understand the work in affectivity and emotions in an intelligent learning system, we need to understand what emotions are and the current state-of-the-art thinking on the psychology of emotions. We also present a brief history on the psychological research on emotion that will increase comprehension of the investigations on emotion.

What are Emotions, Moods and Motivation?

Although the term "emotion" is popularly used for many phenomena of affective order, these phenomena should be denominated by the generic term "affective state" that can be seen as more wide-ranging and also includes other states besides emotions, such as moods (Frijda, 1994; Scherer, 2000). Emotions and moods are the two main kinds of affective states that have been taken into consideration in educational systems.

According to Scherer (2000), emotion is the relatively brief episode of synchronized responses for most or all organic systems for the evaluation of an external or internal event as being of major significance. Some examples of emotions are anger, sadness, joy, fear, shame, pride, and desperation. Ortony, Clore, and Collins (1988) propose a similar but more precise definition for emotions. According to them, emotions are valenced reactions to events, agents, or objects, with their particular nature being determined by the way in which the eliciting situation is constructed. According to this definition, surprise is not an emotion since it does not have a valence. Frijda (1994) considers that the emotion is an intentional mental state, because it is "directed toward" an object, its intentional object. For instance, I am angry with John, but I admire Nicholas.

Another kind of affective state is mood. It is a diffused affective state that consists of changes in subjective feeling, of low intensity but of long duration, without apparent cause (Scherer, 2000). Some examples of moods are: cheerful, gloomy, irritable, listless, depressed, and buoyant. Frijda (1994) considers that moods differ from emotions most strongly in not having an intentional object. Their causes are typically conceptual or evaluative (things are or are not going well).

As we can see, scientists try to differentiate emotions from other affective states; however, there is not a clear and unique definition for emotion. Emotion, which has been well studied, is differentiated from all other affective states through some of its characteristics, such as brief response, result of an evaluation of an event, and others.

The works on affectivity and education have also considered the motivation of the student. Student motivation deals with a student's desire to participate in the learning process (Ames, 1990). According to Ames, students can have extrinsic or intrinsic motivation that determines the reasons for students to engage in learning.

Students that are *intrinsically motivated* are oriented toward developing new skills and abilities, trying to understand their work, improving their level of competence, and learning new things (Ames, 1990). When students are *extrinsically motivated,* they believe that performance is important and want to show that they have abilities (Ames, 1990). They feel successful when they please the teacher or do better than other students, rather then when they learn something new.

Researchers suggest that better learning occurs when intrinsic motivation (learning because it is interesting and useful) is emphasized over extrinsic motivators (learn because it will be on the quiz) (Meece & McColskey, 2001). Students who are more intrinsically oriented tend to take on more challenging tasks, persist longer at a task, handle failure better, and use better learning strategies.

Nowadays, researchers believe that motivation is sensitive to contexts and it can be fostered in the classroom. This way, a lot of works have been developed in the sense of fostering student motivation to learn in educational computing systems (Bercht & Viccari, 2000; De Vicente & Pain, 2002). Some of these works are described in the following sections.

The Different Theories of Emotions

In order to understand the current research on emotion, we present a summary about the historical root of psychological models of emotions.

One of the first studies about emotion was done by Plato around 430 BC. Plato suggested that the soul is a structure with three parts: cognition, emotion, and motivation. Fifty years later, Aristotle discussed this division and suggested an interaction among the different components.

Around 1600, Descartes insisted on the dualist vision that separates the mind from the brain and the body (Damasio, 1994). According to Descartes' conception, the rational soul, a distinct entity from the body, makes contact with the body through the pineal gland of the brain.

Darwin (1965) studied mainly the expression of emotions in the face, body, and voice. In his studies, he evidenced that the emotional phenomena, particularly expression, can be found in different cultures. As pointed out by Darwin and more recently by Ekman (1999), it appears that a set of emotional facial expressions are universal, that is, represent the same emotion in different countries. This led to the birth of the theory of *basic emotions*. Actually, this model has been receiving criticism from some researchers (Ortony et al., 1988) who believe it is vague.

William James (1884) believed that emotion is the perception of different corporal changes. This means that emotion is a result of a corporal reaction to an event. We have an emotion because we perceive body changes. According to James, an emotion has a unique pattern of skeletal muscle and physiological changes, since our experience of emotion is a direct function of feedback from the body. There is little evidence of the postulate of James, since there are different standards of responses for specific emotions.

Nowadays, scientists believe that emotions are not just the result of corporal changes but a composition of several components. They believe (Clore & Ortony, 1999) that the emotions in human beings are characterized by the presence of four main components: a cognitive component, a component of motivation-behavior, a somatic component, and a subjective-experiential component. The *cognitive component* is the representation of emotional meaning or the personal significance of some emotionally relevant aspect in the perceived world of the person. The *motivational-behavioral component* is concerned with inclinations of an individual to act on the construal (interpretation) of the world that these representations represent and their relation to what is actually done. The *somatic component* involves the activation of the autonomic and central nervous systems with their effect in the body. The *subjective-experimental component* is responsible for "subjective feeling" and, therefore, it is more elaborated in human beings who try to label the emotions that they are feeling. This theory is known as *componential model* (Scherer, 1999).

The current focus of psychological research on emotion is the *cognitive component* of emotion, mainly, the elicitation of emotion through antecedent evaluation. According to this approach, emotions are elicited by a cognitive evaluation of antecedent situations and events; it means that emotions are activated by an individual's interpretations in relation to the happy or irritating aspects of an event. This cognitive evaluation is called *appraisal*. This approach, which is known as the *cognitive approach of emotion*, has been influencing several works in affective computing. Based on this cognitive approach of emotion, there is a theory of emotions—the OCC model (Ortony, Clore, & Collins, 1988)—that has been largely used for recognition of users' emotions in computational systems and for implementation of emotion in machine. The OCC model is a theory that explains the origins of 22 types of emotions by describing the cognitive processes that elicit each of them. For example, the feeling of hope appears when a person develops an expectation that some good event will happen in the future.

Pedagogical Point of View: Affectivity and Motivation in Learning

Some pedagogues, such as Piaget (1989), Vygotsky (1962; 1978), Goleman (1995), and John-Steiner (2000), point to *the importance of motivation and affectivity in learning*.

Pursuant to Piaget (1989), the accelerating or disturbing role of affectivity in learning is incontestable. For instance, a considerable number of students who are weak in mathematics fail due to an affective blockage. Piaget believes that there is no cognitive mechanism without an affective element. Affectivity motivates the intellectual activity. There is an intrinsic or extrinsic interest, a necessity. It is through interest that we select our activities.

Goleman (1995) has pointed out the way in which emotional disturbances affect mental life. He recalls the well-known idea that depressed, ill-humored, and anxious students have greater difficulty in learning.

Izard's work (1984) shows that induced negative emotions damage performance of cognitive tasks, and positive emotions have an opposite effect. Coles (1998) presents other studies that showed that inducing a sad mood in very young children increased the time it took them to learn to respond to a task, and also increased their number of errors; opposite results were achieved by inducing happiness. Coles (1998) also highlighted other researchers' works that showed that young children identified as at risk in school completed math problems significantly more accurately under induced positive-mood conditions.

In one of his last publications, Vygotsky (1994) presented a new important concept introducing affectivity in learning—*perezhivanie*. The development of a child depends on the way that the child experiences a situation in the environment, that is "how a child becomes aware of, interprets, and emotionally relates to a certain event" (Vygotsky, 1994, p. 341); Vygotsky called this *perezhivanie*.

Another basic factor to learning is motivation; therefore, without motivation there is no learning. Motivated, students search for answers to their problems and to satisfy their needs. According to Vygotsky (1962), motivation is the reason of the action. It stimulates needs, interests, desires, and particular attitudes of the citizens.

Coles (1998) considers that as a teacher can contribute to the development of the student's cognitive abilities, he can also assist the emotional development of the child through guidance and support. As Coles points out:

Fear of failure may be changed to feelings of self-confidence; motivation may change from low to high; intellectual insecurity may become confidence in one's intelligence. These transformations can occur through a teacher's scaffolding and guidance in the formation of new emotional states a learner can achieve and sustain by him- or herself. (Coles, 2004, Web)

Handling Student's Emotions in E-Learning Systems

As seen in the previous section, emotions interfere positively (when the student is motivated and has positive emotions) and negatively (when the student is depressed and bad-humored, for example) in the student's learning. Therefore, researchers in education believe that the educational environments would be more pedagogically effective if they had mechanisms to recognize and show a student's emotions. As empathic teachers do in their classes, these pedagogical environments should observe students, try to recognize their emotions, and respond affectively to these students, giving them emotional support, motivation, and encouragement.

We can observe that the works in affectivity in the intelligent educational system can be divided into three main research interests: (1) recognition of user's emotions, (2) expression of emotions, and (3) emotions synthesis. In the next sections, we describe some techniques used by these works to recognize, express, and simulate emotions in the machine.

Recognizing and Modeling Students' Emotions

In order for an affective computational system to interact effectively with the student, it should recognize his emotions in order to respond to him appropriately. At present, we observe four main modes of user's emotion recognition: (1) *voice* (prosody) (Kopecek, 2000; Tcherkassof, 1999); (2) *observable behavior* or user's actions in the system's interface (for example, chosen options and typing speed) (Bercht & Viccari, 2000; De Vicente & Pain, 2002; Jaques & Viccari, 2004; Jaques, Viccari, Pesty, & Bonneville, 2004); (3) *facial expressions* (Ekman, 1999; Wehrle & Kaiser, 2000); and (4) *physiological signs* (blood volume pulse, electromyogram—muscle tension, skin conductivity, breathing) (Picard, Vyzas, & Healey, 2001).

In recognition by physiological signs, Rosalind Picard of the MIT Media Lab Computing Group (http://vismod.www.media.mit.edu/ vismod/demos/affect/) achieved good results with physiological recognition on eight emotional states (neutral, anger, hate, grief, platonic love, romantic love, joy, and reverence) with a success rate of about 81% (Picard, 2000). These results were obtained through tests made with one person over the course of 20 days, spanning about five weeks. The signals used were: blood volume pulse, electromyogram (muscle tension), skin conductivity, and breathing.

Emotion recognition mechanisms, such as emotion recognition by the user's facial expressions, are composed of hardware equipment that detects the physiological signs, and a software component that is responsible for decoding the information sent by the hardware. For example, Wehrle and Kaiser (2000) videotaped a user's facial expressions while he played a game and used the software FEAT to automatically analyze the recorded facial behavior.

We can recognize a student's emotions just by analyzing his facial expressions or voice, but, usually, the physiological sensors are not used as the unique mechanism to infer the student's emotions. Since they only yield some evidence on the arousal, valence, and other information about the emotions, they are used as auxiliary mechanisms to infer emotions more accurately, or together. Some examples of evidence detected by physiological sensors are (Conati, 2002; Picard, 1997):

- skin conductivity, which is a very good indicator of the level of arousal; and
- heartbeat (measured by a heart rate monitor), which increases more in the presence of emotion with negative valence.

Emotion can also be inferred by the student's *observable behavior*, that is, the student's actions in the interface of the learning environment. In this case, the system should reason about an emotion-generating situation and try to infer the user's emotion by using a psychological model of emotion. Some examples of observable behavior are: time to accomplish an exercise, success or failure in tasks, request for or refusal of help, and the like. In such cases, generally the system predicts the student's emotions based on a cognitive psychological model of emotions, mainly the OCC model. The idea is to use the information provided by the psychological model in order to build an interpretation of a situation from the user's point of view and to reason about to which emotion this interpretation leads. For example, in order to infer the emotion happy according to the OCC model, the system reasons about the desirable aspect of an event based on goals and preferences of the student. If the student has as a goal pleasing his parents, obtaining a good grade in a task is a desirable event (situation) since it promotes his objective and, in this way, elicits positive emotions, such as joy. Pat (Jaques & Viccari, 2004; Jaques et al., 2004) is a pedagogical agent that infers the student's emotions by his observable behavior in a collaborative e-learning environment.

According to Paiva (2000), although these mechanisms for emotion recognition differ, as they seize different expressions of emotion, they can be seen as being complementary and part of a large multi-modal affective sensory system. Picard (1997) believes that the best recognition is likely to come from the combination of the different modalities and including not only low-level signal recognition but also higher-level reasoning about the situation.

In order for the system to respond appropriately to the user, in addition to recognizing the user's emotions, it must have a student affective model, which is called *affective user modeling* (AUM). Elliott, Rickel, and Lester (1999) define AUM as the capacity of the computational system to model the user's affective states. The affective user model must be dynamic enough to consider the changes in emotional states, since emotion is seen as a dynamic process that happens in the form of episodes delimited in time (Bercht & Viccari, 2000).

One of the first works that proposed the integration of affective modeling in an educational environment is that of Elliott, Rickel, and Lester (1999). This work discusses on how to use the Affective Reasoner (Elliott, 1992) in the pedagogical environment, Design a Plant of agent Herman (Lester & Stone, 1997), in order to model students' emotions. But the model was not implemented, and they do not show how to identify a student's goals, which is necessary according to the OCC model in order to infer emotions. The authors assume that the user's goals and preferences that are necessary to define the outcome of the appraisal should be known.

Conati (2002) propose a probabilistic model to infer students' emotions in an educational computational game. The model is implemented using Dynamic Decision Networks (DDNs) that are an extension of Bayesian networks. The model considers six emotions (joy, distress, pride, shame, admiration, and reproach) that are inferred using the OCC model. The DDN and Bayesian networks have proved to be powerful tools to model emotions since they allow explicit representation of the probabilistic dependencies between causes, effects, and emotional states, enabling the determination of emotions with more accuracy in situations where the user experiences a variety of emotions. On the other hand, it is difficult to define the required prior and conditional probabilities that are necessary in Bayesian networks.

De Vicente and Pain (2002) model students' motivational states based on factors such as control, challenge, independence, fantasy, confidence, sensory interest, cognitive interest, effort, and satisfaction, that are caught through observable student behavior. To determine which actions are indications of these affective factors, they observed recorded interactions in MOODS, an educational computing environment.

Bercht and Viccari (2000) defined a dynamic affective model based on a Belief-Desire-Intention approach (Bratman, 1990) that considers the factors self-confidence, independence, and effort to detect the motivational state of a student.

The Expression of Emotions in Machines

Due to the motivation aspect of lifelike characters, systems have been enriching the interfaces with characters that exhibit facial and body expressions (Johnson, Rickel, & Lester, 2000; Lester, Converse, Stone, Kahler, & Barlow, 1997; Lester & Stone, 1997; Paiva & Machado, 1998). In Education, for example, some works use agents represented by lifelike characters for the presentation of pedagogical content to the student, doing demonstrations, with the aim of engaging the student and motivating him (Elliott et al., 1999; Paiva, Machado, & Martinho, 1999). These agents are known as *animated pedagogical agents*.

The animated pedagogical agents are intelligent agents that have a pedagogical or educational role to facilitate or improve learning and that are personified by lifelike characters that interact with the student. These agents use multimedia resources to provide for the user an animated character with characteristics similar to those of living, intelligent creatures. In this way, which differs from conventional systems, the animated pedagogical agents communication has a more anthropomorphic and social nature. They exploit the natural tendency of people to engage in social interactions with computers, termed "the Media Equation" by Reeves and Nass (1996).

As some examples of animated pedagogical agents, we can mention the agents: Adele (Johnson, Shaw, & Ganeshan, 1998), Steve (Rickel & Johnson, 1998), Vincent (Paiva & Machado, 1998), Cosmo (Lester et al., 1997a) and Herman (Lester & Stone, 1997). In Figure 1, we can see Adele (Johnson et al., 1998) and the educational environment where it exists, Graphical Interface for Medical Simulation.

Since they are represented by lifelike characters, the animated pedagogical agents become powerful tools for the expression of emotions in machine. They can express emotions through face and body signals. For example, the animated agents, Herman (Lester & Stone, 1997) and Cosmo (Lester, Voerman, Towns, & Callaway, 1997), have some emotional facial expressions and movements that are presented according to the interaction with the student.

In order for a lifelike pedagogical agent to express emotions, they show animations composed of emotive facial expressions, body attitudes, and affective utterances. In such cases, the agent chooses their behavior from a library of physical (attitudes) and verbal (speeches) behaviors, or it can generate them dynamically by 3D graphical algorithms.

Pat: An Animated Pedagogical Agent that has the Role of Providing Emotional Support to the Student

Jaques and Viccari (2004) and Jaques et al. (2004) proposed an animated pedagogical agent called Pat (Pedagogical and Affective Tutor) that has the role of providing emotional support to the student—motivating and encouraging him, making him believe in his self-ability, and promoting a positive mood in him, all of which fosters learning. This careful support of the agent, its affective tactics, is expressed through emotional attitudes and by encouragement messages of the lifelike character.

In order to respond appropriately to the student, Pat recognizes the student's emotions (joy/distress, satisfaction/disappointment, anger/gratitude, and shame) from the student's observable behavior, that is, his actions in the interface of the educational system. The inference of emotions is psychologically grounded on the OCC model.

The agent is composed by two main modules: the mind and the body. The *mind* is responsible for the affective diagnosis and the selection of the affective tactics. The

Figure 1. Adele and the educational environment for medical simulation (pictures available at http://www.isi.edu/isd/ADE/ade-body.html)

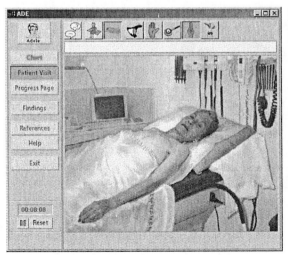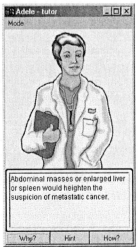

student's affective model and the mind of the agent are implemented in BDI. The BDI model describes an agent as an intentional system, that is, having mental states of Belief, Desire and Intention (Bratman, 1990). In order to infer the student's emotions, the BDI mind reasons, using the information from the OCC model that is provided for the agent in the form of beliefs, about which emotions a situation (an action of the student, for example, providing an incorrect response for an exercise) leads based on student's goals and preferences. The *body* is responsible for selecting, from the database of behaviors, an emotive attitude and speech for the tactic to be applied. In order for the agent to be believable, more realistic, and less robotic, there are several physical and verbal behaviors for each type of tactic. The body was implemented in Java.

As we already said, the affective tactics of Pat, which are chosen according to the student's emotions, have the role of encouraging the student and promoting positive emotions in him. The work is based on the research carried out by psychologists and pedagogues who pointed out that positive emotions have a positive effect on learning (Coles, 1998; Izard, 1994). Jaques and Viccari believe that this role of an affective tutor that cares about the student's progress in learning and that chooses the appropriate affective tactics in order to promote positive emotions in the student (which is better for learning) can be performed by Pat (Jaques et al., 2004). As shown by the Media Equation (Reeves & Nass, 1996), people react socially to a computer, although they think that they do not.

In Figure 2, we can see what Pat looks like (Jaques & Viccari, 2004; Jaques et al. 2004). The lifelike character was developed in Microsoft Agent (http://www.microsoft.com). The character was designed based on a study made by psychologists and pedagogues. For the agent's speech, the Microsoft Speech API was used for the voice synthesizer.

Figure 2. The animated pedagogical agent, Pat (Jaques & Viccari, 2004)

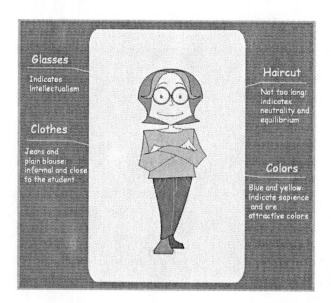

As a case study, the proposed agent was implemented as the Mediating Agent of MACES (Andrade, Jaques, Viccari, Bordini, & Jung, 2001), an e-learning collaborative environment modeled as a multi-agent system and pedagogically based on the Vygotsky sociocultural theory (1962; 1978).

Emotion Synthesis ("Have" Emotions)

In some cases, to exhibit affective behavior in a coherent manner, agents are constituted of models of emotions, which Picard (1997) called "Emotion Synthesis." We can observe a great interest from the research community in studying theories and architectures to obtain "machine emotions."

Many researchers discuss whether computers can have emotions, since emotions in humans are constituted of the integration of mental, cognitive, motivational, and somatic components (Clore & Ortony, 1999). In relation to this question, Picard (1997) says that the affective computing researchers refer to computer emotions in a descriptive sense, for instance, a computer is able to label a state in which it received a lot of conflicting information as "frustration."

One of the first works that suggested the modeling of architecture of emotions in pedagogical agents is that of Elliott et al. (1999). These authors proposed to use the Affective Reasoner Framework (Elliott, 1992; Elliott, 1997) to implement emotions in the lifelike pedagogical agent, Steve. In the Affective Reasoner, the agents are able to generate emotions through a set of rules that follow the OCC model. According to the OCC model, the emotions are the result of a cognitive evaluation that an agent performs based on his goals and principles. In this case, the authors propose a set of goals and principles to Steve that is the basis of the Steve's generation of emotion. For example, one of Steve's purposes is to engage the student, therefore, Steve will be anxious or depressed when the student is bored with the tasks at hand. As we can see, it is necessary for the agent to also infer the student's emotions.

Emotion synthesis can be used not only as a way to obtain more rational behavior, but also to make the lifelike agents more believable, that is, more realistic. Thus, there are several researchers interested in developing emotional agents, such as the works of El-Nasr, Ioerger, Yen, House, and Parke (1999) that are specifically interested in the use of emotions in order to increase the believability of lifelike characters. Other research in this area has been done by Elliott (1997) and Bates (1994).

Conclusion and Future Trends

In this chapter, we presented some of the works that are on-going in the area of Affective Computing, in particular the application of this research matter in teaching and learning systems that can also be applied specifically in Web-based learning systems. Affective Computing is a recent area of research, however, the results are very promising in the Artificial Intelligence area in general and in particular for Computer in Education.

As we have already seen in the research mentioned in this chapter, emotions play an important role in learning and, therefore, cannot be neglected by teachers or educational computing systems. However, to infer students' emotions in computational systems is not an easy task. For instance, we need a psychological model of emotions to ground it. The major challenge is to find a psychological model of emotions that can be implemented computationally. As explained before, a great number of the works mentioned in this chapter is based on the OCC model (Ortony, Clore, & Collins, 1988). This is due to the fact that the OCC model was designed to be implemented computationally, unlike others. Yet in relation to the inference of the emotions, determining the emotional intensity by the student's observable behavior is a difficult and inaccurate task. We believe that the insertion of physiological sensors that detect bodily expressions of emotion can be used with the information inferred from a student's observable behavior (based on a cognitive model of emotions) to determine the intensity of that student's emotions more accurately. The body sensors can be useful to identify when the student is feeling an emotion, the valence, and intensity of these emotions.

It is also important to accomplish a deeper study concerning these physiological sensors in order to choose the one that gives more accurate information on students' emotions and their intensity. Despite the limitations in the detection of emotions and in the computational models for emotions representation, we strongly believe that this area improves the interaction process in a teaching-learning system.

Concerning the affective model of the student, this model must be dynamic enough to consider the changes in emotional states. Since the motivation and the affectivity of the student may vary in a very dynamic way (the student may not feel satisfied at a certain moment and feel more satisfied in another), the use of the BDI approach for the implementation of the student model has proven to be very convenient, because it allows simple revisions and frequent modifications on the information concerning the student (Bercht & Viccari, 2000). The student model is built dynamically from each interaction in real-time. Another approach, the Bayesian networks, has been shown to be a powerful tool to model emotions that are also inferred based on a cognitive model of emotions, since they allow explicit representation of the probabilistic dependencies between causes, effects, and emotional states, enabling the determination of a student's emotions with more accuracy in situations where he or she experiences a variety of emotions.

When it comes to the expression of emotions by a machine, much work can be done in the sense of which messages and attitudes of encouragement an affective agent should apply. As there are not many works that show which affective tactics are best and should be applied, much research should be done in this sense, as, for instance, the studies and interviews done by Cooper, Brna, and Martins (2000) about empathic teachers. In order to design more powerful agents that express emotions, because they are generally represented by lifelike characters, it is necessary to work with a multidisciplinary team that includes cartoon designers, psychologists, pedagogues, Artificial Intelligence experts, and others.

Another future work that could be done is to extend the BDI model in order to also include personality traits, emotions, and moods. According to DeRosis (2002), this approach offers several advantages. One is that it presents the opportunity of driving consistent behaviors of agents from a model of their cognitive state: the system of beliefs, desires, and intentions may trigger emotions, regulate the decision of whether to show or to hide them, and finally, drive externalized actions. In such a case, we are incorporating an architecture of emotions (emotion synthesis) in the agent in order for it to generate a more consistent and believable affective behavior. Jaques and Viccari (2004a) propose the extension of a BDI model and tool, X-BDI (Móra, Lopes, Viccari, & Coelho, 1998), in order to implement emotion synthesis in Pat.

References

Ames, C. (1990). Motivation: What teachers need to know. *Teachers College Record, 91*(3), 409-421.

Andrade, A., Jaques, P., Viccari, R., Bordini, R., & Jung, J. (2001). A computational model of distance learning based on Vygotsky's sociocultural approach. In *Proceedings of AI-ED, 2001 Workshop Papers: Multi-agent Architectures for Distributed Learning Environments,* San Antonio, Texas, May 19-23 (pp. 33-40).

Bates, J. (1994). The role of emotion in believable agents. *Communications of ACM, 37*(7), 122-125.

Bercht, M. & Viccari, R. (2000). Pedagogical agents with affective and cognitive dimensions. In *Congreso Iberoamericnao de Informatica Educativa* 2000, Vina del Mar. Santiago: Universidad de Chile. CD ROM, p. 173.

Bratman, M. E. (1990). What is intention? In P. Cohen, J. Morgan, & M. Pollack (Eds.), *Intentions in communication* (pp. 15-31). Cambridge, MA: MIT Press.

Clore, G. & Ortony, A. (1999). Cognition in emotion: Always, sometimes, or never? In L. Nadel, & R. D. Lane (Eds.), *The cognitive neuroscience of emotion* (pp. 24-61). New York: Oxford University Press.

Coles, G. (1998). *Reading lessons: The debate over literacy.* New York: Hill & Wang.

Coles, G. (2004). Literacy, emotions, and the brain. Retrieved from *http://www.readingonline.org/critical/coles.html*

Conati, C. (2002). Probabilistic assessment of user's emotions in educational games. *Applied Artificial Intelligence, 16*(7-8), 555-575.

Cooper, B., Brna, P., & Martins, A. (2000). Effective affective in intelligent systems: Building on evidence of empathy in teaching and learning. In A. Paiva (Ed.), *Affective interactions: Towards a new generation of computer interfaces* (pp. 21-34). Berlin: Springer.

Damasio, A. (1994). *Descartes' error: Emotion, reason, and the human brain.* New York: G.P. Putnam.

Darwin, C. R. (1965). *The expression of emotions in man and animals.* London: Murray.

DeRosis, F. (2002). Toward merging cognition and affect in HCI. *Applied Artificial Intelligence, 16*(7-8), 487-494.

De Vicente, A. & Pain, H. (2002). Informing the detection of the students' motivational state: An empirical study. In *Proceedings of International Conference on Intelligent Tutoring Systems*, June, Biarritz, France (pp. 933-943). Berlin: Springer-Verlag.

Ekman, P. (1999). Facial expressions. In T. Dalgleish & T. Power (Eds.), *The handbook of cognition and emotion* (pp. 301-320). Sussex, UK: John Wiley & Sons.

Elliott, C. (1992). *The affective reasoner: A process model of emotions in a multi-agent system.* PhD thesis in Computer Science. Institute for the Learning Sciences, Northwestern University, Illinois.

Elliott, C. (1997). Affective reasoner personality models for automated tutoring systems. In *Proceedings of Workshop on Pedagogical Agents, 8th World Conference on Artificial Intelligence in Education,* August, Kobe, Japan (pp. 33-39).

Elliott, C., Rickel, J., & Lester, J. (1999). Lifelike pedagogical agents and affective computing: An exploratory synthesis. In M. Wooldridge & M. Veloso (Eds.), *Artificial intelligence today* (pp. 195-212). Berlin: Springer-Verlag.

El-Nasr, M., Ioerger, T., Yen, J., House, D., & Parke, F. (1999). Emotionally expressive agents. In *Proceedings of Computer Animation,* May 26-28, Geneva, Switzerland (p. 48). New York: IEEE Press.

Frijda, N. (1994). Varieties of affect: Emotions and episodes, moods, and sentiments. In P. Ekman & R. J. Davidson (Eds.), *The nature of emotion* (pp. 59-67). New York: Oxford Univ. Press.

Goleman, D. (1995). *Emotional intelligence.* New York: Bantam Books.

Izard, C.E. (1984). Emotion-cognition relationships and human development. In C.E. Izard, J. Kagan, & R.B. Zajonc (Eds.), *Emotions, cognition, and behavior* (pp. 17-37). New York: Cambridge University Press.

Jaques, P. A. & Viccari, R. (2004). A BDI approach to infer student's emotions. In *Proceedings of IBERAMIA 2004, Advances in Artificial Intelligence. Ibero-American Conference on AI,* November 22-26 (pp. 901-911). Puebla, México.

Jaques, P. A., Viccari, R.M., Pesty, S., & Bonneville, J.-F. (2004). Applying affective tactics for a better learning. In *Proceedings of the 16th European Conference on Artificial Intelligence, ECAI 2004,* August 22-27, Valencia, Spain (pp. 109-113).

James, W. (1884). What is emotion? *Mind, 9,* 188-205.

John-Steiner, V. (2000). *Creative collaborations.* Oxford, UK: Oxford University Press.

Johnson, L., Shaw, E., & Ganeshan, R. (1998). Pedagogical agents on the Web. In *Proceedings of ITS Workshop on Pedagogical Agents* (pp. 2-7). San Antonio, Texas.

Johnson, L., Rickel, J., & Lester, J. (2000). Animated pedagogical agents: Face-to-face interaction in interactive learning environments. *International Journal of Artificial Intelligence in Education, 11,* 47-78.

Kopecek, I. (2000). Emotions and prosody in dialogues: An algebraic approach based on user modelling. In *Proceedings of the ISCA Workshop on Speech and Emotions* (pp. 184-189). Belfast: ISCA.

Lester, J. & Stone, B. (1997). Increasing believability in animated pedagogical agents. In *Proceedings of International Conference on Autonomous Agents* (pp. 16-21). Marina del Rey, CA.

Lester, J., Converse, S., Stone, B., Kahler, S., & Barlow, T. (1997). Animated pedagogical agents and problem-solving effectiveness: A large-scale empirical evaluation. In *Proceedings of World Conference On Artificial Intelligence In Education*, August, Kobe, Japan (pp. 23-30). Amsterdam: IOS.

Lester, J., Voerman, J., Towns, S., & Callaway, C. (1997).Cosmo: A life-like animated pedagogical agent with deictic believability. In *IJCAI: Workshop on Animated Pedagogical Agents,* Nagoya, Japan (pp. 61-69). San Francisco: Morgan Kaufmann.

Meece, J. & McColskey, W. (2001). Improving student motivation. *Serve.* Retrieved from *http://www.serve.org/Products/ProdPub.php*

Móra, M. C., Lopes, J. G., Viccari, R. M., & Coelho, H. (1998). BDI models and systems: Reducing the gap. In *Proceedings of Agents Theory, Architecture and Languages Workshop* (pp. 153-167). Canary Islands. London: Springer-Verlag.

Ortony, A., Clore, G., & Collins, A. (1988). *The cognitive structure of emotions.* Cambridge, UK: Cambridge University Press.

Paiva, A. (2000). Affective interactions: Toward a new generation of computer interfaces? In A. Paiva (Ed.), *Affective interactions—Towards a new generation of computer interfaces* (pp. 1-8). Berlin: Springer.

Paiva, A. & Machado, I. (1998). Vincent, an autonomous pedagogical agent for on-the-job training. In *Proceedings of Conference on Intelligent Tutoring Systems*, San Antonio, TX (pp. 584-593). Berlin: Springer-Verlag.

Paiva, A., Machado, I., & Martinho, C. (1999). Enriching pedagogical agents with emotional behavior: The case of Vincent. In *Proceedings of AIED, Workshop on Life-Like Pedagogical Agents*, Le Mans, France. Berlin: Springer-Verlag.

Piaget, J. (1989). Les relations entre l'intelligence et l'affectivité dans le developpement de l'enfant. In B. Rimé & K. Scherer (Eds.), *Les Émotions. Textes de base en psychologie* (pp. 75-95). Paris: Delachaux et Niestlé.

Picard, R. (1997).*Affective computing.* Cambridge, MA: MIT Press.

Picard, R. (2000). An interview with Rosalind Picard, author of *Affective Computing.* In A. Paiva (Ed.), *Affective interactions—Towards a new generation of computer interfaces* (pp. 219-227). Berlin: Springer.

Picard, P., Vyzas, E., & Healey, J. (2001). Toward machine emotional intelligence: Analysis of affective physiological state. *IEEE Transactions Pattern Analysis and Machine Intelligence, 23*(10), 1175-1191.

Reeves, B. & Nass, C. (1996). *The media equation: How people treat computers, television, and new media like real people and places.* New York: Cambridge University Press.

Rickel, J. & Johnson, L. (1998). Steve: A pedagogical agent for virtual reality. In *Proceedings of International Conference on Autonomous Agents* (pp. 165-172). Minneapolis, MN; New York: ACM Press.

Scherer, K. (1999). Appraisal theory. In T. Dalgleish & T. Power (Eds.), *Handbook of cognition and emotion* (pp. 637-663). New York: John Wiley & Sons.

Scherer, K. (2000). Psychological models of emotion. In J. Borod (Ed.), *The neuropsychology of emotion* (pp. 137-162). Oxford/New York: Oxford University Press.

Tcherkassof, A. (1999). Les indices de préparation à l'action et la reconnaissance des expressions émotionnelles faciales. *Revue Européenne de Psychologie Appliquée, 49*(2), 99-105.

Vygotsky, L. (1962). *Thought and language.* Cambridge, MA: MIT Press.

Vygotsky, L. (1978). *Mind in society.* Cambridge, MA: Harvard University Press.

Vygotsky, L. (1994). The problem of the environment. In R. Vander Veer & J. Vlasiner (Eds.), *The Vygotsky Reader* (pp. 338-354). Cambridge, MA: Blackwell.

Wehrle, T. & Kaiser, S. (2000). Emotion and facial expression. In A. Paiva (Ed.), *Affective interactions - Towards a new generation of computer interfaces* (pp. 49-63). Berlin: Springer.

Chapter VII

Defining Personalized Learning Views of Relevant Learning Objects in a Collaborative Bookmark Management System

Antonella Carbonaro
University of Bologna, Italy

Abstract

In this chapter, we introduce how to use a Web-based hybrid recommender system developed with a collaborative bookmark management system approach. The system combines content analysis and the development of virtual clusters of students and educational sources. It provides facilitation in the use of a huge amount of digital information stored in a distributed learning environment on the basis of the student's personal requirements and interests. By adopting a hybrid approach, the system is able to effectively filter relevant resources from a wide heterogeneous environment like the Web, taking advantage of the common interests of the users and also maintaining the benefits provided by content analysis. The basic idea is to appropriately help students classifying domain-specific information found on the Web and saved as bookmarks, to recommend these documents to other students with similar interests, and to notify users periodically about new, potentially interesting documents. Documents are represented using metadata model.

Introduction

In a distributed learning environment, there is likely to be large number of educational resources (Web pages, lectures, journal papers, learning objects, etc.) stored in many distributed and differing repositories on the Internet. Without guidance, students would probably have great difficulties in finding the reading material relevant to a particular learning task. The meta-data descriptions about learning object representation provide information about properties of the learning objects. However, the meta-data by itself may not provide qualitative information about different objects nor may it provide information for customized views. This problem is becoming particularly important in Web-based education, where the variety of learners taking the same course is much greater.

Conversely, the courses produced using adaptive hypermedia or intelligent tutoring system technologies are able to dynamically select the most relevant learning material from their knowledge bases for each individual student. Nevertheless, generally, these systems can't directly benefit from existing repositories of learning material (Brusilovsky & Nijhavan, 2002). This chapter provides a contribution to this issue. The basic idea is to appropriately gather different agent-based modules that would help students classify domain-specific information found on the Web and saved as bookmarks, to recommend these documents to other students with similar interests, and to notify the students periodically about new, potentially interesting documents. The system is developed to provide immediate portability and visibility from different user locations, enabling access to a personal bookmark repository just by using a Web browser.

Recently, learning objects (LOs) have been the center of attention in e-learning mechanisms and have been designated as atomic units of knowledge (Wetterling & Collis, 2003). In educational settings, learning objects can be of different kinds, for example, from files having static content (like HTML, PDF, or PowerPoint presentation format) to sophisticated interactive formats (like HTML pages loaded with JavaScript or Java applet, etc). Audio files, video clips, or Flash animations also constitute learning objects. An LO comprises a chunk of content material, which can be re-used or shared in different learning situations. LO standards allow the use or re-use of content from one system to another so that these can be adopted across different computer platforms and learning systems. The IEEE Standard for Learning Object Metadata (LOM) (http://grouper.ieee.org/p1484/wg12/files/LOM_1484_12_1_v1_Final_Draft.pdf) is the first accredited standard for learning object technology (http://ltsc.ieee.org).

There are presently countless LOs available for commercial and academic use. CAREO (http://www.careo.org) and MERLOT (http://www.merlot.org/Home.po) are two global

LO repositories, while SPLASH (http://www.edusplash.net/default.asp?page=Home) is an example of peer-to-peer architecture of local repositories. Because of time and capability constraints, however, it is almost impossible for a learner and a teacher to go through all available LOs to find the most suitable one. In particular, learning object metadata tags may facilitate rapid updating, searching, and management of content by filtering and selecting only the relevant content for a given purpose (Carbonaro, 2004). Searchers can use a standard set of retrieval techniques to maximize their chances of finding the resources via a search engine (Recker & Wiley, 2001). But the value of searching and browsing results depends on the information and organizational structure of the repository. Moreover, searching for LOs within heterogeneous repositories may become a more complicated problem. What we argue in this chapter is that one can alleviate such difficulties by automatically filtering and recommending relevant LOs in a collaborative framework, to address issues like trying to determine the type or the quality of the information suggested from the personalized learning environment.

In this context, standard keyword search is of very limited effectiveness. For example, it cannot filter for the type of information (tutorial, applet or demo, review questions, etc.), the level of the information (aimed at secondary school students, graduate students, etc.), the prerequisites for understanding the information, or the quality of the information. The starting point is the use of statistical information extraction and natural language parsing techniques to automatically derive classificatory and metadata information from primarily textual data (Web pages, Word, postscript or similar documents, etc.). While still challenging for large ontologies, text classification methods that semantically categorize an entire document are now relatively well-understood and provide a good level of performance.

The chapter is organized as follows. Firstly, it describes some relevant and recent related works. Then, it illustrates the recommendation process that offers interesting opportunities to introduce the need for personalized criteria. In fact, personalized information classification and filtering facilities are essential basics to use the huge amount of digital information according to the student's personal requirements and interests. In this way, data can be obtained about which material is proving to be most effective in raising student achievement. Following that, the chapter introduces the learning object recommendation process, obtained by considering student and learning material profiles and adopting filtering criteria based on the value of selected metadata fields. Finally, the conclusion of the chapter and some future research directions are presented.

Related Works

Due to the characteristics of the system described in this chapter, relevant related works fall into three main categories: adaptive hypermedia, recommending technical papers, and categorizing search results.

Adaptive hypermedia has been studied extensively in the literature. As pointed out by Paramythis and Loidl-Reisinger (2003), some categories of adaptation in learning environments could be defined. The broad and partially overlapping categories are: adaptive interaction, adaptive course delivery, content discovery and assembly, and, finally, adaptive collaboration support.

The first, adaptive interaction, refers to adaptations that take place at the system's interface and are intended to support the user's interaction with the system, without modifying the learning content itself. The second category, adaptive course delivery, refers to adaptations that are intended to tailor a course to the individual learner (for example, dynamic course structuring, adaptive navigation support, adaptive selection of alternative fragments of course material) (Brusilovsky, 2001). These adaptation techniques are the most common and widely used in learning environments today. The third category refers to the application of adaptive techniques in the discovery and assembly of learning material from potentially distributed repositories. It is necessary to use models and knowledge about users typically derived from monitoring (for example, one's personal learning and interaction history). The fourth and final category, adaptive collaboration support, involves communication between multiple persons and, potentially, collaboration towards common objectives. Collaboration, cooperative learning, communities of learners, and so on, represent an important dimension to be considered (Paramythis & Loidl-Reisinger, 2003). The adaptive techniques of the system described in this chapter are in the last two directions—facilitating the cooperation process, and ensuring a good match between collaborators. In addition, due to the crawler component (see next section for more details), the described system helps the students to discover new learning material from the Web.

There are several related works concerning recommending technical papers. Basu, Hirsh, Cohen, and Nevill-Manning (2001) studied this issue in the context of assigning conference paper submissions to reviewing committee members. McNee et al. (2002) propose the adoption of collaborative filtering techniques to recommend papers for researchers. But making recommendations in an e-learning environment is different from that in other domains; for example, items liked by learners might not be pedagogically appropriate for them (Tang & McCalla, 2003). In the developed system, we organize papers not only based on their main content categories, but also according to their technical levels, discriminating between review papers, workshop papers, or highly technical papers, and so forth (see third section for more details).

One of the main general procedures used to organize documents into topical contexts is by classification. In this approach, statistical techniques are applied to learn a model based on a labeled set of training documents (documents with category labels). The model is then applied to new documents (documents without category labels) to determine their categories. For example, Chen and Dumais (2000) use a Support Vector Machine to classify new Web pages returned from search engines on-the-fly. Moreover, Glover, Tsioutsiouliklis, Lawrence, Pennock, and Flake (2002) describe a method for learning a highly accurate Web page classifier analyzing the relative utility of document text, and the text in citing documents near the citation, for classification and description. In the developed system, the classification process is obtained using a combination of Text Categorization and Relevance Feedback (see next section for more details).

Personalized Learning Environment

In order to foster the development of Web-based information access and management, it is relevant to be able to obtain a user-based view of available information. The exponential increase of the size and the formats of remotely accessible data make it difficult to find suitable solutions to the problem. Moreover, technological advances in wireless communication and mobile devices have challenged educational institution to adopt the opportunities of distributed knowledge acquisition and delivery (Andronico, Carbonaro, Colazzo, & Molinari, 2003; Andronico, Carbonaro, Colazzo, Molinari, & Ronchetti, 2004). Often, today's information access tools are not able to provide the right answers for a user query but, rather, provide large supersets (e.g., in Web-search engines). Search for documents uses queries containing words or describing concepts that are of interest to the user. Most content retrieval methodologies use some type of similarity score to match a query describing the content, and then present the user with a ranked list of suggestions. To obtain a personalized view of (relevant) information, a number of Recommender Systems (RS) have been implemented. The RS recommendations are generated using two main techniques: content-based information filtering, and collaborative filtering (Belkin & Croft, 1992).

If, on one hand, a content-based approach allows the definition and maintenance of an accurate user profile, that is particularly valuable when a user encounters new content; on the other hand, it has the limitation of dealing only with textual resources. Moreover, content-based techniques do not depend on having other users in the system, but they suffer certain drawbacks, including requiring a source of content information and not providing much in the way of serendipitous discovery.

In a collaborative approach, resources are instead recommended based on the rating of other users of the system with similar interests. As there is no analysis of the item content, collaborative filtering systems can deal with any kind of item, not being limited to textual content. This way, users can receive items with content that is different from that received in the past. But for a collaborative system to work well, several users must evaluate each item. So, new items cannot be recommended until some users have taken the time to evaluate them, and new users cannot receive recommendation until the system has acquired some information about the new user in order to make personalized predictions. These limitations often referred to as the scarcity and start-up problems (Melville, Mooney, & Nagarajan, 2002).

By adopting a hybrid approach, the system is able to effectively filter relevant resources from a wide heterogeneous environment like the Web, taking advantage of the common interests of the users and also maintaining the benefits provided by content analysis.

Usually, this idea has been widely and successfully developed for specific domains, such as movie or film recommendations (Hanani, Shapira, & Shoval, 2001; Li & Kim, 2004), and is rarely used for recommending LOs. Our system uses a hybrid approach and suitable representations of both available information sources and user's interests in order to match user information needs, as expressed in his query, as accurately as possible to the available information. In the next paragraph, we describe how to consider LO structure to properly represent learning material and extract metadata information.

Figure 1. Logical architecture of the recommendation system. The red arrows indicate the user feedback that, through learning module, permits to update the user profile. The yellow boxes represent the software components. For each user, the system manages a specific user agent.

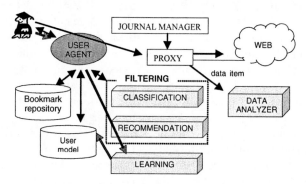

Figure 2. Resource classification and recommendation

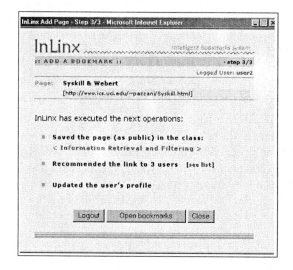

In our system, we have adopted a representation based on the Vector Space Model (VSM), the most frequently used in Information Retrieval (IR) and text learning. Since the resources of the system are Web pages, to obtain a vector representation it is necessary to apply a sequence of contextual processing to the source code of the pages. To filter information resources according to user interests, we must have a common representation for both the users and the resources. This knowledge representation model must be expressive enough to synthetically and significantly describe the information content. The use of the VSM allows the user profile to be updated in accordance to consulted information resources (Salton, 1989).

Figure 3. Resource recommendation

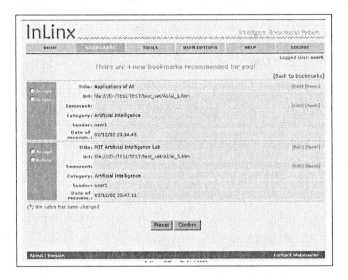

Figure 1 shows the logical architecture of the presented recommendation system. The system includes a process of classification and recommendation feedback (Figure 2), in which the user agent learns from the student and consequently adapts itself according to the changes in the student's interest; this gives the agent the chance to be more accurate in the following classification and recommendation steps (Figure 3). Thus, a high number of students using the system would make the following agent's actions more accurate. This allows the system to be capable of reflecting continuous ongoing changes of the practices of its member, as required by a cooperative framework.

To guarantee a personalized framework, the system needs to construct and maintain user profiles. For a particular user, it is reasonable to think that processing a set of correctly classified relevant and inappropriate documents from a certain domain of interest may lead to identification of the set of relevant keywords for that domain at a certain time. Thus, the user's domain-specific sets of relevant features, called prototypes, may be used to learn how to classify documents. In particular, to consider the peculiarity of positive and negative examples, we define positive prototype for a class c_j, a user u_i at time t, as a finite set of unique indexing terms, chosen to be relevant for c_j, up to time t. Then, we define negative prototype as a subset of the corresponding positive prototype, whereas each element can be found at least once in the set of documents classified as negative examples for class c_j. Positive examples for a specific user u_i and for a class c_j, are represented by the documents explicitly registered or accepted by u_i in c_j, while negative examples are either deleted bookmarks, misclassified bookmarks, or rejected bookmarks that happen to be classified into c_j.

According to traditional IR, we must state our classification problem as a combination of Text Categorization and Relevance Feedback.

Text Categorization

In our system, we have introduced a refinement of the standard similarity measure in order to also consider the distinction between positive and negative prototypes; so we define the similarity between a class c_j and a document D retrieved by the user u_i as:

$$sim_i^!(c_j, D) = (\vec{Q}_{i,j}^{(t)+} \circ \vec{D}_i^{(t)}) - (\vec{Q}_{i,j}^{(t)-} \circ \vec{D}_i^{(t)})$$

where $\vec{Q}_{i,j}^{(t)+}$ is the vector of the term weights of the positive prototype of a user u_i for

the class c_j up to time t and, in the same way, $\vec{Q}_{i,j}^{(t)-}$ is the vector of the term weights of

the negative prototype, while $\vec{D}_i^{(t)}$ is the vector of the term weights of the document D

saved by the a user u_i up to time t.

This equation, intuitively, expresses the idea that a document is similar to a class if it is comparable to the positive prototype of the class and not similar to its negative prototype. In case of equal similarity between two or more classes, the system also takes into account the user's interest in each of those categories and chooses the one for which the user has shown more interest (we will discuss the representation of the user's interest for a class later, in the recommendation section of the chapter). For term weighting, we have chosen the TF-IDF schema (Joachims, 1997), as it is one of the most successful and well-tested methods used in IR.

Relevance Feedback

In order to always reflect the current user's interest upon time, the system handles the feedback provided by the user. The feedback is supplied in an explicit way, by confirming/changing the class suggested in the classification task and by accepting/rejecting a recommended bookmark. The prototype's update is executed every n positive examples classified in a certain category. The feedback algorithm includes two steps.

The first one is the selection of the k most informative features, extracted from the n most recently classified documents. Comparative studies of different features selection techniques for text classification (Yang & Pederson, 1997) show how *Information Gain* (IG) is one of the most efficient for that task. Consequently, we have chosen to use IG for selecting the most informative terms from the corpus of the documents.

The second step is the prototype adaptation to the set of selected features. As traditional IR methods (for example, one of the most well-known is the Rocchio algorithm) do not allow adding or replacing keywords from the prototype, we felt the need to introduce an ad hoc algorithm that takes into account the possibility that the dimension of the profile vector may change over time, in order to reflect the user's current interest. According to our schema, relevant keywords that are not present in the prototype are added to it;

Figure 4. Updating schema of the positive prototype based on the most important words list extracted from positive examples

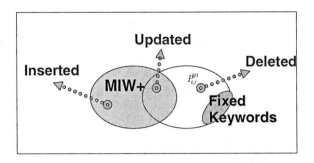

conversely, terms that are in the prototype but not in the list of the most informative terms are removed (unless the term was a core keyword of the class basic profile that cannot be eliminated). The weights of the terms that are present both in the prototype and in the selected feature list, such as the weights of the newly added terms, are updated with respect to the *n* documents processed for this purpose (Figure 4).

To manage the learning content recommendation, we maintain a user vs. category matrix that, for a specific user, stores the number of times he shows interest in a certain class and saves a bookmark in that class. Then, to learn the recommendation receivers, we use a matrix maintaining the user's confidence factor to represent how many documents recommended by a specific user are accepted or rejected by another one. Finally, to evaluate the similarity between users, we have chosen the Pearson-r correlation measure applied to a modified user-category matrix obtained by weighting the similarity between prototypes. This method allows the recommendation of an item to users with sure interest in the topic from which the recommending document depends or is related.

Detailed information about technical characteristics of described system can be found in Bighini and Carbonaro (2004) and Bighini, Carbonaro, and Casadei (2003).

Our experimental tests produce several reasons to expect that the use of the system promotes student information management. First of all, we have tested the classification process. It achieved good results since the first uses of the system, due to used text-learning techniques (stop-list filtering, stemming algorithm, VSM representation, and TF-IDF term weighting) and because fixed category profile never substituted in the student prototype.

Secondly, in order to evaluate the collaborative recommendation techniques, we have considered different initial student profiles. Tests carried out have highlighted the different components that influence the selection of those who receive recommendation:

- student interest in the category of recommended resource,
- confidence level between students, and

- the relation between the class prototype of the recommended resource and the class prototype of other categories.

The experiments performed have shown that the system responds to the "gray sheep problem," which is common in a pure collaborative recommendation system; that is, a student with interests different from those of other students will be able to receive recommendations as well. Moreover, we can consider that in the used test environment each classification produces approximately two recommendations; that is, with respect to the 66 saved documents, the system produces 118 recommendations, showing the importance of the collaborative component of the system.

Finally, to evaluate the crawler component that performs content-based recommendations, we have considered the knowledge needs of a student surfing the Web to find detailed information about a specific subject. For example, we have taken into account several issues of online journals from the Web site of the Kluwer Online (http://www.kluweronline.com). Our classification algorithm executes ad hoc classification of student prototypes, to consider that they can dynamically change over time. So, it is possible that the same document is recommended in two different categories for two different students. We have tested the system using some issues from the *Data Mining & Knowledge Discovery* journal, when students have already saved their bookmarks, and the system has updated prototypes and student profiles.

The E-Learning Recommendation

The automatic recommendation of relevant learning objects is obtained considering student and learning material profiles and adopting filtering criteria based on the value of selected metadata fields. Our experiments are based on Sharable Content Object Reference Model (SCORM)-compliant LOs. For example, we use the student's knowledge of domain concept to avoid recommendation of highly technical papers to a beginner student or popular magazine articles to a senior graduate student. For each student, the system evaluates and updates his skill and technical expertise levels. The pre-processing component developed to analyze the information maintained in LOs is able to produce a vector representation based on term weighting that can be used by the collaborative recommendation system described in previous paragraphs.

In SCORM, the organization and learning resources must be included with the course and placed in an XML file with the name imsmanifest.xml. The structure required for this file is detailed in the SCORM content aggregation specification (http://www.adlnet.org); it consists of four sections:

- a preamble section containing XML pointers to the schemas required for validating this file,

Figure 5. An example of an imsmanifest.xml file for a simple one-lesson course

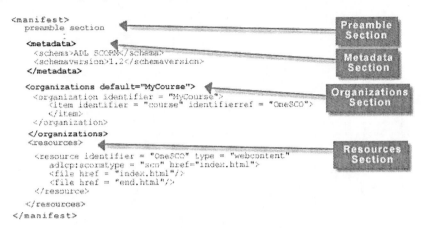

- a metadata section contain global course information, such as its title or its description,
- an organizations section describing course sequencing, and
- a resources section listing all the files used in the course.

Figure 5 shows an example of a simple imsmanifest file for a course with a single lesson.

To obtain the loading of some didactical source and its classification, we analyze the imsmanifest.xml file to extract .htm and .html files and examine the content. We consider the following metadata to provide the corresponding technical level:

- **difficulty:** represents the complexity of the learning material, ranging from "very easy" to "very difficult";
- **interactivity level:** represents the interactive format, ranging from "very low" (only static content) to "very high";
- **intended end-user role:** represents the user type (for example, student or teacher); and
- **context:** represents the instructional level necessary to take up LO.

The difficulty level is explicitly loaded into our database (in most cases, Learning Management Systems use this value). Difficulty and the other values are combined to characterize the technical level of learning material, ranging from 0 to 1 and representing how demanding is the LO. If some of these fields are not present in the manifest file (they are not required), we consider their average value.

Figure 6. Student's home page

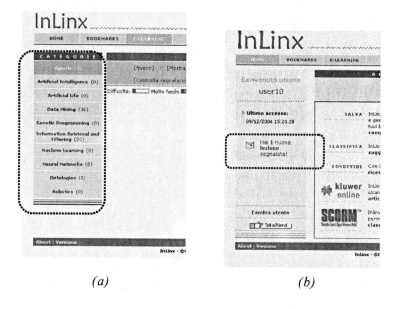

(a)   *(b)*

Figure 7. Learning object recommendation

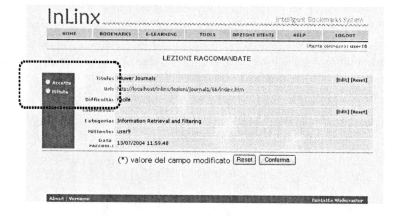

Figure 8. Index.html page of recommended learning object

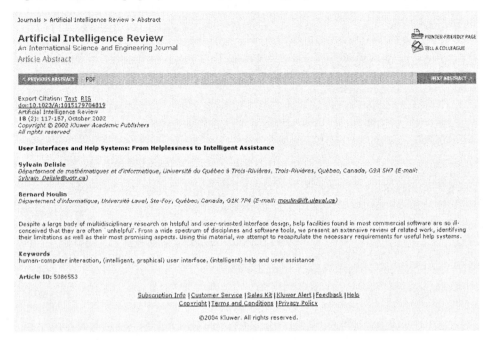

Figure 9. Imsmanifest.xml section of recommended learning object

```
<?xml version="1.0" ?>
- <manifest identifier="MANIFEST1" xmlns="http://www.imsglobal.org/xsd/imscp_v1p1"
    xmlns:imsmd="http://www.imsglobal.org/xsd/imsmd_v1p2" xmlns:xsi="http://www.w3.org/2001/XMLSchema-instance"
    xsi:schemaLocation="http://www.imsglobal.org/xsd/imscp_v1p1 imscp_v1p1p3.xsd
    http://www.imsglobal.org/xsd/imsmd_v1p2 imsmd_v1p2p2.xsd">
  - <metadata>
      <schema>IMS Content</schema>
      <schemaversion>1.1.2</schemaversion>
    - <imsmd:lom>
      - <imsmd:general>
        - <imsmd:title>
            <imsmd:langstring xml:lang="en-US">User Interfaces and Help Systems: From Helplessness to Intelligent
              Assistance</imsmd:langstring>
          </imsmd:title>
        - <imsmd:catalogentry>
            <imsmd:catalog>ISBN</imsmd:catalog>
          - <imsmd:entry>
              <imsmd:langstring>0-534-26702-5</imsmd:langstring>
            </imsmd:entry>
          </imsmd:catalogentry>
        - <imsmd:catalogentry>
            <imsmd:catalog>ISBNX</imsmd:catalog>
          - <imsmd:entry>
              <imsmd:langstring>X-XXX-XXXXX-X</imsmd:langstring>
            </imsmd:entry>
          </imsmd:catalogentry>
          <imsmd:language>en_US</imsmd:language>
        - <imsmd:description>
            <imsmd:langstring xml:lang="en-US">Learning Object generato automaticamente</imsmd:langstring>
          </imsmd:description>
        - <imsmd:keyword>
            <imsmd:langstring xml:lang="en">human-computer interaction, (intelligent, graphical) user interface,
              (intelligent) help and user assistance</imsmd:langstring>
          </imsmd:keyword>
        - <imsmd:coverage>
            <imsmd:langstring xml:lang="en">Sample code</imsmd:langstring>
          </imsmd:coverage>
        - <imsmd:structure>
```

Our system also considers the user's skills to express cleverness as regards different categories. This value ranges from 0 to 1, and it depends initially on the context chosen by the user during his/her registration (primary education, university level, and so on). During the creation of a new category (for example, when a lesson is saved), we consider the user's skill value equal to the resource technical level, presuming that if a user saves learning material then he could be able to make use of it. The user's skill level is updated when a new resource is saved, taking into account its technical level and the user's skills in that category. Starting value for user's skills parameter, its update frequency, the increment or decrement value, and the difference between technical level and user's skills are necessary to obtain a recommendation outcome from the following experimental tests. However, they are easily adaptable.

Despite SCORM's wide use in learning environments, it presence on the Web is very limited; furthermore, most of the LOs that are published are not free. So, we created SCORM-compliant learning material using the abstracts of hundred and hundred of papers in .html version from scientific journals published on the Web. We linked an imsmanifest SCORM file to each paper. Then, we simulated ten users with different initial profiles (based on the field of interest and the skill level) and saved, in four turns, 10 learning resources for each user, obtaining 400 LOs.

Figure 6 shows the personal bookmark page, after the student has logged into the system; the bookmarks are organized in the categories automatically proposed or chosen during the registration of an interesting page (a), and the user can check the received recommendation ("You have a new recommended learning object") in (b). The student can either accept or reject when he is notified of such recommendation (Figure 7).

Figures 8 and 9 show the index.html and the imsmanifest.xml file corresponding to the recommended learning object highlighted in Figure 7.

The precision value (Raghavan & Jung, 1989) of the recommendation phase, calculated considering the resource difficulty and the user's skills, exceeds 80%. It is important to note that the recommendation is made using skill and technical levels (the resource difficulty is one of the parameters, even if the most meaningful); in fact, users rarely know the technical level of a recommended resource; rather, they know about its difficulty. Moreover, the categories of recommended learning material correspond to the user's interests, in almost all of the tests carried out.

Conclusion

This chapter shows how the integration of content-based and collaborative approaches in a virtual community setting has a great impact on the quality of the service. Thanks to the bookmark sharing and recommendation facility, the system contributes to human collaborative works as it supports group collaboration among people involved in a work process, independently of time and space distance, and learns from positive and negative experience in group practice. In fact, recommendation systems can help learners by collaboratively eliminating irrelevant information, operating like mediators between the sources of information, the learning management system, and the learners. We believe that the described system can find application in any context in which the group collaboration is a requisite, and a Web-based learning system is an ideal application domain.

The chapter addresses issues like trying to determine the type or the quality of the suggested information. The automatic recommendation of relevant learning objects is obtained considering student and learning material profiles and adopting filtering criteria based on the value of selected metadata fields. Our experiments to test the system's functionality are based on SCORM-compliant LOs; we use artificial learners to get a flavour of how the system works.

Summarizing, the key elements of the described system could be highlighted as follows. The system provides immediate portability and visibility from different user locations, enabling access to personal bookmark repository just by using a Web browser. The system assists students in finding relevant reading material providing personalized learning object recommendation. The system directly benefits from existing repositories of learning material, providing access to open huge amounts of digital information. The system reflects continuous ongoing changes of the practices of its member, as required by a cooperative framework.

One research direction to pursue is to adopt solutions for user and resources modelling capable of capturing not only structural but also semantics information. Another research direction is to design and evaluate how ontology languages (for example, OWL) can allow for the extension of the description of the LOs with non-standard metadata, thus giving students and students' cluster more flexibility when sharing resources.

References

Andronico, A., Carbonaro, A., Colazzo, L., & Molinari, A. (2004). Personalisation services for learning management systems in mobile settings. *International Journal Continuing Engineering Education and Lifelong Learning, 14*(4/5), 353-369.

Andronico, A., Carbonaro, A., Colazzo, L., Molinari, A., & Ronchetti, M. (2003). Models and services for mobile learning systems. *Lecture Notes in Computer Science, 2954*, 90-106. Berlin-Heidelberg: Springer-Verlag.

Basu, C., Hirsh, H., Cohen, W., & Nevill-Manning, C. (2001). Technical paper recommendations: A study in combining multiple information sources. *Journal of Artificial Intelligence Research, 1*, 231-252.

Belkin, N. J. & Croft, W. B. (1992). Information filtering and information retrieval: Two sides of the same coin. *Communication ACM, 35*(12), 29-38.

Bighini, C. & Carbonaro, A. (2004). InLinx: Intelligent agents for personalized classification, sharing and recommendation. *International Journal of Computational Intelligence, 2*(1).

Bighini, C., Carbonaro, A., & Casadei, G. (2003). InLinx for document classification, sharing and recommendation. In V. Devedzic, J. Spector, D. Sampson, & Kinshuk (Eds.), *Advanced learning technologies: Technology enhanced learning.* Los Alamitos, CA: IEEE Computer Society.

Brusilovsky, P. (2001). Adaptive hypermedia. *User Modeling and User-Adapted Interaction, 11*(1/2), 87-110.

Brusilovsky, P. & Nijhavan, H. (2002). A framework for adaptive e-learning based on distributed re-usable learning activities. In *Proceedings of World Conference on E-Learning, E-Learn 2002,* Canada.

Carbonaro, A. (2004). Learning objects recommendation in a collaborative information management system. *IEEE Learning Technology Newsletter, 6*(4).

Chen, H. & Dumais, S. T. (2000). Bringing order to the Web: Automatically categorizing search results. In *Proceedings of CHI '00, Human Factors in Computing Systems* (pp. 145-152).

Glover, E., Tsioutsiouliklis, K., Lawrence, S., Pennock, D., & Flake, G. (2002). Using Web structure for classifying and describing Web pages. In *Proceedings of the 11th International Conference on World Wide Web,* Hawaii.

Hanani, U., Shapira, B., & Shoval, P. (2001). Information filtering: Overview of issues, research and systems. *User Modeling and User-Adapted Interaction, 11*, 203-259.

Joachims, T. (1997). A probabilistic analysis of the Rocchio algorithm with TFIDF for text categorization. In *Proceedings of the 14th International Conference on Machine Learning ICML '97.*

Li, Q. & Kim, B. M. (2004). *Constructing user profiles for collaborative recommender system. LNCS 3007.* Berlin-Heidelberg: Springer-Verlag.

McNee, S., Albert, I., Cosley, D., Gopalkrishnan, P., Lam, S., Rashid, A., Konstan, J., & Riedl, J. (2002). On the recommending of citations for research papers. In *Proceedings of ACM International Conference on Computer Supported Collaborative Work (CSCW '02)* (pp. 116-125).

Melville, P., Mooney R., & Nagarajan, R. (2002). Content-boosted collaborative filtering for improved recommendations. In *Proceedings of the 18th National Conference on Artificial Intelligence (AAAI-2002),* Canada.

Paramythis, A. & Loidl-Reisinger, S. (2003). Adaptive learning environments and e-learning standards. In *Proceedings of the Second European Conference on e-Learning. ECEL 2003.*

Raghavan, V. V. & Jung, G. S. (1989). A critical investigation of recall and precision as measures of retrieval system performance. *ACM Transactions on Information Systems, 7*(3), 205-229.

Recker, M. & Wiley, D. (2001). A non-authoritative educational metadata ontology for filtering and recommending learning objects. *Journal of Interactive Learning Environments, 9*(3), 255-271.

Salton, G. (1989). *Automatic text processing: The transformation, analysis and retrieval of information by computer.* Reading, MA: Addison-Wesley.

Tang, T. Y. & McCalla, G. (2003). Towards pedagogy-oriented paper recommendations and adaptive annotations for a Web-based learning system. *Workshop on Knowledge Representation and Automated Reasoning for E-Learning Systems. IJCAI 2003,* Mexico

Wetterling, J. & Collis, B. (2003). Sharing and re-use of learning resources across a transnational network. In A. Littlejohn & S. Buckingham Shum (Eds.), Reusing online resources (Special Issue), *Journal of Interactive Media in Education,* (1).

Yang Y. & Pederson J. (1997). Feature selection in statistical learning of text categorization. In *Proceedings of the 14th International Conference on Machine Learning ICML '97.*

Chapter VIII

Hyperbook Features Supporting Active Reading Skills

Tom Murray
University of Massachusetts, USA

Abstract

MetaLinks is a domain independent authoring tool and web server for adaptive textbooks ("hyperbooks") that supports active reading. We show how cognitive and educational research and theory from the areas of text comprehension and active reading strategies can be applied to hyperbooks. Adaptivity and other MetaLinks features allow us to create a single hyperbook that serves multiple purposes. A MetaLinks hyperbook can serve as textbook and reference book; can be equally appropriate for novice and advanced readers, and can be coherently read from a number of thematic perspectives. "Active reading/learning" refers to a set of high level reading, searching, problem solving, and metacognitive skills. We describe the MetaLinks system and how its features support a number of behavioral, cognitive, and metacognitive active reading skills.

Introduction

In this chapter, we show how cognitive and educational research and theory from the areas of text comprehension and active reading strategies can be applied to the domain of hypermedia textbooks ("hyperbooks"). We describe our work on the MetaLinks system, an authoring tool and Web-based server for adaptive hyperbooks. We illustrate how adaptive hyperbooks support active reading skills in ways that traditional texts do not (the focus of the work is on textbooks rather than narrative texts). MetaLinks is an adaptive hypermedia system, and thus composes pages "on the fly" so that the content, style, and/or sequencing of the page are customized to the needs of the particular learner and situation (Brusilovsky, 1998; DeBra & Calvi, 1998; Specht & Oppermann, 1998). Though non-adaptive (static) hypermedia has been popular for over 20 years, it is only recently that Internet data-base technologies that enable dynamic configuration and personalization of Web pages have become common. Adaptivity and other MetaLinks features allow us to create a single hyperbook that serves multiple purposes. A MetaLinks hyperbook can serve as textbook and reference book, can be equally appropriate for novice and advanced readers, and can be coherently read from a number of thematic perspectives.

"Active reading" refers to a set of high-level reading, searching, problem-solving, and metacognitive skills used as readers proactively construct new knowledge. We will sometimes refer to this general process as "active reading/*learning*" to reflect the fact that active readers of textbooks are proactively trying to construct knowledge. Because learners have different background knowledge, learning styles, and goals, and because each learner constructs new knowledge in a personal, idiosyncratic fashion, the best path through a textual resource may differ for each learner. "Active reading" is a term used to emphasize the dynamic, opportunistic processes observed in non-recreational reading of expository texts as done by experts and motivated readers. For example, Marshall and Shipman (1997) discuss dealing with information quantity overload as "information triage," where readers quickly skim or otherwise assess the value and nature of informational components (texts, links, pages, etc.), then sort or categorize them for further use.

Though active reading skills are important because they lead to more efficient and effective comprehension and information finding, these skills are not very advanced in many students (and adults), and it is important to support, scaffold, and teach these skills. We acknowledge that in moving from paper to computer screen many affordances are lost (see Masten, Stallybrass, & Vickers, 1997; Schilit, Price, Golovshinski, Tanaks, & Marshall, 1999), and we do not advocate for the replacement of paper texts with electronic ones, but we are of the opinion that: a) the movement of textual material to electronic form is momentous and inevitable and thus we must engage in efforts to maximize the effectiveness and usability of electronic text, and b) electronic texts have the potential to support active reading in new and significant ways. Johnson and Afflerback (1985) see reading comprehension skills as being "eminently teachable" (also see Levinstein et al., 2003). Existing educational and informational hypermedia does not sufficiently make use of the affordances of the available technology to support and enhance key cognitive processes.

In this chapter, we first give some background in active reading, discussing the importance of considering differences in background knowledge, the importance of supporting local and global coherence, and culminating with a compiled list of 18 active reading skills culled from the literature. We then describe the MetaLinks system and MetaLinks hyperbooks. We illustrate several features unique to MetaLinks, including custom depth control, narrative smoothing, and a set of features that enable "multi-theme hyperbooks." We show how with such features entirely novel (yet highly usable) types of "texts" are possible, beyond what we typically see on the World Wide Web. We then indicate how active reading in general, and each of the 18 active reading skills, are supported in MetaLinks hyperbooks (and by other hypermedia systems). We conclude with some thoughts about the role of cognitive theories and pre-training in performing empirical evaluations of novel hypermedia systems.

Background

In recent times, the traditional behaviorist view of reading as a decoding process leading to the passive acquisition of isolated facts and skills has been replaced with a more cognitively oriented view. Reading is an active, self-regulated meaning-construction process in which the reader interacts with text in a strategic way (Kintsch, 1979, 1998; Mannes & Kintch, 1987). Text reading for comprehension is seen as a process of trying to maintain semantic coherence, that is, fitting new information into existing knowledge structures at both local and global levels. Studies by Foltz (1996) indicate that users reading hypermedia documents are active opportunistic problem solvers who look for cues and navigate with a goal of maintaining semantic coherence. At a *local* level, readers try to fit what they are reading into the context of what they have recently read, making sense of the progression of related ideas. At a *global* level, readers try to assimilate new information into prior knowledge or accommodate prior knowledge to be consistent with the new information. Johnson and Afflerback's (1985) study investigates the process of constructing main ideas from texts, which is generally regarded as the essence of reading

Table 1. Active reading strategies

Behavioral strategies:	Cognitive strategies:
• Skimming (for an overview or "forward planning")	• Summarizing & consolidating (identify main points)
• Scanning (to locate specific content)	• Connecting (creating meaning and relevance for new knowledge)
• Reviewing (looking back to note relevant ideas)	• Planning (what pages to visit next)
• Bookending (looking at the beginning and end of a book or section)	• Evaluating (critiquing and synthesizing)
• Big picturing (using a tool to get a "bird's eye view" of the structure)	• Questioning (determine what needs to be know, explained, or justified)
• Deepening (diving deeper or obtaining additional information on a subject)	• Predicting (anticipating where the author is going)
• Refocusing (on a different level of the text)	**Metacognitive strategies**:
• Exploring (taking tangents not immediately related to a high priority goal)	• Monitoring coherence, understanding, effort, and efficiency
• Writing (note taking, annotating, highlighting, etc.)	• Setting goals and managing goal priorities
	• Deciding which behavioral or cognitive strategy to use next

comprehension. This skill, though universally important to reading at all levels, is actually a complex set of skills that never fully develop in many readers.

In addition to identifying how local and global levels of processing affect text comprehension, the literature identifies *background knowledge as* one of the primary factors determining reading behavior and outcomes. Readers who know more about a domain can more easily: comprehend content as they read, determine what they need to know, decide how to find what they need to know, and anticipate or predict what may come next. They can make bridging inferences when the flow of text lacks coherence, and construct macro-representations (overviews or summaries) of the structure of an entire topic or document (Kintsch, 1998; Royer & Cunningham, 1981). *Learning* from text is related to one's ability to *use* knowledge and integrate it into existing knowledge structures, and requires a larger proportion of the higher level cognitive processes (Royer, Carlo, Dufrense, & Mestre, 1996).

In Table 1, we list a number of active reading strategies culled from the literature (Collins et al., 1989; Foltz, 1996; Mannes & Kintsch, 1987; O'Hara, 1996; Roast, Ritchie, & Thomas, 2002; Schilt et al., 1999) that we have organized into behavioral, cognitive, and metacognitive strategies. As we will illustrate later, this list of skills has a very strong correlation with the types of behaviors and skills that hypermedia can support. Thus we can conceive of new types of "text books" that (a) provide tools that directly support or facilitate active reading for those who *already have* these skills, (b) scaffold active reading skills so that those who are *deficient in* these skills can experience them, and (c) scaffold active reading skills so that those who are deficient in them can *learn* them and *transfer* these skills to "normal" (off-line) reading. The main goal of this chapter is to describe a system with features that directly support most of the active reading skills in Table 1, and thus whose design is supported and informed by cognitive research in text comprehension. Our work on the MetaLinks project to date has demonstrated that hyperbooks with these features are highly usable (Murray, 2003).

Of course, it is also possible that hyperbooks may exacerbate the reading deficiencies of those who have poor active reading skills. Future tests are planned to specifically look at the effects of hyperbook features on active reading skills, and the effects of active reading skills on hyperbook use.

The benefits and problematic issues of hypermedia have been described at length in the literature (for example, see Beasley & Waugh, 1995; Conklin, 1987, Ferguson, Bareiss, Birnbaum, & Osgood, 1992; Plowman, Luckin, Laurillard, Stratfold, & Taylor, 1999; Spiro & Jeng, 1990; Stanton & Baber 1994). In Murray (2003; 2004), we describe how MetaLinks supports learners' exploration and use of hypermedia spaces while ameliorating a number of classic problems (including disorientation, poor narrative flow, poor conceptual flow, and cognitive overload). Most prior research that applies the concept of "active reading" to hypermedia focuses on annotation (highlighting, underlining, marginal comment notes, etc.) as the "active" element in processing information (for example, see Bromerg, 2000; Jayawardana, Hewagamage, & Hirakawa, 2001; Marshall & Shipman, 1997; Obendorf, 2003; Schilit et al., 1998). Compared with most of these studies cited above, which focus one or a small set of specific skills, this work takes a broader view in considering a more complete set of active reading skills found in the reading comprehension literature.

Figure 1. Tectonica Interactive page T.2.4

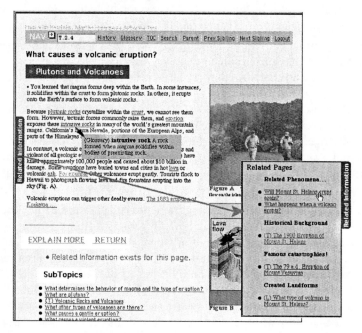

The Metalinks System Description

The MetaLinks software comprises an authoring tool and Web server for adaptive hyperbooks (Murray, 2003; Murray, Condit, & Haugsjaa, 1998; Murray, Piemonte, Khan, Shen, & Condit, 2000). Figure 1 shows a typical MetaLinks hyperbook screen. From top to bottom, it contains the navigation bar, the page title, the page text, "custom depth control" navigation buttons, and a list of links to children pages. The author can include as many figures as desired, and specify a scaling factor for each picture. Green-colored, underlined words (e.g., "intrusive rocks" in Figure 1) correspond to words in the glossary. When the user drags the cursor over one of these words, its definition pops up as shown in Figure 1. When the user clicks on a glossary word, he or she navigates to the page in the book that most fully describes that concept (called the "base page" for that term). Teal- colored underlined words (e.g., "For example" in Figure 1) indicate footnotes, which also appear as pop-up text and graphics. When the user clicks on the "Related Information" tab, he or she sees a list of links to thematically related pages, as shown in the insert to the right of the figure. The user can navigate through the book hierarchically using parent, subtopic, and sibling topic links, and can navigate associatively, through the list that pops out in the "Related Information" menu.

In addition to the main screen shown in the picture, the system has screens (separate browser windows) for a table of contents (TOC), search engine, navigation history tool, and glossary tool (see the buttons near the top of the main screen). The system includes an authoring tool that makes it easy to manage content, media (graphics, applets, etc.), and hyperlinks (see Figure 2). The MetaLinks authoring tool and Web server is built using a FileMaker Pro and JavaScript/DHTML coding. All user behavior is recorded in a database to allow for adaptivity and to facilitate experimental data collection.

The authoring tool is a highly usable graphical interface for authoring all aspects of MetaLinks books. It automates many design steps such as the creation of the TOC, glossary links, and section numbering. Our representational framework has been purposefully limited to features that can be easily portrayed in the GUI and authored by anyone with minimal training (one hour). All of the features mentioned above come practically "for free" when the author enters the text and graphics and defines links between pages.

To date, MetaLinks has been used to author four hyperbooks. Tectonica Interactive, in the domain of introductory geology, is the largest, with approximately 400 pages, 500 graphics, and 320 glossary entries. Our evaluation studies have all been done with Tectonica, shown in Figure 1. The second MetaLinks hyperbook authored was the MetaLinks Users Guide. The remaining two hyperbooks were created as part of two Hampshire College service learning classes. College students in the classes used MetaLinks to build hyperbooks in collaboration with two community-based organizations. The first was "Famous Women Mathematicians," which was built in collaboration with Amherst Middle School teachers for use by an eighth-grade class. The second was

Figure 2. MetaLinks Authoring Tool

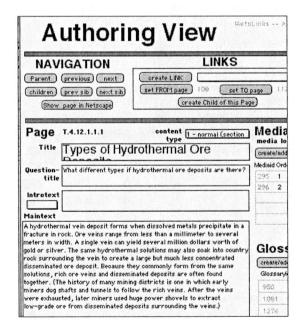

Figure 3. Custom depth control

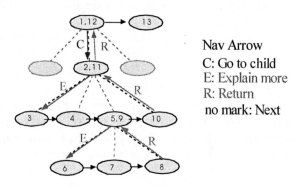

Nav Arrow
C: Go to child
E: Explain more
R: Return
no mark: Next

"Early 20th Century Children's Games," a hyperbook built in collaboration with a group of senior citizens enrolled in a computer literacy class in Holyoke, Massachusetts. The project became somewhat of an oral history project, as seniors told us their memories of the games they played as children, and we organized this material thematically for the hyperbook. Both of these college-class-built hyperbooks are on the order of 30-50 pages large. Though the authoring and usage of these four hyperbooks, we have gained confidence in the usability of the system, have had the benefit of user-participatory design iterations, and have demonstrated its application in several domains.

Results of MetaLinks evaluation studies can be found in Murray (2003) and Murray et al. (2000). We are now creating a new version, MetaLinks II, which will include collaborative annotation and "schema-based page template" features, and will first be used for a college-level hyperbook for a concept-based chemistry course.

Supporting Narrative, Hierarchical, and Associative Forms

We can describe text books as being structured according to three co-existing ubiquitous "epistemic forms" (Collins & Ferguson, 1993): narrative, network, and hierarchy. The interplay between these three epistemic forms provides an essential tension from both the designer's and the user's perspective. Below, we describe three features that map to these three epistemic forms: "custom depth control" supports *hierarchical* conceptualizations of content; "thematic links" support *associative* conceptualizations of content; and "narrative smoothing" supports *narrative* coherence in reading.

Horizontal Reading and Custom Depth Control

In MetaLinks hyperbooks, the default narrative flow (a linear navigation path for which the reading or organization of the content is most natural or perspicuous) is organized for "horizontal reading," which differs from traditional books and most other hyperbooks. The default "next" page is the sibling page, so if one is reading the introduction to Section 3.1, the default next page is the introduction to Section 3.2, which is navigated to with the "Next" button (Figure 3). The text is written (or rewritten, in the case of converting a traditional book to a hyperbook, as we did with Tectonica Interactive) to flow in a breadth-first fashion as opposed to the depth-first fashion needed in traditional texts. Thus the default path is to continue reading "sibling" pages at the same level of generality and then, as explained next, to the "parent" page.

Horizontal reading sets the stage for an innovation called "custom depth control." To the left of the Next button is the "Explain More" button. This button begins a path across the children of the current page (by pushing the children on a stack). When the last child in a sibling sequence is reached, the Next button becomes a Return button, so that the user can easily return to the parent page where he or she originally pressed the Explain More button. Thus, the user has continuous control over the level of depth at which he or she is reading. They can choose to read "across" or "deeper" at any point. Horizontal reading creates what amounts to an alternative rhetorical structure for texts. The "introduction" "body" "conclusion" linear rhetorical flow of standard texts is replaced with an "overview" and "more depth" structure in horizontal reading.

For example, Figure 3 shows a path in which a user does the following: Upon reading a page (1) the reader is interested in a particular subtopic as seen in the children links. He navigates to that child page (2). He becomes interested in even more detail on that subject and presses "Explain More." He begins a traversal across sibling pages (3) using the Next button. He become particularly interested in the third sibling page (5) and presses "Explain more" a second time for more depth on *that* topic. The Next button changes to a Return button when he reaches the last sibling (at 8, 10, and 11), and he is eventually led back to where he began, and can continue on from there.

Supporting Thematic Relationships Among Content

Hierarchies do not capture the conceptual richness of most domains. Each topic is related to others in numerous ways. Each MetaLinks page has a set of thematic links (non-hierarchical, associative, or "tangential" links) to other pages, accessed via a pop-out menu by clicking on the "Related Information" tab (see Figures 1 and 4). Unlike most other hypermedia, the links are "typed" or categorized to indicate the type of relationship they represent. The authoring tool provides a list of possible link types, but the author can create her own types for each hyperbook. They allow the learner to maintain a path through the material that responds to his or her curiosity and inquiry goals. Here are some of the approximately 20 link types we defined for the geology hyperbook:

- "Where in the world?"

- "Are scientists sure?"

- "Extreme cases and famous catastrophes."

Figure 4. MetaLinks "Famous Women Mathematicians" hyperbook

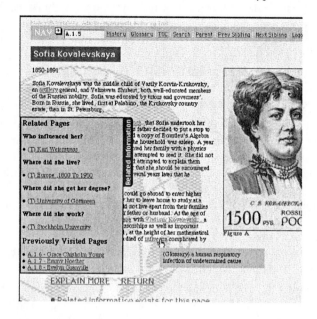

- "Geologists used to think…"

- "How is it measured?" and

- "What do I need to know first?"

In a MetaLinks hyperbook about Women Mathematicians (see Figure 4), the link types include:

- "Who influenced her?"

- "Where did she get her degree?"

- "Where did she live?"

- "About the time period" and

- "How her work affects in our lives."

Authors can use the link types to organize their content creation. Thematic links encourage the learner to assimilate domain knowledge structures that reflect the relationships and themes important to the author/expert. Link types can also act as author prompts that remind or inspire the creation of related content or the creation of more links among existing content.

Inquisitory Page Titles

To support our goal of inquiry-based and exploratory navigation, MetaLinks pages have an *inquisitory title* in addition to the regular title (see the corresponding field in the Authoring Tool Figure). For example, the page T.2.1.1.1, titled "Earth's Layers: The Crust," has a question title "What are the properties of the earth's crust?" The inquisitory page title appears in small font just above the page title. The main purpose of inquisitory titles is their use in page links. Another page with a related link to T.2.1.1.1 will have "What are the properties of the crust?" as the link text, rather than "Earth's Layers: The Crust." Using inquisitory titles gives the navigational interaction a conversational feeling, adding to the narrative flow of the experience. Upon navigating to a page that addresses one question, new links answering new questions are available, giving the interaction a feeling of a question and answer dialog. (The author can also define the text/question for each specific link, overriding the link's target page inquisitory page title.)

Narrative Smoothing

As mentioned, the narrative of the hyperbook is written to flow most perspicuously for users using horizontal reading and custom depth control. If the reader navigates using any other feature, for example, thematic links or the search engine, then the narrative would have a discontinuity. We have a simple but elegant adaptive solution to the narrative flow problem that we call "narrative smoothing." Each page has associated with it an "intro text" paragraph (see the Authoring Tool Figure). This paragraph eases the reader into the subject of the page, giving a little background, context, or introduction. If the user jumps to that page in a non-standard way, that is, one that does not follow horizontal reading, the intro-text is pre-pended to the main text of the page (otherwise it is not included).

Adaptivity

Several of the features mentioned above involve adaptivity, which is possible because the content is stored in a modular form in a data base and the components of each page are combined specifically for each page request. The narrative smoothing feature adds the introductory paragraph to pages conditioned upon whether the navigation path was "horizontal." The TOC is annotated to show which pages have been visited and the "you are here" page. Each main page also has an indication of whether it has been visited before. Pages links are shown using the page title or the "question title," based on the type of link. The links in the annotated history page are annotated with the link types, or "reasons" why the page was visited.

The functioning of custom depth control and the adaptive Next and Return buttons relies on an internal "goal stack" that keeps track of the user's nested implicit goals. Pressing Explain More signals a goal to visit all of a node's children, and the child nodes are pushes onto the goal stack. Using a thematic link (and other navigation methods) indicates a goal to take a tangent, which we assume implies eventually returning to where one left off, so the current node is pushed onto the goal stack when such a tangent is taken. The goal stack consists of tokens that store node IDs and the context in which the node was put on the stack. Both the visibility and the function of the Next and Return buttons adapt according to what is currently on the top of the goal stack. If the top node represents a continuation of an Explain More traversal across siblings, then Next will navigate to that node. If the top node represents the end of an Explain More traversal, or a return from a tangent, then the Return button will take the user in that direction. The adaptivity allowed by the goal stack allows the user to nest goals within goals and remain oriented. Later, we mention the "dual space overlay student model" feature that enables additional adaptivity.

Multi-Theme HyperBooks

Active reading involves using a text in multiple ways and conceptualizing it in multiple modes. Learning about or doing research in a subject area usually involves using several texts, with different focal themes and organizational styles. Though we do not expect that a single hyperbook will ever be able to serve the purpose of all of the books that one might need in learning or researching a subject, we illustrate below how one hyperbook can serve the purpose of several text books with different thematic approaches to a subject.

Figure 5 shows a page from the "Century Games" hyperbook and its Table of Contents from that book. Century Games Chapter 2 contains stories and reminiscences from our elderly collaborators (all natives of Holyoke, Massachusetts, with diverse socio-economic backgrounds) about their childhood play in the early 1900s, grouped by story author. These stories mention places in Holyoke, time periods, events, specific games, and some themes that we found recurring among many of the stories. As the TOC illustrates, the college student co-authors did additional research to create chapters that focus on the rules and history of certain games (such as Hop Scotch and Red Rover), and the History of Holyoke in the early 1900s. They also created a Themes chapter with sections synthesizing topics such as how people crafted their own toys and games during the Great Depression; how girls and boys interacted in past times vs. modern times; and how the logistics of neighborhoods and transportation affected who played what games with whom. The pages in all of these chapters are connected using thematic links. For example, a person's story will link to pages describing the game, the time period, relevant themes, etc. A section describing a particular game will link to the stories that mention that game, and so on for every other appropriate relationship between pages of the different chapters.

This may seem like a logical but not particularly innovative way to organize a book. However, upon closer inspection we can see that, due to the navigation features provided by MetaLinks, this book has characteristics very different than most ordinary texts. Someone interested in the personal stories and histories of our elderly collaborators can read Chapter 2 and take short tangents out to the other chapters as his or her interest

Figure 5. Century Games Hyperbook main page and TOC

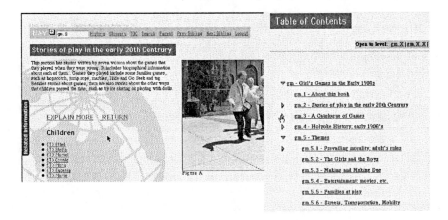

Figure 6. Navigation in a multi-theme hyperbook

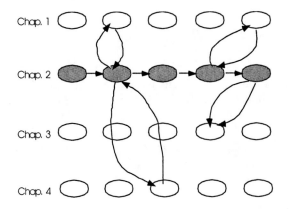

dictates, always returning to the main narrative of Chapter 2 (see illustration in Figure 6). Someone interested in games of olden times can read Chapter 3, taking short tangents to Chapters 2, 4, 5, or 6 as needed, always returning to the main narrative of Chapter 3. In a similar way the book supports readers interested in the history of Holyoke or in the general themes that we uncovered. Thus the Century Games hyperbook is not meant to be read "front to back." It is like four different books ("Chapters" 2, 3, 4, 5) each with a different perspective on the material. Each "chapter" references the three other chapters, as if they were hyperlinked appendices or reference material.

Supporting Active
Reading and Learning

Below we describe how MetaLinks features relate to several important active reading and learning issues: coherence, reading strategies, background knowledge, and exploration.

Supporting Local and Global Coherence

MetaLinks includes a number of features that support coherence in reading and, thus, better comprehension. Features that support local coherence include narrative smoothing, inquisitory page titles in links, pop-up footnotes and glossary definitions (which alleviate the need to digress to another page to read a footnote or definition), and custom depth control (which allows reading or skimming at any level without interrupting the narrative). To support global coherence, MetaLinks has an annotated table of contents (TOC), visual content maps, a page-numbering scheme that identifies a page's position in the hierarchy, and thematic links that reify the key thematic dimensions of a domain.

Supporting Active Reading Strategies

In the move from text to hypertext, some issues are trivialized, some are problematized, and new issues are introduced. The basic features of MetaLinks hyperbooks practically trivialize the "behavioral" set of active reading strategies in Table 1. *Skimming* is directly supported with the horizontal reading feature. *Scanning* (looking for a specific thing) is done easily with the search engine. *Reviewing* involves returning to a previous page (a Back or Return button) and is supported by the annotated history tool. *Bookending* in MetaLinks books is done automatically due to its rhetorical structure and custom depth control feature. *Big picturing* involves using the TOC tool and content maps. *Deepening* and *refocusing* are supported directly with custom depth control. *Exploring* is supported with thematic links. *Writing and annotating* were not supported by MetaLinks v. I, but are supported by MetaLinks v. II (see below).

Hyperbooks also support the (non-behavioral) cognitive and metacognitive strategies in Table 1, but the support of these also depends heavily on how the author organizes the content and/or what types of prompts and activities are provided by an author or teacher. *Summarizing* is supported through horizontal reading and the alternative rhetorical structure of our hyperbooks. *Connecting* is supported through the thematic links, which reify important connections and allow readers to learn about a connected topic as soon as they become aware of or interested in the connection, and through inquisitory page titles. *Planning* and *monitoring* are supported by features mentioned above that give students "big picture" information and by the explicit "types" in the thematic links.

Evaluating, questioning, predicting, and all of the cognitive and metacognitive active reading strategies are supported to the extent that local and global coherence are supported (as described above). When reading is more coherent, it consumes less cognitive resources, and these resources are freed up for higher-level processes. We are currently building a new version, MetaLinks II, which contains collaborative annotation tools and supports peer evaluation (skills listed in Table 1). This supports more active practicing of skills in evaluating, critiquing, questioning, and connecting.

More could be done technologically to support the cognitive and metacognitive skills. Our prototype implementation of a "dual-space overlay student model" (implemented but not put to use yet) will allow MetaLinks to tag pages that are ready, or not ready to be read (similar to the adaptive link annotation used in Brusilovsky, Schwartz, and Weber (1996). This will help learners *monitor* their understanding and better *set goals* related what to read next. Extending this feature, we have also designed a set of coaching and prompting rules meant to help students with cognitive strategies by pointing out important parts of the book they have not seen yet and warning them when they may be on unproductive tangents.

Accounting for Background Knowledge and Prerequisites

As mentioned above, background knowledge has a significant impact on learning, coherence, navigation, comprehension, and strategies. The MetaLinks system includes several features that allow readers with multiple levels of expertise to use the text, and it allows readers with low expertise or missing prerequisite knowledge to learn what they need to learn. Skimming in the custom depth feature allows readers to read at a level of depth and detail that fits their prior knowledge. Thematic links can be used to create "prerequisite" links between pages, making it explicit to readers what material should come first, and whether or not they have read this material (the color of the link text shows if they have been there). The glossary pop-up feature assists the reader in filling in small gaps in knowledge. The glossary base page feature allows easy access to additional information.

Supporting Exploratory Navigation

Above, we identified exploration as one of the strategies used in active reading. Though most hypermedia projects focus on goal-directed learning and information- finding tasks, MetaLinks aims to provide strong support for behavior that has been called inquiry-based or exploratory. Many learning tasks involve an initial convergent stage of articulating and refining the goal or question and then divergently exploring potential sources of information before returning to convergent thinking and focused search (Wallace, Kuperman, Krajcik, & Soloway, 2000). Exploratory navigation is particularly appropriate for open-ended questions and/or learning in ill-structured domains in which the richness of the content suggests multiple themes or perspectives (Heller, 1990; Jacobson & Archodidou, 2000; McAleese, 1989; Spiro & Jehng, 1990). MetaLinks supports exploratory and curiosity-driven behavior in several ways. Thematic links and inquisitory page titles facilitate exploring related but tangential topics. Custom depth control and glossary base pages make it easy for the reader to "dive deeper" into topics she is curious about. Finally, to the degree that many features minimize hypermedia "side effects," they make it easier to explore tangents while maintaining coherence and orientation.

Conclusion and Future Directions

MetaLinks is a domain-independent authoring tool and Web server for adaptive hyperbooks. Its design supports the goals and strategies of active reading. Its implementation of "horizontal reading," "custom depth control," "thematic links," and "narrative smoothing" are novel and further advance and differentiate hyperbooks from traditional textbooks toward truly novel expository tools. Our formative evaluations indicated that our hyperbook representational formalism and navigation tools are usable and sufficient, at least for the domain tested. Though research in cognitive science has informed MetaLinks design, so far our formative evaluations have studied only usability factors, which did not gather detailed data on cognitive processes. In the future, we plan to conduct additional investigations to: (1) push the tasks and content to more difficult levels and in more domains; (2) directly measure learning effects, (3) study the interaction between active reading skills and hyperbook tool use, (4) study the authoring process; and (5) develop and test MetaLinks hyperbooks in authentic classroom situations. We would also like to test how MetaLinks supports different instructional methods such as spiral teaching and case-based instruction using "landscape crisscrossing" (Jacobson & Spiro, 1995; McAleese, 1989; Spiro & Jehng, 1990).

In our studies of active reading skills, we will be particularly interested in whether the active reading behavior scaffolding provided by MetaLinks acts in a compensatory or capitalizing way; that is, when a particular task is made easier, does this lead to better comprehension in students who already have the related skill (a capitalizing effect) and/ or does it lead to better comprehension in students who are weak in the related skill (a compensatory effect)?

General Suggestion for Hyperbook Evaluation

Research literature meta-analyses by Dillon and Gabbard (1998) and by Chen and Rada (1996) point to an overall lack of consistent or rigorous approaches to the research, including the lack of shared taxonomies for describing tasks and system features, as a major barrier to finding more conclusive evidence concerning the most effective uses and design principles for hypertext. Certainly such rigor would advance the field. However, comments by Charney (1994) suggest a parallel concern of equal importance. After summarizing the cognitive research on reading and hypertext, he notes that there is an "enormous tension" between the creative, open-ended aspects of hypertext and the conservative "normalizing forces" and predictable patterns of orientation and use we are accustomed to with paper textbooks. Though most learners these days are quite familiar with the affordances of HTML and the World Wide Web, almost all hypermedia studies look at fairly novel hypermedia features. In studying the use of new technologies for which users have not learned effective use strategies, we may be inadvertently guaranteeing non-significant or negative results concerning hypermedia effectiveness. Ideally, in comparing the benefits of advanced hyperbooks to textbooks or standard hypermedia, a fair comparison requires that the advanced hypermedia users already be familiar and comfortable with the novel technology. Thus, to find more convincing evidence supporting new hypermedia technologies, evaluation subjects should first be sufficiently trained in the use of the technology. In the context of our focus on active reading, we mentioned earlier that learners often have weak active reading strategies, and that instruction in active reading strategies has beneficial results (for paper texts). It seems clear that adaptive hypermedia holds great promise for supporting active reading strategies, but it may be that these benefits will only be realized if users are first made aware of the affordances of the new tools and are supported in learning active reading skills in hypermedia. We plan to use this approach in evaluating MetaLinks II.

Acknowledgments

This material is based upon work supported by the National Science Foundation under Grant No. NSF DUE-9652993, and by the Office of Naval Research AASERT Grant No. ONR/N00014-97-1-0815. Disclaimer: Any opinions, findings, and conclusions or recommendations expressed in this material are those of the author(s) and do not necessarily reflect the views of the National Science Foundation or the Office of Naval Research.

References

Beasley, R.E. & Waugh, M.L (1995). Cognitive mapping architectures and hypermedia disorientation: An empirical study. *Journal of Educational Multimedia and Hypermedia, 4*(2/3), 239-255.

Bromerg, A. (2000). *Learners as knowledge workers—Text-Col and FOCO, two tools to put into their toolboxes.* Department of Computing Science Technical Report. Umea University, Sweden.

Brusilovsky, P. (1998). Methods and techniques of adaptive hypermedia. In P. Brusilovsky, A. Kobsa, & J. Vassileva (Eds.), *Adaptive hypertext and hypermedia* (Chapter 1, pp. 1-44). The Netherlands: Kluwer Academic Publishers.

Brusilovsky, P., Schwartz, E., & Weber, G. (1996). A tool for developing adaptive electronic textbooks on the WWW. In *Proceedings of WebNet-96 - World Conference of the Web Society,* October 16-19, San Francisco (pp. 64-69). AACE.

Charney, D. (1994). The impact of hypertext on processes of reading and writing. In S. Hilligoss & C. Selfe (Eds.), *Literacy and computers* (pp. 238-263). New York: Modern Language Association.

Chen, C. & Rada, R. (1996). Interacting with hypertext: A meta-analysis of experimental studies. *Human-Computer Interaction, 11*(2),125-156.

Collins, A. & Ferguson, W. (1993). Epistemic forms and epistemic games: Structures and strategies to guide inquiry. *Educational Psychologist, 28*(1), 25-42.

Collins, A., Brown, J. S., & Newman, S. E. (1989). Cognitive apprenticeship: Teaching the craft of reading, writing and mathematics. In L. B. Resnick (Ed.), *Knowing, learning, and instruction.* Hillsdale, NJ: Erlbaum.

Conklin, J. (1987). Hypertext: An introduction and survey. *IEEE Computer,* September, 17-41.

De Bra, P. & Calvi, L. (1998). AHA: A generic adaptive hypermedia system. In *Proceedings of the Second Workshop on Adaptive Hypertext and Hypermedia, Hypertext '98,* June 20-24, Pittsburgh, PA. Retrieved from *http://www.contrib.andrew.cmu.edu/~plb/HT98_workshop/*

Dillon, A. & Gabbard, R. (1998). Hypermedia as an educational technology: A review of the quantitative research literature on learner comprehension, control, and style. *Review of Educational Research, 68*(3), 322-349.

Ferguson, W., Bareiss, R., Birnbaum, L, & Osgood, R. (1992). ASK systems: An approach to the realization of story-based teachers. *Journal of the Learning Sciences, 2*(1), 95-134.

Foltz, P.W. (1996). Comprehension, coherence, and strategies in hypertext and linear text. In J.F. Rouet, J.J.Levonen, A. Dillon & R.J. Spiro (Eds.), *Hypertext and cognition.* Hillsdale, NJ: Lawrence Erlbaum.

Heller, R. (1990). The role of hypermedia in education: A look at the research issues. *Journal of Research on Computing in Education, 22,* 431-441.

Jacobson, M.J. & Archodidou, A. (2000). The design of hypermedia tools for learning: Fostering conceptual change and transfer of complex scientific knowledge. *Journal of the Learning Sciences, 9*(2),145-199.

Jacobson, M.J. & Spiro, R.J. (1995). Hypertext learning environments, cognitive flexibility, and the transfer of complex knowledge: An empirical investigation. *Journal Educational Computing Research, 12*(4), 301-333.

Jayawardana, C., Hewagamage, K.P., & Hirakawa, M. (2001). Personalization tools for active learning in digital libraries. *The Journal of Academic Media Librarianship,* Summer, *8*(1). Retrieved from *http://wings.buffalo.edu/publications/mcjrnl/v8n1*

Johnson, P. & Afflerback, P. (1985). The process of constructing mean ideas from text. *Cognition and Instruction, 2*(3&4), 207-232.

Kintsch, W. (1979). On modeling comprehension. *Educational Psychologist, 14,* 3-14.

Kintsch, W. (1998). *Comprehension: A paradigm for cognition.* New York: Cambridge University Press.

Levinstein, I., McNamara, D., Boonthum, C., Pillarisetti, S., & Yadavalli, K. (2003). Web-based intervention for higher-order reading skills. In *Proceedings of World Conference on Educational Multimedia, Hypermedia and Telecommunications (EDMEDIA 2003)* (Issue 1, pp. 835-841).

Mannes, S. & Kintsch, W. (1987). Knowledge organization and text organization. *Cognition and Instruction, 4*(2), 91-115.

Marshall, C. & Shipman, F. (1997). Effects of hypertext technology on the practice of information triage. In *Proceedings of ACM Hypertext '97*, Southampton, UK, April (pp. 124-133). New York: ACM.

Masten, J., Stallybrass, P., & Vickers, N. (Eds.) (1997). *Language machines: Technologies of literary and cultural production.* New York: Routledge Press.

McAleese, R. (1989). Navigation and browsing in hypertext. In R. McAleese (Ed.), *Hypertext: Theory into action* (Chapter 2). Norwood NJ: Ablex Publishing.

Murray, T. (2003). MetaLinks: Authoring and affordances for conceptual and narrative flow in adaptive hyperbooks. *International Journal of Artificial Intelligence in Education, 13*(2-4), 199-234.

Murray, T. (2004). Content design issues in adaptive hyperbooks. *International Journal of Computer-Aided Technology, 1*(2), 203-218.

Murray, T., Condit, C., & Haugsjaa, E. (1998). MetaLinks: A preliminary framework for concept-based adaptive hypermedia. In *Proceedings for ITS-98 Workshop on WWW-Based Tutoring,* San Antonio, August.

Murray, T., Piemonte, J., Khan, S., Shen, T., & Condit, C. (2000). Evaluating the need for intelligence in an adaptive hypermedia system. In C. Frasson & G. Gautheir (Eds.), *Proceedings of Intelligent Tutoring Systems 2000* (pp. 373-382). Springer-Verlag: New York.

Obendorf, H. (2003). Hypertext annotation, evaluation, metadata, active reading. In *Proceedings of Hypertext 2003.* Retrieved from *www.ht03.org/session6.html*

O'Hara, K. (1996). *Towards a typology of reading goals.* Xeros Park Technical Report EPC-1996-107.

Plowman, L., Luckin, R., Laurillard, D., Stratfold, M., & Taylor, J. (1999). Designing multimedia for learning: Narrative guidance and narrative construction. In *Proceedings of CHI '99*, May 15-20, Pittsburgh, PA (pp. 310-317). ACM.

Roast, C., Ritchie, I., & Thomas, S. (2002). Re-creating the reader: Supporting active reading in literary research. *Communications of the ACM, 45*(10), 109-111.

Royer, J. M., Carlo, M. S., Dufrense, R., & Mestre, J. (1996). The assessment of levels of domain expertise while reading. *Cognition and Instruction, 14,* 373-408.

Royer, J. M. & Cunningham, D. J. (1981). On the theory and measurement of reading comprehension. *Contemporary Educational Psychology, 6,* 187-216.

Schilit, B.N., Price, M.N., Golovshinski, G., Tanaks, K., & Marshall, C.C. (1999). The reading appliance revolution. *IEEE Computer*, January, 65-73.

Specht, M. & Oppermann, R. (1998). ACE—Adaptive courseware environment. *New Review of Hypermedia and Multimedia, 4,* 141-162.

Spiro, R.J. & Jehng, J.C. (1990). Cognitive flexibility and hypertext: Theory and technology for the nonlinear and multidimensional traversal of complex subject matter. In D. Nix & R. Spiro (Eds.), *Cognition, education, and multimedia* (pp. 163-205). Hillsdale, NJ: Erlbaum.

Stanton, N.A. & Baber, C. (1994). The myth of navigating in hypertext: How a "band-wagon" has lost its course! *Journal of Educational Multimedia and Hypermedia*, *3*(3/4), 235-249.

Wallace, R.M., Kuperman, J., Krajcik, J., & Soloway, E. (2000). Science on the Web: Students online in a sixth grade classroom. *Journal of the Learning Sciences*, *9*(1), 75-104.

Chapter IX

Knowledge Representation in Intelligent Educational Systems

Ioannis Hatzilygeroudis
University of Patras and
Research Academic Computer Technology Institute, Greece

Jim Prentzas
Technological Educational Institute of Lamia and
Research Academic Computer Technology Institute, Greece

Abstract

In this chapter, we deal with knowledge representation in Intelligent Educational Systems (IESs). We make an effort to define requirements for Knowledge Representation (KR) in an IES. The requirements concern all stages of an IES's life cycle (construction, operation, and maintenance), all types of users (experts, engineers, learners) and all its modules (domain knowledge, user model, pedagogical model). We also briefly present various KR schemes, focusing on neurules, a kind of hybrid rules integrating symbolic rules and nuerocomputing. We then compare all of them as far as the specified KR requirements are concerned. It appears that various hybrid approaches to knowledge representation can satisfy the requirements in a greater degree than that of single representations. Another finding is that there is not a hybrid scheme that can satisfy the requirements of all the modules of an IES. So, multiple representations or a multi-paradigm representation environment could provide a solution to requirements satisfaction.

Introduction

Recent developments in computer-based educational systems resulted in a new generation of systems encompassing intelligence, to increase their effectiveness; they are called Intelligent Educational Systems (IESs). Intelligent Tutoring Systems (ITSs) constitute a popular type of IESs. ITSs take into account the user's knowledge level and skills and adapt the presentation of the teaching material to the needs and abilities of individual users. This is achieved by using Artificial Intelligence (AI) techniques to represent pedagogical decisions as well as domain knowledge and information regarding each student. ITSs were usually developed as stand-alone systems. However, the emergence of the WWW gave rise to a number of Web-based ITSs (Brusilovsky, 1999), which are a type of *Web-Based Intelligent Educational System* (WBIES) (Hatzilygeroudis, 2004).

Adaptive Educational Hypermedia System (AEHS) (Brusilovsky, Kobsa, & Vassileva, 1998) are another type of educational system. These systems are specifically developed for hypertext environments such as the WWW. The main services offered to their users are adaptive presentation of the teaching content and adaptive navigation by adapting the page hyperlinks. Compared to ITSs, they offer a greater sense of freedom to the user, since they allow a guided navigation to the user-adapted educational pages. Furthermore, they dynamically construct or adapt the educational pages, in contrast to ITSs where the contents of pages are typically static. Enhancing AEHSs with aspects and techniques from ITSs creates another type of WBIES.

A crucial aspect in IESs (hence, WBIESs) is making decisions on the proper adaptation of the system to the user needs. This is mainly done by mimicking corresponding human decision making. So, a crucial aspect in the development of an IES, and hence of a WBIES, is how related knowledge is represented and how reasoning for decision making is accomplished. Various knowledge representation (KR) schemes have been used in IESs. An aspect that has not received much attention yet is defining requirements for knowledge representation in IESs. The definition of such requirements is important, since it can assist in the selection of the suitable KR scheme(s).

In this chapter, we present an effort to specify a number of requirements that a KR scheme that is going to be used in an IES should meet in order to be adequate. Based on them and a comparison of various KR schemes, we argue that hybrid schemes satisfy those requirements to a larger degree than single schemes. Such a hybrid scheme, called *neurules*, is presented as an example. However, our final argument is that only multiple representations or a multi-paradigm environment would be adequate for the development of an IES. This chapter is an extension of the work of Hatzilygeroudis and Prentzas (2004b).

The chapter is organized as follows. The following section specifies the KR requirements. Then, a number of KR schemes and how they satisfy the requirements are presented. The next section compares the KR schemes and, finally, we end the chapter with our conclusions.

KR Requirements

Introductory Aspects

As in other knowledge-based systems, we distinguish three main phases in the life cycle of an IES: the *construction phase*, the *operation phase,* and the *maintenance phase*. The main difference from other knowledge-based systems is that an IES requires a great deal of feedback from the users and iteration between phases. Three types of users are involved: *domain experts*, *knowledge engineers*, and *learners*. Each type of user has different requirements for the KR scheme(s) to be used. We call them *user requirements*, since they mainly concern the needs of the users.

Some of the user requirements are related to the general requirements for a KR language, such as efficiency and naturalness. Efficiency mainly refers to how quickly conclusions are drawn, whereas naturalness refers to how easy it is to construct and understand sentences of a KR language as well as inference steps (Reichgelt, 1991).

On the other hand, the system itself imposes a number of KR requirements. An IES (as well as a WBIES) consists of three main modules (see Figure 1): (a) the *domain knowledge*, which contains the teaching content and meta-information about the subject to be taught, (b) the *user model*, which records information concerning the user, and (c) the *pedagogical model*, which encompasses knowledge regarding various pedagogical decisions. Each component imposes different KR requirements. We call them *system requirements*, since they are related to the system components.

Figure 1. The basic structure of an Intelligent Educational System (IES)

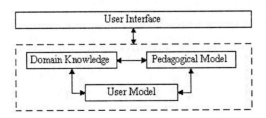

User Requirements

Domain Expert

The domain expert provides knowledge concerning the application domain. He/she is a person who has in-depth knowledge about the possible problems, the way to deal with them, and various practices obtained through his/her experience. In IESs, the domain experts are mainly the tutors. Tutors are highly involved in the construction and maintenance stages. However, in most cases, their relation to AI or even to computers is rather superficial. This may potentially make them restrained in their interactions with the knowledge engineer. Furthermore, the teaching theories to be incorporated in the system are rather difficult to express.

So, it is evident that one main requirement that tutors impose is *naturalness* of representation. Naturalness facilitates interaction with the knowledge engineer and helps the tutor in overcoming his/her possible restraints with AI and computers in general. In addition, it assists the tutor in proposing updates to the existing knowledge.

Also, expert is involved in checking the validity of the represented knowledge—a tedious task. So, the capability of *providing explanations* is another requirement from the expert, which is of great help in checking represented knowledge.

Knowledge Engineer

The knowledge engineer manages the development of an IES and directs its various phases. The main tasks of the knowledge engineer are: acquire knowledge from the domain expert and/or other knowledge sources, select the implementation tools, and effectively represent the acquired knowledge. He/she is the one who chooses (or designs) the KR scheme to be employed. Finally, he/she maintains the produced knowledge base.

Obviously, *naturalness* is again a basic requirement. The more natural the KR scheme, the easier it is for the knowledge engineer to transfer expert knowledge. Furthermore, during construction, tutors may frequently change part (small or big) of the represented knowledge. Also, even if the system's operation is satisfactory, changes and updates of the incorporated expert knowledge may be required. This demands *ease of updates*.

Additionally, the KR scheme should facilitate the knowledge acquisition (KA) process. KA is usually a bottleneck in the development of a knowledge-based system. Facilitation can be achieved if the KR scheme allows acquiring knowledge from alternative (to experts) sources, such as databases of empirical data or past cases, in an automated or semi-automated way. So, *ease of knowledge acquisition* is another requirement.

In developing knowledge-based systems, a prototype is usually constructed before the final system. The prototype includes a small part of the whole knowledge. The rest of it is gradually added to the system. This is called *incremental development* of the system, and it is a desirable feature. Furthermore, testing the continually incremented prototype can call for arduous efforts. In this context, two important factors are the inference engine performance and the capability of providing explanations. *Efficient inferences* reduce the time spent by the knowledge engineer. Also, *provision of explanations* is important, because it can assist in the location of deficiencies in the knowledge base.

End-User

An end-user (learner) is the one who uses the system in its operation stage. The basic requirement for KR, from the point of view of end-users, concerns time efficiency. IESs are highly interactive knowledge-based systems requiring time-efficient responses to the users' actions, which mainly depend on inference engine responses. In the case of WBIESs, time performance is even more crucial, since the Web imposes additional time constraints due to multiple users and the restricted communication bandwidth. In addition to efficiency, the inference engine should also be able to reach *conclusions from partially known inputs*. During a learning session, the user may not be able or does not want to provide values for all parameters. However, the system should be able to make inferences without having all inputs known.

System Requirements

Types of Knowledge

System requirements refer to representation of the knowledge involved in the components of an IES. These requirements are mainly based on the required type(s) of involved knowledge, since different types of knowledge are more easily represented in different KR schemes (Reichgelt, 1991).

A first type of knowledge is called *structural knowledge*. Structural knowledge is concerned with types of entities (i.e., concepts, objects, etc.) and how they are interrelated. It reflects the structure of the domain knowledge. Often, those relationships are hierarchical, that is, they concern generalization/specialization relationships, for example, "math is a form of an academic course, which itself is a form of a course."

Another type of knowledge is *relational knowledge*. Relational knowledge concerns relations between entities of the domain. Those relations may be causal relations, for example, "smoking causes cancer" or dependency relations, for example, "mark depends on the number of attempts and the help asked."

From another point of view, there is *heuristic knowledge*. It is knowledge in the form of "rules of thumb"—practical knowledge about how to solve problems based on experience. Sometimes, knowledge is not clear enough, but *uncertain* or *vague*. For example, values "low" and "medium," used to characterize the knowledge level of a student are vague, since their boundaries are not clear. Also, knowledge may be not certain, but may have a degree of certainty.

Domain Knowledge

The domain knowledge module contains knowledge related to the subject to be taught as well as the actual teaching material. It usually consists of two parts: (a) knowledge model, and (b) course units. Knowledge model refers to the basic concepts that constitute the subject to be taught and the types of relationships between them, for example, the "prerequisite" or "specialization," relationships. Finally, they are associated with course units, which constitute the teaching content.

Usually, concepts are organized in a type of structure. So, it is evident that the KR scheme should be able to naturally represent *structural and relational knowledge.*

User Model

The user model (or student model) records information about the learner's knowledge state and traits. This information is vital for the system to be able to adapt to the user's needs. The process of inferring a user model from observable behavior is called "diagnosis." There are many possible user characteristics that can be recorded in the user model. One of them is the knowledge that the user has learned. In this case, diagnosis refers to an estimation (or evaluation) of the learner's knowledge level. Diagnosis of other characteristics such as learning ability and concentration means estimations based on learner behavior while interacting with the system.

Diagnosis of learner's characteristics is not a clear process. Also, there is not a clear-cut distinction between various levels (values) of the characteristics. So, it is quite obvious that a representation scheme for the user model should be able to deal with *uncertain* and *vague knowledge.* Also, representation of *heuristic knowledge* is needed to make estimations about the values of the student characteristics.

Pedagogical Model

The pedagogical model represents the teaching process. It provides the knowledge infrastructure in order to tailor the presentation of teaching content according to the information recorded in the user model. The pedagogical model of a "classical" IES mainly performs the following tasks: (a) course planning (or knowledge sequencing), (b) teaching method selection, and (c) learning content selection. The main task in (a) is planning, that is, selecting and appropriately ordering the concepts to be taught. The main task involved in (b) and (c) is also selection, for example, how a teaching method is selected based on the learner's state and the learning goal. This is a reasoning process whose resulting conclusion depends on the logical combinations of the values of the user model characteristics, which is a function of *heuristic knowledge.* Furthermore, selection is not always clear, so *uncertain knowledge* representation may be required.

The above analysis of the requirements of knowledge representation for an IES is depicted in Tables 1 and 2.

Table 1. Users' requirements

USERS' REQUIREMENTS		
Expert	**Engineer**	**Learner**
• naturalness • explanations	• naturalness • ease of updates • incremental development • ease of knowledge acquisition • explanations	• efficient inferences • partial input inferences

Table 2. System requirements

SYSTEM REQUIREMENTS		
Domain Knowledge	**User Model**	**Pedagogical Model**
• structural knowledge • relational knowledge	• vague knowledge • uncertain knowledge • heuristic knowledge	• heuristic knowledge • uncertain knowledge

Knowledge Representation Schemes

In this section, we investigate satisfaction of the requirements specified above by various KR schemes. We distinguish between single and hybrid KR schemes.

Single Schemes

Structured Representations

Semantic nets and their descendants (*frames* or *schemas*) (Negnevitsky, 2002) represent knowledge in the form of a graph (or a hierarchy). Nodes in a semantic net graph represent concepts and the edges represent relations between the concepts. Nodes in a frame hierarchy also represent concepts, but they have internal structure that describes the corresponding concept via a set of attributes. They are very natural and well suited for representing structural and relational knowledge. They can also make efficient inferences for small to medium graphs (hierarchies). However, it is difficult to represent heuristic knowledge, uncertain knowledge, and make inferences from partial inputs. Also, explanations are not provided and knowledge updates are difficult. *Conceptual graphs* are similar to semantic nets, whereas *ontologies* (Staab & Studer, 2004) refer to a representation scheme similar to frames, but more restrictive.

In IESs, semantic networks have been used mainly for the representation of the domain knowledge structure.

Symbolic Rules

Symbolic rules are one of the most popular KR methods (Negnevitsky, 2002). They represent general domain knowledge in the form of if-then rules: if <conditions> then <conclusion>, where the term <conditions> represents the conditions of a rule, whereas the term <conclusion> represents its conclusion. The conditions are connected with one or more logical operators such as "and," "or," and "not." The conclusion of a rule is derived when the logical function connecting its conditions results to true. *Expert systems* constitute the most well-known type of rule-based systems. The main parts of a typical expert system are: rule base, inference engine, working memory, and explanation mechanism.

The inference engine uses the knowledge in the rule base as well as facts about the problem at hand to draw conclusions. Typically, facts are provided by the user during inference. There are two main inference methods: backward chaining (guided by the goals) and forward chaining (guided by the data). The explanation mechanism provides explanations regarding the drawn conclusions.

Rules are natural (easy to comprehend) and rule-base updates (removing/inserting rules) can be easily made. Also, incremental development of a rule base is a quite natural process. In addition, heuristic knowledge is naturally represented by rules. However, a major drawback is the difficulty in acquiring them. KA may turn out to be a bottleneck. Furthermore, the acquired rules may be imperfect. Efficiency of the inference process depends on the length of the inference chains. Additionally, conclusions cannot be derived if some of the inputs are unknown. Finally, pure rules cannot represent uncertain or vague knowledge and are not suitable for representing structural and relational knowledge.

Symbolic rules have been used in IESs mainly to diagnose the learner's characteristics and to perform various pedagogical tasks (Simic & Devedzic, 2003; Vassileva, 1998). The system described by Vassileva (1998) uses heuristic knowledge in the form of rules (classified into groups with different functionality) to manage course generation based on learner's performance and the domain knowledge.

Case-Based Representations

Case-based representations (Leake, 1996) store a large set of past cases with their solutions in the *case base* and use them whenever a similar new case has to be dealt with. A case-based system performs inference in four phases: (1) retrieve, (2) reuse, (3) revise, and (4) retain. In the retrieval phase, the most relevant stored case(s) to the new case is (are) retrieved. Similarity measures and indexing schemes are used in this context. In the reuse phase, the retrieved case is combined with the new case to create a solution. The revise phase validates the correctness of the proposed solution. Finally, the retain phase decides on retention (or not) of the new case.

Cases are usually easy to obtain and, unlike other schemes, case acquisition can also take place during the system's operation. Cases are natural. Explanations cannot be provided in a straightforward way as in rule-based systems, due to the similarity functions. Even if some of the inputs are not known, conclusions can be reached through similarity to stored cases. Updates can be easily made. However, the efficiency of the inference process depends on the size of the case base. Finally, cases are not suitable for representing structural, uncertain, and heuristic knowledge.

In IESs, case-based reasoning has been used in the user model to assess the learner's knowledge and in the pedagogical model to perform instructional tasks (Guin-Duclosson, Jean-Danbias, & Norgy, 2002; Shiri, Aimeur, & Frasson, 1998). The approach described by Guin-Duclosson et al. (2002) uses case-based reasoning to teach problem-solving methods. The system enables modeling the knowledge observed in learners by explicitly defining a problem classification, the reformulation, and the solution knowledge associated with it. According to that model, an expert in the teaching domain defines a hierarchy of problem classes and reformulation knowledge for the classification of a new problem based on discriminating attributes.

Neural Networks

Neural networks represent a totally different approach to AI, known as connectionism (Gallant, 1993). A neural network consists of many simple interconnected processing units called *neurons*. Each connection from neuron u_j to neuron u_i is associated with a numerical weight w_{ij} corresponding to the influence of u_j to u_i. The output of a neuron is based on its inputs and corresponding weights. Usually, neural networks are organized in three levels: input, intermediate (or hidden), and output level. The weights of a neural network are determined via a *training* process using empirical data. Input neurons are fed with the input values of the problem. These values are propagated through the network and produce the outputs by activating the corresponding neurons.

Neural networks are very efficient in producing conclusions, since inference is based on numerical calculations, and can reach conclusions based on partially known inputs due to their generalization ability. On the other hand, neural networks lack naturalness of representation, that is, the encompassed knowledge is incomprehensible, and explanations for the reached conclusions cannot be provided. It is also difficult to make structural updates to specific parts of the network. Neural networks do not possess inherent mechanisms for representing structural, relational, and uncertain knowledge. Heuristic knowledge can be represented to some degree via supervised training.

The system described by Tchetagui and Nkambou (2002) employs a neural network to classify the learner into a knowledge level.

Belief Networks

Belief networks (or *probabilistic nets*) (Russell & Norvig, 2003) are graphs, where nodes represent statistical concepts and links represent mainly causal relations between them. Each link is assigned a probability, which represents how certain is it that the concept where the link departs from causes (leads to) the concept where the link ultimately arrives. Belief nets are good at representing causal relations between concepts. Also, they can represent heuristic knowledge to some extent. Furthermore, they can represent uncertain knowledge through the probabilities and make relatively efficient inferences (via computations of probabilities propagation). However, estimation of probabilities is difficult, making the KA process a problem. For the same reason, it is difficult to make updates. Also, explanations are difficult to produce, since the inference steps cannot be easily followed by humans. Furthermore, their naturalness is reduced.

In IESs, belief networks have been used mainly in user modeling (Jameson, 1995; Tchetagui & Nkambou, 2002; Vanlehn & Zhendong, 2001). The system described by Tchetagui and Nkambou (2002) uses Bayesian reasoning to aggregate performance values throughout the network of the domain knowledge structure.

Hybrid Schemes

Hybrid schemes are integrations of two or more single KR schemes. In this section, we focus on the most popular ones.

Fuzzy Rules

Fuzzy logic is good at representing imprecise and fuzzy terms, like "low" and "high." Fuzzy logic extends traditional logic and set membership by defining membership functions over the range [0.0, 1.0], where 0.0 denotes absolute falseness and 1.0 absolute truth. *Fuzzy expert systems* constitute the most popular application of fuzzy logic. In such systems, sets of *fuzzy rules* (Dubois, Pride, & Yager, 1993) are used to infer conclusions based on input data. Fuzzy rules include fuzzy variables. Inference process includes three phases: fuzzification of inputs (via membership functions), application of fuzzy rules, and defuzzification (to produce the output).

Given the above, fuzzy rules are good at representing vagueness. However, fuzzy rules are not as natural as symbolic rules (due to membership functions), a fact that complicates the KA process and the updates to the rule base. It is difficult to specify membership functions. Inference is more complicated and less natural than in simple rule-based reasoning, although its overall performance is not worse (because a fuzzy rule corresponds to more than one simple rule). Provision of explanations is feasible, but not all reasoning steps can be explained.

Fuzzy rules have proven quite helpful in the user modeling component of various ITSs (Hwang, 1998; Nkambou 1999). The Web-based ITS described by Hwang (1998) employs a fuzzy expert system to assess learner characteristics and guide the learning process. The user model records fuzzy characteristics (like knowledge level, concentration, etc.) and non-fuzzy characteristics (like total session time, effective learning time, etc.). The non-fuzzy characteristics are used to determine the values of the fuzzy ones. Fuzzy rules are used for subject material selection.

Connectionist Rule-Based Representations

A number of neuro-symbolic approaches have been developed, but we concentrate here on *connectionist expert systems*, because they satisfy more requirements. *Connectionist expert systems* (Gallant, 1993) combine neural networks with rule-based expert systems. The knowledge base is a network whose nodes correspond to domain concepts. Dependency information regarding the concepts is used to create links among nodes. The network's weights are calculated through a training process using a set of training patterns. In addition to the knowledge base, connectionist expert systems also consist of an inference engine and an explanation mechanism. Compared to neural networks, they offer more natural representation and can provide some type of explanation. Naturalness is enhanced due to the fact that most of the nodes correspond to domain concepts.

Neuro-Fuzzy Representations

There are various ways to integrate neural networks and fuzzy logic (Nauck, Klawonn, & Kruse, 1997). We are interested in integrations where the two component representations are indistinguishable. Such integrations are the *fuzzy neural networks* and the *hybrid neuro-fuzzy representations*. Fuzzy neural networks are fuzzified neural networks—they retain the basic properties and architectures of neural networks and "fuzzify" some of their elements (i.e., input values, weights, activations, outputs). In a hybrid neuro-fuzzy system, both fuzzy techniques and neural networks play a key role. Each does its own job in serving different functions in the system. Hybrid neuro-fuzzy systems seem to satisfy KR requirements to a greater degree than fuzzy neural networks. They retain more benefits of their component representations in a more satisfactory way.

The system described by Magoulas, Papanikolaou, and Grigoriadou (2001) is an Adaptive Educational Hypermedia System, which uses neural and fuzzy modules to accomplish its tasks. Neural and fuzzy modules are used in the domain knowledge, the learner evaluation, and the pedagogical model. This hybrid approach enables the representation of incomplete, imprecise, and vague information about the learner and also exploits the generalization capability of neural networks.

Integrations of Rules and Cases

Another trend in hybrid knowledge representation is the *integrations of rule-based reasoning with case-based reasoning* (Golding & Rosenbloom, 1996). We refer here to approaches where one method (either rules or cases) dominates and not to balanced approaches, because reasoning in them is more complicated. In such systems, naturalness of the underlying components is retained. Compared to "pure" case-based reasoning, their key advantage is the improvement in the performance of the inference engine and the ability to represent heuristic and relational knowledge. Furthermore, the synergism of rules and cases can cover up deficiencies of rules (improved knowledge acquisition) and also enable partial input inferences. The existence of rules in such hybrid schemes makes updates more difficult than "pure" case-based representations. Also, explanations can be provided but not as easily as in pure rule-based representations, given that similarity functions are still present.

Description Logics

Description Logics (DLs) (Baader, Calvanese, McGuiness, Nardi, & Patel-Schneider, 2002) combine aspects from frames, semantic nets, and logic. They consist of two main components, the Tbox and the Abox. Tbox contains definitions of concepts and roles (i.e., their attributes) called *terminological knowledge*, whereas ABox contains logical assertions about concepts and roles called *assertional knowledge*. DLs offer clear semantics and sound inferences. They are usually used for building and maintaining ontologies and for classification tasks related to ontologies. Also, DLs can be built on existing Semantic Web standards (XML, RDF, RDFS), so they are quite suitable for representing structural and relational knowledge. Also, being logic-based, they can represent heuristic knowledge. Furthermore, their Tboxes can be formally updated. Their representation is natural, but not as much as that of symbolic rules. Inferences in DLs may have efficiency problems. Explanations cannot be easily provided.

Neurules

Syntax and Semantics

Neurules are a type of hybrid rules integrating symbolic rules with neurocomputing (Hatzilygeroudis & Prentzas, 2000, 2001a). In contrast to other hybrid approaches, the constructed knowledge base retains the modularity of rules, since it consists of autonomous units (neurules), and also retains their naturalness in a great degree, since neurules look much like symbolic rules.

The form of a neurule is depicted in Figure 2a. Each condition C_i is assigned a number sf_i, called its significance factor. Moreover, each rule itself is assigned a number sf_0, called its bias factor. Internally, each neurule is considered as an adaline unit (Fig. 2b). The inputs C_i ($i=1,...,n$) of the unit are the conditions of the rule. The weights of the unit are the *significance factors* of the neurule and its bias is the *bias factor* of the neurule. Each input takes a value from the following set of discrete values: [1 (true), 0 (false), 0.5 (unknown)]. The output D represents the conclusion of the rule. The output can take one of two values ('-1', '1') representing failure and success of the rule respectively.

The general syntax of a condition C_i and the conclusion D is:

<condition/conclusion>::= <variable> <predicate> <value>

where <variable> denotes a *variable*, for example, "mark-level," "solution-attempts," and so on. <predicate> denotes a symbolic (is, isnot) or a numeric (<, >, =) predicate (not

Figure 2. (a) Form of a neurule; (b) corresponding adaline unit

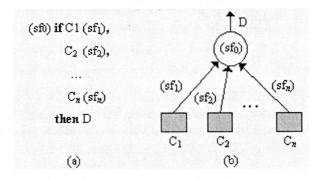

(a)

(b)

Table 3. A neurule for assigning examination marks

(-9.7) **if** assistance-times is 1 (4.7),
assistance-times is 0 (4.6),
solution-attempts is 2 (4.6),
requested-examples is >1 (3.2),
requested-examples is 1 (1.4)
then mark is average

used in conclusions). <value> denotes a value (a symbol or a number). The significance factor of a condition represents the significance (weight) of the condition in drawing the conclusion. Table 3 presents an example of a neurule used in assigning examination marks to a student.

Neurules can be constructed either from symbolic rules (Hatzilygeroudis & Prentzas, 2000), thus exploiting existing symbolic rule bases, or empirical data (Hatzilygeroudis & Prentzas 2001a). Each adaline unit is individually trained via the Least Mean Square (LMS) algorithm.

A neurule-based system consists of the same basic components as a rule-based system. The neurule-based inference engine is based on a backward chaining strategy and uses neurules and facts (typically acquired from the user) to draw conclusions. Evaluation of a neurule is based on special neurocomputing measures (Hatzilygeroudis & Prentzas, 2001b). A neurule fires if the output of the corresponding adaline unit is computed to be "1" after evaluation of its conditions. A neurule is said to be "blocked" if the output of the corresponding adaline unit is computed to be "-1" after evaluation of its conditions.

Experiments have shown that the neurule-based inference process not only does better than simple rules but also better than other similar systems, like MACIE (Gallant, 1993). Neurules are also associated with an explanation mechanism capable of providing explanations of various types in the form of if-then rules. Experiments have shown that neurules' explanation mechanism produces more natural explanations with less rules (Hatzilygeroudis & Prentzas 2001b).

Using Neurules in an ITS

We constructed an intelligent tutoring system using neurules as its main knowledge representation scheme (Hatzilygeroudis & Prentzas 2004a; Prentzas, Hatzilygeroudis, & Garofalakis, 2002). Neurules were used for representing knowledge in the user modeling unit and the pedagogical unit. In the user modeling unit, neurules were used for user classification in some stereotype and for student evaluation. In the pedagogical unit, they were used for three tasks: method selection, concept selection, and unit selection. There is a neurule-based expert system, which makes pedagogical decisions during the learning process, with a neurule-based inference engine, and a neurule base consisting of five partial neurule bases, distributed between the user modeling and the pedagogical unit.

An important characteristic of the ITS is the existence of a special unit, called knowledge management unit (KMU). KMU has facilities for (a) acquiring knowledge from various sources (experts, existing symbolic rule bases, empirical data), and (b) updating the knowledge stored in the neurule bases.

The use of neurules in the development of the ITS revealed a number of benefits:

- Neurules can be acquired in a semi-automated way from various sources, such as symbolic rules, empirical data, or an expert. This is very important for IESs, given that KA is harder than other systems due to the existence of more than one knowledge-based module.

- Neurules support incremental development of the neurule bases. One can easily add new neurules to or remove old neurules from a neurule base. This is difficult for other hybrid approaches.

- Neurules are space-efficient; they produce much smaller knowledge bases compared to simple rules. The size reduction in the ITS was 35-40%.

- Neurules can make robust inferences. In contrast to simple rules, neurules can derive conclusions from partially known inputs. This feature is useful because, values of some parameters may be unknown during a learning session.

- Neurules provide a more time-efficient inference engine than simple rules. This is very important, since an IES is a highly interactive knowledge-based system.

- Neurule bases can be efficiently updated, that is, without thorough reconstruction of them. This is quite helpful during the construction and maintenance stage, where many updates are required. Knowledge base updates constitute a bottleneck for other hybrid approaches.

Table 4. Comparison of KR schemes

	USERS' REQUIREMENTS						SYSTEM REQUIREMENTS				
	Naturalness	Ease of Update	Efficient Inference	Explanations	Knowledge Acquisition	Partial input inferences	Structural knowledge	Relational knowledge	Uncertain knowledge	Vague knowledge	Heuristic knowledge
Semantic nets/frames	√+	√-	√+	-	√	-	√+	√+	-	-	-
Symbolic rules	√+	√+	√	√+	√-	-	-	√-	-	-	√+
Case-based representations	√+	√+	√	√	√+	√	-	√	-	-	-
Belief networks	√-	-	√+	-	√-	-	√	√+	√+	√-	√-
Neural networks	-	-	√+	-	√+	√+	-	√-	-	-	√-
Fuzzy rules	√	-	√	-	√-	-	-	√-	√-	√+	√+
Connectionist expert systems	√-	√-	√+	√-	√+	√+	-	√-	-	-	√-
Neurofuzzy representations	√-	-	√	-	√	√-	-	√-	√-	√+	√
Cases and rules	√+	√	√	√	√	√	-	√	-	-	√
Description logics	√	√-	√-	√-	√	-	√+	√+	-	-	√
Neurules	√	√	√+	√+	√+	√+	-	√-	-	-	√+

Despite the above benefits, we experienced some difficulties too. First, we could not use neurules to represent domain knowledge, due to its structural nature. So we had to rely on degenerate (hence, weak) representation methods like relational tables. Another difficulty was that we could not represent vague knowledge. So we had to use clear cut distinctions among various classes of a test mark level or the knowledge level of a student (low, average, high, etc.).

Comparison of KR Schemes

Table 4 compares the KR schemes discussed in the previous sections, as far as satisfaction of KR requirements for IESs is concerned. Symbol "-" means "unsatisfactory"; "√-" "average"; "√" "good"; and "√+" "very good."

A conclusion that can be drawn from the table is that none of the single or hybrid schemes satisfies all the requirements for an IES. However, some of them satisfy the requirements of one or two modules of an IES. So, taking into account only the learner's and system requirements, one can say that semantic nets, frames, description logics, and belief networks are more suitable for representing knowledge in the domain model. Also, fuzzy rules, belief networks, and neuro-fuzzy representations are more suitable for the student modeling module. Finally, symbolic rules and neurules are more suitable for the pedagogical model. Hybrid schemes, in general, demonstrate improvements compared to most or all of their component schemes and therefore are preferable. However, a solution to the representational problem of an IES could be the use of different representation schemes (single or hybrid) for the implementation of different IES modules. Hence, the idea of a multi-paradigm development environment seems to be interesting.

Conclusion

In this chapter, we make an effort to define requirements for knowledge representation in an IES. This work was motivated by the fact that we found symbolic rules inadequate to construct an ITS. The requirements concern all stages of an IES's life cycle (construction, operation, and maintenance), all types of users (experts, engineers, and learners), and all its modules (domain knowledge, user model, and pedagogical model). According to our knowledge, such requirements have not been defined yet in the IES literature. However, we consider them of great importance as they can assist in choosing the KR schemes for representing knowledge in the components of an IES. To this end, we briefly present and compare various KR schemes. Our decision about the satisfaction level of a requirement by a KR scheme is based on advanced basic research results from the literature.

It appears that various hybrid approaches to KR can satisfy the requirements to a greater degree than that of single representations. The use of hybrid approaches to knowledge representation in IESs can become a popular research trend, although, until now, few IESs employed hybrid KR schemes. Another finding is that there is not a hybrid scheme that can satisfy the requirements of all of the modules of an IES, but rather, each one individually. So, multiple representations or a multi-paradigm representation environment could provide a solution.

References

Baader, F., Calvanese, D., McGuiness, D., Nardi, D., & Patel-Schneider, P.F. (2002). *The description logic handbook: Theory, implementation and applications*. Cambridge, UK: Cambridge University Press.

Brusilovski, P. (1999). Adaptive and intelligent technologies for Web-based education. In C. Rollinger & C. Peylo (Eds.), *Kustliche Intelligenz*, Special Issue on Intelligent Systems and Teleteaching, *4*, 19-25.

Brusilovsky, P., Kobsa, A., & Vassileva, J. (Eds.) (1998). *Adaptive hypertext and hypermedia*. The Netherlands: Kluwer Academic Publishers.

Dubois, D., Pride, H., & Yager, R. R. (Eds.) (1993). Fuzzy rules in knowledge-based systems. In *Reading in fuzzy sets for intelligent systems*. San Francisco: Morgan Kaufmann.

Gallant, S.I. (1993). *Neural network learning and expert systems*. Cambridge, MA: MIT Press.

Golding, A.R. & Rosenbloom, P.S. (1996). Improving accuracy by combining rule-based and case-based reasoning. *Artificial Intelligence*, 87, 215-254.

Guin-Duclosson, N., Jean-Danbias, S., & Norgy, S. (2002). The AMBRE ILE: How to use case-based reasoning to teach methods. In S.A. Cerri, G. Gouarderes, & F. Paraguacu (Eds.), *Sixth International Conference on Intelligent Tutoring Systems. Lecture Notes in Computer Science* (Vol. 2363, pp. 782-791). Berlin: Springer-Verlag.

Hatzilygeroudis, I. (guest editor) (2004). Special Issue on AI Techniques in Web-Based Educational Systems. *International Journal on AI Tools (IJAIT)*, *13*(2).

Hatzilygeroudis, I. & Prentzas, J. (2000). Neurules: Improving the performance of symbolic rules. *International Journal on Artificial Intelligence Tools*, *9*, 113-130.

Hatzilygeroudis, I. & Prentzas, J. (2001a). Constructing modular hybrid rule bases for expert systems. *International Journal on Artificial Intelligence Tools, 10*, 87-105.

Hatzilygeroudis, I. & Prentzas, J. (2001b). An efficient hybrid rule based inference engine with explanation capability. *Proceedings of the 14th International Florida Artificial Intelligence Research Society Conference* (pp. 227-231). Menlo Park, CA: AAAI Press.

Hatzilygeroudis, I. & Prentzas, J. (2004a). Using a hybrid rule-based approach in developing an intelligent tutoring system with knowledge acquisition and update capabilities. *Journal of Expert Systems with Applications, 26*, 477-492.

Hatzilygeroudis, I. & Prentzas, J. (2004b). Knowledge representation requirements for intelligent tutoring systems. In J.C. Lester, R.M. Viccari, & F. Paraguacu (Eds.), *The 7th International Conference on Intelligent Tutoring Systems (ITS 2004). Proceedings. Lecture Notes in Computer Science* (Vol. 3220, pp. 87-97). Berlin: Springer-Verlag.

Hwang, G.-J. (1998). A tutoring strategy supporting system for distance learning on computer networks. *IEEE Transactions on Education, 41*(4), 1-19.

Jameson, A. (1995). Numerical uncertainty management in user and student modeling: An overview of systems and issues. *User Modeling and User-Adapted Interaction, 5*(3-4), 193-251.

Leake, D.B. (Ed.) (1996). *Case-based reasoning: Experiences, lessons & future directions*. Menlo Park, CA: AAAI Press/MIT Press.

Magoulas, G.D., Papanikolaou, K.A., & Grigoriadou, M. (2001). Neuro-fuzzy synergism for planning the content in a Web-based course. *Informatica, 25*, 39-48.

Nauck, D., Klawonn, F., & Kruse, R. (1997). *Foundations of neuro-fuzzy systems*. New York: John Wiley & Sons.

Negnevitsky, M. (2002). *Artificial intelligence: A guide to intelligent systems*. Reading, MA: Addison Wesley.

Nkambou, R. (1999). Managing inference process in student modeling for intelligent tutoring systems. In *Proceedings of the Eleventh IEEE International Conference on Tools with Artificial Intelligence* (pp. 19-23). Los Alamitos, CA: IEEE Computer Society Press.

Prentzas, J., Hatzilygeroudis, I., & Garofalakis, J. (2002). A Web-based intelligent tutoring system using hybrid rules as its representational basis. In S.A. Cerri, G. Gouarderes, & F. Paraguacu (Eds.), *Sixth International Conference on Intelligent Tutoring Systems. Lecture Notes in Computer Science* (Vol. 2363, pp. 119-128). Berlin: Springer-Verlag.

Reichgelt, H. (1991). *Knowledge representation: An AI perspective*. Norwood, NJ: Ablex Publishing.

Russel, S. & Norvig, P. (2003). *Artificial intelligence, A modern approach*. Englewood Cliffs, NJ: Prentice Hall.

Shiri, M. E., Aimeur, E., & Frasson, C. (1998). Student modelling by case-based reasoning. In B. P. Goettl, H. M. Halff, C. L. Redfield, & V.J. Shute (Eds.), *Fourth International Conference on Intelligent Tutoring Systems* (Vol. 1452, pp. 394-404). Berlin: Springer-Verlag.

Simic, G. & Devedzic, V. (2003). Building an intelligent system using modern Internet technologies. *Expert Systems with Applications, 25*, 231-146.

Staab, S. & Studer, R. (Eds.) (2004). *Handbook on Ontologies*. Berlin: Springer-Verlag.

Tchetagui, J. M. P. & Nkambou, R. (2002). Hierarchical representation and evaluation of the students in an intelligent tutoring system. In S.A. Cerri, G. Gouarderes, & F. Paraguacu (Eds.), *Sixth International Conference on Intelligent Tutoring Systems. Lecture Notes in Computer Science* (Vol. 2363, pp. 708-717). Berlin: Springer-Verlag.

Vanlehn, K. & Zhendong, N. (2001). Bayesian student modeling, user interfaces and feedback: A sensitivity analysis. *International Journal of AI in Education, 12*, 155-184.

Vassileva, J. (1998). Dynamic course generation on the WWW. *British Journal of Educational Technologies, 29*, 5-14.

Chapter X

Modeling of Adaptive Tutoring Processes

Alke Martens, University of Rostock, Germany

Abstract

In this chapter, a formal, adaptive tutoring process model for case-based Intelligent Tutoring Systems (ITSs) is described. Combining methods of Artificial Intelligence and Cognitive Science led to the development of ITSs more than 30 years ago. In contrast to the common agreement about the ITSs' architecture, components of ITSs are rarely reusable. Reusability in ITSs is intimately connected with the application domain, that is, with the contents that should be learned and with the teaching and learning strategy. An example of a learning strategy is case-based learning, *where the* adaptation *of the learning material to the learner plays a major role. Adaptation should take place automatically at runtime, and thus should be part of the ITS's functionality. To support the development of ITSs with reusable components and the communication about and the evaluation of similar ITSs, a* formal approach *has been chosen. This approach is called the tutoring process model.*

Introduction

Using machines to support teaching and training has a long tradition. One of the earliest approaches is said to be the machine developed by S.L. Pressey in the 1920s: "a simple apparatus which gives tests and scores and teaches" (Pressey, 1960). The beginning of using a computer in educational settings can be dated from the late 1950s (Kruse, 2000). The first systems developed were strongly influenced by the behavioristic research. Thus, most of the time, simple drill-and-practice programs were realized. Many years of research, a paradigm shift in learning theory, cognitive science, and new technology like the WWW have led to the current state of the art. Nowadays, a large variety of system types are part of what is called e-learning, for example, Computer-based Training System (CBT), Web-based Training System (WBT, also known as Web-based Education or WBE), Learning Management System (LMS), Adaptive Hypermedia System (AH), Intelligent Tutoring System (ITS), to name but a few. This chapter focuses on the ITSs.

Since Clancey described the ITS architecture (1984), a kind of common agreement about the constituents of an ITS exist. Accordingly, an ITS consists of the components: expert knowledge model, pedagogical knowledge model, learner model, and user interface. Based on the common agreement about the ITS architecture, assumptions are that ITSs are comparable, that the reuse of components is possible, and that communication about ITS realizations is easy. However, in the process of developing an ITS, some problems arise. Often, ITSs are not comparable and components are normally not reusable. Furthermore, communication with other ITS developers reveals heterogeneous views on the ITS architecture. These problems are mainly based on the fact that the interpretation of the role of each ITS component varies. A closer look at the components' tasks described in different theoretically and practically oriented papers reveals the fact that content and delivery are not separated in the ITS components. Moreover, there exists no clear description of which components have the task to provide content and which components are responsible for delivery, steering, and control of the tutoring process. This decision is made individually by the system developers, which leads to a quite heterogeneous usage (see Martens, 2003a).

Thus, a revision of the ITS architecture is necessary. The revised architecture differentiates between content, provided by the classical ITS components, and delivery. The "delivery" is taken over by a new component, called the tutoring process model. Located in the center of the ITS architecture (Martens, 2003b), the new component interacts with each of the other components. It is responsible for adaptation and delivery of content to the learner, and for steering the interaction with the learner. Based on a formal description (Martens, 2004a; Martens & Uhrmacher, 2004), the tutoring process model is independent of the application domain and of programming languages. The clear description facilitates communication about the model, independent of the application domain. As a side effect, the separation of content and delivery in the ITS leads to reusable components and concepts.

In this chapter, the focus lies on the formal tutoring process model. The tutoring process model is developed to support case-based learning. In the following section, the theoretical background of case-based learning is sketched. Case-based learning makes certain demands on an ITS, especially regarding the contents' adaptability and the automatic adaptation of contents to the learner at runtime. The underlying idea of supporting two cognitive processes is depicted. In the next section, the discussion about the ITS architecture is sketched, and the new component's interaction with the classical ITS components is described. The subsequent section contains the formal tutoring process model. The formal model is based on a mathematical description, which is close to automata theory. The next section describes exemplarily a practical realization of the theoretic approach. Based on the formal tutoring process model and the new architecture, the Web-based and case-based ITS Docs 'n Drugs—The Virtual Hospital (http://www.docs-n-drugs.de) has been developed. Docs 'n Drugs teaches clinical medicine in a case-based way. It has been established as part of the medical curriculum at the University of Ulm, Germany. The system has been used since 2000 by hundreds of students. A conclusion of the described approach finalizes this chapter.

Case-Based Training, Adaptation and ITS

In this section, the theoretical background of the formal tutoring process model is described. The section consists of a short introduction to case-based training, a description of the role of adaptability, and how to realize adaptability in case-based training with an ITS.

Case-Based Training

Case-based training means interacting with close to real-life situations that are provided in a narrative manner. In the training case, the learner takes on a certain role. For example, in a medical training case, the learner has to act and react like a physician who gives a patient medical treatment.

Being traditionally part of the education in law, business, and medicine, case-based training can look back on a long history—in law education, it has been used since the late 19th Century, in business schools it has been part of the curriculum since the early 20th Century (Merseth, 1991). Training cases provide concrete application scenarios instead of abstract theoretical descriptions. They engage the learner to interact with the offered information, to make decisions, and to behave in complex and probably changing situations. The learner trains to apply the theoretical knowledge acquired in traditional lectures to concrete scenarios. In contrast to training and practice in real-life, the (computer-based) training case offers a safe environment that takes the learner's knowledge into account as it adapts to his abilities, and that allows the learner to make mistakes and to learn from these mistakes.

Training cases can be developed in different complexities. A distinction can be made with respect to the required level of expertise of the learner (e.g., ranging from beginner to expert), the kind of information embedded in the training case (e.g., correct facts, wrong

Figure 1. Types of training cases (Martens, 2004)

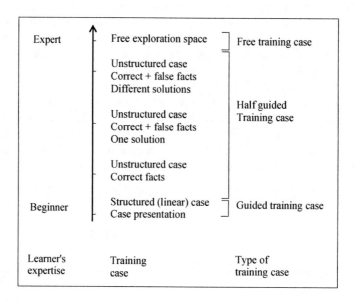

facts, misleading facts), and the amount of decisions about next steps in the training case (e.g., ranging from a fixed sequence of steps with no freedom of choice, to a free navigation without restriction). These different types of training cases are sketched in Figure 1. The distinction is close to classifications in instructional theories (e.g., see Gage & Berliner, 1991).

Due to the fact that the development of ITSs has historically been interwoven with the research in cognitive science, it lends itself to the adoption of insights in cognitive science for the construction of an ITS. Especially in the domain of clinical medicine, some work is available that can be used as theoretical basis. Here, the work of Patel, Kaufman, and Arocha (1995) and Patel and Kushniruk (1998) plays an important role, as it analyses the different behaviour of experts and beginners in interaction with patients. Taking the results of their research, it can be concluded that case-based training should at least support the training of two cognitive processes, namely:

1.   The process of general knowledge application, that is, how to act and react in an appropriate manner in a changing environment; and

2.   The process of diagnostic reasoning, that is, how to deduce diagnoses from given facts.

Martens (2003a) has shown that the two processes also occur in other than medical application scenarios. Thus, the conclusion is that case-based ITSs in general should support these two processes. To support the training of the process of general knowledge application, the learner should have the ability to decide about how to proceed in a given situation. This can be easily realized in ITSs by offering an amount of actions to the learner, for example, in form of a menu or a set of navigation options. The learner has to select an action. The chosen action determines the development of the training case. To allow for training of diagnostic reasoning, the ITS should support an additional "diagnosis task," which is permanently available for the learner. In such a task, the learner can, for example, collect his suspected diagnoses. He might have correction facilities available. The correction of the learner's selected list of diagnoses should always take into account the learner's current state of knowledge, for example, a diagnosis should be perceived as "possible" as long as facts that prove the diagnosis to be false have not been collected by the learner.

Adaptation

To optimally support the process of general knowledge application and the process of diagnostic reasoning, the ITS must adapt the contents and the navigation of the training case to the learner and to the learner's decisions. Distinguishing two aspects of adaptation, namely, adaptation of content and adaptation of navigation, has been suggested by several other researchers (e.g., Brusilovsky, 2000). Also, Kinshuk and Lin (2003) state: "The design of an adaptive educational system requires adaptation of both navigation and content" (p. 22). Martens and Harrer (2004) take this one step further, distinguishing three dimensions of adaptation:

- Object of adaptation (What will be adapted?);
- Object of influence (What leads to the adaptation, why is the adaptation necessary?); and
- Time of adaptation (When does the adaptation take place?).

The objects of adaptation in the ITS's training case are at least the content and the navigation (i.e., the actions mentioned in the last subsection). It is also possible to adapt the help, feedback, and correction functions. For example, in the context of diagnoses, the functions help, feedback, and correction should always take into account the learner's current state of knowledge in the training case.

The objects of influence for the adaptation in the training case are the logical coherence of the training case and the learner. Regarding the learner, there can be two aspects distinguished: the learner's profile information and information the learner has collected in the training case. The latter can be perceived as the learner's continuously changing state of knowledge about the training case's contents.

In case-based training, the time of adaptation can be initial adaptation, that is, the complete training case is initially adapted to the learner, and continuous adaptation at runtime. A combination of both adaptation mechanisms is possible.

These different aspects of adaptation are realized in the adaptive tutoring process model.

Intelligent Tutoring Systems

This section gives a short sketch of the history of ITSs and of the ITS architecture. It explains the different views of the ITS architecture, which has led to heterogeneous and incomparable systems. The architecture with tutoring process model, which is one step towards reusability and homogenization, is described.

Historical Background

ITSs can be traced back to the early 1970s, when Carbonell (1970) made the first attempts to combine methods of Artificial Intelligence (AI) with Computer-Aided Instruction (CAI). Thus, the first generation of ITSs are more or less a kind of "intelligent" CAI. Their main task is stated by Lelouche (1999): "The basic principle of 'intelligent' CAI is that it should know the taught material" (p. 6). Knowledge about the taught material is embedded in the ITS in form of expert systems, that is, the expert knowledge model. The integration of insights of cognitive science in ITSs (e.g., see Woolf & McDonald, 1984) has led to what today is called an Intelligent Tutoring System. In addition to the knowledge about the taught material, these systems have knowledge about pedagogical strategies and knowledge about the learner, realized as pedagogical knowledge model and learner model, respectively.

The ITS Architecture

The classical ITS architecture, first described by Clancey (1984), consists of the components expert knowledge model, pedagogical knowledge model, learner model, and user interface. The naming of the components varies. Sometimes, depending on the training domain, a component for automatic generation of exercises is also part of the ITS. This classical ITS architecture can be found in a lot of theoretical ITS descriptions, for example, Corbett, Koedinger, and Anderson (1997); Harrer (2000); Lelouche (1999); Lusti (1992); Martens (2003a); Peylo (2002); and Puppe (1992), and in a lot of existing ITS, for example, Alpert, Singley, and Fairweather (1999); Gertner and VanLehn (2000); Mayo, Mitrovic, and McKenzie (2000); and Shaw, Ganeshan, and Johnson (1999).

Whereas the ITS's constituents seem to be part of common agreement in the ITS community, the role and the functionality of each of the components varies a lot. The reason for this can partly be seen in the different application domains. One can easily imagine that training in mathematics places different demands on ITSs than clinical medicine training. Another reason might be the realization of different learning theories in ITS. Case-based learning, described in the former section, places special demands on an ITS that are somewhat different in problem-oriented learning. These reasonable aspects often necessarily lead to heterogeneous and incomparable systems. But even in the same application domain and based on the same learning style, ITSs are often not comparable and based on a complete different interpretation of the same architecture.

Moreover, regarding only the ITS architecture on a more abstract level, it becomes hard to find reasons for heterogeneous realizations at all. A mixture of content and delivery functions, which is seemingly not based on insights of research but on traditions of ITS development, can be found in ITS realizations. Traditionally, the expert knowledge model is realized like in GUIDON, where Clancey (1984) used MYCIN as the underlying expert system. Thus, in a lot of ITS (e.g., the system D3, http://www.d3web.de/), the expert knowledge base is still implemented as a system with own database and own functionality. In other ITSs, the expert knowledge base is a simple database without own functionality (e.g., Docs 'n Drugs). The same situation can be found in the different ways the pedagogical knowledge model is realized and embedded in the ITS. Thus, there are ITSs that consist of a set of interacting and more or less separate subsystems, and there are ITSs consisting of passive components plus a component that encapsulates the execution. Execution in this context contains the interaction with the learner, the evaluation of the learner's behaviour and success, and the provision of contents and navigation. Thus, two perspectives on the same architecture can be found, reflecting different interpretation of the same models:

1.   ITS architecture consists of separate independent subsystems; and
2.   ITS architecture consists of passive components with centralized execution system.

Surely, both perspectives have their advantages and disadvantages. However, the underlying system's philosophy regarding the realization of the components should be made explicit to provide for comparability of ITSs and reusability of ITS components.

Docs 'n Drugs realizes expert knowledge model and pedagogical knowledge model as databases without their own execution functionality, that is, as passive components. The system's functionality is embedded in the ITS in an extra component—the tutoring process model. The advantage of this approach is that the central steering component might be reused in different ITSs, as it is clearly separated from the databases and the user interface. In Figure 2, the suggested ITS architecture with the tutoring process model is sketched.

Figure 2. ITS architecture with tutoring process model

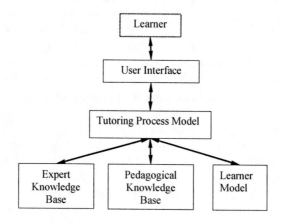

Formal Tutoring Process Model

In this section, the formal tutoring process model will be described. The tutoring process model is realized as the abstract tutoring process model with two extensions, namely, the basic tutoring process model and the adaptive tutoring process model. Firstly, the abstract tutoring process model will be explained. This is followed by a description of the basic tutoring process model, which does not support runtime adaptation. Finally, the adaptive tutoring process model is depicted. The adaptive tutoring process model embeds a learner model and provides adaptation capabilities to the learner. Additionally, the adaptation can provide a logical coherent development of the storyline in case-based training.

Abstract Tutoring Process Model

The abstract tutoring process model consists of a training case *C* and the two additional functions *show* and *enable*:

$$TPM = <C, show, enable>$$

with: *C* is the training case, *show* is the show state function, and *enable* is the enable action function.

The training case C is a structure itself:

$$C = <Q, A, q_0, F, B, \delta, select, allow >$$

with: Q is a finite set of states, A is a finite set of actions, $q_0 \in Q$ is the start state, $F \subset Q$ is a finite set of final states, B is a finite set of bricks, δ is the state transition function, *select* is the select brick function, and *allow* is the select action function.

The basic parts of a training case are the states Q and actions A. Each training case contains a start state q_0 and a set of possible final states $F \subset Q$. Each state Q is composed by a set of bricks B. Bricks are the actual multimedia elements (e.g., text or picture) that form the page displayed to the learner. Bricks can be distinguished in information elements and interaction elements. Whereas information elements should only be read or regarded by the learner, the interaction elements require the learner to interact, for example, to answer questions or to mark regions in pictures. A learner's display is constituted by one brick or by a set of bricks. The learner's navigation (e.g., menu or navigation bar) is composed of the actions A. The learner steers through the training case by selecting appropriate actions from the set of allowed actions.

The state transition function δ of the training case determines which state will be reached if an action is selected in a certain state:

$$\delta : Q \times A \rightarrow Q \cup \{\perp\}$$

Here, the symbol $\perp$ stands for NIL. In the context of the tutoring process model, the symbol denotes that there exists no transition for the given 'state action pair.' This is the case for all final states $q_f \in F \subset Q$, as final states have no associated actions. If the learner has reached a final state, the training case terminates.

$$\forall q_f \in F, a \in A : \delta(q_f, a) = \{\perp\}$$

As mentioned above, each state consists of a set of bricks. After the state transition function has determined the subsequent state, the *select* function derives which subset of the set of bricks is related to the new state. These are the bricks that can potentially be shown to the learner:

$$select: Q \rightarrow 2^B$$

For each state $q \in Q$ there must be at least one brick: $\forall q \in Q: select(q) \neq \emptyset$

This means that no empty states are allowed.

In addition to the bricks, the set of actions that should be active in the subsequent display must be determined. This is realized by the *allow* function:

$$allow: Q \to 2^A$$

Here, two conditions must be met. The first condition says: if an action a is not part of a set of actions derived by applying the *allow* function on a state q, then there is no state transition:

$$\forall\ a \in A,\ q \in Q:\ a \notin allow(q) \neq \varnothing \Rightarrow \delta(q,a) = \{\bot\}$$

The second condition says: the *allow* function applied on a final state q_f leads to the empty set, as finals states have no actions associated:

$$\forall\ q_f \in F:\ allow(q_f) = \varnothing$$

To these elements of a training case C, the tutoring process model *TPM* adds two more functions. These functions are the *show* and the *enable* function. As mentioned above, the *select* function of the training case is responsible for selecting the bricks associated with a state. The *show* function is responsible for determining which subset of these bricks will actually be shown to the learner. Thus, the *show* function is part of the adaptation process and will be extended in the adaptive tutoring process model. The *enable* function plays the same role with regard to the actions. The set of actions, derived by the *allow* function of the training case, is taken as input. From this set of actions, the *enable* function determines which subset of actions will actually be shown to the learner. Thus, the enable function is the second part of the adaptation process, that is, adapting the amount of subsequent steps the learner has available. In the adaptive tutoring process model, this function will also be extended.

Basic Tutoring Process Model

The basic tutoring process model, having the same structure as the abstract tutoring process model, is described as:

$$TPM_{basic} = <C, show, enable>$$

It can be used for defining, steering, and controlling the execution of training cases without a learner model being part of the tutoring process. This basic tutoring process model is not adaptable in the broad sense. It is possible to initially adapt a complete training case to a learner's profile, but there is no adaptation process that takes a continuous adaptation to a learner into account. This is reflected in the two functions of the tutoring process model.

The *show* function, which determines the subset of bricks that should be shown to the learner, is defined as:

$$\forall\ q \in Q : show(q) \equiv select(q)$$

Thus, all the available bricks of the training case will be shown to the learner.

The *enable* function, which is responsible for determining the subset of actions that should be available in this state, is similarly defined as:

$$\forall\ q \in Q : enable(q) \equiv allow(q)$$

Thus, all the actions that are available for a state will be shown to the learner.

For the author of a training case, which is steered and controlled by the basic tutoring process model, this has the following consequences:

1. The author must foresee all navigation paths the learner should be able to take, that is, he must predefine the set of actions that should be available at each state.

2. The author must foresee all the content elements, that is, the bricks that should be displayed to the learner. Furthermore, the author must care for the logical coherence of the training case—for all possible paths the learner might choose.

Comprising this large amount of authoring work will most likely lead to training cases with only a small amount of next-step choices for the learner. Guided training cases can easily be constructed with this kind of tutoring process model. However, training cases constructed with the basic tutoring process model are closer to classical computer-based training (CBT) applications than to ITS.

Adaptive Tutoring Process Model

To provide for adaptation capabilities, as a first step a learner model should be integrated directly into the tutoring process model. Thus, the adaptive tutoring process model is a structure:

$$TPM_{adapt} = <C, LM, show, enable>$$

Here *LM* is the learner model.

In the following, a prototypical learner model is described. This learner model can be easily extended, for example, with regard to new insights in user modelling. The learner model consists of at least two parts. One part specifies the learner's profile *LP* and the other part reflects the learner's knowledge *LW*. Thus, the learner model *LM* is a structure consisting of:

$$LM = <LP, LW>$$

LP and *LW* are structures themselves. The learner's profile *LP* should at least contain the identification of the learner *id*, and information about the learner's expertise in the application domain *expertise*. Thus, *LP* is a structure:

$$LP = <id, expertise>$$

The knowledge of the learner *LW* in the training case capsules information, such as the path the learner has chosen so far in the training case (denoted by the partial path *Lpath*), the results the learner has achieved in interaction elements (described as the set of results *Lresult*), and the facts the learner has acquired so far (given by the set of facts *Lacq*). The notion of paths and facts will be explained later. Thus, *LW* is a structure:

$$LW = <id, Lpath, Lresult, Lacq>$$

In addition to the embedded learner model, actions and bricks are extended in the adaptive tutoring process model. Both actions and bricks are now structures. All actions $a \in A$ consist of the action's identification *id*, the action's name *name*, and a set of preconditions *PRE*:

$$\forall\ a \in A: a = <id, name, PRE>$$

A brick's structure ($\forall\ b \in B$) is composed of the brick's identification *id*, a list of the brick's multimedia contents *con*, a set of preconditions *PRE* that must be met to allow to select the brick for the next display, and a set of postconditions *POST* that are valid after the brick has been selected for display.

$$\forall\ b \in B : b = <id, con, PRE, POST>$$

The action's and the brick's preconditions *PRE* and the brick's postcondition *POST* are well-defined expressions that are constructed according to a syntax and that are interpretable. They can be constructed as logical expressions. The elements of the set of preconditions *PRE* can be profile information or facts. Profile information denotes which entry in the learner's profile *LP* must be given to allow the display of the brick or the action. For example, a precondition "expert" denotes that the according brick should only be displayed if the learner's *expertise* is "expert."

The elements of the set of postconditions *POST* are also facts. These facts stem from two information sources. Some of the facts will be taken from the general knowledge, that is, they stem from the expert knowledge base of the ITS. In a medical training case, as realized by Docs 'n Drugs, the expert knowledge base contains general medical knowledge. The facts are, for example, "headache" or "abdomen." Some other facts will be taken from the knowledge base, which is directly related to a training case and which can be realized as the pedagogical knowledge base of the ITS. In a medical training case, these facts are often given by attributes of the general facts, for example, attributes of "headache" can be "date: yesterday, intensity: bad, location: left, duration: 1 hour." The properties (i.e., "date, intensity, location, duration") are part of the general medical knowledge, whereas the attributes are strongly related with a concrete training case.

After a certain brick has been selected to be part of the display, the set of facts of the brick's postcondition *POST* become part of the set of facts in the learner's knowledge *LW*, that is, they are stored in the set of facts *Lacq*. Here, the assumption is that the learner might have "learned" the fact. Thus, the learner's subsequent behaviour in the training case will be evaluated taking this assumed knowledge into account. For selection of the actions that should be displayed, the learner's profile *LP* and the learner's knowledge *LW* is used to evaluate the preconditions *PRE* of the actions that could be displayed. Only the actions with fulfilled preconditions will form the actual display. After the learner has selected an action, that is, the learner has chosen a subsequent step in the training case, the next state will be derived. According to the evaluation of the preconditions of the actions, the brick's preconditions will be evaluated to determine which bricks will form the actual display. Thus, both selection of actions and selection of bricks take place at runtime and are based on the current state of knowledge of the learner and the learner's profile. The learner's collection of facts in the training case leads to a continuous change in *LW*, which is automatically considered in the process of selecting actions and bricks. The same can be realized with respect to the learner's profile *LP* via changing the learner's level of expertise in *LP* or other profile information, for example, reflecting the learner's current behaviour in the training case. Thus, as the learner selects the appropriate steps, his level of expertise might raise, whereas a repeated selection of wrong steps might lead to a lower level of expertise. Accordingly, the "beginner" might, for example, get a restricted set of actions, whereas the "expert" gets a larger set of correct and wrong actions (Martens & Uhrmacher, 2002).

To allow for the adaptation of bricks and actions, as sketched above, the *show* function (for the selection of the bricks that should form the display) and the *enable* function (for the selection of the actions that should be available to the learner) must be extended in the adaptive tutoring process model. Both functions must now take the entries in the learner model *LM* into account. As described above, the preconditions *PRE* are evaluated via the learner's profile information *LP* (especially the learner's *expertise*) and the learner's knowledge *LW* (especially the facts the learner has acquired so far *Lacq*). Thus, both parts of the learner model have to be integrated into the two functions. The *show* function is changed to:

> *show: $2^B \times LP \times LW \to 2^B$*
>
> *show(B_q, expertise, Lacq) = B_a*

Here, B_q is the set of bricks determined by the *select* function, *expertise* is the entry in *LP*, *Lacq* is the set of acquired facts, which are entries in *LW*, and B_a is the set of bricks determined by the *show* function.

The *enable* function is changed accordingly to:

> *enable: $2^A \times LP \times LW \to 2^A$*
>
> *enable(A_q, expertise, Lacq) = A_a*

Here, A_q is the set of actions determined by the *allow* function, *expertise* is the entry in *LP*, *Lacq* is the set of acquired facts, which are entries in *LW*, and A_a is the set of bricks determined by the *enable* function.

With the integrated learner model, the extensions of actions and bricks, and the extension of the two functions of the adaptive tutoring process model, the automatic adaptation process is formalized. Additionally, the formal description of the notion of paths in the training case is required, as mentioned above in the description of the learner model. Paths can be used, on one hand, to facilitate the training case's development; the training case author might get a tool to graphically relate states to paths (see, e.g., Reichmann [2000], who used workflow for a preliminary work in this direction). The according preconditions and postconditions of actions and bricks can be derived automatically and might be fine-tuned by the authors at a later stage of development. On the other hand, paths can be used to evaluate the sequence of steps chosen by the learner. This sequence of steps can be used to reason about the learner's process of general knowledge application and about the learner's "mental plan" (Martens & Uhrmacher, 2002). In addition to actions and bricks, help and correction can be adapted to the insights resulting of the investigation of the path chosen by the learner.

The sequence of actions chosen by the learner constitutes the learner's path in the training case. Thus, each path is a sequence:

> *path = $(q_0, a_1, a_2, ..., a_{n-1}, a_n, q_f)$*

with: $q_0 \in Q$ is the start state, $a_i \in A$ are actions with $0 < i < n$, $a_n \in A$ is an action leading to a final state, and $q_f \in F$ is a final state. Each path has to start with a start state and has to lead to at least one final state (definitions see Martens, 2003a). Accordingly, the shortest path is given by: *path* $= (q_0, a_n, q_f)$. This shortest path makes no sense, regarding a realistic training case. Moreover, usually training cases consist of more than one path. The only exception is the guided training case, which has exactly one path from the start state to a final state.

If the training case is not a guided training case, the set of allowed paths in a training case is described by

$PATH_C = \{p \mid p$ is an allowed path $path\}$

with: $PATH_C \neq \emptyset$ and $|PATH_C| \geq 1$

To allow for a recording of the path the learner has chosen from a start state to the current state, that is, a recording of the learner's progress at runtime, the notion of partial paths must be introduced. Until the learner has not reached a final state, the *path* is perceived to be a partial path, named *part*. Thus, it is:

part is an allowed partial path

$$<=> ((\, part = (q_0,\, a_1) \wedge a_1 \in allow(q_0) \wedge a_1 \notin A_F)$$
$$\vee (part = part' \circ a_i \wedge path' = (q_0, a_1 ..., a_{i-1}) \text{ is allowed partial path} \wedge a_i \in allow(q_{i-1}) \wedge a_i \notin A_F))$$

with: $q_0 \in Q$ is the start state, $a_1, a_i, a_{i-1} \in A$ are actions with $0 < i < n$, $a_n \in A$ is an action leading to a final state, and A_F is the set of actions leading to a final state.

Every time the learner chooses an action, the partial path has to be actualized. The result is stored in the learner model in *Lpath*.

Sequence of Steps in Adaptation

Due to the update functionality in the learner model, the sequence of steps in the process of adaptation is important. After the learner has selected an action, the following sequence of steps must be guaranteed by the tutoring process execution:

1.   The next state related with the action chosen by the learner has to be determined by the state transition function δ.

2.   Take this new state and derive the set of associated bricks, using the *select* function.

3.   The set of bricks determined by *select* has to be taken by the *show* function, to determine which bricks will constitute the actual display of the learner.

4.   Actualize the learner model with the post conditions of the bricks determined by *show*.

5.   Based on the actualized learner model, determine the amount of actions associated with the new state, using the *allow* function.

6.   Take the set of actions determined by *allow* and derive with *enable*, which subset of actions will be available to the learner in the new state.

This sequence of steps is important because, after the learner has the new information of the new display available, his state of information changes. Thus, the actual state of information must be taken into account to determine the amount of available next steps.

Example: Docs 'n Drugs

Part of the medical curriculum at the University of Ulm since the year 2000, Docs 'n Drugs —The Virtual Hospital (http://www.docs-n-drugs.de) is a Web-based ITS for case-based training of clinical medicine. As the system is integrated into the regular curriculum, it has already been used by several hundreds of students. An evaluation is currently running. First results are that students like to work with the program, as it offers training settings that are close to real life.

Case-based training should be part of the education in clinical medicine from an early stage. However, reality seldom meets this requirement. Due to the fact that case-based training has an inherent complexity, it can hardly be realized in education at the university. Thus, students and lecturers perceive training with Docs 'n Drugs as an important supplement to traditional lectures and courses. Training cases are currently developed in German only, however, the system is not restricted to the German language; potentially, the system is open to English training cases as well. The authors of the training cases are physicians working at the University Hospital at Ulm. Most of the time, the training cases are based on existing patient records, which are changed and adapted to provide for anonymity of the original patients.

The system Docs 'n Drugs has been implemented based on the formal tutoring process model, and it is based on the architecture with the centralized tutoring process model, as described earlier. Thus, Docs 'n Drugs components lend themselves to re-use. The ITS itself is implemented in Java. The expert knowledge model of Docs 'n Drugs is a hierarchically organised ontology that contains case-independent medical knowledge. The medical knowledge is constructed based on classifications, nomenclatures, and thesauri (for example, the ICD-10, 1992). The pedagogical knowledge model of Docs 'n Drugs contains the didactically elaborated training cases. Each of the content elements of a training case—in the tutoring process model's terminology, each of the *bricks*—is related to at least one entry in the expert knowledge model. Thus, relations and dependencies of the medical knowledge can be used to evaluate the learner's behaviour, as described above (see: facts in the tutoring process model). The tutoring process model is the central component, responsible for steering and interaction of the training case. The learner model in Docs 'n Drugs is currently quite simple and will be part of future research.

In Figure 3, a screenshot of a training case in Docs 'n Drugs can be seen. The user interface of Docs 'n Drugs is subdivided into the parts navigation (on the right), content (in the center), and situation description (on top). The situation description is a pedagogical element that is used to introduce the learner in different situations. For example, it contains a description of the learner's current environment and his role. The situation description and the situation navigation are not part of the tutoring process model and thus will not be described in more detail.

The training case's navigation distinguishes between permanently available actions and temporarily available actions (the latter are those mentioned in the tutoring process model). Permanently available actions, that is, the "Diagnosis," the "Tip," the "Findings Folder," and the "Close" button, are always available to the learner. The "Diagnosis"

Figure 3. Screenshot of Docs 'n Drugs (Martens, 2004)

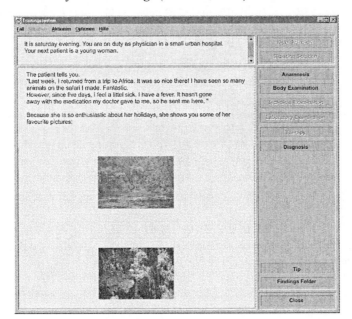

button leads to a special task, where the learner can note and correct his current suspected diagnoses. Here, the process of diagnostic reasoning, mentioned in the section about case-based training, is trained. The 'Findings Folder' provides a protocol of the findings the learner has collected; that is, here, the results of the examinations are noted, some pictures can be revisited, and some of the patient's utterances can be recorded. The "Findings Folder" is close to the patient record at hospital. The "Tip" button provides additional functionality for help, feedback, and correction. The answers given by the so called "intelligent tutor" underlying the "Tip" button are automatically generated, taking the entries in the learner model into account.

The temporarily available actions are part of the adaptation process of the tutoring process model. Thus, inactive and active actions are distinguished in this part of the navigation. In half-guided adaptable training cases, the number of active and the number of inactive actions might change with every decision of the learner. By selecting one of the actions, the learner steers the training case's progress. Here, part of the cognitive process of general knowledge application, mentioned in the section about case-based training, is trained.

In the screenshot shown in Figure 3, temporarily available actions are distinguished in the medical categories "Anamnesis," "Body Examination," "Technical Examination," "Laboratory Examination," and "Therapy". Each of the buttons leads to a menu consisting of submenus and actions. If all temporarily available actions in a category are inactive, the whole category gets inactivated as shown in Figure 3. However, it is also possible to inactivate single actions in the submenus.

In the screen's center, the information is shown. The content of the page displayed is constituted by the bricks. If the training case is based on the adaptive tutoring process model, the subset of bricks shown to the learner is determined at runtime. In the Figure 3, one text brick and one picture brick are selected. The picture brick consists of the two photos shown in Figure 3.

Application Example

To give an example of the interaction and the adaptation from the tutoring process model's perspective, a short sequence of a medical training case is formally sketched (Martens & Uhrmacher, 2004). The example is much shorter than a situation in a real training case, that is, there are only a few bricks and only a few actions shown for demonstration purposes.

The learner "Hugo", who is Learner Number 9 in the ITS, has selected the Training Case Number 11. In this training case, the task of the physician is to find out that the patient suffers from malaria. The case starts with a young female patient, having a fever and telling a story about her last holiday in Africa. Hugo is a beginner in the training domain. Thus, his learner model $LM = <LP, LW>$ contains the following information in the learner profile: $LP = <9, 'beginner'>$. After Hugo has read the initial information, he has correctly selected the 'Travel anamnesis', which can be found at the second menu level at the 'Anamnesis'. Hugo currently sees the screenshot shown in Figure 3. Thus, he has the information about the patient's journey available. As subsequent steps, he can choose between the temporarily available actions 'Anamnesis' and 'Body Examination.' The current state of the entries in the learner's knowledge is:

$$LW = <11, (q_0, a_{travel}), \varnothing, \{sun\text{-}tanned\ skin, fever, africa\}>$$

This information in LW is constructed in the following way: The learner works with Training Case 11. He has seen the start state q_0 and he has chosen the action a_{travel}, thus currently his valid partial path is (q_0, a_{travel}). He has not visited any interaction elements yet, thus his set of results in interaction elements is empty. The fact 'sun-tanned skin' has been part of the information in the start state's brick. The currently displayed bricks in the state $q_{travel} \in Q$ are related to the facts 'fever' and 'africa'. Because the learner has selected the suspected diagnoses 'malaria' and 'amoebic colitis' (both of which he has noted in his list of suspected diagnoses), he decides to check whether the patient has prepared correctly for her trip to Africa. Thus, he decides to select the 'Inoculation anamnesis,' which he finds at the menu related to 'Anamnesis', i.e. $a_{ino} \in A$.

After Hugo has made his click on the button 'Inoculation anamnesis', the tutoring process makes the following steps: The state transition function δ determines the next state, which will be reached from the state q_{travel} after the selection of the action a_{ino}. The next state reached is the state q_{ino}: $\delta(q_{travel}, a_{ino}) = q_{ino}$

The state $q_{ino} \in Q$ consists of four bricks, that is, $select(q_{ino}) = \{b_1, b_2, b_3, b_4\}$
The bricks have the following structure:

b_1 = <1, (text, 'The patient made malaria prophylaxis with the medication noted in her certificate of vaccination. Check in the Internet, whether this kind of medication is appropriate.'), 'beginner', 'malaria prophylaxis' >

b_2 = <2, (picture, vaccination card malaria, Ø, Ø>

b_3 = <3, (text, 'The patient smiles and sais: "Sure, I have made malaria prophylaxis."'), 'expert', Ø>

b_4 = <4, (text, 'The vaccination card tells you, that the patient has made a malaria prophylaxis. Try to find out, if the medication noted down in the card might have effected the headache.'), 'headache', 'malaria prophylaxis'>

The brick b_1 is suitable only for beginners, as it provides some extra information. Brick b_2 has an empty precondition, thus it will always be part of the learner's display. The information in brick b_3 is unsubtle, and thus only suitable for a learner with more experience in the application domain, for example, an expert. The brick b_4 should only be displayed if the learner's knowledge LW contains the fact '*headache*'. Based on the entries in the learner model, the function *show* determines the bricks b_1 and b_2 to be displayed:

$show(\{b_1, b_2, b_3, b_4\}, \text{'beginner'}, \{\text{sun-tanned skin, fever, africa}\}) = \{b_1, b_2\}$

After the bricks have been derived by the *show* function, the learner model is updated. Only brick b_1 has a post condition ('*malaria prophylaxis*'), which becomes part of the facts in the learner's knowledge LW. Thus, LW is now:

$LW = <11, (q_0, a_{travel}), Ø, \{\text{sun-tanned skin, fever, africa, malaria prophylaxis}\}>$

With this updated learner model, the tutoring process now determines which actions will be active. The function *allow* derives which actions are related to the state q_{ino}:

$allow(q_{ino}) = \{a_{ana}, a_{th}, a_{lab}\}$

Here, the example is shortened due to comprehensibility—usually, there are a lot more actions available in each state. The set of actions determined by *allow* is used by *enable*, which together with the learner knowledge derives which subset of actions will be active for Hugo. To see how *enable* works, the structure of the actions has to be shown:

a_{ana} = <1, 'Anamnesis', Ø>

a_{th} = <2, 'Therapy', 'expert'>

a_{lab} = <3, 'Laboratory Examination', ' malaria prophylaxis '>

The action a_{ana} is always available, as it has an empty precondition. The action a_{th} is only active if the learner is an expert. If the learner has the entry ' *malaria prophylaxis* ' in his learner model, the action a_{lab} will be active. Because Hugo is a beginner in the application domain and has acquired the fact ' *malaria prophylaxis*', the function *enable* determines the actions a_{ana} and a_{lab} to be active.

enable({a_{ana}, a_{th}, a_{lab}}, 'beginner', {sun-tanned skin, fever, africa, malaria prophylaxis}) = {a_{ana}, a_{lab}}

Conclusion

In this chapter, different aspects of ITS have been highlighted under the perspective to develop and use a formal tutoring process model as central component of an ITS. After a short introduction into the history of ITS, case-based learning with ITSs is explained. Case-based learning is a special learning style, where the learner takes over a certain role in the training case and should act and interact in the training case scenario. The training case is usually provided in a narrative manner. Two cognitive processes that can be trained in the case-based scenario are the process of general knowledge application and the process of diagnostic reasoning. To optimally support the training of these two processes, the ITS should adapt the training case at runtime to the learner's expertise, his knowledge, and his decision about how to proceed in each step.

In the development of an ITS that supports training in the described way, some problems arise. One of the problems is that ITS components are usually not reusable. Another problem is rooted in the question, which one of the ITS components should take over the role of steering the adaptation? Thus, an excursion into the ITS architecture was necessary. This excursion revealed that the interpretation of the role and functionality of each of the components of an ITS is quite heterogeneous. A reason for this can be seen in the mixture of content and delivery in most of the components.

Based on the tutoring process model, the direction of development has been to clearly separate content and delivery in the ITS. The classical expert knowledge model and the pedagogical knowledge model are reduced to simple databases without delivery functions. The tutoring process model is introduced into the architecture as the new central component for steering the interaction between system and learner, and for adaptation of the training case at runtime. To allow for a reusable, domain-independent, and application-independent tutoring process model, the model has been described formally. The two extensions of the formal tutoring process model are the basic tutoring process model and the adaptive tutoring process model.

At the end of the chapter, the ITS Docs 'n Drugs, which is based on the new architecture and the tutoring process model, has been sketched. A short example of a training case is given to visualize the adaptation functionality of the adaptive tutoring process model.

The learner model, which is part of the formal tutoring process model, is currently at a rather coarse level and can easily be extended. This should be part of future research. Also part of future research should be to integrate interaction bricks, to investigate the formalization of permanently available actions (like diagnosis), and to formalize help or feedback functions.

The tutoring process model lends itself to be reused in other ITSs. Currently, application domains like the teaching of computer science (especially teaching of modelling and simulation; see Martens & Himmelspach, 2005) and teaching of music theory are investigated. Furthermore, the tutoring process model can be used as the basic steering component of an authoring system. Here, the tutoring process model can be used as the basis for training case development and for making test runs with prototypical learner models.

References

Alpert, S.R., Singley, M.K., & Fairweather, P.G. (1999). Deploying intelligent tutors on the Web: An architecture and an example. *International Journal of Artificial Intelligence in Education, 10*(2), 183-197.

Brusilowsky, P. (2000). Adaptive hypermedia: From intelligent tutoring systems to Web-based education. In *Proceedings of the 5th International Conference ITS 00. Lecture Notes in Computer Science 2000* (pp. 1-7). Berlin: Springer-Verlag.

Carbonell, J. R. (1970). AI in CAI: An artificial intelligence approach to computer-assisted instruction. *IEEE Transactions on Man-Machine Systems, 11*(4), 190-202.

Clancey, W. J. (1984). Methodology for building an intelligent tutoring system. In W. Kintsch, P.G. Polson, & J.R. Miller (Eds.), *Methods and tactics in cognitive science* (pp. 51-84). Hillsdale, NJ: Lawrence Erlbaum Associates.

Corbett, A.T., Koedinger, K.R., & Anderson, J.R. (1997). Intelligent tutoring systems. In M. Helander, T. K. Landauer, & P. V. Prabhu (Eds.), *Handbook of human-computer interaction* (pp. 849-874). New York: Elsevier Science B.V.

Gage, N. & Berliner, D. (1991*). Educational psychology* (5th ed.). New York: Houghton Mifflin

Gertner, A.S. & VanLehn, K. (2000). Andes: A coached problem solving environment for physics. In *Proceedings of the 5th International Conference on ITS* (pp. 133-142). Lecture Notes in Computer Science 1839. Berlin: Springer-Verlag.

Harrer, A. (2000). *Unterstuetzung von Lerngemeinschaften in verteilten intelligenten Lernsystemen.* University of Munich, Munich, Germany.

ICD-10 (1992). International classification of diseases (10th revision). Retrieved from *http://www.who.int/classification*

Kinshuk & Lin, T. (2003). User exploration based adaptation in adaptive learning systems. *International Journal of Information Systems in Education, 1*(1), 22-31.

Kruse, K. (2000). Web-rules: Information is not instruction. Retrieved from *http://www.learningcircuits.org*

Lelouche, R. (1999). Intelligent tutoring systems from birth to now. *KI—Kuenstliche Intelligenz, 4*, 5-11.

Lusti, M. (1992). *Intelligente Tutorielle Systeme*. Munich: Oldenbourg Verlag GmbH.

Martens, A. (2003a). *Ein Tutoring Prozess Modell fuer Fallbasierte Intelligente Tutoring Systeme*. University of Rostock, Rostock, Germany. infix: DISKI 281.

Martens, A. (2003b). Centralize the tutoring process in intelligent tutoring systems. In *Proceedings of the Fifth International Conference on New Educational Environments ICNEE 2003*.

Martens, A. (2004). Case-based training with intelligent tutoring systems. In *Proceedings of the Fourth IEEE International Conference on Advanced Learning Technologies ICALT 2004*.

Martens, A. & Harrer, A. (2004). Adaptivitaet in e-learning standards—ein Vernachlaessigtes Thema? In *Proceedings of the Deutsche e-Learning Fachtagung der Gesellschaft fuer Informatik* (pp. 163-174).

Martens, A. & Himmelspach, J. (2005). Combining intelligent tutoring and simulation systems. In *Proceedings of the International Conference SIMCHI 2005* (pp. 65-70).

Martens, A. & Uhrmacher, A.M. (2002). Adaptive tutoring processes and mental plans. In *Proceedings of the International Conference on Intelligent Tutoring Systems ITS 2002* (pp. 71-80).

Martens, A. & Uhrmacher, A.M. (2004). Formal tutoring process model for intelligent tutoring systems. In *Proceedings of the 16th European Conference on Artificial Intelligence ECAI 2004*.

Mayo, M., Mitrovic, A., & McKenzie, J. (2000). CAPIT: An intelligent tutoring system for capitalization and punctuation. In *Proceedings of the International Workshop for Advanced Learning Technologies IWALT 2000* (pp. 151-157).

Merseth, K. (1991). The early history of case-based instruction. *Journal of Teacher Education, 42*(4), 243-249.

Patel, V.L., Kaufman, D.R., & Arocha, J.F. (1995). Steering through the murky waters of a scientific conflict. *Journal AI in Medicine, 7*, 413-438.

Patel, V.L. & Kushniruk A.W. (1998). Understanding, navigating and communicating knowledge: Issues and challenges. *Methods on Information in Medicine*, 460-470.

Peylo, C. (2002). *Wissen- und Wissensvermittlung im Kontext von Internetbasierten Intelligenten Lehr- und Lernumgebungen*. University of Osnabrueck, Osnabrueck, Germany. infix.

Pressey, S. R. (1960). A simple apparatus which gives tests and scores and teaches. In A.A. Lumsdaine & R. Glaser (Eds.), *Teaching machines and programmed learning* (pp. 35-41). Washington, DC: National Education Association.

Puppe, F. (1992). Intelligente Yutoringsysteme. *Informatik Spektrum, 15*, 195-207.

Reichmann, D. (2000). *Visual Workflow—Ein Java-Beans Basiertes Werkzeug zur Grafischen Workflowmodellierung.* Diploma thesis, University of Ulm, Germany.

Shaw, E., Ganeshan, R., & Johnson, W. L. (1999). Building a case for agent-assisted learning as a catalyst for curriculum reform in medical education. In *Proceedings of the International Conference on AI in Education AI-ED '99.*

Woolf, B.P. & McDonald, D.D. (1984). Building a computer tutor: Design issues. *IEEE Computer*, 61-73.

Chapter XI

Ontologies and Contracts in the Automation of Learning Object Management Systems

Salvador Sánchez-Alonso
University of Alcalá, Spain

Miguel-Ángel Sicilia
University of Alcalá, Spain

Elena García-Barriocanal
University of Alcalá, Spain

Abstract

Current standardized e-learning systems are centred on the concept of learning object. Unfortunately, specifications and standards in the field do not provide details about the use of well-known knowledge representations for the sake of automating some processes, like selection and composition of learning objects, or adaptation to the user or platform. Precise usage specifications for ontologies in e-learning would foster automation in learning systems, but this requires concrete, machine-oriented interpretations for metadata elements. This chapter focuses on ontologies as shared knowledge representations that can be used to obtain enhanced learning object metadata records in order to enable automated or semi-automated consistent processes inside Learning Management Systems. In particular, two efforts towards enhancing automation are presented: a contractual approach based on pre- and post-conditions, and the so-called process semantic conformance profiles.

Introduction

Current standardized e-learning systems are centred on the concept of learning object (Wiley, 2001), which can be defined as "an independent and self-standing unit of learning content that is predisposed to reuse in multiple instructional contexts" (Polsani, 2002). This concept of *learning object* is at the centre of a new instructional design paradigm for Web-based learning—a new paradigm that emphasizes reuse as a quality characteristic of learning contents and activities. Most referenced definitions in the field explicitly include the term reuse, including the abovementioned definition by Polsani or the one provided by Wiley (2001), namely, "any digital resource that can be reused to support learning." At the same time, Polsani's definition and others consistent with it (such as those of Sosteric and Hesemeier [2002] and Hamel and Ryan-Jones [2002]) evidence the necessity of including metadata together with the objects. A metadata instance attached to a given learning object provides information on its contents, which undoubtedly facilitates its reusability.

Several interrelated standardization efforts—including the IEEE, ADL SCORM, and the IMS Consortium (Anido et al., 2002)—are devoted to promoting reuse by producing and refining specifications oriented to fostering consistency in learning contents and related elements. These specifications currently cover learning object packaging and metadata, sequencing and composition of activities, and the definition of specialized types of learning objects like questionnaires, among other aspects. Regarding metadata, LOM (IEEE LTSC, 2002) represents the most important initiative from the learning object point of view and might be consequently considered a promising step towards the reusability objective.

However, when machine-understandability is required, for example, to build software modules that automatically retrieve and combine learning objects to form higher-level units of instruction, reusability means having precise metadata records that contain detailed usage considerations. In this context, more research is needed to come up with rigorous approaches to metadata annotation, enhancing machine understandability. Nevertheless, current specifications do not provide details about the use of well-known knowledge representations for the sake of automating some processes like selection and composition of learning objects, or adaptation to the user or platform. In addition, the information schemas provided in such specifications are not free of controversial interpretations (Farance, 2003), which seriously hamper the possibility of implementing standardized "intelligent" behaviours.

Ontologies are shared knowledge representations that form the basis of the current Semantic Web vision (Berners-Lee, Hendler & Lassila, 2001) and are becoming widespread thanks to the availability of common languages like OWL and associated modelling and development tools (Fensel, 2002). Ontologies have been described elsewhere (Lytras, Tsilira, & Themistocleous, 2003; Qin & Paling, 2001; Stojanovic, Staab, & Studer, 2001) as enablers of more flexible and advanced learning systems, but the mere use of ontologies does not guarantee that consistent Learning Management Systems (LMS) functionality will become available in the future: a specification effort about the uses of ontologies in each particular learning technology scenario is also required. Precise and unambiguous usage specifications for ontologies in e-learning would eventually result in a higher level of automation in learning systems. But preciseness requires a clear separation of responsibilities for the participants in each scenario, along with concrete, machine-oriented interpretations for metadata elements, which are not the focus of current specification efforts.

Some previous research has started to devise contract-based specification approaches to metadata (Sánchez-Alonso & Sicilia, 2003; Sicilia & Sánchez-Alonso, 2003) as a technique to produce machine-oriented specifications. In addition, the role of ontologies in process descriptions has been described recently (Sicilia, Pagés, García, & Sánchez-Alonso, 2004). These are examples of research aimed at more convenient specifications for automated or semi-automated learning systems that address the issues of completeness of metadata records, largely neglected in current approaches (Pagés, Sicilia, García, Martinez, & Gutiérrez, 2003).

This chapter focuses on ontologies as shared knowledge representations that can be used to obtain enhanced learning object metadata records —according to existing criteria (Duval, Hodgins, Sutton, & Weibel, 2002)—and also to enable automated or semi-automated consistent processes inside learning management systems. Contract-based metadata design is described as a technique for the definition of metadata that clearly delineates the responsibilities of each participant in a learning process, thus avoiding misuses or misinterpretations of metadata elements. The contractual approach combined with metadata enables the definition of conformance profiles for LMS-based processes that entail a given degree of "intelligence"—understood as the capability to automatically adapt or change their behaviour in a number of situations involving the selection, delivery, and composition of learning objects—and can be used to specify consistent and predictable LMS behaviours. This would broaden the scope of current learning technology standards to include specific types of well-known intelligent techniques.

The rest of this chapter is structured as follows. In the first section, the limitations of automation with current standards and specifications will be briefly described, along with the motivation for the use of contractual approaches and usage descriptions of ontologies in learning object-based systems. Then, the roles of ontologies in learning object descriptions will be studied, and the concrete idioms and usage patterns for ontologies within current learning technology specifications described. Later a contractual approach based on pre- and post-conditions will be analysed as a way to provide machine-oriented metadata to enable automated or semi-automated profiles, including the use of ontologies in those descriptions that require flexible knowledge representation formalisms due to their nature. Later on, we will speak about semantic conformance profiles (SCP) as they constitute a means to integrate required metadata elements, concrete uses of ontologies, and expected outcomes for the processes. Finally, a summary of contributions and findings about the theme of the chapter as well as an overview on the potential future research developments in the area will be provided.

Role of Automation in Learning Design

Designing learning materials as standard reusable learning objects (RLO) provides a number of advantages, such as reducing the cost and time of creating new contents or making available the possibility of creating personalized learning resources by assembling existing ones, among others. But while learning object reusability is certainly a must, we should aspire to more ambitious objectives. In a similar way to what occurred in other fields (e.g., the automotive industry), writing standards that allow the construction of standardized (and sometimes reusable) components should not be seen as an end that allows their easy combination, but rather as a means towards an improved development process. Improving the development process means that several tasks in the process of creating and delivering learning experiences to a learner can be automated. However, as Mohan and Brooks (2003) say, "there has not been any significant work done so far in automating the discovery and packaging of learning objects based on variables such as learning objectives and learning outcomes" (p. 196). This is probably because, as these authors remark, "...automating these processes is also a knowledge-intensive activity likely to require the application of artificial intelligence techniques such as knowledge representation and reasoning" (p. 196).

Routine tasks are not for humans. We usually hand them over to machines as our time is better spent in creative activities that can not be reduced to repetitive sequences of simple steps. In learning design, composing existing materials in order to create a brand new course is not a particularly exciting task. Well, it is, but part of the process can be extremely time-consuming, in particular, browsing through hundreds of learning objects to select and reuse a few of them. Instead, it would be practical to delegate this task to a software agent that could automatically obtain a preliminary solution containing a reduced number of learning objects, provided a given criteria or learning objectives. Such software could, for example, produce a tentative list consisting of 50 candidates recovered from an original repository with approximately 10,000 learning objects, like MERLOT (http://www.merlot.org). This process of previous filtering would help humans to concentrate on those subjective tasks that are difficult to automate, for example, fine-grain filtering of fuzzy criteria such as difficulty level, look and feel issues, or accessibility considerations. Ideally then, in such a process of composition, human activity would be limited to validating whether the proposal returned by the automatic system fits in with the expressed learning objectives or not. If the agent proposal is found to be valid, refinement would be necessary before the final material could be delivered in the form of a course to the final user.

Some authors in the literature (Mortimer, 2002) see a future in which learning materials are automatically assembled on the fly from reusable chunks stored in a public repository, personalized, and then delivered to the end user without human intervention. This futuristic view of the learning design process is, in our opinion, difficult to attain. Human intervention will always be needed when creating new materials. It would ensure non-tangible features such as, for example, the new content consistence and attractiveness. However, we agree with those authors when it comes to the possibility of automating a number of processes such as some of the aforementioned. We will use the term *semi-automation* to designate the automation of time consuming and repetitive processes for which the use of computers rather than humans is proposed, although human creativity still plays a relevant role in the overall creation process.

Currently, learning management systems are not capable of automatically adapting their behaviour in a number of situations involving the selection, delivery, and composition of learning objects. Following is a list of tasks that could be automated:

- Selecting the right version of a RLO from the information on the age of the intended user, provided that more than one version—each addressing different levels of difficulty—of the same content is available.

- Selecting the more appropriate RLO for the user platform where it is to be delivered, supposing that similar objects guarantee the same objectives.

- Delivering a RLO that is part of a higher-level RLO that is to be delivered.

- Recommending a particular learning content depending on the user profile or existing knowledge records.

- Interpreting a given RLO according to the specific characteristics or preferences set in a particular LMS.

- Classifying a given RLO according to a specific process profile in order to cause a known sequence of semantic behaviours when the RLO is dealt with as part of the process.

All the examples above correspond to a prototypical subprocess to be performed by an LMS. In particular, we assume that the full process of designing, composing, and delivering a new learning experience from existing RLOs can be divided into the following subprocesses: gathering data on the learner itself, gathering data on the learner platform, gathering data on the learning objectives to be accomplished, searching and selecting the appropriate RLOs from a repository, composing the new materials from the retrieved objects, assessing the materials, and, finally, delivering the RLOs to the learner. From this list of processes, at least three can be fully automated, and it is not difficult to introduce some degree of automation in the others.

In the following sections, we will see how ontologies can help to design learning management systems capable of adapting their behaviour in a number of situations that will allow human actors to concentrate on tasks that are difficult or impossible to automate. In particular, two recent research lines address the lack of support for automation in current metadata standards and specifications, and rely on ontologies to reach their aim: learning object design by contract and semantic conformance profiles.

Role of Ontologies in Process Descriptions

Ontologies, understood as shared representations of the concepts used in a given domain, formally establish the structures and kinds of objects in the domain, as well as their properties and possible relations. The elements inside an ontology have meaning because of a definition, but also because of the relationships they hold and the potential inferences that can be made from those relationships. Noy and McGuinness (2001) define an ontology as "...a common vocabulary for researchers who need to share information in a domain. It includes machine-interpretable definitions of basic concepts in the domain and relations among them" (p. 1). Therefore, ontologies play an important role wherever there are applications that use the definitions in a domain to process the content of an information item instead of just presenting that information to humans. In this sense, ontologies represent a promising step towards fostering automation in learning management systems, as they can be useful in a number of areas:

1.   Including the notion of learning object type inside an ontology, which is beneficial as it introduces different, specialized metadata description schemas and facilitates pedagogical selection (Sicilia, 2004).

2.   Mapping metadata items to ontology elements will allow definition of specific behaviour linked to each item through logical statements, enabling richer semantic descriptions that would foster inference on metadata descriptions, ontology-based composition, and semantic search.

3.   Defining lists of appropriate values for learning object metadata items (vocabularies), fostering the reasoning capabilities of learning management systems from metadata information.

In particular, the description of explicit types of learning objects inside ontologies would provide a means to formally specify specialized variants of metadata records and implicitly classify learning objects in an arbitrary number of dimensions aimed at pedagogical selection. The main benefits of such approach are the reuse of existing explicit type definitions, and the flexibility in adding implicit categories that can be freely overlapped due to their logical and precise characterization.

However, the reformulation of current metadata schemas in ontology description languages requires the provision of semantic interpretations oriented to providing higher degrees of "machine-understandability." For example, "mandatory" and "recommended" conditions of target users should be clearly separated, and the intended outcomes of a learning object should be expressed through ontology elements in a way that by itself enables the automated design of personalized learning paths.

In this direction, interesting work towards providing a formal and more comprehensive content description of learning resources is being carried out by Bennacer, Bourda, and Doan (2004). Their work, particularly focused on the semantic relationships between learning resources, makes use of ontologies to allow better reusability and retrievals and has adopted OWL (http://www.w3.org/TR/owl-features/) as the language of choice. OWL is a description logics-based ontology language for the Semantic Web developed by the W3C that provides powerful expressiveness as well as computational capabilities for reasoning systems. However, although this work is closely related to ours, it is more specific as it is mainly focused on retrieval and query reasoning capabilities. Our work, which will be described in the following sections, aims at providing the necessary logics to enhance all kinds of reasoning about learning resources, such as adaptation to platform and user requirements or semi-automatic composition of learning contents.

Description of Learning Object Types in Ontological Structures

Knowledge representation requires a representation language; candidates range from natural languages to logic-based languages. Natural languages such as Spanish are very expressive, but also ambiguous and imprecise as some sentences can include not always obvious nuances, idioms, or hidden implications. The rich expressiveness of natural languages can lead to problems. Logic-based languages offer a simplified, more efficient approach to better formulate rules about common concepts. The advantages of logic-based knowledge representation include precision, adequate expressiveness, and a use-neutral representation that makes the represented knowledge more reusable. Ontologies use logic-based languages for concept representation both because they use the represented knowledge in reasoning and because reasoning requires precision of meaning. In the following discussion, CycL will be our ontology language of choice, even though other ontology languages such as OWL and others could also have been used.

OpenCyc (http://www.opencyc.org) is a general knowledge base and commonsense reasoning engine. OpenCyc assertions are written in CycL, a formal language that derives from first-order predicate calculus. In order to express common sense knowledge, the vocabulary of CycL consists of a set of terms, such as constants, non-atomic terms, variables, and other types of objects:

- CycL constants, prefixed by the string '#$', denote specific individuals or collections, such as individual relations, individual people or types of buildings; for example, #$Spain, #$Country or #$isA.

- A CycL formula is a relation applied to some arguments enclosed in parentheses. The formula (#$BirthFn #$JesusChrist) gives us a new term that refers to a particular event: the birth of Jesus Christ.

- A sentence is a well-formulated formula that has a truth value, that is, it is must be either true or false. This is an example of formula: (#$isA #$Spain #$Country).

In OpenCyc, terms are combined into expressions, which are used to make assertions in the knowledge base.

The learning object type has been recently pointed to as a key factor in the automation of a good number of processes: location, composition, selection, and personalization (Sicilia, Pagés et al., 2004). Describing taxonomies of learning objects inside ontological structures allows the clear establishment of the "reasoning" processes that are applicable to each kind of learning object, classifying RLOs in a semantic multidimensional structure aimed at fostering selection processes based in pedagogical criteria. The main benefits derive from having a universally acknowledged and public definition of the type *LearningObject*, as well as the ability to inherit properties from other types in the ontology, and the almost unlimited facility to create new types of learning objects by extending other definitions. Regarding the automation of the subprocesses mentioned in the preceding section, the definition of a hierarchy of learning objects would ease the automation of selection processes based on type. An example follows.

A learner wishes to perform an interactive activity to improve her listening and comprehension skills of spoken Spanish. She feeds the LMS with the basic information on her current skills and the desired type of activity. This information (and any other that would be automatically retrieved, for example, from the platform information) is used by the LMS to look for `Learner-Instructor Interaction`* (in what follows, ontology terms, properties, and other constants are in Courier font) instances in the repositories listed in the LMS settings. `Learner-Instructor Interaction` is a particular type of learning object that expresses interaction as an implication from the fact that the tutor has a role in the learning object execution (`actorInvolved`). This can be defined in OpenCyc like this:

```
(#$implies
    (#$and  (#$isa  ?X  #$LearningObject)
       (#$actorInvolved  ?X  #$Tutor))
    (#$isa  ?X  #$LearnerInstructorInteraction)
)
```

So, if the search engine finds an RLO that ensures the learning objectives set by the learner, and the type of such an object is `LearnerInstructorInteraction` or any of its subtypes, it would be considered a good candidate, and the search will stop here. On the contrary, it would be discarded, and the search process would continue until an appropriate object is found.

Mapping Metadata Items to Ontology Elements

Metadata attributable to any kind of learning object can be defined through properties or functions related to the `LearningObject` class. Using LOM (IEEE LTSC, 2002) as the standard metadata annotation reference, elements such as `title`, `language` and `keywords`, can be mapped to `IDStrings`, connections to `HumanLanguage` instances, and the `topicOfIndividual` predicate, respectively. Other mapping examples for LOM metadata elements are described by Sicilia, García et al. (2004). It is important to mention that the reformulation of current metadata schemas (for example, LOM) in ontology description languages requires the provision of semantic interpretations specifically oriented to providing higher degrees of "machine-understandability."

In the previous example, the RLO found has Spanish as the value for the language element, and this implies two important behaviours. First, the object is selected because it fits in with the learning objectives. Second, the learner platform will be asked to support the Spanish character set before the object can be delivered. Preparing the learner platform to support Spanish is transparent to the user, and is a task automatically launched in the LMS by the semantic implications in the ontology.

As the basis for this example, the language used within the RLO to communicate to the intended user (LOM element 1.3.Language) has to be specified through a binary predicate in OpenCyc, like this:

```
(#$isa #$isInLanguage #$BinaryPredicate)
   (#$arg1Isa #$isInLanguage #$LearningObject)
   (#$arg2Isa #$isInLanguage #$HumanLanguage)
```

Ontology-integrated learning object metadata provides a formal basis to enhanced metadata specification, which can thus enable selection and composition of learning objects based on other consistently specified elements, for example, taking into account cost, keywords, and typical learning time.

Defining Vocabularies

LOM defines vocabulary as "a list of appropriate values for a learning object metadata item." Vocabularies allow controlling the range of values that can be used in completing metadata instances and, for that reason, are useful when computer systems need to identify a RLO from its metadata, as they represent a qualitative step forward compared to textual descriptions. Defining vocabularies inside an ontology helps to establish a universally acknowledged set of values for a given metadata element, which is very helpful, in particular, to automate search processes. But the major difference from the LOM model of lists is the added value through the definition of deeper semantics in describing learning objects, both conceptually and relationally (Qin & Paling, 2001).

Provided that vocabularies are defined inside a given ontology, a number of tasks become easier to automate. Let us think about using the information on the operating system running on the user's computer to select the right version of a RLO. In this case, we would make use of the corresponding LOM vocabulary for the 4.4.1.2.Name element (provided that 4.4.1.1.Type = operating system):

```
pc-dos, mac-os, ms-windows, unix, multi-os, none
```

This vocabulary would be linked to the LOM metadata item OperatingSystemName defined in the ontology. Using DAML+OIL (http://www.daml.org) to define an enumeration class as an example of a simple vocabulary for this element we should obtain something like:

```
<daml:Class  rdf:ID="OperatingSystem">
    <daml:oneOf  rdf:parseType="daml:collection">
        <OperatingSystem  rdf:ID="pc-dos"/>
        <OperatingSystem  rdf:ID="mac-os"/>
        . . .
    </daml:oneOf>
</daml:Class>
```

Considering that the same metadata element can be linked to different vocabularies depending on the application domain or other considerations, OperatingSystemName could be linked to other defined vocabularies. Links between classification systems can be asserted inside Cyc to provide a kind of mapping when disparate classifications are used for objects in similar domains.

Learning Object Design by Contract

Ontology-integrated learning object metadata provides a formal basis to contract-based approaches to metadata specification. Meyer (1996) defines contracts in the following way: "… the Design by Contract theory suggests associating a specification with every software element. These specifications (or contracts) govern the interaction of the element with the rest of the world." Design by Contract, originally a semi-formal method for the specification of objects in Object-Oriented Programming (OOP), has been proposed in recent research studies (Sánchez-Alonso & Sicilia, 2003; Sicilia & Sánchez-Alonso, 2003) as a means of introducing formalization in RLOs by specifying responsibilities and circumstances of use. The innovative contribution of this research is adapting this well-known technique, bringing in new approaches to foster reusability in learning objects.

A Brief Description of the Method

Learning object contracts are used to formally express metadata elements in an assertion-based syntax that can be sketched as follows:

```
rlo   <URI>
      require
            precondition1
            precondition2
            ...
      ensure
            postcondition1
            ...
```

Preconditions under the require label formally indicate the requirements that have to be met before the object can be used. These requirements are classified in three different categories: the learner, the system where the learning object is due to be executed, and the context of use. The format of a precondition assertion is as follows:

```
[level] subject.element(attribute)<operator>
```

Where level refers to the level of priority and can take the values mandatory, recommended or optional. The preconditionId corresponds to one of the mentioned categories (learner –lrn–, system –sys–, and context –ctx–), while element maps to a LOM metadata element. Attribute is an optional information that allows adding additional information. Using this syntax to write a partial learning object contract stating requirements on the operating system would include assertions like:

```
[recommended] sys.operating_system = ms-windows
```

Postconditions, under the ensure label, are specifications on outcomes. Mainly, these outcomes refer to learner knowledge, although other results might also be considered. The format of postconditions is similar to the format of preconditions:

```
subject.element(attribute)<operator>
```

Where postconditionId again corresponds to one of the mentioned categories. It should be noted that postconditions include the so-called *degree of credibility*. This item notes the fact that some learning objects may be credited to be more appropriate than others due to authoritative revisions or evaluation processes, like, for example, the peer-review assessments being carried out in MERLOT. An example of a partial learning object contract including a postcondition might be:

```
lrn.knows (QuickSort_Sorting_Algorithm) [90]
```

To sum up, applying design by contract to RLOs consists of specifying a formula in the form *{C}RLO{O} [θ]* for each learning object. This formula means that using the RLO in a learning context *C*—that includes a description of the learner and system profiles as well as specific context requirements—facilitates the acquisition of some kind of learning outcome *O* to a certain degree of credibility *θ*.

How Design by Contract Benefits Automation Processes

In the preceding sections, we divided the full process of designing, composing, and delivering a new learning experience into seven subprocesses. Three of them were related to gathering data on the learner side: data on the learner itself, data on the learner platform, and data on the learning objectives to be accomplished. These subprocesses precede RLOs search, retrieval, composition, and delivery. We think that these processes are fully automatable, for example, the platform requirements can be gathered by adding introspective features to the LMS. Therefore, if learning object authors incorporated metadata in the form of contracts in RLOs, and the contracts themselves were publicly accessible in the repositories where the RLOs are stored, search engines would easily decide whether a particular RLO matches the data previously gathered. Under these premises, the search process can be automated since it is reduced to a comparison of the assertions in every candidate object with the assertions automatically composed on the learner side.

An example of this follows. Using its introspective capabilities, a LMS has gathered the following data from the user platform:

```
Browser = Netscape v8.0
Operating system = unix
```

This data, together with the rest of the data about the learner and the learning objectives will form a comparison criteria that will be used by the search engine to infer whether a RLO can be considered as appropriate or not. Now, suppose that a RLO with the following contract is found during the search process:

```
rlo <http://www.object-repository.org/ExampleRLO.html>
  require
    recommended sys.requires(browser) >= Netscape8
    mandatory sys.requires(operatingSystem) = unix
    ...
```

This is a promising candidate, as the preconditions in its contract match the searching criteria. In a semi-automated composition process, the search engine will probably include this object in a list of candidates from which a human expert will select the best ones following personal preferences, educational guidelines, and so forth. Another benefit of contracts is the possibility of recommending certain materials to learners according to their profile or previous background. In a complex learning environment, different roles can be defined for the users to play, according to their preferences or skills. In such role-play environments, contracts can be used to express the preconditions that a user must hold before the role can be played and the expected outcomes after the play ends. An example of role modelling through contracts can be a simulation activity aimed at training emergency workers on handling radioactive waste. Performing this activity will increase learner previous practical knowledge, marked in the contract as `lrn.knows(-1)increases`:

```
role <WasteHandlerTrainee>
  require
    mandatory lrn.knows >=Handling_Waste_Theoretical_Basics
    mandatory lrn.language = en
  ensure
    lrn.knows(handleRadioactiveWaste) >
      lrn.knows(-1)(handleRadioactiveWaste) increases [90]
```

The contract presupposes that the learner has previously acquired a theoretical under-standing of the basics of handling waste, as this is a prerequisite in the WasteHandlerTrainee role contract. This is because this role is specifically designed to increase practical knowledge through an activity—where the directions are provided in English—that would be difficult to perform without any previous knowledge. From this contract, an LMS can recommend this course to a learner engaged in a full-training program on emergency activities depending on her knowledge records.

Learning Object Relationships

Learning object relationships, as currently defined in LOM, are a problematic issue. The fact is that a shared consensus does not exist on the kind of relations that can be established between RLOs. On the other hand, a clear determination of the runtime implications of the diverse kinds of relationships is critical to attaining consistent LMS behaviour. In the particular case of a multipart object that is composed of others, delivery must take into account a number of commitments detailed in Sánchez-Alonso and Sicilia (2004b), the most relevant being availability of the parts. This is expressed in a contract as a precondition on the delivery context, like this:

```
rlo <http://../QuickSortLesson.html>

  require

    [mandatory] lrn.language = en

    [mandatory] sys.browser = MS_IExplorer6

    [recommended] ctx.time = 2h

    [mandatory] ctx.hasPart = ("http://../Animation.html")

      ...

  ensure

    lrn.knows(QuickSortAlgorithm) [90]

      ...
```

Stating information on relationships in the aggregates by making use of the value hasPart for the LOM element 7.1.Relation.Kind allows informing on semantic aggregations, which forces LMS to check the related resources. In the example, the full lesson on the QuickSort algorithm includes an animation that displays the partition table state to the learner as an example array is sorted. Before delivering the QuickSortLesson RLO, the LMS will need to check whether *Animation* is available or not, because it will be delivered at any time from then on because it is part of the full lesson, as stated in the above contract.

Semantic Conformance Profiles

The concept of semantic conformance profile (SCP) is a recent proposal for the definition of learning processes in a broad sense, integrating the ideas of learning object design by contract and pointing to the use of ontological structures as an integral part of the definition of the processes. SCPs have been described as a way to specify internal processes required or enacted by learning management systems like RLO location, trading, aggregation or device-adaptation (Sicilia, Pagés, et al., 2004). They are intended to complement existing standards, broadening their scope to operations that are internal to learning management systems, at the same time and providing a contract-based specification that clarifies their runtime semantics. Formal languages and knowledge representations should become an integral part of the approach in order to enable the construction of Semantic Web applications.

An SCP can be defined as a contract-based specification of a basic LMS process, oriented towards its automation. The contractual approach is intended to specify the prerequisites or pre-conditions required for the process to take place, as long as the expected outcomes or post-conditions resulting from its execution. Such an approach clearly delineates the responsibilities the LMS assumes if the required preconditions are satisfied, and thus forms a basis for normative conformance with regards to the effects of the process being carried out.

As a first step towards providing a full catalogue of profiles covering common automation processes, five basic SCPs have been sketched. These basic profiles are not the only possible ones, as they can in turn be used to define more complex SCPs. A brief description of each basic SCP follows:

- PUB-1 (Basic publication): enumerates a number of basic requisites for a learning object to be used through a repository.

- ACQ (Acquisition): this profile describes the automated or semi-automated purchase of an RLO to fulfil a given learning objective inside an LMS.

- CMP-1 (Basic composition): it is intended for situations in which an LMS decides to automatically aggregate two or more RLOs into the same learning-oriented structure.

- U-SEL (User selection): it is aimed at capturing the semantics of targeted searches of an RLO for given needs.

- P-SEL (Platform selection): this profile is intended to select RLOs according to their technical requirements, provided that the LMS is able to self-describe the devices it uses to deliver learning contents.

Semantic conformance profiles are specified in terms of required metadata elements (the metainformation items that are required for the given functionality), metadata idioms (requirements for its specification), and runtime commitments (the actions that are expected to be carried out by the systems that support the functionality). In addition, we need to describe in which points such definitions can be integrated with Semantic Web ontologies, as this enables richer semantic descriptions and, eventually, inference on metadata descriptions. As an example, a basic conformance profile SCP is described in Table 1.

The *Acquisition profile* (ACQ) is intended to describe the automated or semi-automated buy of an RLO to fulfil a given learning objective inside an LMS. The cost, buying conditions, and copyright considerations must be specified in the metadata record to enable the automated transaction. Moreover, such items must be localized or "localizable" to the conditions of the buyer, and the seller system(s) requires a specified protocol P to carry out the transaction (e.g., using an e-commerce infrastructure like ebXML). The LMS can be expected to validate the account to be charged and the proper functioning of the seller, and it should check the conditions and audit the transaction. Finally, the transaction must be justified from the viewpoint of the stakeholder. This latter commitment is largely system-dependant (as denoted by the braces) and may involve complex decision procedures.

Curly braces are used in Table 1 to denote effects that are complex to specify and thus open to different degrees of conformance, due to their inherent vague or multifaceted nature. As a result of profile specification, learning object metadata could be classified according to the profiles that can be fulfilled with a particular metadata record. This way, for example, a learning object with no cost information would not fulfil the criteria of completeness for ACQ shown in Table 1 and would not, consequently, launch the described buying process.

The ACQ(O1, SS1, LMS1) profile is a typical example of LMS-initiated process that is very close to current specifications for B2B e-commerce like *OAGIS* or *RosettaNet*. Basic information needed about the learning object being bought comprises localized cost (not only the fact that it is subject to payment, but its amount) and also copyright and other buying conditions. Note that such specification is complex in the general case, involving rights transfer and legal regulation, as addressed, for example, by the XrML language(http://www.xrml.org). In addition, the seller system SS1 must be available, including complete binding information.

The minimal commitments for the ACQ profile include the following:

- A "Charge Unit" at the buyer (LMS1) should be validated for permission for the transaction.

- Buying conditions must be attainable according to the criteria of LMS1. This entails consideration of available budget.

- The operation must be audited both at LMS1 and SS1 sides, to support traceability of business operations.

- The buy must be "justified" according to some kind of individual or organizational need. This "explainability" of the decision to buy LO1 could be simple or complex, depending on the system, and it ideally connects a "knowledge gap" identified to the knowledge the learning object is supposed to facilitate.

This last consideration of learning objects as commodities requires an explicit account of learning objects outcomes that could be expressed in terms of categorizations or as "post-conditions," as described in learning object contracts. This should be reflected in the profile as part of the {justified} verb information. ACQ processes could be the result of learning object selection processes, in which case the process is explainable in terms of the associated SEL process(es).

Table 1. The ACQ Semantic Conformance Profile

Required Elements	Idioms	Runtime commitments
LOM 6.1. Cost. LOM 6.2. Copyright and other. [Buying conditions] [Seller System]	a) Localized cost and copyright. b) [Seller System] available through a public protocol (P)	a) Charge_Unit validated. b)[Seller System] functioning. c) [Buying conditions] attainable d) Audit enabled. e) Buy {justified}

Conclusion and Future Research Directions

Current e-learning specifications provide a convenient way to achieve interoperability between learning management systems, and they play a critical role in the advancement of the e-learning industry. Nonetheless, metadata in such specifications are usually described in highly general terms, which makes the standardization of LMS behaviour that could be considered "intelligent" difficult. In this chapter, the use of ontologies as a knowledge representation formalism for learning object management has been analyzed, focusing on their realistic integration with existing standards. In addition, a contract-based approach to the design of learning object metadata has been described as an enhancement for existing annotation practices, aimed at providing precise, machine-oriented semantics to metadata records. The concept of semantic conformance profile applies the same philosophy to processes that are common to learning management systems functioning.

The techniques described here can be considered as concrete examples of what can be done in standardizing "intelligent" learning management systems behaviour, understood as functionality that makes use of knowledge representation systems to support diverse levels of advanced functions. Consequently, future work in the direction described here should address the development of standards and specifications that add to existing ones concrete guidelines for the integration of ontologies. Since it is difficult to have only one vision for such integration, the concept of "conformance profile" can be used to produce scenario-oriented specifications, enabling competition among vendors as a result of the existence of diverse specifications with different "degrees of intelligence", that is, that have varying degrees of exploitation of the underlying ontologies.

References

Anido, L.E., Fernández, M. J., Caeiro, M., Santos, J. M., Rodríguez, J. S., & Llamas, M. (2002). Educational metadata and brokerage for learning resources. *Computers & Education, 38*(4), 351-374.

Bennacer, N., Bourda, Y., & Doan, B. (2004). Formalizing for querying learning objects using OWL. In *Proceedings of ICALT 2004, Fourth IEEE International Conference on Advanced Learning Technologies*. Los Alamitos, CA: IEEE Computer Society.

Berners-Lee, T., Hendler, J., & Lassila, O. (2001). The Semantic Web. *Scientific American, 284*(5), 34-43.

Duval, E., Hodgins, W., Sutton, S.A., & Weibel, S. (2002). Metadata principles and practicalities. *D-Lib Magazine, 8*(4). Retrieved June 20, 2005, from *http://www.ao.uiuc.edu/ijet/v3n1/html*

Farance, F. (2003). IEEE LOM standard not yet ready for "prime time." *IEEE LTTF Learning Technology Newsletter, 5*(1), 22-23.

Fensel, D. (2002). Language standardization for the Semantic Web: The long way from OIL to OWL. In *Proceedings of the Fourth International Workshop on Distributed Communities on the Web*, Lecture Notes in Computer Science, 2468 (pp. 215-227). Berlin: Springer-Verlag.

Hamel, C.J. & Ryan-Jones, D. (2002). Designing instruction with learning objects. *International Journal of Educational Technology, 3*(1).

IEEE LTSC (Learning Technology Standards Committee). (2002). Learning object metadata (LOM). IEEE 1484.12.1-2002.

Lytras, M., Tsilira, A., & Themistocleous, M.G. (2003). Towards the semantic e-learning: An ontological oriented discussion of the new research agenda in e-learning. In *Proceedings of the Ninth Americas Conference on Information Systems* (pp. 2985-2997). AIS.

Meyer B. (1996). Building bug-free O-O Software: An introduction to design by contract. *Object Currents, SIGS Publication, 1*(3). Retrieved June 20, 2005, from *http://www.learningcircuits.org/2002/apr2002/mortimer.html*

Mohan, P. & Brooks, C. (2003). Learning objects on the semantic Web. In *Proceedings of ICALT 2003, the Third IEEE International Conference on Advanced Learning Technologies*.

Mortimer, L. (2002). (Learning) Objects of desire: Promise and practicality. *ASTD Learning Circuits*, April.

Noy, N. F. & McGuinness, D. L. (2001). *Ontology development 101: A guide to creating your first ontology*. Stanford Knowledge Systems Laboratory Technical Report KSL-01-05 and Stanford Medical Informatics Technical Report SMI-2001-0880.

Pagés, C., Sicilia, M. A., García, E., Martínez, J. J., & Gutiérrez, J. M. (2003). On the evaluation of completeness of learning object metadata in open repositories. In J. A. Mesa Gonzalez & J. Mesa Gonzalez (Eds.), *Proceedings of the Second International Conference on Multimedia and Information & Communication Technologies in Education (mICTE03)* (pp. 1760-1764).

Polsani, P. R. (2002). Use and abuse of reusable learning objects. *Journal of Digital Information, 3*(4). Retrieved June 20, 2005, from *http://jodi.ecs.soton.ac.uk/Articles/v03/i04/Polsani/*

Qin, J. & Paling, S. (2001). Converting a controlled vocabulary into an ontology: The case of GEM. *Information Research, 6*(2). Retrieved June 20, 2005, from *http://informationr.net/ir/6-2/paper94.html*

Sánchez-Alonso, S. & Sicilia, M. A. (2004a). Relationships and commitments in learning object metadata. In *Proceedings of ITHET 2004, the Fifth International Conference on Information Technology Based Higher Education and Training*.

Sánchez-Alonso, S. & Sicilia, M. A. (2004b). On the semantics of aggregation and generalization in learning object contracts. In *Proceedings of ICALT 2004, the Fourth IEEE International Conference on Advanced Learning Technologies*.

Sicilia, M. A. & Sánchez-Alonso, S. (2003). On the concept of learning object "design by contract." *WSEAS Transactions on Systems, 2*(3), 612-617.

Sicilia, M. A., Pagés, C., García, E., & Sánchez-Alonso, S. (2004). Specifying semantic conformance profiles in reusable learning object metadata. In *Proceedings of ITHET 2004, the Fifth International Conference on Information Technology Based Higher Education and Training* (pp. 900-901). Los Alamitos, CA: IEEE Computer Society.

Sicilia, M.A., García, E., Sánchez-Alonso, S., & Rodríguez, E. (2004). On integrating learning object metadata inside the OpenCyc knowledge base. In *Proceedings of ICALT 2004, the Fourth IEEE International Conference on Advanced Learning Technologies.*

Sosteric, M. & Hesemeier, S. (2002). When is a learning object not an object: A first step towards a theory of learning objects. *International Review of Research in Open and Distance Learning, 3*(2). Retrieved June 20, 2005, from *http://www.irrodl.org/content/v3.2/soc-hes.html*

Stojanovic, L., Staab, S., & Studer, R. (2001). E-learning based on the Semantic Web. In *Proceedings of the World Conference on the WWW and Internet (WebNet 2001)* (pp. 1-10). New York: ACM Press.

Wiley, D. A. (Ed.) (2001). *The instructional use of learning objects*. Bloomington, IN: Association for Educational Communications and Technology.

Endnote

[1]   Curly braces are used to denote effects that are complex to specify and thus open to different degrees of conformance, due to their inherent vague or multifaceted nature.

Chapter XII

The Role of Metadata in E-Learning Systems

Juha Puustjärvi
Lappeenranta University of Technology, Finland

Abstract

The fast development of technologies requires specialised and complex skills that need to be renewed frequently. Thus the role of continuing education and lifelong learning is becoming even more important. E-learning adapts well to continued education, as it can be done in parallel to other work. This in turn sets new requirements for universities: they have to build e-learning infrastructures and course material has to be in digital form. Moreover, the e-learning systems should be designed in a way that they provide easy access to courses and course material. A cornerstone of easy access is the metadata attached to courses and other relevant elements. However, the mere metadata itself is not very useful without the ontology that gives the semantics for the metadata. In this chapter, we will give an overview of the role of metadata and ontologies in e-learning systems. We will also consider the standards of educational metadata and consider the utilization of metadata and ontologies in three e-learning systems.

Introduction

The idea of e-learning offers several interesting advantages for both the universities as course providers and for the students. The main advantage for universities is the possibility of surviving the competition for students by offering courses in their special areas of competence, research, and expertise via the Internet. Students are interested on e-learning as it provides flexible ways to combine work and studying. Thus, e-learning can be defined as an information technology-enabled and supported form of distance learning in which the traditional restrictions of classroom learning have disappeared (Liu, Chan, Hung, & Lee, 2002). Moreover, a virtual university can enhance organizational learning and bring competitive advantages by continuously developing the skills and knowledge of employees (Teare, Davies, & Sandelands, 1999).

Current e-learning systems have been developed at different times; they are based on a variety of technologies; and they may provide very heterogeneous functionalities and user interfaces. However, the learner should be able to access all the virtual universities in a similar way or, more ideally, there should be a global e-learning portal through which a learner could access every virtual university as simply as accessing one. In order to achieve this goal, the e-learning system should support the following functions:

- hide the heterogeneity of various e-learning systems, and
- provide advanced querying and searching features.

The support of these functions requires appropriate technologies, but the technology can only be utilized if learning objects' standardized metadata descriptions and ontologies are commonly used.

In this chapter, we will restrict ourselves to the meaning of metadata and ontologies in the context of e-learning systems. First, we consider different approaches for representing the content and searching learning objects. In particular, we want to emphasize the significance of the type of services the system supports, and thereby motivate the need for advanced searching and querying functions. Then, we give an overview of ontologies and explain why and which kinds of ontologies are required in e-learning systems. Also, the notions of metadata and educational metadata as well as their standardization issues are discussed. The LOM standard is analysed in most detail, as is the most powerful and most widely used metadata standard for educational information systems. Then, three metadata based e-learning systems, namely, the ARIADNE Knowledge Pool-system, the CUBER-system and the ONES-system, are introduced. These systems support metadata-based searching of learning objects, but they have essential differences in the methods they use and the services they provide. Next, we discuss the dynamicity of ontologies. In particular, we consider how the dynamicity of ontologies affects learning objects' metadata descriptions and what kinds of problems it causes for metadata based searching. A solution for the problem is also proposed. Finally, the future trends of metadata and learning object ontologies is discussed.

Figure 1. Relevant documents and retrieved documents

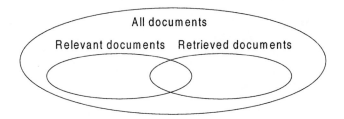

Representing and Searching Learning Objects

The representation and organization of documents (e.g., learning objects) should provide an easy access to the documents. Ideally, the system should be able to retrieve all the documents that are relevant while retrieving as few non-relevant documents as possible (Figure 1).

This kind of quality of information retrieval system is usually measured by the following fractions (Baeza-Yates & Ribeiro-Neto, 1999):

- **Recall:** the fraction of the relevant documents that have been retrieved.

- **Precision:** the fraction of the retrieved documents that are relevant.

The values of these fractions are highly dependent on the way the query and the content of document are presented. In order to illustrate this, we distinguish between three approaches for representing queries and the content of documents: *full-text indexing, extracted keywords, and weighted keywords.*

Full-Text Indexing

Document content is traditionally represented through keywords, which are extracted directly from the document. It is also possible to represent the document by first automatically eliminating its articles, connectives, adjectives, adverbs, and verbs and then extracting all its remaining words to keywords. In such a case, we say that a document is represented by full-text indexing.

Assume now that full-text indexing is applied to learning object descriptions. Hence, the description of each learning object is a set of keywords. Now, if a learner is interested in learning objects focusing on Web technologies, he enters the keyword "Web technologies." Then the search engine returns all the learning objects where the keyword "Web technologies" is stated.

Probably the quality of this retrieval is not very good. For example, a document containing the statement "Web technologies will not be considered in this course" will be returned. On the other hand, it is obvious that there may be a lot of documents discussing Web technologies but without explicitly stating that term. So the probability of missing many relevant documents is rather high.

Extracted Keywords

Within full indexing a reason for missing many relevant documents is that the keywords used with queries and documents descriptions are not standardized. In order to standardize semantic metadata, specific ontologies are introduced in many disciplines. Typically, such ontologies are hierarchical taxonomies of terms describing certain topics. For example, in Figure 2, an ontology for learning objects is presented.

Now, if this ontology is used and a learner is interested in learning objects focusing on Web technologies, he picks from the hierarchy the keywords that he considers to be related to Web technologies (e.g., XML, XML-schema and Semantic Web) and enters them into the retrieval system. (It is also possible to increase the expression power of the query by representing it by a Boolean expression [Baeza-Yates & Ribeiro-Neto, 1999], where the keywords are connected by "and," "or," and "not" operands.) Then, the retrieval system returns the documents having one or more of the keywords in their description. Now the recall and precision fractions are obviously higher than with full indexing, as the same keywords are used in queries and documents descriptions.

Weighted Keywords

The weighted keywords approach differs from the extracted keywords approach only in that weights are assigned to the extracted keywords such that the sum of the weights equals to one. Mathematically, such a description is a vector. Hence, each document

Figure 2. An ontology for learning objects

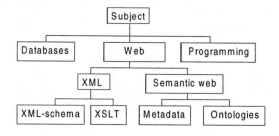

description and learner's query is a vector, that is, a point in the vector space determined by the nodes in the ontology hierarchy. The answer of a query is an order list of learning objects where the order is determined according to the distance between a query and the document. The idea behind the weighted keywords approach (i.e., the vector model) is that it is possible to define queries and documents' descriptions more accurately. For example, the learner who is interested in courses focusing on Web technologies may give weight 0.3 to XML, 0.2 to XML-Schema and 0.5 to Semantic Web. As a result of the query, the documents are sorted in the order determined by the similarity, that is, the document having the best match with the query is presented first. The number of the documents in the result should be restricted by requiring a certain degree of similarity.

Ontologies for Learning Objects

An ontology provides a general vocabulary of a certain domain (Fridman Noy & McGuinness, 2001), and it can be defined as "an explicit specification of a conceptualisation" (Gruber, 1993). So ontologies provide a systematic way to standardize the used metadata items, that is, they provide a shared and common understanding of the metadata items (Davies, Fensel, & Harmelen, 2002).

Essentially, the used ontology must be shared and consensual terminology, as it is used for information sharing and exchange. A salient feature of ontologies is that—depending on the generality level of conceptualization—different types of ontologies are needed. Each type of ontology has a specific role in information sharing and exchange. In accordance with the increasing expression power of ontologies, we distinguish between four types of ontologies (Daconta, Orbst, & Smith, 2003): taxonomy, thesaurus, conceptual model and logical theory (Figure 3).

Taxonomy

We already discussed the used of hierarchical taxonomies in the context of searching learning objects. In a taxonomy, as we have seen, the semantics of the relationship

Figure 3. The ontology system

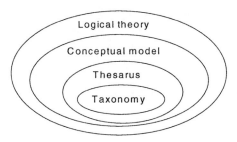

between a parent and a child node are relatively underspecified. Typically, the relationship is the *subclass of* relation or the *part of* relation. For example, in Figure 2, the relationship between the node Semantic Web, and its children Ontology and Metadata is *part of* rather than *subclasses of* as the node Semantic Web may also have other subclasses.

Thesarus

A thesaurus differs from a taxonomy in that the relationships between terms are clearly displayed and identified by standardized relationship indicators. The relationships are *equivalence, homographic, hierarchical,* and *associative.*

The primary purpose of *equivalence* and *homograph* in the context of e-learning systems is to manage semantic heterogeneity, namely, the cases where different terms are used with the same meaning and vice versa. For example, it may be necessary to state that "Database course" is equivalent with "DB-course" (equivalence) or that the course "Principles of Programming" within the examination of Mathematics and within the examination of Physics is not the same course (homographs).

Hierarchical relationships can be used to specify the relationships between a parent and its children (hierarchic parent of), or between a child and its parent (hierarchic child of). For example, we can specify that the term XML is broader than XSLT, or that XSLT is narrower than XML. Associative relationship between two terms means that there are some unspecified relationships between the two terms. For example, a book may be associated with a course.

Conceptual Model

A conceptual model has more expression power than a thesaurus has. Essentially, a conceptual model is a model of a domain. It represents the primary entities of the domain, their relationships, and the attributes of the entities. The process of designing a conceptual schema begins with an analysis of what information the ontology must hold and the relationships among the entities. The structure of the conceptual schema is specified in one of several languages or notations suitable for expressing design, for example, entity-relationship (ER-model) (Ullman, 1998), Object Definition Language (ODL) (Ullman & Widom, 1998), and Unified Modelling Language (UML) (Ullman & Widom, 1998).

In the context of learning, a conceptual model may specify, for example, that a course may have one or more lecturer and that each course has a name, a unique code, and credit units. It is also possible to specify the execution order of the courses and the structures of the examinations.

Logical Theory

The main idea behind representing ontologies as logical theories is that some ontology tools can perform automatic reasoning using ontological theories and hence provide advanced services to intelligent applications. Logical theories are built on axioms and inference rules, which, in turn, are together used to prove theorems about the domain. Logical theories can be specified by the ontology languages (e.g., DAML+OIL and OWL) developed for the Semantic Web (Daconta, Orbst, & Smith, 2003).

Representational and Domain Ontologies

The previous classification of ontologies is based on the expression power of ontologies. It is also useful to classify ontologies based on their use. Hence, we also make a distinction between representational and domain ontologies.

- Representational ontologies provide representational entities without stating what should be represented, that is, they do not commit to any particular domain. For example, the ODL-language and the ER-model, which define concepts such as entities, attributes, and relations, can be considered as representational ontologies.
- Domain ontologies capture the knowledge valid for a particular type of domain, for example, on learning domain.

Further, we divide domain ontologies into two subclasses:

- Domain meta-ontology, which captures the model or schema of the domain. For example, an ER-schema capturing knowledge of learning objects is a domain meta-ontology.
- Domain instance ontologies represent an instance of a domain meta-ontology. For example, a list of courses represented according to an ER-schema is domain instance ontology.

Metadata and Educational Metadata Standards

Metadata

The term metadata has variable interpretations depending upon the circumstances in which it is used. In short, metadata is "data about data." Metadata can also be defined as descriptive and classifying information about the object. It describes certain important characteristics of its target in a compact form. Further, metadata can be described by meta-metadata, which is descriptive information of the metadata itself.

Metadata can be classified in many ways. For example, metadata can be divided into *structural metadata, descriptive metadata,* and *semantic metadata.* Structural metadata describes the structural characteristics of object, such as the format of the object. A salient feature of descriptive metadata (e.g., language and author) is that it is external to the meaning of the document, that is, it describes the creation of the document rather than the content of the document.

The metadata describing the content of the document is commonly called semantic metadata. For example, the keywords attached to many scientific articles represent semantic metadata. Hence, the notions of *extracted keywords* and *weighted keywords* also represent semantic metadata. To standardize descriptive and semantic metadata, specific taxonomies and ontologies are introduced in many disciplines.

Dublin Core

The Dublin Core metadata elements represent descriptive metadata. They are intended to facilitate discovery of electronic resources, especially from the Web. Dublin Core (http://www.dublin.core.org) is a widely known metadata standard that has been developed since 1995 by a series of workshops. The standard includes 15 metadata elements that describe the content, the intellectual property rights, and the instantiation of the object. For example, the standard includes the following elements: Creator, Date, Description, Subject, and Language. Although the Dublin Core does not contain any educational metadata elements, it has been used as a basis for many educational metadata projects. In addition, proposals to extend the standard by educational elements have been done. For example, the proposed extensions include the following educational elements: Audience, Interactivity type, Interactivity level, and Typical learning time.

Educational Metadata

Educational metadata describes any kind of educational objects, such as study courses. The pedagogical features of the course, the contents, special target groups, and the technical requirements of the study course can be described with the help of educational metadata. Well-designed and sufficient metadata facilitates the learners' decision-making process and aids the educational institutions to provide suitable information about their course supply. Educational metadata is, by nature, semantic metadata. It can be used by educational institutes and professionals as well as by learners in order to describe, for example, the content, structures, and relationships of the learning objects and to search for educational objects (Stojanovic, Staab, & Studer, 2001).

Educational metadata is needed to improve the retrieval of learning objects, to support the management of collections of learning objects, and to support the decision process of the learners looking for educational resources. Metadata is also useful when guiding non-experienced users through a large collection of learning resources (Strijker, 2001). LOM is the most powerful and most widely used metadata standard for educational information systems (Lamminaho, 2000).

Learning Object Metadata (LOM) Standard

The main aim of standardization is to achieve interoperability between systems from different origins. A standard does not impose a particular implementation but, rather, a common specification that establishes an opportunity for collaboration by diverse groups.

Learning object metadata (LOM) standard (LOM, 2002) specifies a conceptual model that defines the structure of a metadata instance for a learning object. A learning object is defined as any entity—digital or non-digital—that may be used for learning. The main purpose of the LOM standard is to facilitate search and use of learning objects, for instance, by automated software processes. In addition, the standard facilitates the sharing and exchange of learning objects by enabling the development of catalogues and inventories while taking into account the diversity of cultural and lingual contexts in which the learning object and their metadata will be exploited.

In LOM, the metadata elements describing a learning object are grouped into categories. The categories are:

a.   The *General* category, which groups the general information that describes the learning object as a whole. For example, the metadata elements *title, language,* and *keywords* belong to this category.

b.   The *Lifecycle* category, which groups the features related to the history and current state of the learning object and those who have affected the learning object during its evolution. For example, the metadata elements *contribute* (e.g., people or organizations that have contributed the learning objects), *role of contribution,* and *date of contribution* belong to this category.

c.   The *Meta-Metadata* category, which groups the information about the metadata instance itself rather than the learning object that the metadata instance describes. This category describes how the metadata instance can be identified, and who created the metadata instance. For example, the metadata element *metadata schema* (the name and version of the authoritative specification used to create the metadata instance) belongs to this category.

d.   The *Technical* category, which groups the technical requirements and technical characteristics of the learning object. For example, the metadata elements *size* (the size of the digital learning object in bytes) and *requirements* (the technical capabilities necessary for using the learning object) belong to this category.

e.   The *Educational* category, which groups the educational and pedagogic characteristics of the learning object. For example, the metadata elements *Interactivity Type* (predominant mode of learning supported by the learning object), *Difficulty* (how hard it is to work with or through the learning object for the typical intended target audience) and *Semantic Density* (the degree of conciseness of a learning object) belong to this category.

f.   The *Rights* category, which groups the intellectual property rights and conditions of use for the learning object. For example, the metadata elements *cost* (whether the use of the learning object requires payment) and *copyright* (whether copyright or other restrictions apply to the use of this learning object) belong to this category.

g.   The *Relation* category groups features that define the relationship between the learning object and other related learning objects. For example, the metadata element *kind* belongs to this category. The possible values of this element may be, for example, *is part of, is version of*, and *is based on*. To define multiple relationships, there may be multiple instances of this category.

h.   The *Annotation* category provides comments on the educational use of the learning object and information on when and by whom the comments were created. This category enables educators to share their assessments of learning objects and suggestions for use. For example, the data elements *entity* (e.g., people or organization that created the annotation) and *description* (the content of the annotation) belong to this category.

i.   The *Classification* category describes the learning object in relation to a particular classification system, for example, the ACM classification. To define multiple classifications, there may be multiple instances of this category.

IMS Global Learning Consortium's Metadata Specifications

Instructional Management System (IMS) Project (IMS, 2002) is a global consortium of several educational institutions, commercial entities, government agencies, and developers in the area of distance education. The aim of IMS is to develop and promote open specifications for facilitating online distributed learning activities such as locating and using educational content, tracking learner progress, reporting learner performance, and exchanging student records between administrative systems.

IMS is a major contributor to the LOM. It has introduced the use of XML for representing metadata. IMS also uses the LOM as its basis for metadata work. IMS has also contributed to LOM by introducing best practice guides for metadata developers and implementers.

Metadata-Based E-Learning Systems

In this section, three metadata-based e-learning systems are introduced and compared. The systems are the ARIADNE Knowledge Pool System (ARIANDE, 2001), the CUBER System (Personalized Curriculum Builder in the Federated Virtual University of the Europe of Regions) (CUBER, 2002), and the ONES System (One-Stop e-Learning Portal) (Puustjärvi & Pöyry, 2003). They all support metadata-based searching of learning objects. However, they have essential differences in the way they are implemented and in the services they provide. Through these systems, we will illustrate and analyse how the ingredients of a metadata-based e-learning system (paradigms, methods, technologies) can be put together to form a working system. In particular, we will view these systems from information retrieval models, architectures, and metadata standards points of view. We first present a short comparison of the design principles of these systems. A more detailed description of these systems is given in later sections.

- **Information retrieval model:** The ARIADNE Knowledge Pool System and the CUBER System is based on the Boolean-model, whereas the ONES System is based on the vector-model.

- **Architecture:** The ARIADNE Knowledge Pool System is based on a distributed database, the CUBER System is based on a centralized knowledge base, whereas the ONES System is a distributed system based on a mediator.

- **Metadata standards:** The ARIADNE Knowledge Pool System is based on extended LOM standard, the CUBER System is based on the LOM standard, whereas the ONES System is based on LOM and on specific ontologies that extend the LOM.

ARIADNE Knowledge Pool System

The Ariande Project (ARIANDE, 2002) was focused on developing tools and methodologies for enabling computer-based education. The ARIADNE Knowledge Pool System (ARIANDE, 2001) is a distributed repository for learning objects that encourages the share and reuse of learning objects. An indexation and query tool uses a set of metadata elements to describe and enable search functionality on learning objects.

The repository contains about 4000 metadata instances for learning objects from different science types, languages, contexts, and granularities. The instances are described in nine human languages of the multilingual ARIADNE community.

A result of the project is the metadata work carried out in order to enable and facilitate producing, managing, and reusing the pedagogical elements. The project has also analysed metadata information provided by indexers when they introduce new learning objects into the Knowledge Pool System. The analysis gave a clear indication about their understanding of metadata elements and their values.

The project has used LOM as its basis. Particularly, the project has added more educational metadata elements to the original LOM schema. In order to ensure simplicity and adaptability, metadata elements are grouped into six categories (Najjar, Ternier, & Duval, 2003):

a. **General:** groups the general information that describes the learning objects, such as document title and document language.

b. **Semantics:** groups elements that describe the semantic classification of the learning object, like the science type, main discipline, and subdiscipline.

c. **Pedagogical:** groups elements that describe the pedagogical and educational characteristics of the learning object, such as semantic density and interactivity.

d. **Technical:** groups elements that describe the technical requirements and characteristics of the learning object, like operation system version and required disk space.

e. **Indexation:** groups elements that describe the general information about the metadata itself of the learning object, such as the identifier of the metadata instance, metadata creation date, and creator.

f. **Annotations:** groups elements that describe people or organization notes about learning objects, like annotator, language of annotations, and date of annotation.

The CUBER System

The CUBER System (Pöyry, Pelto-Aho, & Puustjärvi, 2002; Pöyry & Puustjärvi, 2003) is designed to become a broker system that supports the search for study courses from European universities. It facilitates the access of various kinds of learners to a vast collection of higher education courses offered by European course providers, in particular by distance teaching universities.

The CUBER System has been designed to be a search engine or a broker system that enables many kinds of potential students to search for study units from institutions providing higher education. CUBER aims at matching the needs of the learners with characteristics of the courses offered by the universities. The architecture of the CUBER System consists of three main components: knowledge base, search engine, and authoring interface (Figure 4).

The knowledge base is a centralized database that includes the metadata descriptions of the learning objects and an ontology describing a conceptual schema of learning objects. The used metadata elements follow the LOM standard. Fundamentally, the ontology provides a shared and common understanding of CUBER's metadata items, which is necessary for a fruitful communication between learners and the CUBER system

The basic elements of the conceptual schema (ontology) are learning objects.

There are four types of learning objects: programme, package, course, and material. These can include each other in the following ways: Material is its own element. Course can contain material. Package consists of courses and might include other packages. Programme consists of packages and courses, but can contain another programme (for

Figure 4. The architecture of the CUBER system

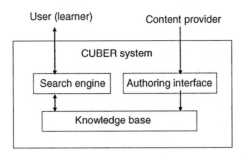

example, a B.Sc. programme can be included in an M.Sc. programme). All the learning objects (e.g., a course or a course package) have metadata attached to them. All of these metadata fields and their corresponding data types are defined in a separate metadata specification.

Through the authoring interface, the content provider (e.g., a teacher) attaches metadata descriptions for learning objects. As the information retrieval model of the CUBER System is the Boolean model, the description is comprised of a set of keywords. Also, a learner represents queries by a set of keywords and the search engine then returns the learning objects having at least one of the entered keywords.

The ONES System

The main goal of the ONES System (Puustjärvi, 2004) is to integrate e-learning systems in a way that the learner can access the integrated systems as a single system. Consequently, the main functions of the ONES System are the following: (1) to hide the distribution and heterogeneity of e-learning systems, (2) to allow the reusability of learning objects, and (3) to provide advanced querying and searching support..

The ONES System deploys many new technologies and paradigms such as Web services (Newcomer, 2002), mediators (Garcia-Molina, Ullman, & Widom, 2000), Resource Description Framework (RDF) (Davies et al., 2002), Resource Description Language Schema (RDFS) (Davies et al., 2002) and OWL Web Ontology Language (Daconta et al., 2003).

Metadata Elements in ONES

The ONES System is based on LOM. However, certain querying and searching features have required minor extensions to LOM. First, a new data element, called subject is introduced. Second, the types of list the LOM supports are extended. The LOM standard supports the following lists:

- **Ordered list:** the order in which data items appear in the list is significant, and
- **Unordered list:** the order of the data elements in the list bears no meaning.

These types are extended by introducing weighted unordered list. In particular, the value of the data element (attribute) *subject* is weighted unordered list. So the weighted keywords can be exploited.

The ONES System deploys multiple representational and domain ontologies. OWL, RDF Schema, and Object Definition Language (ODL) are used as a representational ontology. Further, there is a domain meta-ontology called *learning object ontology* and a domain instance ontology called *subject ontology*.

The *learning object ontology* is represented by ODL. This ontology is rather simple in that it consists of two classes, called *learning_object* and *profile_element*. The attributes of the class *learning_object* are the data elements defined in the LOM. The class *learning_object* has two relationships: *precedes* and *includes*. Using these ingredients, it is possible to model the structures of larger learning objects (e.g., examinations) and the constraints concerning the execution orders of learning objects.

The class *learning_object* has a many-to-many type relationship to the class *profile_element*, which has the attributes *weight* and *node*. Using this class, it is possible to specify the profile of a learning object, namely, a weighted unordered list.

Subject ontology describes the terms that can be used in the profiles of learning objects. Originally, the Subject ontology is the ACM Computing Classification System, which is used to standardize the keywords attached to articles of computer science. Similar to the ontology presented in Figure 2, it is a hierarchy (a tree) in which the nodes represent the used keywords.

LOM provides rather rich expression power to attach metadata to learning objects. However, in some cases, there may be a need to attach such data elements to learning objects that are not defined in LOM. In order to allow such flexibility the ONES System deploys RDF and RDF Schema. RDF provides a means for attaching semantics to a resource (e.g., on a learning object) without making any assumptions about its structure. The relationship of XML (Harold & Means, 2002) and RDF is that XML provides a way to express RDF-statements. A RDF-statement may express, for example, that the lecturer of the previous Database course was John Smith or that the language of the Database course has been changed to English.

Although RDF defines a language for attaching semantics to resources in terms of named properties and values, it provides no mechanisms for modelling these properties; that is the role of RDF vocabulary description language, RDF Schema (a representational ontology). It defines classes and properties that may be used to describe classes, properties and other resources. Hence, there is a straight correspondence between RDF schema and object oriented design languages (e.g., ODL).

OWL Web Ontology Language has more facilities for expressing meaning and semantics than RDF and RDF Schema, and thus OWL goes beyond these languages in its ability to represent machine interpretable content on the Web. In particular, it adds more vocabulary for describing properties and classes, for example, relations between classes, cardinality of relationships, and equality of classes and instances. OWL provides three increasingly expressive sublanguages—OWL Lite, OWL DL, and OWL Full—designed for use by specific communities of implementers and users. In ONES, OWL is mainly used for managing semantic heterogeneity. In particular, the following OWL Lite language constructions are used in modelling the semantic heterogeneity of local e-learning systems:

- **equivalentClass:** Two classes may be stated to be equivalent. For example 'course' can be stated to be equivalentClass to 'learning-object.'

- **equivalentProperty:** Two properties may be stated to be equivalent. For example, 'isPredecessor' may be stated to be the equivalentProperty to 'precedes.'

- **sameAs:** Two individuals may be stated to be the same. For example, 'DB-course' may be stated to be the same individual as 'Database-course.'

OWL Lite is also used for specifying ontology inclusions. The inclusion construction is needed as single e-learning systems cannot join to ONES System before their ontology includes the Ones ontology. After the inclusion-operation is performed, the above language constructions are used to solve the possible semantic heterogeneity.

Incrementality of Ontologies

A feature of ontologies is that they are more or less incremental. That is, as the domain of the ontology changes, the ontology must also be updated accordingly. In particular, as new concepts emerge, they must be included into the appropriate ontologies. For example, by adding the concept "XML-databases" to the ontology presented in Figure 2, we get the ontology presented in Figure 5.

An interesting feature of this ontology is that it is no longer a tree. Instead, as the concept "XML-databases" has two parents, the structure is a directed acyclic graph. Omitting one of these parents would keep the tree structure, but it would not be semantically correct.

This simple example shows that even though many domain ontologies are originally trees they may become directed acyclic graphs after a new concept is inserted to the structure. The main problem of this incremental feature lies in that we cannot compute the distance of a query and a document if their profiles (vectors) are not specified against the same ontology (vector space).

We can solve this problem by using a profile reducer, which decreases the dimensions of a vector in a way that it corresponds to an earlier version of the ontology. To illustrate this, assume that a user defines a query against the extended subject ontology and the documents profiles are specified against the original subject ontology. Assume that in user's query (vector), the node "XML-databases" has weight 0.6. Now this weight is inserted to its parent nodes so that the weights of the Databases-node and the XML-node are increased by 0.3. We can also state this exactly as follows: if there is weight w, on concept t, which does not appear in the earlier ontology, and t has n parents in the ontology, then the weights of each t's parent is increased by w/n. This practice ensures that the sum of the weights of the new reduced vector equals to one (assuming that the sum of the weights of the original vector equals to one).

Future Trends in Using Learning Objects' Metadata

So far, we have mainly discussed the use of metadata in the context of searching learning objects. Metadata can also be used for other purposes, such as learning object reusability, automatic composing of learning objects into larger units, and sophisticated query processing. Such features, however, cannot be implemented based on the current standards like LOM and Dublin Core, as they do not provide enough semantics of learning objects. Therefore, a standard that would give semantics for the concepts related to learning objects (i.e., standardized ontology for learning objects) would be of high importance. For now, in the absence of standard ontologies, single e-learning systems develop their own ontologies.

The use of standard learning object ontology would ensure that the concepts in various e-learning systems would share the same semantics. This in turn would allow searches spanning over e-learning systems and including automatic reasoning. In addition, the ontology would allow flexible way for composing larger learning objects of single objects located at different e-learning systems. The composition also brings a new problem: what is an appropriate size for a learning object? Basically, object size could be a paragraph, topic, section, chapter, lesson, or a course. From objects reusability point of view, smaller objects allow more reusability. On the other hand, small object size increase the burden of producing metadata descriptions as each unit must have its own metadata description; otherwise automatic composition would not be possible.

The composition of learning objects also allows learner-specific courses. Such courses would be very useful, but, on the other hand, personalized courses set strong require-

Figure 5. An extended ontology for learning objects

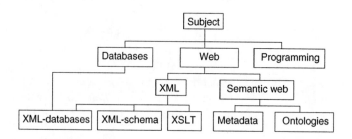

ments on learning objects metadata, learning objects ontology, and on the way personalized object is described. It is not enough that the application only returns a set of learning objects, but the objects must also have an appropriate sequence. In addition, in composing objects the application should have information about learner's previous courses and how they are related to other courses.

Conclusion

E-learning sets new requirements for universities—they have to build global learning infrastructures, course material has to be in digital form, and learners must have access to various virtual universities. Separate e-learning systems may provide very heterogeneous functionalities and user interfaces. However, the learner should be able to access all the virtual universities in a similar way, or more ideally, there should be a global e-learning portal through which a learner could access every virtual universities as simply as one. In order to achieve this goal, the integrated e-learning system should hide the heterogeneity of various e-learning systems and provide advanced querying and searching features. The support of these functions require appropriate technologies, but the technology can only be utilized if learning objects' standardized metadata descriptions and ontologies are commonly used.

Ontologies provide a systematic way to standardize the metadata items. Essentially, the used ontology must be shared and consensual terminology, as it is used for information sharing and exchange. A salient feature of ontologies is that, depending on the generality level of conceptualization, different types of ontologies are needed. Each type of ontology has a specific role in information sharing and exchange.

The term metadata has variable interpretations depending upon the circumstances in which it is used. Educational metadata describes any kind of educational objects, such as study courses. The pedagogical features of the course, the contents, special target groups, and the technical requirements of the study course can be described with the help of educational metadata. Well-designed and sufficient metadata facilitates the learners' decision-making process and aids the educational institutions in providing suitable information about their course supply.

The main aim of standardization is to achieve interoperability between systems from different origins. A standard does not impose a particular implementation but, rather, a common specification that establishes an opportunity for collaboration by diverse groups. The LOM (Learning Object Metadata) standard specifies a conceptual model that defines the structure of a metadata instance for a learning object. A learning object is defined as any entity—digital or non-digital—that may be used for learning. The main purpose of the LOM standard is to facilitate search and use of learning objects, for instance by automated software processes. A deficiency of the LOM standard is that it does not provide enough semantics of learning objects. Therefore, a standard ontology that would give semantics for the concepts related to learning object would be of high importance.

References

ARIADNE (2001). ARIADNE Foundation. Retrieved from *http://ARIADNE-eu.org/*

ARIADNE (2002). The ARIADNE Project. Retrieved from *http://ariadne.unil.ch/Metadata*

Baeza-Yates, R. & Ribeiro-Neto, B. (1999). *Modern information retrieval.* New York: Addison Wesley.

Cuber (2002). Personalized curriculum builder in the federated virtual university of the Europe of Regions. Retrieved from *htttp://www.cuber.net*

Daconta, M., Obrst, L., & Smith, K. (2003). *The Semantic Web.* Indianapolis, IN: John Wiley & Sons.

Davies, J., Fensel, D., & Harmelen, F. (2002). *Towards the Semantic Web: Ontology driven knowledge management.* West Sussex, UK: John Wiley & Sons.

Fridman Noy, N. & McGuinness, D. L. (2001). *Ontology development: A guide to creating your first ontology.* Stanford Knowledge Systems Laboratory Technical Report KSL-01-05, Stanford Medical Informatics Technical Report SMI-2001-0880.

Garcia-Molina, H., Ullman, J., &. Widom, J. (2000). *Database system implementation.* Englewood Cliffs, NJ: Prentice Hall.

Gruber, T.R. (1993). Toward principles for the design of ontologies used for knowledge sharing. *Padua workshop on Formal Ontology.*

Harold, E.R. & Means, W.S. (2002). *XML in a Nutshell.* Sebastapol, CA: O'Reilly & Associates.

IMS Global Learning Consortium. (2002). Retrieved from *http://www.imsproject.org/metadata/index.html*

Lamminaho, V. (2000). *Metadata specification: Forms, menus for description of courses and all other objects.* CUBER Project: Deliverable D3.1.

Liu, J., Chan, S., Hung, A., & Lee, R. (2002). Facilitators and inhibitors of e-learning. In L.C. Jain, R.J. Howlett, N.S. Ichalkaranje & G. Tonfoni (Eds.), *Virtual environments for teaching and learning: Series on innovative intelligence* (Vol. 1, pp. 75-109). Singapore: World Scientific.

LOM—Learning Object Metadata. (2002). Retrieved from *http://ltsc.ieee.org/doc/wg12/LOM_1484_12_1_v1_Final_Draft.pdf*

Najjar, J., Ternier, S., & Duval, E. (2003). The actual use of metadata in ARIADNE: An empirical analysis. In *Proceedings of the Third Annual ARIADNE Conference* (pp. 20-21). Leuven, Belgium: K.U.Leuven,

Newcomer, E. (2002). *Understanding Web services.* Boston: Addison-Wesley.

Pöyry, P., Pelto-Aho, K., & Puustjärvi, J. (2002). The role of metadata in the CUBER system. In *Proceedings of the Annual Conference of the SAICSIT 2002* (pp. 172-178).

Pöyry, P. & Puustjärvi, J. (2003). CUBER: A personalised curriculum builder. In *Proceedings of the Third IEEE International Conference on Advanced Learning Technologies (ICALT 2003)* (pp. 326-327).

Puustjärvi, J. (2004). Integrating e-learning systems. In *Proceedings of the International Conference on Web-Based Education (WBE2004)* (pp. 417-421).

Puustjärvi, J. & Pöyry, P. (2003). Searching learning objects from virtual universities. In *Proceedings of the International Workshop on Multimedia Technologies in e-Learning and Collaboration (WOMTEC)*.

Stojanovic, L., Staab, S., & Studer, R. (2001). E-learning based on the Semantic Web. In *Proceedings of WebNet2001—World Conference on the WWW and Internet*, Orlando, FL.

Strijker, A. (2001). Using metadata for re-using material and providing user support tools. In *Proceedings of ED-MEDIA 2001*, Tampere, Finland.

Teare, R., Davies, D., & Sandelands, E. (1999). *The virtual university—An action paradigm and process for workplace learning.* Cassell Publishing.

Ullman, J. & Widom, J. (1998). *Principles of database systems.* Englewood Cliffs, NJ: Prentice Hall.

Chapter XIII

AWLA:
A Writing
E-Learning Appliance

Manuel Ortega Cantero
Universidad de Castilla La Mancha, Spain

Pedro Pablo Sánchez-Villalón
Paseo de la Universidad, Spain

Abstract

As e-learning gets more widespread, its definition is becoming more distinctive, implying the use of the Web for learning. The Web's original functionality was to provide access to materials located in servers. This has been the core strategy for e-learning. However, the Web is becoming more versatile. The new interactive Web functionalities are organized in services offered to users. The content-based Learning Management Systems are evolving into more interactive systems providing agent-like learning services rather than only learning content. By designing an interactive environment with a learning objective, we can develop an effective e-learning appliance: the application of strategic Web functionalities on a technologically enhanced learning environment. Designed under the constructivist perspective, A Writing e-learning Appliance (AWLA) is an organized set of interactive Web-based utilities that, when applied in a technologically enhanced learning environment, allow learners to develop their writing skill in language learning and fulfil writing activities in any other discipline, both individually and in collaboration.

Introduction

Education has been enhanced by the use of technologies as they have progressively appeared. Pen, paper, blackboards, and printed books are common in traditional class-rooms. New technologies such as audiovisual devices and photocopiers have also helped to improve the learning environment. The advent of the Internet and the Information and Communication Technologies (ICT) is influencing learning in a fast qualitative way. Learning is based on information and communication; computers even supported the learning environment in the first instance and were seen as the panacea for self-directed learning and distance learning. The evolution of computing into a more ubiquitous and interactive application to learning involves an exponential change. Information-based tools such as diskettes and CD-ROMs, which led to Computer Based Instruction (CBI) and Computer-Assisted Learning (CAL), were enhanced with commu-nication capabilities first in intranet-extranet systems and finally with the Internet. Thus, information and communication technologies integrated in the learning environment offer new possibilities and potential for learning. By analysing the technological, organizational, and pedagogical aspects of the evolution of the technologically en-hanced learning environments into e-learning, we present an innovative Web-based writing environment for learning that provides learning not only with easy access to content or to learning objects but also with a socially interactive tool to internalize the ability to communicate through writing on the Web.

Definitions and
Implications of E-Learning

Although a broad definition of e-learning refers to new online ways of learning (European Commission, 2002), it currently involves using electronic technologies to deliver learning content and facilitate interactive learning resources. Clark (2003) points out the interac-tion feature and claims that e-learning exploits interactive technologies and communica-tion systems to improve the learning experience. The Learning and Teaching Support Network (LTSN) Generic Centre (LTSN, 2003) defines e-learning as "learning facilitated and supported through the use of information and communication technologies (ICT)," being essential that it is "pedagogically sound, learner-focussed and accessible by all." It includes digital content, it is experienced through a technology interface, and it is Internet-enabled (Zastroky, 2000). E-learning may be implemented in various ways, depending on the aspects on which it focuses: technological, organisational, or peda-gogical aspects.

Technological Aspects

Before the emergence of the Internet, to be online was to use network-connected computers. However, the application of Computer-Mediated Communication (CMC) technology has been scarce in schools. Previous attempts to adapt the classroom to a computer room when trying to implement Computer-Based Instruction (CBI) and, in particular, Computer-Assisted Language Learning (CALL) have not been as successful as expected (Warschauer, 1997). Providing classrooms with networked computers does not, in and of itself, make e-learning. The integration of computers into the traditional classroom has been difficult. The computing components used in the classroom (mainly Desktop PCs) seem to hinder the learning activity (Ortega et al., 2001). The result is that students always work alone, both in class or using the computer from a distance. The paradigm of Ubiquitous Computing (Weiser, 1991) allows us to break down the border transitioning the computational environment into the learning environment, whether at school, at work, or at home. The Internet has contributed to ubiquity by providing information availability and communication capabilities anywhere anytime.

The use of computers and the Internet in education has enhanced some modes of learning, such as Distance Learning, Life-long Learning, and self-directed learning. The use of ICT has made possible other new modes of learning: Computer-Based Learning, Blended Learning, Mobile Learning, and what we could call Ubiquitous Learning. U-Learning consists of the application of Ubiquitous Computing to learning, with the online connection of diverse computational mobile devices inside and outside the educational institution, thus creating a really ubiquitous learning environment.

Organizational Aspects

In conventional learning environments, learning has been based on transmitting information (knowledge transfer) (Grady & Turner, 2002). Initially, Computer- Assisted Learning (CAL) has focused on learning as providing access to information by using the available technologically enhanced information and communication tools (ICT tools), and integrating them in the learning environment.

Loads of exercises, tutorials, and drill-and-practice activities are transferred from textbooks onto CD-ROMs and over the Internet, mirroring printed materials in digital form. The provision of this material in an organised way gave birth to what has been called Learning Management Systems (LMS). LMS are centered on the delivery of content and materials, more specifically Learning Content Management Systems (LCMS), where access to course materials is the core strategy. This perspective guides the very popular BlackBoard and WebCT systems. These Management Learning Environments (MLE) focus on the organizational issues, mainly facilitating access to content and course administration. These systems help teachers and learners with a repository of resources and contents and allow organizing and browsing of the material.

The content offered by these systems is considered learning objects. To allow reuse of these objects in different LMS, a series of educational interoperability standards (Britain & Liber, 2004) are being developed in order to keep different elements related and accessible between them. Instructional Management System (IMS) and Sharable Content Object Reference Model (SCORM) specifications allow teachers or designers to describe a learning object in a standardised way to be accessible in a variety of learning environments. The interoperability of these objects enhances the organization of e-learning.

Pedagogical Aspects

Considering methodology, Britain and Liber (2004) state that these first online learning environments:

support a model of teaching and learning interactions that was strongly based around information transmission via the provision of structured content from teacher to learners and the subsequent testing of learners on the content with little consideration given to the activities that the learners themselves might engage in. (p. 3)

Then, with LMS, the methodology seems to have stepped backwards to conductism or behaviourism. The teacher transmits the knowledge organizing its provision through selected contents made available to learners in close learning environments. Most exercises are based on mere repetition (drilling quizzes, accessing materials to be read and memorized, and so forth) (Jonassen, Peck, & Wilson, 1999). All LMS take advantage of the attractive motivation that learning with computers and the accessibility to information involve, but because they focus on information transmission as their pedagogical model, they neglect the use of the authentic communicative facility that computers can provide. Interaction and collaboration, although available in these systems, are kept to a minimum.

Some more learner-centered, constructivist learning environments such as COSE and MOODLE provide flexible learning activities together with content, and enable monitoring the learners' actions during the learning process.

More interactive learning environments have emerged such as the Communities of Practice or Learning Communities (Jonassen, Peck, & Wilson, 1999; Kaplan, 2002), whose participants share the same interests and goals for learning. The most outstanding feature of these communities is that they provide participants with some communication facilities via chats, forums, and e-mail. Although these communicative systems are all Internet-based, they use different technologies—IRC or Java for chats, newsgroups for forums, and the e-mail protocol for message exchange—while the interface for content presentation is achieved via the World Wide Web. However, the Web can also integrate all these communication facilities or services in a Web-only interface. Although the Web is only a part of the Internet, it is becoming more versatile (Sandholtz, Ringstaff, & Dwyer, 1997) and allows not only access to information by browsing, but also interaction through communication. Web users can communicate in a more integrating way: chatting, sending, and receiving e-mail messaging with webmail, getting and offering access to multimedia, and even writing on the Web (with Wikis and Blogs), so that Web users can write their own texts on open-access Web pages without previous knowledge of HTML coding required. While Web users can communicate with natural written language on the Web, Web development languages such as CGI or DHTML with JavaScript and CSS allow for the design of server-client interactions with which designers can develop chats, Web page-based threaded discussions, and webmail.

Collaboration is also a common feature of learning communities. It is usually achieved through the communication facilities. Some communities and educational institutions use commercial collaborative tools that run on vendor-specific applications such as Microsoft NetMeeting and SharePoint, but these are not easily integrated into Web-based e-learning environments. A more Web-integrating technology for collaboration is the Wiki technology (Leuf & Cunningham, 2001).

Derived from the Wiki philosophy, A Writing e-Learning Appliance (AWLA) integrates the information and communication services with the ubiquitous and collaborative facilities for writing in a technology-enhanced e-learning environment, where the students as participants can be mentored by the teacher or tutor as the organizer of the learning process through writing activities.

E-Learning as Interaction

The Web not only offers browsable access to information or content (learning objects), but also facilitates interactive agent-like services. E-learning currently tends to shift to more interactive environments. This kind of interactions provides e-learning systems with technology-based educational activities that can be integrated into the online learning environments and adapted to the interface required by any specific discipline. In these interactive learning environments, as the previous section points out, the pedagogical aspects are of outmost importance, since there must be an integration of the technological and organizational issues within a theoretical learning background. The interactive components (facilities, functionalities, services, or applications) must contribute to the learners' knowledge development in an organized (teacher-designed) technology-enabled learning environment. It is the job of the teacher to organize them into tasks and design the learning activities to accomplish the teaching objectives.

For that purpose, a categorization and organization of services available on the Web will be necessary. Technical and methodological standards now include the definition of these facilities and functionalities, whether identified as resources, events, tools, skills, services, or instructional strategies (Hirumi, 2002). The ARIADNE specification project seems to have taken into consideration the categorization of these resources. The integration through XML will enable different applications and environments to communicate and share these services.

Following Laurillard's (1993) conversational model, based on the Vygotskyan theory, some functionalities can be implemented and become services and resources for communicating and collaborating (interaction, discussion, adaptation) and providing access to content for reflection. These actions help learners to develop their knowledge

Figure 1. The AWLA infrastructure

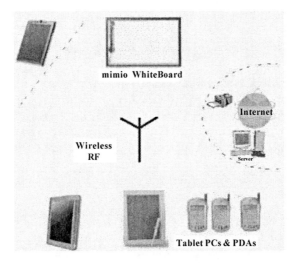

in a social context with the help of ICT. There is here an evolution to Technology-Enhanced Learning, where technology enables other more communicative, constructivist concepts of learning. Thus, learning is achieved through social interaction (European Commission, 2002), closer to socialization, where an individual internalizes knowledge by collaborating in common activities and by sharing the means of communication (Vygotsky, 1978), hence the centrality of language, communication, and collaboration in learning with technologies (McLoughlin, 1996).

Currently, access to content and its management is seen as only one of the diverse services the Web can provide for learning. There is a tendency to design more open, interactive learning environments, where the content delivery is not as central as the fact of facilitating access to services, whether digital libraries, Web searches, communication facilities, or any tool for interacting with partners and teachers. Teachers are not transmitters of knowledge but guiders or mentors who facilitate learning. It is the learning experience that matters and the teacher gives guidance through the learning activities he/she designs to help the learners develop the knowledge required in a discipline. These learning activities may involve more interactive techniques, such as problem solving (Bravo et al., 2003), communication techniques, understanding of concepts or mechanisms through simulations of multimedia representations (such as DOMOSIM-TCP) (Redondo, Bravo, Bravo, & Ortega, 2003), and authentic scenario-based learning contexts (Kindley, 2002). Some learning activities will be realizable by isolated users while others will require the collaboration between peers or with experts.

Other services and functionalities depend on the discipline to learn, on the methods or techniques traditionally involved in its learning, and also on new methods or techniques enabled by the use of ICT in education. Writing is one of the techniques used to communicate information, common in almost all disciplines (reports, exams, research

Figure 2. AWLA user interface: Opening page with a list of working scenarios

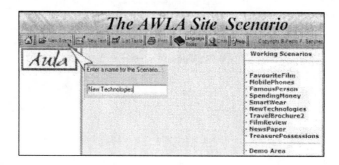

papers, etc.). The use of a Web-based writing environment will help the learning process, enhanced by the ICT in almost all disciplines, both in any ICT-improved traditional learning activity that may involve writing as well as in new technology-enabled uses of writing, mainly collaborative writing. This is the objective of AWLA, to be used to help the learning process by integrating writing on the Web in an interactive e-learning environment.

The AWLA System

AWLA tries to contribute to the provision of Web-based services and functionalities to e-learning by establishing an infrastructure of functionalities (called an "appliance") combining ubiquitous technology with a set of Web-based functionalities for constructivist e-learning. AWLA bases its methodology on tasks achieved in teacher-designed scenarios where the focus is on the organization and development of the users' learning process, not on content (although access to learning materials and objects can also be easily provided by the teacher when organizing the writing tasks).

AWLA's specific proposal consists of offering learning through interactive writing facilities with the online connection of diverse computational mobile devices appropriate for a really communicative environment. Interaction in AWLA fosters participation and the constructivist learning approach (Jonassen, Peck, & Wilson, 1999). With AWLA, we have also applied the principles of knowledge development based on Schank's Schema Theory (Schank & Abelson, 1977), designing the practice of the writing process in a structured and distributed way. As a constructivist learning environment, the AWLA system represents the natural complexity of the real world, presents authentic tasks (in real contexts and situations rather than through simulations), provides real-world, scenario-based learning environments (Kindley, 2002), and focuses on context- and activity-dependent knowledge construction in a collaborative way through communication as social negotiation (Soloway et al., 1999).

The AWLA Infrastructure

Initially designed for mobile learning, A Ubiquitous Learning Appliance (AULA) evolved into AWLA, and it is based on the Web and on Technology-Enhanced Learning (TEL) as an e-learning environment enhancing language communication. AWLA has been designed for Blended Learning, to be used in a TEL classroom environment with mobile computing devices wirelessly interconnected to an Internet access point. Taking mobile computing devices—laptop computers, Personal Digital Assistants (PDA), or TabletPCs and a projector with an electronic Whiteboard—to any classroom with wireless access to the Internet (see Figure 1) makes the classroom technologically enhanced and cost-effective (in contrast to CBI, which usually requires a classroom lab with a sophisticated network of desktop computers). It improves availability, providing access to e-learning, whenever and wherever it is required. The system makes the communication tools permanently accessible to the learner in a pervasive way.

The facilities the AWLA appliance provides are presented in a DHTML-designed user interface with CGI-based interaction, fully integrated in the Web. The application is located at the Computer Human Interaction and Collaboration (CHICO) Web server (http://chico.inf-cr.uclm.es/ppsv/awla.html), so that the teacher and the learners can have access to it from anywhere with any computing device with an Internet connection, facilitating blended learning in the widest sense, namely, ubiquitous learning or "U-Learning."

Learning How to Write by Writing with AWLA

One of the most active learning skills is writing, mainly in communicative environments. Writing is a common tool for interaction and communication in all disciplines. Web technology can help learners communicate actively through writing and thus learn more effectively. Learners will be able not only to have access to information but also to create it, share it, and communicate synchronously or asynchronously by writing on the Web from anywhere at anytime. There is a profusion of Web sites that give guidance via tutorials on how to write, but they do not provide a tool for writing. AWLA offers the writing facility and let tutors guide the writing.

The AWLA writing activities are basically organized in scenarios designed by the tutor or teacher. It requires the interaction of the teacher and the learners to create information. The teacher is the organizer of the learning experience, guiding and mentoring the learners in the learning process. For this purpose, the teacher establishes the assignment, names the scenario (by clicking the "New Scene" button on the top menubar in the interface). This turns the scenario into a domain subdirectory that will serve as the content repository for the written texts and associated tracking files.

Under this technological and organizational infrastructure, AWLA was pedagogically designed for a specific discipline—Foreign Language learning, and with a specific objective—to develop the Writing Skill. This e-learning appliance enables Collaborative Writing in an online, skill-based environment with synchronous and asynchronous

Figure 3. AWLA user interface areas: Opening a text in a scenario

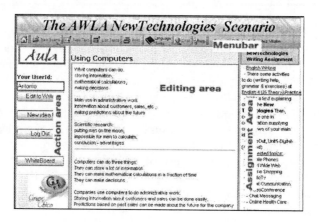

communication and edition facilities or tools, where ideas are shared, access to information is provided, and the writing process can be developed individually or in collaboration.

When a learning activity involves writing, the learners can get online from their technology-enhanced location (the classroom, the workplace, or their home) and enter the AWLA writing environment. The user interface is divided into four main areas (Figure 3): the Utilities menubar on the top, the Actions area, the Editing area, and the Assignment area.

On the right is the Assignment area, where the teacher edits the permanently visible Assignment file with the appropriate information for the learners to follow the writing process. It includes the description of the task, the target group of learners, the knowledge level required to fulfil the task, internal or external links to content (tutorials, practice material, and exercises), and any other information the teacher wants to communicate to all the learners during the learning process.

A secondary window (Figure 4) opens when access to content or to language and communication tools is required. The teacher can modify this Assignment at any time during the writing activity (Figure 5).

The Utilities menubar offers a set of tools to help the learners in the creation of the text:

- A chat facility, with which they can negotiate collaboration;

- A set of language reference facilities: dictionaries, a lexicon, and an image search facility;

- A printing utility; and

- Facilities to access and create content in the scenario and in the system.

Figure 4. List of texts in New Technologies Scenario and secondary window with access to external content and language tools

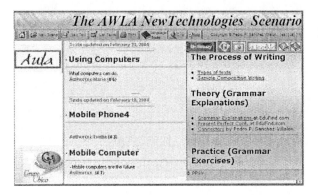

Figure 5. Editing a text in New Technologies Scenario with Chat facility in secondary window

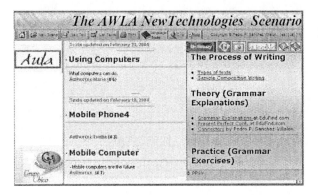

The chat facility allows both synchronous and asynchronous communication. The language tools are based on reference tools, mainly online dictionaries. They provide hyperlinked lexical information at all stages in the writing process, from the brainstorming phase to the final draft phase, at the final stage of revision.

The learners, then, create their text files by clicking on the "New Text" menu button and they edit the text in the central area, where it will display upon registration and whenever they save it (by clicking the adaptive action buttons on the left-hand side area). Only a basic level of computing skills is required for writing with AWLA.

The Actions area shows an adaptive interface that displays different action buttons depending on the user who logs in. Usually, it first displays buttons to log in and then, if a learner logs in, buttons to edit, save, or read the text (Figures 3 and 5). If it is the teacher

Figure 6. The teacher's assessment tools

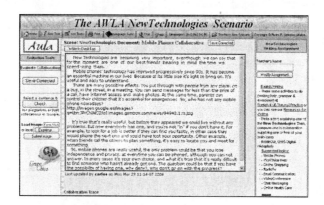

Figure 7. Corrected version of the text (with a case of plagiarism)

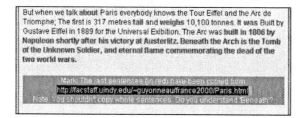

(Fig. 6) who logs in, the system displays specific buttons for the teacher to evaluate and correct the text: a table with the different contributions and modifications made by the learners, and a button to check for plagiarism or cheating (Figure 7).

Discovering plagiarism on the Web is as easy as cheating on the Web. Just select a sequence of at least three words and check them against a reliable search engine such as Google. It will display the documents or Web pages where the expression appears.

An important feature that AWLA has is that it provides monitoring and assessment facilities for the teacher to evaluate the resulting written texts. A tracking feature allows him/her to discern, in collaborative assignments, who contributed to the texts, what, when, and how they did it (with new ideas, extending ideas into sentences, connecting sentences or paragraphs, or correcting others' contributions). After the correction, the learners can access the corrected version (with mistakes corrected in red, as usual) and contrast it with their final version (Figure 7).

The AWLA Newspaper Scenario: A Case Study

The AWLA system is being used by learners of English as a Foreign Language at the Escuela Oficial de Idiomas de Ciudad Real, with seven writing scenarios (three of which are collaborative writing assignments named "NewsPaper," "TravelBrochure," and "NewTechnologies"), ranging from 12 to 40 writings from 20 to 40 participants each. The first prototype scenario was the assignment called "NewsPaper." The students were first assigned to write an online newspaper for the English Language class. This was carried out with Spanish students over 18-years-old with an Elementary Level of knowledge of English. Any student at any time could propose a title for an article, and also participate in brainstorming, develop draft paragraphs, and revise the news items proposed. Their attendance was three 50-minute sessions in general. Some could not attend one or two sessions; however, they continued contributing and revising from their homes, or their university or workplace.

As a result, they proposed seven news items, of which two became discussion lists and five were really news items written collaboratively. Every time a student entered the editing area, his or her name was registered and displayed on the chat area, so that all the participants could see there was a new member of the group collaborating.

As to the writing process, the natural tendency of freewriting merged with some structured writing techniques (as demanded by the teacher).

No roles were assigned a priori in this experience. During the sessions, most students took the role of authors, contributing with notes, sentences, and whole paragraphs, while others preferred to participate as reviewers, making corrections. Some of them even made balanced contributions with proposals as well as corrections (see Figure 8).

Most students followed the instructions and produced really uniformed multi-authored documents (5 news items). The teacher had to clearly point out certain features of collaborative writing, mainly to establish a common ground in order to avoid writing expressively about personal experiences and opinions as much as possible. So the students need to approach collaborative writing with a good understanding of the written discourse conventions and strategies and of the appropriate dynamics of writing multi-authored texts.

The results indicate that:

- the students were highly motivated and interested in working with the ICT;

- they interacted and collaborated well in the writing process, using the chat facility to negotiate collaboration;

- they contributed with their notes, sentences, and paragraphs to uniform collaborative texts, although there were a few cases of informally written dialogue exchanges;

- they revised the news articles correcting their classmates' contributions, using the language tools available;

Figure 8. The students' participation

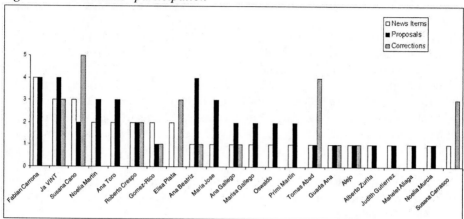

- the tracking mechanism allowed teacher assessment of every student's participation in the writing activity; and

- the system supported the collaborative writing activity successfully.

Following this first experience, others have been carried out (7 in total, 3 for collaborative writings and the 5 remaining are individual writing scenarios). The individual writing assignments, due to their quality of dealing with personal information, were not adequate as topics for collaborative writing. These dealt with Treasured Possessions or opinions on Smart Wear. The system proved quite efficient and equally motivating when used for individual writing. The students spent one session less than when collaborating, since there was no chatting and they are more accustomed to writing individually.

It is also currently being used at the Escuela Universitaria de Ingeniería Técnica Agrícola (Technical Agricultural Engineering University College), at the University of Castilla La Mancha (in Spain), in a course for university lecturers and researchers entitled "Writing Research Papers in English" with ten participants and ten research papers in progress in December 2004. The participants greatly appreciate the easy-to-use interface, the flexibility of the system, and the accessibility to online language tools for reference offered.

Conclusion

The age of learning based on knowledge transfer is coming to an end. Learning lies now on knowledge construction. Content-based systems promote the extension of the traditional transmissionist learning process, while ICT and the Web allow for new perspectives in teaching and learning processes: mentored learner-controlled learning activities developed in collaboration though interaction, with open access to information, which promotes critical thinking, in a constructivist communicative learning environment.

In order to achieve effective learning, the traditional learning environment can be enhanced with ICT developing a technologically enhanced learning environment where learners can access information, communicate with the teacher and their fellow students, and collaborate in developing common knowledge. The Web provides a series of technologies and functionalities that should be structured and delivered in Web-based e-learning environments to help learners of any discipline. Writing is one of the new services the Web facilitates, and AWLA organizes a set of tools and writing resources to help learners in their knowledge development.

Originally designed for the development of academic writing skills, AWLA is adaptable to any discipline where collaborative writing is involved, establishing an infrastructure of ubiquitous computing, applied to education, that creates an enhanced environment of collaborative e-learning. It provides interactive techniques such as collaborative writing, Web searches, and communication in real contexts based on tasks and integrated in a ubiquitous e-learning infrastructure, transforming traditional learning environments into scenario-based online learning environments.

The main contribution that AWLA offers to e-learning is the use of the Web for learning not just by browsing organized content but mainly by facilitating writing on the Web as a pedagogically grounded activity. One of its outstanding novel features is that the AWLA system makes collaborative writing possible while still allowing the teacher's assessment, thanks to the facility that tracks every participant's specific contributions to the resulting collaborative text. Another aspect to point out is that learners can write with a social purpose to be read by a real audience on the Web. The e-learning environment established with AWLA helps learners communicate actively and thus learn more effectively.

References

Bravo, C., Redondo, M.A., Bravo, J., Ortega, M. (2003). Organizing problem solving activities for synchronous collaborative learning of design domains. In J.M Cueva, B. Martín, L. Joyanes, J.E. Labra, & M. P. Paule (Eds.), *Web Engineering, Proceedings of the Third International Conference of Web Engineering,* LNCS 2722 (pp. 108-111). Berlin: Springer-Verlag.

Britain, S. & Liber, O. (2004). *A framework for the pedagogical evaluation of eLearning environments.* Report to JISC Technology Applications Programme. Retrieved May 28, 2004, from *http://www.cetis.ac.uk/members/pedagogy/files/4thMeet_framework/VLEfullReport*

Clark, C. (2003). Towards a unified e-learning strategy: Consultation document. Nottingham: DfES Publications. Retrieved July 1, 2004, from *http://www.dfes.gov.uk/consultations2/16/docs/towards%20a%20unified%20e-learning%20strategy.pdf*

European Commission (2002). Towards a knowledge-based Europe. Retrieved May 22, 2004, from *http://europa.eu.int/comm/publications/booklets/move/36/en.pdf*

Grady, R. & Turner, D. (2002). E-learning and knowledge transfer. *E-Learning and Knowledge Transfer Conference 2002.* Retrieved March 23, 2003, from *http://www.bath.ac.uk/iohm/gradyturnerw.doc*

Hirumi, A. (2002). A framework for analyzing, designing and sequencing planned eLearning interactions. *The Quarterly Review of Distance Education, 3*(2).

Jonassen, D.H., Peck, K.L., & Wilson, B.G. (1999). *Learning with technology. A constructivist perspective.* Englewood Cliffs, NJ: Prentice Hall.

Kaplan, S. (2002). Building communities—Strategies for collaborative learning. Retrieved May 28, 2004, from *http://www.learningcircuits.org/2002/aug2002/kaplan.html*

Kindley, R.W. (2002). Scenario-based e-learning: A step beyond traditional e-learning. Retrieved May 22, 2003, from *http://www.learningcircuits.com/2002/may2002/kindley.html*

Laurillard, D. (1993). *Rethinking university teaching—A framework for the effective use of educational technology.* London: Routledge.

Leuf, B. & Cunningham, W. (2001). *The Wiki way: Quick collaboration on the Web.* Boston: Addison-Wesley Longman.

LTSN Generic Centre. (2003). *e-Learning Series.* York, UK: LTSN Generic Centre.

McLoughlin, C. (1996). Technology supported learning environments: Opportunities and challenges. In *Proceedings of HERDSA Conference,* Perth, Western Australia. Retrieved March 23, 2003, from *http://www.herdsa.org.au/confs/1996/mcloughlin.html*

Ortega, M., Redondo, M.A, Paredes, M, Sánchez-Villalón, P.P., Bravo, C., & Bravo, J. (2001). Ubiquitous computing and collaboration: New paradigms in the classroom of the 21st century. In M. Ortega & J. Bravo (Eds.), *Computers and education: Towards an interconnected society* (pp. 261-273). Dordretch, The Netherlands: Kluwer Academic Publishers.

Redondo, M.A., Bravo, C., Bravo, J., & Ortega, M. (2003). Organizing activities of problem-based collaborative learning with the DomoSim-TPC system. In M. Llamas, M.J. Fernández, & L.E. Anido (Eds.), *Computers and education: Towards a lifelong learning society.* Dordretch, The Netherlands: Kluwer Academic Publishers.

Sandholtz, H.J., Ringstaff, C., & Dwyer, D.C. (1997). *Teaching with technology: Creating student centered classrooms.* New York: Teachers College Press.

Schank, R. & Abelson, R. (1977). *Scripts, plans, goals, and understanding: An inquiry into human knowledge structures.* Hillsdale, NJ: LEA Publishing.

Soloway, E., Grant, W., Tinker, R., Roschelle, J., Mills, M., Resnick, M., Berg, R., & Einseberg, M. (1999). Science in the palms of their hands. *Comm ACM, 42*(8), 21-27.

Vygotsky, L.S. (1978). *Mind in society: The development of higher psychological processes.* Cambridge, MA: Harvard University Press.

Warschauer, M. (1997). Computer-mediated collaborative learning: Theory and practice. *Modern Language Journal, 81*(3), 470-481.

Weiser, M. (1991). The computer for the twenty-first century. *Scientific American, 265*(3), 94-104.

Zastroky, M. (2000). Distributed learning, e-learning and e-business: What do they mean and where's the content? Retrieved May 22, 2004, from *http://www.globaled.com/articles/ZastrockyMichael2000.pdf*

Section II

Chapter XIV

Effects of Teaching Science through Immersive Virtual Environments

Lisa M. Daniels, North Dakota State University, USA

Jeff Terpstra, North Dakota State University, USA

Kimberly Addicott, North Dakota State University, USA

Brian M. Slator, North Dakota State University, USA

Donald P. Schwert, North Dakota State University, USA

Bernhardt Saini-Eidukat, North Dakota State University, USA

Phillip McClean, North Dakota State University, USA

Alan R. White, North Dakota State University, USA

Abstract

The North Dakota State University (NDSU) World Wide Web Instructional Committee (WWWIC) is an inter-disciplinary research team, which has, since the 1990s, developed multi-user, interactive virtual environments (IVEs) to teach the structure and process of various branches of science. The most developed of these include the "Geology Explorer" and the "Virtual Cell," (VCell). This chapter describes the key features the Virtual Cell and the Geology Explorer, the underlying philosophy and educational theory guiding their development, and results of large controlled experiments that investigate their effectiveness on student learning. Additionally, ongoing projects and experiments of the team relevant to the development and dissemination of these software programs are explored. The underlying purpose of our IVEs is to increase student achievement and scientific problem-solving skills while providing students with opportunities to learn-by-doing in a real-world context. Research findings collected for almost a decade demonstrate the positive impact of our IVEs on science students.

Introduction

Immersive virtual environments (IVEs) offer a computer-based method for science instruction that provides a number of advantages over traditional instruction. Students are invited into simulated worlds that offer interactivity, authentic experiences, and, in the best cases, an adventure in learning. The World Wide Web Instructional Committee (WWWIC) at North Dakota State University (NDSU) has been researching and developing IVE systems of this sort since the 1990s.

The most developed of these include the "Virtual Cell," (VCell)(White, McClean, & Slator, 1999) where students enter into a 3D cell simulation and perform experiments on various biological functions, and the "Geology Explorer" (Schwert, Slator, & Saini-Eidukat, 1999) where students land on a foreign planet and perform geologic tests while exploring the environment.

Each of these IVEs has been used in college-level courses at multiple universities where they were rigorously studied regarding their effectiveness on student learning, both in content knowledge and problem-solving skills. Results consistently indicate that IVE students perform higher on various assessments than their counterparts in a traditional setting. Further, there is anecdotal evidence that IVE students enjoy the learning more. While collecting and analyzing data on student learning, WWWIC has continued to evaluate the IVEs and improve their effectiveness using standard software evaluation procedures. As a result, both programs have continued to evolve and have a range of modules planned and under development.

More recent WWWIC projects include the development of both 2-dimensional and 3-dimensional world building, teacher assistance Web pages for module development, and the inclusion of many new modules for teaching students a broader range of topics within each of the virtual worlds. Technically speaking, WWWIC simulations are hosted on a LambdaMOO server (Curtis, 1997) coupled with a client developed for each particular environment. To accommodate easy use on the Internet, the clients have been developed mainly in Java and VRML (Borchert et al., 2003), and are delivered to students using Java applets.

The IVEs described here are a combination of simulation and multi-user networked game. The student player is immersed in an authentic science learning context that is populated by other users and software agent avatars acting as tutors and guides. This defines a virtual world that synthesizes but does not replicate a large number of competing approaches. For example, the "SimCity" game is a single-user resource management game that provides a problem-solving context that is powerful but non-authentic. The "Oregon Trail" game provides a more authentic context, but is limited to resource management without an overriding science teaching agenda. The hugely popular "Everquest" simulation provides many of the attractions of socially situated experiences, but is not aimed towards teaching science content of any sort.

The WWWIC IVE systems are all constructed on the client-server model. A central server hosts a simulation of geological or biological processes. A client is launched as a Java applet through a Web browser. This approach keeps the client system safe from intrusion, because of the Java security model. The simulations are built on top of the publicly available LambdaMOO software.

Server-to-client communication is accomplished through a system of low-bandwidth text-based directives. These directives control the client-side view of the simulation.

Developing IVEs for science education is both time intensive and expensive. It takes the concentrated effort of a team of content experts, designers, and computer specialists to develop a Geology Explorer or a Virtual Cell. The evidence, however, suggests that this effort and expense is worth the cost. Though the IVEs were originally intended as supplements to the classroom, they are designed to be self-explanatory and portable. Thus, students can interact with other users, virtual artifacts, and software agents from anywhere via the Internet. The efficiency of the program in terms of time and cost are designed to induce instructors to employ this form of instruction and further employ the embedded assessments built into each one.

From a practical point of view, these systems deliver considerable benefit, but at considerable cost. First, it takes a team of researchers and developers to construct each module. The "game play" must be designed with a view towards pedagogical goals, and this means a careful "storyboard" needs to be written before implementation can begin. Then, content experts, graphic artists, and software developers must be employed to implement the plan and create the necessary simulation. Finally, these systems must be extensively tested and vetted to insure the student experience is both authentic and educationally sound. In other words, these projects have a normal "software lifecycle," which means they are both labor intensive and expensive to produce. Once a system is "shipped," there are a number of additional issues to manage. It is inevitable that users (students) will find problems not detected in the testing phases of the project. These need to be fixed in as timely a manner as possible. Instructors will sometimes find they need assistance with advanced customizing options, or will want student data organized in ways not anticipated by the design team. These, too, are not unusual in the software lifecycle of a complex project.

The main message is that these virtual environments for education are both unique and mainstream at the same time. The approach to pedagogy is novel and interesting, with many advantages. The software management is quite pedestrian in most respects. Systems need to be designed, developed, supported, and maintained. This is both axiomatic and expected in contexts where software development and delivery are central to the success of the project. These are advanced software systems, and they require resources, both to build and to maintain.

Each WWWIC environment is guided by a number of principles that guide their design. These principles include role-based, goal-oriented, learn-by-doing, spatially oriented, exploratory, game-like, highly interactive, multi-user/multi-player, and immersive. Our environments are based on the hypothesis that total immersion increases learning acquisition. Therefore, both the VCell and the Geology Explorer are designed to immerse students in virtual worlds where the language of science, including experimentation and the scientific method, are spoken. As each game progresses, students encounter successively harder goals that are completed by using the tools of the discipline and the scientific method to solve problems.

When learners join the IVE, they are assigned goals appropriate to their experience. Goals are assigned point values, and learners accumulate objectively measured scores as they achieve their goals. As game play progresses, goals become increasingly more difficult. Certain goals are required while others are optional. In this way, designers ensure that highly important concepts are thoroughly covered while allowing the maximum flexibility to the learner, whose outcomes are assessed in terms of performance of specific and authentic tasks. This is the particular strength of learn-by-doing immersive environments—that a learner's success in achieving his or her goals provides an automatic measure of personal progress.

The premise for developing these virtual environments was to discover alternative methods for teaching students to "think like scientists." This involved constructing authentic activities that provide experiences with doing science. One implication of this strategy is there are no multiple choice exams in WWWIC systems. Rather, the theory of role-based learning calls for assessing students on two criteria: their ability to perform the tasks of a scientist, for which they score points within the games, and their ability to demonstrate transfer of the skills learned via authentic assessments.

Theoretical Background

WWWIC projects are designed to engage students in active learning (Reid, 1988). This approach has a number of implications for design and development. Student motivation is a key concern, since systems that do not "engage" the student will ultimately fail the final test—the students will not play them. Student motivation and ways to promote are critical to the success of educational technology in all its many forms.

Technology and Student Motivation

A main concern in education is student motivation. The uninspired student often creates difficulties for instructors. Many studies have demonstrated a positive correlation between student motivation to learn and classroom integration of technology (Backes, 1994; Cardon, 2000). Encouragingly, recent studies indicate that the use of technology in the classroom not only increased student motivation, but also improved achievement (Blume, Garcia, Mullinax, & Vogel, 2001).

Yet simply incorporating technology into traditional, teacher-centered instruction will not achieve either goal. One of the largest concerns regarding the use of technology in classrooms is that too often the technology only provides a new way to do the same old thing. Further, this approach to "technology in the classroom" has actually contributed to the "digital divide" between socioeconomic groups. Students from higher socioeconomic backgrounds are more likely to use computers in innovative ways and use advanced technologies. Their lower socioeconomic counterparts, however, are frequently limited in their technological savvy as they often use computers for simple rote exercises, thus creating road blocks in their process of "social inclusion" in a digital society (Warschauer, 2003). Integrating the IVEs into these environments may be a way to shrink this "digital divide."

While there is a certain body of research that indicates students are more engaged and actively learning when using computers (Barone, 2002), WWWIC goes beyond technology for the sake of technology. We do not recreate traditional classroom activities (i.e., research on the Web as opposed to research in the library); instead, the approach is to provide authentic experiences, similar to those of professional scientists. WWWIC IVEs not only motivate students to learn, but also keep them actively engaged in critical thinking as they learn-by-doing in a real-world, albeit virtual, context.

Constructivist Learning Theory and Authentic Assessment

Constructivist approaches to education hold that true learning occurs only when learners construct their own meaning about a given topic. Consequently, instruction needs to be focused on the learners; it needs to be student-centered. The use of student-centered technology in the classroom will boost motivation and promote true learning. The use of IVEs in instruction is an exceptional way to incorporate student-centered technology.

Learning was once believed to be a passive undertaking—that mastery of a subject meant identifying specific pieces of knowledge. Therefore, concepts were broken down into dissectible bits that, it was believed, could be easily measured (Dietel, Herman, & Knuth, 1991). The problems with this are well-known. Not only is motivation negatively affected, but cognitive and learning science research indicates that information is most securely encoded and best retrieved when it is embedded in a web of meaning; in fact, humans resist learning fragmented facts that are presented in isolation (Caine & Caine, 1991). Unfortunately, a fundamental problem in science education is that it is frequently taught as sets of disconnected facts rather than allowing students opportunities to construct their own understanding of science principles.

We now know that learning is an active process, requiring learners to construct knowledge themselves (Pellegrino, Chudowsky, & Glaser, 2001). The role of the instructor, then, is to provide guiding experiences—hands-on, "minds-on" activities—so that students can explore and come to discover learning objectives, as best possible, on their own (Jorgenson &Vanosdall, 2002). When this is done, instructors are providing what is called "authentic instruction." The brain processes many things at the same time, and holistic experiences are recalled more quickly and easily. Thus, learning is believed to occur faster and more thoroughly when it is presented in meaningful contexts, with an experiential component (Lake, 1997).

Such authentic contexts are the premise upon which WWWIC IVEs are built. The immersive virtual environments allow students to take on the active role of a scientist discovering science in a problem-solving context. Ideally, authentic instruction is followed by authentic assessment in which students perform meaningful tasks similar to those they would be expected to perform as a professional in the field (National Academy of Sciences, 1995). Authentic assessments contain an active learning component, although they may still be used in a summative manner. One such form of authentic assessment is scenario-based.

Scenario-Based Assessment

Scenario-based assessment of student learning has long been a part of formal educational evaluations. Historically, scenario-based assessments have taken various forms. For instance, some mathematical word problems, open-ended questions at the end of history textbook chapters, and writing prompts for English exams have scenario-based components. Vocational-technical schools have also adopted scenario-based assessments, using workplace-derived measures of competent performance to teach and assess students (Losh, 2000). Such performance-based assessment has been a part of medical education for many decades, and, beyond the educational setting, scenario-based assessments are used for training by the FBI, major business corporations, and multiple crisis management organizations (Swanson, Norman, & Linn, 1995).

The attraction to such assessment is its effectiveness. Employing scenario-based assessments helps to better ensure that students are not feigning competence because there is little separation between "test performance" and real learning (Shepard, 2000). Scenario-based assessments are a part of a larger category of evaluation called "authentic assessment," which means that student performance on intellectual tasks is directly examined (Wiggins, 1990). Students benefit in having the opportunity to engage in authentic work and receive feedback that speaks directly to their capabilities as scientists, historians, and so on. Additionally, the exploration of in-depth situations encourages students to develop problem-solving and higher-order thinking abilities (Lockwood, 1991). Evaluation of student learning in the IVEs has been accomplished through scenario-based assessments from the beginning. Results of this assessment data are later described.

Software Tutoring Agents

Software tutoring agents are a key feature in WWWIC's immersive virtual environments. These agents generally work by "looking over the shoulder" as students attempt to complete their goals. The agents engage in various forms of remediation as students encounter difficulties and make mistakes. This strategy is a form of scaffolding in that the role of the "teacher" or "tutor" decreases as the learners' abilities increase.

Figure 1. Screenshot of tutoring agent in Planet Oit advising a player where to travel

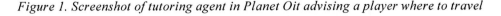

Figure 1 is a screenshot depict a tutoring agent in Planet Oit advising a player where to travel.

Scaffolding is embedded in the constructivist philosophy that guides the development of WWWIC virtual worlds for teaching science (Borchert et al., 2003). With the impetus on the students to acquire new knowledge, the learning environment must be one in which students are in a state of "relaxed alertness" (Caine, 2000). If the experience is too easy or too hard, students are in either "low arousal" or "high arousal" states and not in their Zone of Proximal Development (ZPD). Students may be considered in a state of "moderate arousal" (appropriate for their ZPD) when learning goals are challenging, but attainable. In other words, each student can reach the goal, but not without stretching. Because of the vast differentiation among learner readiness, individualization of the learning environment is necessary (Tomlinson, 2001).

Our software tutors provide for this by manipulating the learning environment in terms of the level of support offered. Those students at a lower state of readiness may be provided more assistance, while those at a higher level receive less guidance. However, in any case, it is an important component of constructivism that only prompts and guidance be given. Giving students an answer that they can simply memorize reverts back to a behaviorist approach, which is less effective for authentic, long-term learning.

Typically, an interaction with one of our tutoring agents results in a hint to guide the student. Recently, we have begun experimenting with a "fading" strategy that provides a staged sequence of hints, giving more specific guidance as a student's struggle continues past the initial remediation.

Think Aloud Interviews

Although the research collected over the past several years has indicated a positive effect on student learning, WWWIC research aims to more fully understand the learning process that takes place within the virtual environment. Understanding this process would help to improve and develop further modules and assessments. In order to understand the learning process, WWWIC researchers needed to know what the students were thinking while they were immersed in the IVEs. Because most students do not make their thought processes known, a system for revealing these—the think-aloud interview—was implemented. The think-aloud interview allowed the WWWIC researchers to envision the progression of learning that took place while students were playing the IVEs.

The procedure for the think-aloud interviews is fairly simple. WWWIC researchers recruit volunteers for the study. The participants register and complete the pre-game activities on their own. Then, a WWWIC researcher sits with an interview participant and encourages him/her to "think aloud" while playing the game. Furthermore, the interviewer encourages thinking aloud by asking why a student took a certain action. The interviewer also takes notes describing the participants' actions. This serves as a complement to the tape-recorded interview. After the game is finished, the participant completes the post-game activities. After all the interviews are completed, WWWIC researchers transcribe the recordings and combine them with the notes taken during the interview. Then, the transcripts are independently analyzed using phenomenological techniques. During the same time, the pre- and post-assessments are scored and analyzed.

The first set of think-aloud interviews was conducted in the fall of 2003 with the Geology Explorer. WWWIC researchers solicited volunteers from a larger Geology Explorer study taking place in GEOL 105 "Physical Geology," an introductory Geology course at NDSU. There were six interview participants. Similarly, 14 volunteers were recruited from introductory level biology courses at NDSU for the VCell think-aloud interviews held in the Spring of 2004.

Each participant completed the pre-game activities prior to participating in up to two interview sessions, each lasting approximately one hour. Portions of the game were played outside of the interview sessions. After completing the game, the participants completed the post-game activities.

Improvements to the IVEs based upon this initial analysis have been implemented and are proving beneficial. One of the more intriguing findings in the think-aloud process was the discovery that participants with a natural disposition toward the think-aloud process (those participants who articulated their thought process with no prompting by the interviewers) completed the modules in approximately one-third of the time of the average user. This has prompted us to explore the correlation between verbal metacognition and achievement, specifically whether building metacognitive activities within the IVEs may not only teach students science principles but how to *learn* science. WWWIC is currently in the process of designing tools and experiments to test this hypothesis.

The Virtual Cell

VCell is a goal-oriented biology game situated within a virtual cellular research lab. Students are "transported" to a virtual cell through which they "navigate" using submarine-like controls (http://vcell.ndsu.edu/). During this exploration of the cell, students perform assays (experiments) in order to identify cell organelles. To the student, the Virtual Cell looks like an enormous, navigable space populated with 3D organelles. In this environment, experimental goals in the form of question-based assignments promote diagnostic reasoning and problem-solving in an authentic visualized context.

The initial point of entry for the Virtual Cell is a VRML-based laboratory (see Figure 2). Here the learner encounters a scientific mentor and receives a specific assignment. The student then navigates to the inside of a cell or cellular organelle to perform a series of experiments. It is here that experimental science meets virtual reality. As the project progresses, students revisit the laboratory to receive more assignments.

In addition, students watch and interact with animations detailing various cellular processes, such as photosynthesis and the electron transport chain. After studying these animations, students perform various tasks to identify damaged or mutant organelles or complexes. In performing these tasks, students reach a deeper understanding of the cellular processes. The following screenshot is of the Electron Transport Chain animation (Figure 3).

Figure 2. Screenshot of a VRML-based laboratory, the initial point of entry for the Virtual Cell

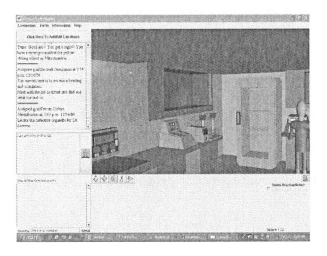

Figure 3. Screenshot of the Electron Transport Chain animation in VCell

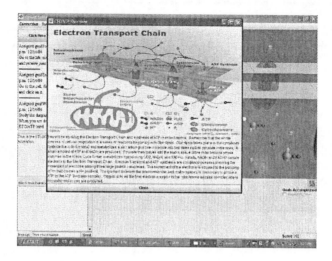

The VCell consists of modules designed to teach the principles and practices of cell biology. All of the VCell modules address the biology standards as outlined by the American Association for the Advancement of Science in its Project 2061 (http://www.project2061.org/). The VCell animations are available online at http://vcell.ndsu.edu/animations/.

Effects of VCell on Student Learning

In the fall semester of 2000, a large controlled study was conducted to determine the impact VCell had on student learning. The results of this study (McClean, Saini-Eidukat, Schwert, Slator, & White, 2001) indicate a statistically significant positive effect on the experimental group (VCell) compared to students in a control group (no Web-based activity) and an "alternative exercise" group (Web-based instruction). Student learning was evaluated using a pre/post scenario-based assessment to determine if students could solve problems in the manner of a cell biologist. To study the effectiveness of the VCell on student learning, the answers of three groups were compared. Scenario-based testing asks the student to solve a practical problem, one they would face as a practicing biologist.

The experimental design includes three test groups: (1) students who address specific questions based on additional textbook readings; (2) students who complete a WWW activity consisting of content similar to that found in the VCell modules; and (3) students who completed two VCell modules. Students were assigned to test groups to ensure each group was equally balanced with respect to computer ability, previous enrollment in a biology laboratory course, and gender. The experiment described below consists of

Table 1. Mean post-intervention scenario scores for Virtual Cell Experiment with NDSU Biology 150 (General Biology) students

Mean	Organelle Identification	Cellular Respiration
Control[a]	17.4a	10.6a
WWW	19.7b	13.7b
Vcell	22.7c	17.3c

Treatment Population sizes are: Control=145; WWW=94; and Virtual Cell=93.

Within any column, any two means followed by the same letter are not significantly different at P=0.05 using the LSD mean separation test (McClean et al, 2001).

students from two sections of General Biology (Biology 150, NDSU). A different instructor taught each section. A total of 332 students participated in the experiment.

Students answered scenario questions both before and after engaging in their group activities. Two different graders, who had been trained against a standard, graded the scenarios. A score of 100 represents an answer a PhD in cell biology would provide. Because a highly significant correlation ($r=0.81$) was observed between the scores of the two graders, the average score of the two graders was used as the experimental observation. A significant difference was observed between the scenario scores among the three experimental groups. Those students using the VCell scored significantly higher ($p < 0.05$) on post-scenario assessments than the other two groups (Table 1).

When the scores for the different subcomponents were analyzed, the students in the VCell experimental group demonstrated a significantly higher level of general knowledge than students in the other two groups. This leads to the conclusion that the VCell is a valuable tool for the delivery of cell biology content. Our extensive testing has conclusively demonstrated that the VCell experience not only provides students with necessary course content, but also supports higher-order thinking skills.

Animations

As mentioned previously, 3D animations are an intricate part of the VCell environment. Animations are also available for independent viewing or supplemental instruction outside the IVE. Animations in this context are developed in order to provide software developers with the content they need to create new modules, and also provide students with a visualization of cellular processes in advance of their interactive simulation experience.

The choice of what animations to build was informed by workshops held with university and Grade 7-12 science teachers who were asked to identify cellular processes that would be best supported by high-quality animations (McClean et al, 2005). Currently, these animations represent the following processes: transcription; translation; bacterial gene expression; mRNA processing; mRNA splicing; protein transport into an organelle;

Figure 4. The Lac Operon advanced look

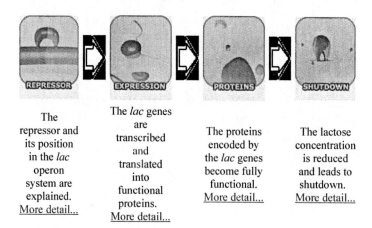

The repressor and its position in the *lac* operon system are explained. More detail...	The *lac* genes are transcribed and translated into functional proteins. More detail...	The proteins encoded by the *lac* genes become fully functional. More detail...	The lactose concentration is reduced and leads to shutdown. More detail...

Table 2. Treatment groups for VCell animation experiment

Group	Treatment
AlAi (n=14)	Animated Lecture/Animated Individual—Lecture augmented with animation followed by individual study of animation
TiAl (n = 14)	Text Individual/Animated Lecture—Individual study of text material followed by lecture augmented with animation
TlAi (n = 15)	Traditional Lecture/Animated Individual—Lecture augmented with overheads followed by individual study of animation
TiTl (n = 12)	Text Individual/Traditional Lecture—Individual study of text material followed by lecture augmented with overheads

photosynthesis; the Lac Operon; the electron transport chain; and the use of a biological gradient to drive ATP synthesis (http://vcell.ndsu.nodak.edu/animations/).

These animations are integrated with an educational module that consists of "First Look" and "Advanced Look" components that feature captioned stills from the animation representing the key steps in the processes at varying levels of complexity. A decision was made to develop animations at a level of detail that would be understood by an advanced undergraduate or graduate student. Within this level of detail, instructors have several options. For instance, they can teach just the basic principles without commenting on the fine-level detail, as appropriate for introductory level courses. On the other hand, instructors in more advanced courses can teach all of the details. Figure 4 depicts the Lac Operon Advanced Look.

In the Spring 2004 semester, a controlled experiment was conducted to determine if students who interacted with animations (like those found in IVEs) performed better on assessments than students who had the same content presented to them in a strictly traditional manner. The protein translation animation was tested at NDSU with the

Education 321 (Introduction to Teaching) class. This class is required of all education majors at NDSU and is typically a mixture of students training to be teachers in the full range of Grade 7-12 disciplines. It is therefore an appropriate group to test the value of animations to aid in the learning of a complex topic by a diverse group of students (McClean et al., 2005).

The participants for the study were selected from two introductory education classes and presented with the same content (the cellular process of protein synthesis), but in different ways. The two classes were each split in half, forming four groups (Table 2). All groups received a lecture given by a college professor. However, for two of the four groups, the lecture was augmented with an animation of protein synthesis while the professor explained what was happening in that animation. The other two groups received a traditional-style lecture by the same professor. Additionally, all groups received an independent assignment, either individual reading of an assigned text or individual viewing of the animation with a voice-over narration describing the protein synthesis process.

Participants completed a four-item assessment on protein synthesis both before and immediately following the treatment. For each item, students were also asked to rank how confident they were in their answer (low, medium, high). Results were stunning. Not only did the group exposed to the most technology significantly outperform the others, but their post-test confidence scores were twice as high.

Analysis

When the pre-treatment test scores among the four treatment groups were compared, no significant difference among the means was detected (P=0.489). By contrast, a significant group effect was noted for the post-treatment mean (P=0.005). To determine which treatments were most significant, the P value associated with each pairwise contrast was calculated (Table 3). In all cases, Group AlAi (animated lecture combined with animated individual study) performed significantly better than any other group. (Note that all

Table 3. Mean student post-treatment performance and group contrasts for the four lecture/individual study treatments. Maximum score is 4. Significant (P<0.05) contrasts are noted with asterisks.

Group	Mean	Treatment group contrast P value			
		vs. AlAi	vs. TiAl	vs. TlAi	vs. TiTl
AlAi	3.54	-	0.0442*	0.0150*	0.0004*
TiAl	2.73	0.0237*	-	0.5612	0.0823
TlAi	2.50	0.0036*	0.4881	-	0.2824
TiTl	2.07	0.0046*	0.4669	0.9409	-

Table 4. Mean student post-treatment confidence levels and contrasts for the four lecture/individual study treatments. Maximum score is 12 (1-3 scale for each of four questions). Significant (P<0.05) contrasts are noted with asterisks.

Group	Mean	Treatment group contrast *P* value			
		vs. AlAi	Vs. TlAi	vs. TiAl	vs. TiTl
AlAi	10.38 (5.92)	-	0.5096	0.3277	0.0002*
TlAi	9.83 (5.33)	0.4438	-	0.7726	0.0024*
TiAl	9.60 (4.36)	0.0381*	0.1995	-	0.0033*
TiTl	7.27 (2.67)	<0.0001*	0.0007*	0.0210*	-

treatment contrast *P* values were less than 0.05.) This result strongly suggests that the animation was a significant component in improving student retention of content material.

Confidence level for test answers gave a somewhat different result (Table 4). There is no significant difference in self-reported confidence among the four groups during the pre-treatment test ($P=0.3424$). On the other hand, there is a significant confidence difference among the groups with the post test ($P=0.001$). When individual group comparisons were made, it is seen that the mean confidence level of group TiTl (individual study of text material followed by a lecture supported by overheads) was significantly less than all other groups.

In this case, the confidence of any group that contained an animation activity (Groups AlAi, TiAl, and TlAi) was significantly greater than the group (TiTl) without an animation support of learning. Although the data is not entirely consistent, one observation can be made: student confidence is significantly improved when an animation is used at some point during the educational experience (McClean et al., 2005).

Two weeks later, the students were given the same quiz to see how much of the instruction they retained. Again, they were asked to report their confidence level (1=low, 2=medium, 3=high) for each answer, and the correlation between confidence levels and correct answers was calculated.

The TiAl group maintained a consistently high correlation between confidence levels and correct answer response throughout the four-item quiz. For Questions 1 and 3, the AlAi group showed the most improvement from Pre to Post, and the most retention for the Late. Contrast that with the TiTl group, who maintained the lowest correlation for Questions 1 and 3 throughout. The TlAi group was mostly middle-of-the-pack.

The results from this study encourage us to believe we are progressing in the right direction for positively impacting student learning. This also guides the formation of new research questions regarding the use of technology tools for the teaching of science, which will be examined in upcoming studies.

Figure 5. Geology Explorer screenshot illustrating the completion of a mineral identification

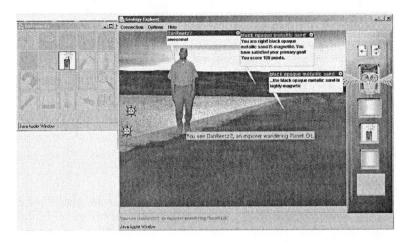

Geology Explorer

The Geology Explorer is a goal-oriented computer game in which students learn about geology by acting like scientists exploring a new world (http://oit.cs.ndsu.nodak.edu/menu/home.ie.htm). Within this virtual world, students "travel" to the imaginary Planet Oit in order to gather geologic data about this newly discovered planet. Students act as geologists by performing various tests in order to identify unknown rocks and minerals. After completing five initial identifications, students move on to geologic mapping. They use identified outcrops to create a geologic map, which serves as an interpretation of the underlying geology of the area. The screenshot illustrates the completion of a mineral identification (Figure 5). The panel on the left illustrates the standard set of tools with which players are equipped.

To play the game, students are transported to the planet's surface and acquire a standard set of field instruments. Students are issued an "electronic log book" to record their findings and are assigned a sequence of exploratory goals. These goals are intended to motivate the students to view their surroundings with a critical eye, as a geologist would. The students make field observations, conduct small experiments, take note of the environment, and generally act like geologists as they work towards their goals. A scoring system has been developed, so students can compete with each other and with themselves (Borchert et al, 2003).

Students must first identify a mineral, then a rock, then any combination of the above until they have mastered the topic, then they are able to continue on to more advanced modules, like map making and determining landform structure. The module and goal structure has been created so that the instructor can decide which goals are appropriate for their students to complete, thus allowing for an individualized educational experience.

One can give a set of relatively easy goals to secondary school students and a larger, harder set to graduate-level college students. The environment allows for full customizability.

Effects of Geology Explorer on Student Learning

In controlled experiments (n=281), where assessment measures of the "Planet Oit" group were compared to both a WWW group (alternative Web-based instruction) and a Control group (traditional instruction without computers), a two-way main effects MANOVA model indicated a significant Group effect (p = 0.0143). In order to investigate the nature of this significant result, simultaneous confidence intervals contrasting the different groups across different graders were constructed. Since this involved the generation of several (say m) simultaneous intervals, we controlled for the overall experimental error rate (a = 0.05) using the well-known Bonferroni technique; that is, each interval was calculated using a 100(1-a/m)% confidence level. The interested reader is referred to Sections 5.4 and 6.6 of Johnson and Wichern (1998) for further details. The Bonferroni intervals indicated that the Oit group outperformed both the WWW group and the Control group. For instance, the mean net improvement intervals contrasting Oit and WWW (for Graders 1 and 2) were [0.10, 20.43] and [6.07, 25.39], respectively. It is interesting to note that the Bonferroni intervals contrasting the WWW and Control groups all contained the value of zero; that is, there were no significant differences in mean net improvement between these two groups. Hence, due to large sample sizes and sound statistical analyses that control for the overall experimental error rate, we can conclude that virtual worlds are benefiting student-learning ability.

Teacher Workshop

Although continuing to implement, test, and improve IVEs at the college level, in 2003, WWWIC members saw the opportunity to expand their aim and make these educational environments available for use at a secondary school level. This task, WWWIC realized, was very different from their previous undertakings. Middle schools and high schools are very different from colleges and universities; they have different types of students, teachers, problems, goals, and so on. Because it was unsure of what, specifically, these differences were and how to address them, WWWIC decided to gather information and feedback from Grade 6-12 educators in workshops held in the summers of 2003 and 2004.

The purpose of the workshops was to train the teachers on the use of these IVEs, and solicit responses on the potential usefulness of these virtual environments in their 6-12 grade classes. The responses were very positive, and we have testimony from many of them stating they would like to (or plan to) incorporate one or more of the IVEs into their lessons. Some have already successfully done so.

Twenty-five teachers were selected to participate in the workshop. The official purpose of the workshop was to teach Grade 6-12 science teachers how to implement these IVEs into their biology or earth science curriculum. The participants would learn how IVEs are designed and implemented, the theory supporting the use of IVEs in science classrooms, the issues dealing with assessment of learning in IVEs, and other aspects of how IVEs function. The participants would then have time to use the IVEs and become familiar with how they work. Finally, the participating teachers would assist WWWIC in implementing the IVEs into science classrooms by creating unit plans that incorporate the IVEs into their curriculum, by designing new lessons based on the IVEs, and by constructing assessment and evaluation tools to be used with the IVEs. Each participant would submit their documents to the committee within two weeks of the workshop.

After the workshop, the participating teachers turned in their unit plans. A few of these teachers created exceptional products and eagerly incorporated the IVEs into their Grade 7-12 classrooms the following academic year. However, many of these unit plans were fairly basic; they just met the requirements of the assignment and did not contain outstanding activities or particularly interesting curriculum integration. This, however, was to be expected. After all, these teachers were just beginning to be familiar with the virtual environments themselves. Furthermore, the unit plan was not directly applicable in many of their classrooms due to the difficulty level of some modules in the IVEs. Consequently, many teachers created the unit plans simply to receive credit for the course.

Despite being relatively basic, WWWIC did learn something from these unit plans; it saw that rather than designing their own activities, many of these unit plans used pre-designed hands-on activities. The teachers may have acquired these activities from textbook supplements, on the Internet, or from other teachers. This trend indicated that teachers not only see the value in incorporating these hands-on learning experiences, but like using them in their classrooms. However, they may not have the time or desire to create their own. Therefore, the prior supposition that we needed to create and provide curriculum materials in order to get teachers to implement the IVEs was confirmed. The participating teachers indicated that if they were provided engaging and effective curriculum materials, they would use them. Furthermore, providing curriculum materials increases the likelihood of teachers using the IVEs in their classrooms, which, obviously, is a necessary step in gathering data at the secondary level.

Noting the interest of the teachers in our workshop in using these IVEs in their Grade 7-12 classrooms, in the Spring 2004 semester, we began developing a Teacher's Manual, complete with standards-based lesson plans and assessments to accompany the Geology Explorer software. Since the IVEs were originally designed for use in higher education classrooms, we realized that modifications needed to be made for them to be most relevant to secondary teachers.

A multi-disciplinary team consisting of educators, geologists, computer scientists, and graphic artists created the curriculum. The curriculum, designed to make the implementation process as easy and convenient as possible, consists of three lesson plans, multiple worksheets, and classroom materials. Experienced educators created these plans to be effective, engaging, and easy to use. Furthermore, the lessons appeal to multiple learning styles and serve as valuable supplements to the Geology Explorer software.

Perhaps most importantly, the Geology Explorer curriculum is flexible. The curriculum can be used in its entirety or can be broken apart into separate lessons. The lessons are adaptable to individual curricular needs and can be modified to fit various schedules. This flexibility allows the teacher to choose the most appropriate and appealing lessons for a class's specific needs.

This Spring, eight science teachers throughout the state of North Dakota implemented these materials in their classrooms. Overall, their reactions have been encouraging. They note high levels of student motivation, which are matched with high levels of understanding.

Conclusion

The underlying purpose of our IVEs is to increase student achievement and scientific problem-solving skills while providing students with opportunities to learn-by-doing in a real-world context. Research findings collected for almost a decade demonstrate the potential impact of our IVEs on secondary science students. There is also reason to believe the IVE approach to science education will increase achievement, not only in science but also technical literacy.

The theoretical and research potential of environments in which students are actively involved with learning in ways that have authenticity and relevance have been major themes in the cognitive and learning sciences for more than a decade. The IVEs we describe provide a suite of enabling technologies for developing, implementing, and doing research with immersive and virtual learning environments that advance what is currently available in the research communities. The overall research context touches on issues of knowledge acquisition, knowledge transfer, conceptual change, attitudes, teacher education and professional development, classroom use of developed systems, and content alignment with state and national standards.

The large experiments described here indicate that the virtual world experiences have a significantly positive effect on the ability of students to solve problems in the manner of scientists. They also provide evidence of the effectiveness of authentic instruction and assessment. The National Science Foundation has noted that these IVEs have wide applicability to a variety of workforce and education initiatives. We are pleased with all that has been accomplished thus far, and look forward to completing future studies to improve the effectiveness of our IVEs on the teaching of science.

Acknowledgments

Support for these projects was provided by the U.S. Department of Education (FIPSE) grant #P116B011528 (Geology Explorer) #P166B000734 and #P116B030120 (Virtual Cell) and the National Science Foundation grant #EIA-0086142.

References

Backes, C. (1994). Motivating students. *Technology Teacher, 54*(1), 9-12.

Barone, C.A.(2002). WINWINI and the next killer App: An interview with Carl F. Berger. *Educause Review,* March/April, 21-26.

Blume, J., Garcia, K., Mullinax, K., & Vogel, K. (2001). *Integrating math and science with technology.* Master of Arts Action Research Project, Saint Xavier University and Skylight Professional Development Field-Based Masters Program. ERIC_NO: ED454088.

Borchert, O., Bergstrom, A., Brandt, L., Brantsig, R., Burns, W., Clark, J.T., et al. (2003). Advances in immersive virtual worlds for science education. In *Proceedings of the Midwest Instructional Computing Symposium (MICS),* April 11-12, Duluth, MN.

Caine, R. N. (2000). Building the bridge from research to classroom. *Educational Leadership,* November, *58*(3), 59-65.

Caine, R.N. & Caine, G. (1991). *Making connections: Teaching and the human brain.* Alexandria, VA: Association for Supervision and Curriculum Development.

Cardon, P. (2000). At-risk students and technology education: A qualitative study. *Journal of Technology Studies, 26*(1), 49-57.

Curtis, P. (1997). *High wired: On the design, use and theory of educational MOOs.* Ann Arbor, MI: University of Michigan Press.

Dietel, R.J., Herman, J.L., & Knuth, R.A. (1991). *What does research say about assessment?* Oak Brook, IL: North Central Regional Educational Laboratory.

Johnson, R. A. & Wichern, D. W. (1998). *Applied multivariate statistical analysis* (4th Ed.). Upper Saddle River, NJ: Prentice Hall.

Jorgenson, O. & Vanosdall, R. (2002). The death of science? What we risk in our rush toward standardized testing and the three R's. *Phi Delta Kappan,* April, 601-605.

Lake, K. (1997). Integrated curriculum. *School improvement program: School improvement research series.* Portland, OR: Northwest Regional Educational Laboratory.

Lockwood, A. T. (1991). *Authentic writing and literature instruction focus in change.* Madison, WI: The National Center for Effective Schools.

Losh, C.L. (2000). Using skill standards for vocational-technical education curriculum development. *Information Series,* No. 383. ERIC Identifier: ED440295.

McClean, P., Johnson, C., Rogers, R., Daniels, L., Reber, J., Slator, B., Terpstra, J., & White, A. (2005). Molecular and cellular biology animations: Impact on student learning. *Cell Biology Education, 4*(2). Retrieved from *http://www.cellbioed.org*

McClean, P., Saini-Eidukat, B., Schwert, D., Slator, B., & White, A. (2001). Virtual worlds in large enrollment biology and geology classes significantly improve authentic learning. In J. A. Chambers (Ed.), *Selected Papers from the 12th International Conference on College Teaching and Learning (ICCTL-01)*, April 17-21 (pp. 111-118). Jacksonville, FL: Center for the Advancement of Teaching and Learning.

National Academy of Sciences (1995). *National science education standards*. Washington, DC: National Academy Press.

Pellegrino, J., Chudowsky, N., & Glaser, R. (Eds.) (2001). *Knowing what students know: The science and design of educational assessment.* Committee on the Foundations of Assessment. Board on Testing and Assessment; Center for Education, Division of Behavioral and Social Sciences and Education, National Research Council. Washington, DC: National Academy Press.

Schwert, D.P., Slator, B.M., & Saini-Eidukat, B. (1999). A virtual world for earth science education in secondary and post-secondary environments: The Geology Explorer. In *Proceedings of International Conference on Mathematics/Science Education & Technology*, March 1-4, San Antonio, TX (pp. 519-525).

Shepard, L. (2000). The role of assessment in a learning culture: Using assessment in the process of learning. *ER Online*, October. Retrieved March 23, 2003, from *http://www.aera.net/publications/?id=331*

Swanson, D.B., Norman, G.R., & Linn, R.L. (1995). Performance-based assessment: Lessons from the health profession. *Educational Researcher, 24*(5), 5-11, 35.

Tomlinson, C. A. (2001). *How to differentiate instruction in mixed-ability classrooms* (2nd Ed.). Alexandria, VA: Association for Supervision & Curriculum Development.

Warschauer, M. (2003). Demystifying the digital divide. *Scientific American, 289*(2), 42.

White, A. R., McClean, P.E., & Slator, B.M. (1999). The Virtual Cell: An interactive, virtual environment for cell biology. *Proceedings of the World Conference on Educational Media, Hypermedia and Telecommunications (ED-MEDIA '99)*, June 19-24, Seattle, WA (pp. 1444-1445).

Wiggins, G. (1990). The case for authentic assessment. *ERIC Digest*. ERIC Identifier: ED328611.

Chapter XV

An Integrated Platform for Educational Virtual Environments

Christos Bouras
University of Patras and
Research Academic Computer Technology Institute, Greece

Eleftheria Giannaka
University of Patras and
Research Academic Computer Technology Institute, Greece

Maria Nani
Research Academic Computer Technology Institute, Greece

Alexandros Panagopoulos
University of Patras and
Research Academic Computer Technology Institute, Greece

Thrasyvoulos Tsiatsos
Research Academic Computer Technology Institute, Greece

Abstract

In this chapter, we present the design and implementation of an integrated platform for Educational Virtual Environments. This platform aims to support an educational community, synchronous online courses in multi-user three-dimensional (3D) environments, and the creation and access of asynchronous courses through a learning content management system. In order to offer synchronous courses, we have implemented a system called EVE-II, which supports stable event sharing for multi-user 3D places, easy creation of multi-user 3D places, H.323-based voice- over IP services fully integrated in a 3D space, as well as many concurrent 3D multi-user spaces.

Introduction

The formation of communities among individuals who shared common characteristics goes along with the evolution and socialization of the mankind. This inherent need for communication and collaboration, in combination with the swift growth of the technology, resulted in the development of services that could meet the above-mentioned needs. In particular, the maturation of the Internet services and the melioration of the network bandwidth, along with the users' familiarization with the powerful means of distant communication and collaboration, formed the basis for the widespread establishment of online communities. These communities are described by the term "virtual communities" in order to define their "online" substance.

The definition of a virtual community is comprised of the following fundamental characteristics: (a) people who want to interact socially to satisfy needs, perform roles, and so forth; (b) a shared purpose, which provides a reason for the community; (c) policies, which guide human interaction; and (d) computer systems to support and mediate social interaction. These basic characteristics define the framework as well as the context of the constituted communities and entitle the scope, the concepts, and the intended milestones. In particular, in the case where the shared purpose of these virtual communities is learning, we address them as virtual learning communities.

Currently, the need for a paradigm change in e-learning has been identified, but which has not yet taken place (Laister & Koubek, 2001). In the past, Information and Communication Technologies (ICT) have been developed in a technology-centered way, but we are currently undergoing a change towards more human-centered concepts of using information technology for business, learning, and communicating with each other. However, Resource-Based Learning (RBL), which focuses on the interaction between human and computer, still prevails. Although, the RBL approach has several advantages for supporting individual learning by providing interactive, media-rich resources for learning, several disadvantages have been identified. Some of these disadvantages involve the lack of peer contact and interaction of students working alone, and the need for flexible, available tutorial support. Moreover, interactive distributed learning facilitates the acquisition of a higher level of understanding by the students than passive distributed learning, thus enabling the learning process to be more active and more explorative.

It becomes clear that the key concept of learning, which qualifies a virtual learning community, requires a balanced combination of technology with the human factor. Therefore, a virtual community should be supported by a computer system that should be able to facilitate delivery of e-learning content, collaboration, and distance learning services, both in the industrial and the educational field. We address such an educational technology system as an Educational Virtual Environment.

The main scope of this chapter is the presentation of an integrated platform for the support of Educational Virtual Environments, which has been designed and implemented in order to integrate the current RBL concepts with collaborative e-learning strategies through advanced technological solutions. The above concept has been chosen in order to overcome the limitations of current e-learning applications, as they were described previously.

In order to exploit the advantages of RBL and interactive distributed learning and, in parallel, overcome their disadvantages while still encouraging communication and collaboration among the participants, the platform provides and supports a variety of synchronous and asynchronous services. In regard to the kind and type of functionality that are intended to be offered, these services are dispersed in the system, which consists of the following components:

- **A Web-based e-learning community (EVE Community):** This component constitutes the central part of the platform, which offers to the users (students, tutors, etc.) the necessary tools for asynchronous interactions (as forums, private messages, etc.), accessing lessons and e-learning content, as well as the users roles and rights management.

- **EVE-II Networked Virtual Environments system, which supports 3D multi-user virtual classrooms:** EVE-II is used to provide the multi-user substance of 3D virtual classrooms for collaborative e-learning in order to offer a collaborative work system or, in other words, a collaborative workspace. Using Networked Virtual Environments (NVEs) as communication media, the members of these virtual communities are given the advantage of creating proximity and social presence, thereby making participants aware of the communication and interaction processes with others. In particular, the awareness of other users and the awareness of learning objects and material constitute a critical factor for the Educational Virtual Environments. In addition, based on the fact that users are influenced by the virtual representation, the 3D multi-user component was selected so as to facilitate the e-learning process and offer all the tools necessary to simulate a real classroom. Furthermore, the EVE-II system supports stable event sharing for multi-user 3D places, easy creation of 3D multi-user places, H.323-based voice-over IP services integrated in 3D spaces, and many concurrent 3D multi-user spaces.

- **A Web-based Learning Content Management Element (LCME):** This component offers tools for facilitating tutors to easily develop learning objects consisting of a variety of content formats and build online courses so as to serve their distant students' needs. These tools support the metadata elements defined in Sharable Content Object Reference Model (SCORM). Using the LCME, RBL is facilitated, and searching and retrieval of e-learning content and tracking of students' interactions with the content are supported. Also, the e-learning content can be reused within different learning objects and asynchronous courses.

The EVE Community aims to provide a virtual learning environment that can simulate in an efficient way the interactions, educational material, and learning process of a real educational environment as realistically as possible.

The remainder of this chapter is structured as follows. We initially describe the state of the art in Educational Virtual Environments. We then present the platform from a technical point of view, describing the overall architecture. Afterwards, we describe the EVE community model, structural components, and the hierarchy of the roles and rights that regulate the platform. We then continue with a detailed presentation of the functionality that the community provides. The section that follows is engaged with the description of the Learning Content Management Element that the platform provides for the access, creation, and manipulation of the content. Finally, we present the usage scenarios for the platform, some concluding remarks, and our vision for the next steps.

Related Technologies and Research Work on NVEs

Currently, there are many commercial platforms that support NVEs. The most significant are:

- Active Worlds (http://www.activeworlds.com/),
- Sense8 (http://www.sense8.com),
- ParallelGraphics solution (http://www.parallelgraphics.com/),
- Moove' s Rose (http://www.moove.com),
- SmartVR's SmartVerse (http://www.smartvr.com/), and
- Worlds (http://www.worlds.com/).

In general, commercial products target large groups of users: "the more people, the better" (Greenhalgh, 2000). This leads commercial platforms to be reliable, attractive, and easy to use, as well as to work on available networks, mainly aiming at leisure or 3D chat. However, the generality that characterizes commercial systems makes their use for educational purposes premature, as most of them do not support audio-video and multimodal user communication. Furthermore, an attempt to modify them by integrating additional components may not be cost effective, because most of them are not based on open standards, and in addition, their development toolkits are very expensive.

The area of NVEs has drawn increased research and development interest. This resulted in systems, tools, protocols, and a variety of platforms for networked virtual environments. The most significant prototypes and research work in the field of NVEs are the following:

- Distributed Interactive Virtual Environments-DIVE (http://www.sics.se/dive/) (Carlsson & Hagsand, 1993),

- Scalable Platform for Large Interactive Environments- SPLINE (http://www.merl.com/projects/spline/),

- Virtual Life Network- VLNET (Pandzic, Capin, Magnenat-Thalmann, & Thalmann, 1996; Pandzic, Magnenat-Thalmann, & Thalmann, 1998), and

- SmallTool (Broll, 1998).

Research platforms emphasize specific research issues such as facial communication, support of heterogeneous networks (Broll, 1997; Pandzic, Joslin, & Magnenat-Thalmann, 2000), or reliability, and tend to be limited in breadth (Greenhalgh, 2000). Furthermore, they focus on particular applications, and their re-usability is limited (Oliveira, Crowcroft, & Slater, 2000). This gives rise to a proliferation of independent, often partial systems, which renders them inappropriate for educational purposes. The solution of integrating or combining effort from different groups tends to be very difficult because of the different philosophies and assumptions, which condition each of these efforts.

To summarize, there are several platforms to support online virtual communities. However, current platforms rarely support both educational communities and the previously discussed goals. The current 3D multi-user communication platforms do not really take advantage of their (theoretical) potential for supporting collaborative e-learning. They are mainly dedicated to avatars movement and text chat collaboration. Features that aim to transport content or support collaborative work are neither integrated nor enhanced. Thus, the increased social presence is not accomplished. These reasons led to the design and implementation of a new platform to support educational virtual environments.

Overall Architecture

A high-level overview of the main components of platform EVE-II is presented in this section. As previously mentioned, the platform is supported by an EVE-II system, a Web-based community, and an LCME system.

The architecture of the platform is depicted in Figure 1. It is based on an n-tier model where each server is used for supporting specific services. These components are presented in detail in later sections of the chapter.

Client

The client is the end-user's computer with an Internet connection and a Web browser. The user utilizes the Web browser as well as necessary plug-ins (such as a VRML 97

Figure 1. Overall architecture

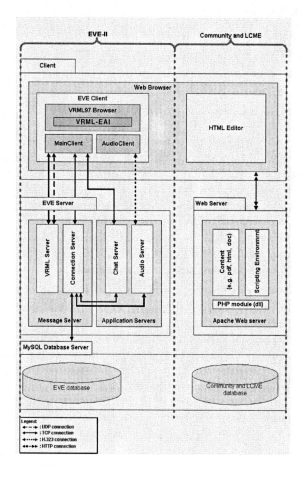

browser and an HTML editor) and/or Java applets (such as VRMLClient and MainClient, which are described later) so as to enter the system and exploit the offered functionality.

Server(s)

Our platform utilizes a set of servers in order to offer the desired functionality:

- **Web server and scripting environment:** The Web server is responsible for storing the learning content as well as for storing and executing the scripts of the scripting environment. It interacts with the Web browser through the HTTP protocol and with the database by means of the scripting environment. We use the Apache Web server (http://httpd.apache.org/) as it is free of charge; it runs on almost every platform; it supports a variety of scripting languages; it is reliable; it has good performance; and it is widely adopted.

The scripting environment is one of the basic components of the system architecture. It constitutes the link through which the other system components can communicate with each other and contributes to the smooth and effective delivery of the appropriate content. It supports interaction with the database, system administration, user authentication, manipulation and extraction of the user's role(s) and access rights in the system, whereas it supports the personal desk of the EVE Community and the LCME (which are described in subsequent sections). For the scripting environment, we have mainly used the (server-side) PHP scripting language (http://www.php.net) in combination to the JavaScript. PHP is open source, cross-platform, and extensible. It has excellent connectivity and high performance. JavaScript is also an open scripting language that is supported by all popular Web browsers. The main functionality offered by the scripting environment is: interactions with the database; system administration; user authentication; manipulation and extraction of the user's role(s) and access rights in the system; support of the Web-based community and the LCME.

- **EVE-II server**: As described in the following section, the EVE-II server is divided into multiple servers and it is used in order to support multi-user 3D virtual environments that are enhanced with voice and text chat communication. This server is totally implemented in Java, and it is characterized by scalability and openness.

- **Database:** The database management system constitutes the core of the whole system, where the majority of the available information is stored and organized. For the presented platform MySQL server (http://www.mysql.com) has been used, which is supported by PHP and many other scripting languages; it can be integrated with the majority of the Web servers (including Apache) and is supported by the majority of the available platforms. The database is responsible for management information regarding the users, the messages exchanged, the content that corresponds to each module, and the events taking place in each area. Furthermore, it is necessary for storing information about the available learning resources, namely, their metadata elements, their relationships, and information about the students' interactions with the content. In order to provide a common understanding regarding the pieces of content that will be used within the system, we distinguish three types of learning content model components: Assets, Learning Objects (including assessments), and Courses.

Table 1. Interrelations between system and SCORM content model components

System content model component	SCORM content model component
Asset	Asset
Learning Object (including assessments)	SCO
Course	Content Aggregation

These are defined as follows:

- **Assets:** Assets comprise the basic constitutive element of the courseware. They refer to raw media files that can be viewed by a Web browser, such as slides, flash objects, exercises, and 3D simulations.

- **Learning Objects/Assessments:** A learning object refers to the learning content launched by the learning management element and delivered to the end-user during a courseware learning experience. It can be either a collection of one or more assets or an assessment object. Assessments may contain a question of at least four types, namely multiple-choice (true-false and multiple answer are also included), matching, fill-in-the-blanks, and open short-answer questions (including short-paragraph questions).

- **Courses:** One or more learning objects or even courses can be aggregated together to form a cohesive unit of instruction, that is, an asynchronous course. Within a course, the learning objects and courses will be listed sequentially in a tutor-defined order. Using a course as part of another course, tutors have the ability to develop courses nested in any depth and, thus, apply learning taxonomy hierarchy.

To meet the requirements for content accessibility and reusability, the system provides compatibility with SCORM metadata specification (http://www.adlnet.org). In order to apply SCORM conformant metadata to the content model components adopted by the presented system, the interrelations depicted in Table 1 are assumed (Bouras, Nani, & Tsiatsos, 2003).

EVE-II System

The multi-user VR system used is a platform for supporting NVEs called EVE-II. EVE-II is based on open technologies (VRML, Java, MySQL, and PHP). It offers stable sharing of VRML events, text chat, and voice chat communication among the users represented by avatars in 3D virtual worlds. The main characteristics of the EVE-II platform are the flexibility and extensibility of the architecture, its stability, and the support of an easy way for transforming standalone 3D worlds to multi-user places.

The technologies used for the implementation of EVE-II, the system architecture, the main system components, and their interaction are presented in this section.

EVE-II architecture (Figure 1) is based on a client-multi-server model. The current form of EVE-II constitutes an open and flexible architecture of simple structure, which allows and supports the basic functionality that the platform is intended to offer. Therefore, the servers on which the platform relies are the message server and two application servers, a text chat and a voice chat server. This model offers scalability and flexibility to the EVE-II architecture, because if needed, more application servers could be integrated in order to offer more functionality. Furthermore, the selection of the above-mentioned architecture results in the distribution of the processing load among the above set of servers.

In addition, EVE-II is characterized by openness due to the fact that is based on open technologies and international standards. More specifically, the implementation of EVE-II is mainly based on:

- Virtual Reality Modeling Language (VRML), for the representation of the 3D worlds and the description of the 3D objects;

- VRML External Tutoring Interface (VRML-EAI) (http://www.web3D.org/), for implementing an interface between the 3D worlds and the external tools;

- Java, for the development of the client-server model, and the network communication among the different components of the platform; and

- H.323 (http://www.itu.int), for offering audio conferencing services through the Internet.

EVE-II is the second version of a system for NVEs (called EVE), which mainly improved on the sharing of events and on audio communication among the users. Concerning the sharing of multi-user events, EVE-II goes beyond EVE and other platforms (Bouras & Tsiatsos, 2004). In particular, the VRML data-sharing mechanism in EVE was based on the usage of an SVE file, which maintained every shared event and shared object in order to facilitate the multi-user communication and the initialization process. This updated approach for the sharing of the multi-user events is based on a VRML parser that has been implemented. The VRML parser runs on the server side; it is an extension of the SVE parser and helps the server to recognize the shared events without the usage of an SVE file. Using this approach, EVE-II presents the following improvements over EVE:

- It offers enhanced stability through an improved interface with EAI as well as a better support of avatar and avatars' gestures.

- It supports a facile creation of a multi-user space from a standalone, through the integration of the VRML parser. In particular, the shared events are commented out (i.e., marked with a "#") in the original VRML file, and thus the standalone world is transferred to a multi-user one.

- It offers server-side syntax checking of 3D spaces in order to support better and faster sharing of multi-user events.

- It supports execution of shared scripts and VRML routes and full support of script sharing (both on JavaScript and Java format).

- It supports server-side execution of scripts, which offers better sharing of events, even in cases that are based on time triggering.

- It supports dynamic insertion of shared objects in multi-user places.

- It supports specific PROTOs (such as "chair" for avatar's sitting).

- It supports better initialization process.

Concerning audio communication, H.323 protocol is supported. H.323 is an ITU recommendation that defines a network architecture and the necessary associated protocols to voice and multi-media calls establishment. H.323 is a protocol suite that can be used for establishing, modifying, and terminating multimedia sessions or calls. These multimedia sessions include both point-to-point and multipoint conferences and Internet telephony applications. The main reason for this choice has been the H.323's modular structure, which offers flexibility and allows the usage of many well-known codecs and mechanisms for the transmission of the data. Furthermore, H.323 supports much more services than voice-over IP, such as videoconferencing, which could be integrated into future versions of the EVE-II platform

In the following paragraphs the main components of EVE-II architecture are described.

Server Side

The servers on which the platform relies are the message server and two application servers (a chat and an audio server).

Message Server

The message server is responsible for the manipulation of the virtual worlds that constitute the training area of the platform. In addition, this server creates and supports the illusion to the participants that they share a common space by updating the view of the world every time that a shared object is modified. Two servers, each of which is used for a specific sequence of operations, constitute the message server. These servers are the Connection server and the VRML server:

- **Connection server:** This server maintains a database, which the system accesses in order to authenticate the user and allow him/her to enter the virtual space of EVE-

II. In addition, the connection server reports every entry or departure that takes place in the platform to all other servers.

- **VRML server:** This server monitors and records every event that takes place in the virtual space and reports these changes to all participating clients of the platform. Thus, by performing these continuous updates, the system assures that the users will have the illusion of sharing a common space. The VMRL server also constantly maintains an updated copy of the world, which is sent to the clients when they enter the system. In this way, the incoming users share the same updated view as the existing users.

Application Servers

The application servers are responsible for providing specific functionality to the participants of the virtual world. In the current form of EVE-II, there are two application servers available, a chat server and an audio server.

- **Chat server:** This server is responsible for the text chat support. It allows group chat, which means text chatting between multiple users, or whispering, which allows the one-to-one communication between two users.

- **Audio server:** This server is responsible for the audio communication between the users of the system. The audio server uses H.323 as its main protocol. H.323 is a powerful multimedia communications protocol, which can transfer voice, video, or data over IP networks, and is especially fitted for this application. The main audio service offered by the system is the audio communication among all participants in a virtual world or between pairs of them. So, the audio server is, in fact, an H.323 Multipoint Conference Unit (MCU), which supports audio conferencing among the users. By using H.323, compatibility with a large range of H.323 audio servers and clients is achieved, and the use of audio as a separate service of EVE-II is permitted, while the numerous applications of H.323 can enrich the functionality of the platform—for example, by the future addition of video conferencing capabilities.

Client Side

As depicted in Figure 1, in order for the users' client to communicate with EVE-II servers and have access to the provided functionalities, they need a Web browser, a VRML browser, the main EVE-II client, and an audio client.

- **Web Browser:** The Web browser is used for the communication with the Web server of the system, which provides an initial interface and entry point between the user's client and EVE-II environment.

- **VRML Browser:** The 3D environment of EVE-II is implemented using the VRML language. Therefore, a VRML browser, a plug-in, is essential in order to allow the navigation of the user's avatar in the virtual training space. ParallelGraphics Cortona VRML browser is a tested solution.

- **Main Client:** This client is responsible for the primary connection of the user to the Message Server, the interaction between the user's avatar and the 3D virtual space of EVE-II, as well as the text chat communication between the users of the same virtual space. In particular, the main client, which is a Java applet, makes an initial connection to the connection server, which allows it to present the current connection status and, when the user is authenticated, it passes it on to the VRML server.

  During an initialization phase, the list of the current participants in the virtual space is retrieved, as well as some information about the user avatar. Then, the normal message exchange with the VRML server begins. The first message received always contains the world, in its current state, and the users' avatars, so that the initialization phase can be completed and the standard operation be started.

  During normal operation, this client is responsible for the interaction between the user's avatar and the 3D virtual space of EVE-II. In particular, every time that a user acts on an object, this client reports the modification and interaction to the VRML server of the platform that performs the update and transmits it to all connected participants.

  The main client also includes a chat client. This part of the main client is responsible for the text chat communication between the users of the same virtual space. Every time that a message is sent from the client's side, it is passed to the chat server that, in turn, transmits it to the appropriate destinations.

- **Audio Client:** The audio client is a Java applet that records the audio stream from the user's side and transmits it to all appropriate destinations, allowing the audio communication between participants of the same space. As already described, H.323 is used to support the audio services. The audio client communicates only with the audio server, which is used as an MCU, handling and mixing the audio streams sent by the clients and forwarding them to the correct destinations.

Network Communication

The network communication of EVE-II, like its architecture, is focused on providing the available functionality at the best possible performance. Therefore, for the transmission of the packets and the achievement of the communication of the connected clients with the host servers (message server, audio server, and chat server), as well as for the server-to-server communication, there are three types of communication supported. Each of these types is found to be optimum for certain kinds of messages. Thus, the messages exchanged in the EVE-II system have been categorized into four basic categories: (a) the messages related to the initial connection of a client to a server, as well as the messages exchanged between the servers of the platform; (b) the position messages that are related with the avatars' position and orientation in the virtual environment; (c) the important messages, which correspond to messages that are vital for the consistency of the networked virtual environment (for simplicity reasons, we consider important messages to be all messages except for the position messages); and finally, (d) messages related to audio streams.

In the following subsections, we describe why a connection type is selected for the corresponding category of messages described above.

TCP Communication

The main characteristic of the TCP communication is the reliability of the transmission of information packets. Therefore, this type of communication is selected for the cases where the reliable delivery of the exchanged messages is essential and vital to the maintenance of the consistency of the networked virtual environment, even if that introduces some delay in the transmission. For the EVE-II system, this type of communication is selected for the following messages: (a) the server-to-server communication; (b) the initial connection of a client to the message server, which includes the authentication; and (c) the messages that are vital for the consistency of the NVE, including the messages that create the 3D world and the avatars when a new client enters the system.

A possible failure or loss of the delivery of this type of messages could cause serious inconsistencies in the presentation of the virtual environment and could introduce security issues to the EVE-II system.

UDP Communication

The main characteristic of this type of communication is the high speed in the transmission of the information packets. However, one of the main drawbacks of the simple UDP communication is that it cannot assure the reliable and correct delivery of the data packets. Therefore, this type of communication is selected for the transmission of messages where their possible loss or failure of delivery would not have a severe impact on the consistency of the virtual world of the connected clients. Such messages are the position message, which carries information about the avatars' position and orientation in the virtual world, since their failure of delivery does not create important scene inconsistencies to the participants.

H.323 Based Voice Communication

As described above, H.323 protocol suite can be used for audio communication, while the transfer protocol used to actually transfer the audio data is the Real Time Protocol

(RTP). A client exchanges RTP packets with the audio server. As already described, the audio server mixes the audio streams and forwards them to the clients, making sure that sounds generated by a client are not sent back to it.

Eve Community

EVE Community (http://ouranos.ceid.upatras.gr/vr/) is a prototype that has been developed to meet the requirements of an Educational Virtual Environment. EVE Community aims to provide the necessary, synchronous and asynchronous e-learning functionalities to its members in order to simulate a real learning environment. In particular, EVE community forms a collaborative educational social space where members have the capability to gain knowledge through dynamic procedures and activities. The system focuses on interaction between the users and encourages communication among them by providing synchronous and asynchronous means of communication and collaboration. A critical factor for the Educational Virtual Environments is the awareness of other users and the awareness of learning objects and material (Bouras & Tsiatsos, 2002). In order to enhance the awareness of the users, especially in the synchronous interaction, EVE community uses multi-user 3D environments, where the users are represented by 3D avatars (Bouras, Psaltoulis, Psaroudis, & Tsiatsos, 2001). Therefore, the community, based on the fact that users are influenced by the virtual representation, is supported by a 3D platform that can facilitate the e-learning process and offers all the tools necessary to simulate a real classroom. Every synchronous course is held in a 3D world, which virtually consists of all the "physical" equipment that could be found in a real classroom. Thus, the platform supports a whiteboard, a presentation table, and chairs where the avatars, which represent the users, sit. In addition, as an educational collaboration space, EVE-II platform supports a variety of communication and collaboration tools that actualize the interaction among the students and the tutor. Text chat, audio chat, and brainstorming are some of the components that forward to this direction. Another important element that EVE community takes into account is the role of the student in the community. The entity of students has advanced capabilities, which allow the users of this role to contribute to the formation of the social and information space. More specifically, students can use all the asynchronous means of communication that are contained in their personal desks, as well as the synchronous means of collaboration within the fields of the virtual classroom, when the tutor allows it. The most important functionality, which takes the student from an active entity to an actor, is the ability to add knowledge material through the uploading of files and his/her ability to create and form courses in the community, as well as becoming a tutor in some courses. EVE community, stepping in the path that educational requirements specify, tries to use available standards and technologies in order to provide an integrated solution.

Community Model

When designing and implementing a Virtual Collaboration Space, there are two main issues that should be taken into account. The first one concerns the fact that the hosted users may not be computer experts nor have a great deal of experience on how to act and navigate in such systems. Thus, the community architecture should offer a friendly to use interface and well-distinguished functionalities, which will guide the user through the learning process without spending much of his/her time on trying to figure out for what each component is used. EVE community is, therefore, structured in sections, where each user, depending on his/her role, can access and use the functionalities offered. The second issue concerns the consistency and efficiency of the hierarchy used in the framework of the community. In order to obtain and maintain a well-structured hierarchy, EVE-II stratified the involved entities and assigned rights of access to each of them. The main concepts that EVE community adopts are the concept of "Organization" and the concept of "Place." The first one is used for organizing the (asynchronous and synchronous) courses offered by the EVE community. The second one is used for the virtual areas that can be visited by the user. Therefore, we could describe EVE community as a set of Organizations that provide e-learning courses and Places that can be used privately by each member or concurrently by groups of users who attend a class. An Organization constitutes the entity that can provide knowledge through courses and can be an educational institute, a University, or even a company. Every Organization has the capability to develop and create categories and subcategories of online asynchronous and synchronous courses, which can be accompanied by e-learning material. These courses are available to all members of the community who can navigate in the system, through a friendly to use interface, and have the capability to view and choose from all the available courses those that meet their interests, as well as view information about the courses for which students or tutors are already registered. The model for organizing the courses offered by the community is hierarchical, and the terms of reference for the levels of the hierarchy (organization-category-subcategory-course) contribute to the flexibility and easy scalability of the community. Also, from the developer point of view, this hierarchy contributes to the consistency of the database schema and the organization of the learning material. EVE community adopts the concept of places in order to simulate and actualize the learning process. The community area is therefore distinguished in three places. The first one, called "Personal Desk," constitutes the user's personal workplace, which is enhanced with asynchronous features; the second one, called "Training area," constitutes the place where synchronous courses are realized; and the third one, called "Courseware area," constitutes the place where the user can access e-learning content in the form of asynchronous online courses. These three types of places are described in detail in the two following paragraphs.

Personal Desk

This term refers to a 2D place that contains all the asynchronous features (apart from the asynchronous courses) a user can access. The personal desk constitutes the unique, for each member, central place where he or she can administer personal holdings. Regardless of the user's role in the system, every member can navigate through the available (asynchronous and synchronous) courses and join the classes in which he or she is registered as a student, and view details about all other courses that he or she wishes to attend. In addition, the characteristic of the personal desk, as part of a Virtual Collaboration Space, is comprised of tools, which allow the asynchronous communication between the members of the community and contribute to the expanding and sharing of knowledge. Therefore, every member can access his/her personal messages, manage his/her profile and view other users' profiles, view and add information on his/her private and public calendars, upload/download files to/from his/her personal directory in the system, and view, post, and reply to messages in the community's forum. Also, a member can create a course and (if this course is approved) become a tutor for that course. The access levels in this space are altered in proportion to the user's role in the community. Thus, the roles that maintain more privileges from others can view additional features when entering their personal desk. Therefore, the user interface diversifies according to each role. As it is obvious, the personal desk facilitates the support of different access levels of the community. Furthermore, it contributes to make the users active due to the fact that they are free to choose the classes that they wish to attend.

Training Area

This place constitutes the virtual classroom where the synchronous courses take place. In EVE community, this place adopts a 3D representation based on the fact that 3D environments reflect positively on users' performance by creating a sense of presence and realism. Therefore, just as in real classrooms, the virtual classrooms must obtain all the prerequisites necessary for the conduction of the learning courses. Thereby, every course deals with a dedicated tutor, who is responsible for the management and the organization of the learning material, of the students and the course, in general. In addition, the students that attend the class and are represented by avatars have the capability to view the other users in the 3D multi-user virtual classroom, and thus maintain a scene of a real course. Furthermore, the 3D Collaboration world offers tools that contribute to the realization of a virtual course. These features, which according to their functionality and the need for realism, can either be 2D (for example, the text chat and the uploading and downloading of files) or 3D (for example, the whiteboard and brainstorming, as well as some extended functionalities such as audio chat), and access to the content repository are some of the components that develop the environment for the simulation of the real classroom. These features are going to be presented in detail later in this chapter.

Courseware Area

In this area, the student can access the courseware (series of online asynchronous courses), search and retrieve content of his/her preference, access his/her personal and academic records and information about his/her interactions with the content of an asynchronous course, and get support from a tutor responsible for the particular asynchronous course. There the student can see the table of contents of the asynchronous course in the form of a hyperlink tree. Furthermore, he or she can see a related resources list, which includes all the resources to which the current learning object relates.

User Roles and Rights

An important factor to be taken into account is the definition of the users' roles in the community, as well as the levels of access that each role involves. More specifically, in EVE Community there are six, well-defined user roles, each of which is associated with certain privileges. These user roles are the following:

Visitor

This type refers to users who have not yet been registered to the system. The users in this category can only view information (mainly static) and demos about EVE community and what it can offer, without being able to navigate and test the systems' functionalities. In addition, they have the capability to register with the system by completing a registration form, which will assign them to the member role.

Member

Members of the community are considered to be users who have not yet joined any of the available courses but who are registered with the system, which means that each has a unique username and password, wherefrom they are recognized. These users have the capability to navigate though the available classes and post registrations for the courses that correspond to their interests. In addition, they have the capability to use all the asynchronous features that the community provides, which include the forum, a personal calendar, send and receive messages, maintain their personal profile, and view other members' profile. However, these users, since are not registered for any class, cannot enter the 3D virtual world, the virtual classroom, where the courses take place.

Student

This user role corresponds to members that have registered for at least one class. Therefore, these users have all the capabilities mentioned above (forum, calendar, uploading/downloading of files), as well as some additional collaboration features that arise from their registration for a class. These features involve the insertion of the user into the 3D virtual classroom, his/her representation of avatars, his/her ability to communicate and collaborate with the other students of the course through collaborative tools, such as the use of a whiteboard, the brainstorming, text and voice chat, the dynamic uploading and sharing of files, and access to the courseware.

Tutor

The tutor role is assigned to only one person per course (asynchronous and/or synchronous). This user must be a member of EVE community, without necessarily being registered for a course as a student. As the concept of the hierarchy implies, the users who are assigned to be tutors in a certain course conserve the capabilities of the student category but obtain some additional "privileges" in relation to the lower levels of the hierarchy. Regarding the tutor's role, it should be distinguished in two instances. The first one consists of the asynchronous components that this kind of role can manipulate. More specifically, the users assigned as tutors have the capability to manage the learning material of each asynchronous and/or synchronous course that he or she created, create examinations and tests, view the users who have registered for the course, access information about each student's interaction with the content of a course, and upload files in the synchronous course's directory. The second one is related to the existence of the tutor in the 3D virtual classroom. In this place, the tutor is the most privileged among the users, as the management of the course falls to his/her jurisdiction. In particular, the tutor can create groups of students, assign them tasks, which he or she supervises during the class, and decide what will be presented on the whiteboard. Furthermore, the tutor is the floor manager of the classroom, which means that every time a student wishes to speak or pose a question, he or she must get the tutor's approval. In general, this type of user is responsible for the efficient realization of the course and the management of the students, who he or she has the ability to expel in cases thought necessary.

Course Manager

Each organization appoints a course manager, a person who is responsible for the creation and management of the categories, the subcategories, and the courses, in general. This entity is authorized to set a tutor for every course and decide which members, who displayed interest in the course, will become registered students. In addition, the course manager can view the users' profiles, consider their research areas, and create new categories, subcategories, and courses that correspond to the majority's interests. Like the tutor, the course manager is responsible for the organization and management of all students, in addition to tutors who have subscribed to any synchronous course of the organization that the course manager represents. Thus, this user can add or delete users, accept or deny requests for the creation of courses by tutors, and accept or deny requests for the attendance of a course by students. Moreover, a course manager can view any change in the asynchronous learning material and approve or reject it accordingly. The course manager is also responsible for the administration of the asynchronous means of communication and collaboration, such as the forum and the calendar of events. Regarding these components, the course manager is responsible for the selection of the topics that are going to be posted on the forum and the calendar. Through an administrative console, this user receives the submissions posted by the users (members, students, and tutors) of the community and decides which of the received information can contribute to the community's facilitation and to the learning process, in order to post it and make it accessible by all members.

EVE Administrator

There is only one person who holds this role, and he or she is the platform owner. Hierarchically, the administrator presents full access to the system, in which he or she can add, remove, and modify functionalities, fix possible weaknesses of the system, and create new organizations. In addition, the EVE administrator is responsible for the management of the course managers and the users of the community, in general.

In Table 2 the access rights of each role are presented. Also, Figure 2 depicts the hierarchy of courses in the EVE community according to organization concept and their relation to the roles and rights that EVE community supports.

What should be significantly emphasized is that the privileges that accompany the role of the tutor stand only for the courses to which this user is assigned. Similarly, the attributes of the course manager stand for the organization that this user represents. For every other entity, these users are treated by the system as members.

Table 2. Table of rights and roles

Place	Rights	EVE administrator	Course manager	Tutor	Student	Member
Organization	Create Organization	v				
	Delete Organization	v				
	Edit Organization's info	v	v			
	Assign course managers	v				
Course category / subcategory	Create Course Categories		v			
	Delete Course Categories		v			
	Edit Course Categories info		v			
	Create Course Subcategories		v			
	Delete Course Subcategories		v			
	Edit Course Subcategories info		v			
Courses (synchronous / asynchronous)	Create Courses		v	v		
	Delete Courses		v			
	Assign Tutors		v			
	Validate Course creation		v			
	Edit Courses' info		v	v		
	Accept / Delete Students		v			
	Register for Course			v	v	v
	Attend Course			v	v	

Figure 2. Roles and rights in EVE Community

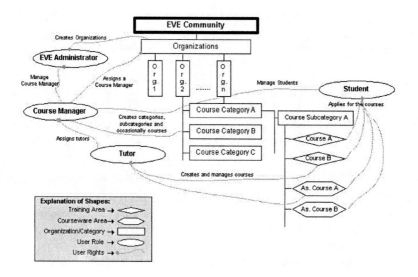

Functionality

The main goal of an Educational Virtual Environment is to provide all the tools, applications, and conditions necessary to make up an efficient space where communication and collaboration can be used for the maintenance and exchange of rich knowledge. Thus, EVE community, trying to simulate the learning process from its very beginning until its completion, is enhanced with the tools necessary for the advising, the notification, the encouragement, and interaction of the users, as it would happen in real educational communities.

In the following paragraphs the functionality of our platform is presented, except the functionality of the courseware area, which is presented in the subsequent section.

Personal Desk Services

These services (Figure 3) constitute, in a way, the anteroom, which prepares the users before attending a class (synchronous course), and is mainly comprised of asynchronous features. This space and the information provided are always available for the users, even if no courses are taking place at the time, and contribute to his/her advising, notification, reminding, and troubleshooting in the scope of the community.

Forum

One of the main services of the EVE's personal desk, as well as of every virtual community (Ganesan, Edmonds, & Spector, 2002), is a forum, which comprises a mean of asynchronous communication. Every registered member can post a topic to the forum with information that he or she thinks is important, and this message is posted to the administrator who ultimately decides whether this message could contribute to the community or not.

Calendar of Events

The calendar of events is a timetable that stores a collection of events and lists them in chronological order. It is an asynchronous mean of communication that can be used for the scheduling of events that take place in the virtual learning community. Each registered user can create a private calendar of events—a calendar in which only the user can see the contents and add posts. The calendar provided by EVE community can support three types of events: public, private, and those related to each course. In the public calendar of events, the members can post their announcements to the administrator, who, in turn, will decide if the announcement is "qualified" to be posted. Furthermore, there can be a course calendar that includes class schedules and venues, schedules assignments, examinations, and topics to be covered. The calendar consists of three views. The day view, which is also time scheduled, the month view, and the year view.

Text Chat

This feature allows participants to communicate in a synchronous mode. It is important to notice that text, as well as voice chat, are also supported in the 3D worlds where the students communicate with each other and with the tutor. However, the text chat described in this section can take place among members who do not join the same courses and are not bound to insert into a 3D world. In the framework of collaborative learning environments, text chat has proven to be extremely helpful for members who meet outside of the virtual classroom and discuss issues that concern them, pose questions, and generally interact without being supervised and rated. In addition, a group of people who share common interests can create its own chat rooms. This component also allows users to send private messages in the chat room that cannot be seen by the other members.

User Profiling

As the term indicates, a collaborative learning environment should motivate the communication between its members. In particular, better communication can be achieved between members who share common ideas and interests. Therefore, every member of the community, at the time of his or her subscription to the system, enters personal information that includes his/her interests, hobbies, the research areas that he or she

Figure 3. Personal desk services

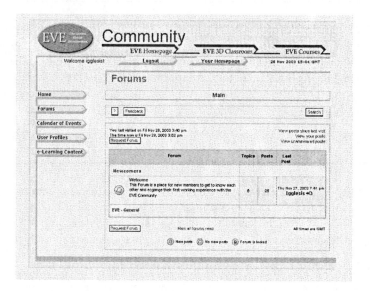

prefers, and so forth. Thereby, a profile for each user is created that is constantly enriched with additional information that arises from the selection of courses that the user decides to attend. An intelligent collaborative environment should be able to match users with common interests and encourage the communication between them. This functionality could be achieved with multiple queries in the users' profiles and selections of courses in order to track down areas of mutual interest, which will contribute to the distribution and extension of knowledge. In addition, a system should be able to compare the users' profiles, and especially the fields of research interests, with the available courses and suggest some possible alternatives. These functionalities could contribute to the interplay between the community members and the system, which, in turn, could result in effective distribution of knowledge.

Manipulation of E-Learning Content

A simulation of a real classroom presupposes that the tutor of the class has the capability to add and manage learning content, which should be dynamically changed, and dispose knowledge to the students, providing them the capability to have and process this learning material. In addition, there could be no efficient simulation if the students did not have the capability to maintain their own notebook, which in terms of an e-learning environment means a directory with files and folders for personal use. Such functionality can be supported by two basic operations—the uploading and downloading of files—in the framework of the collaborative virtual environment.

Training Area Services

The training area is exploited in order to host synchronous e-learning sessions. It combines 2D and 3D features in order to provide the users with communication and collaboration capabilities and necessary tools for realizing collaborative e-learning scenarios. There is one training area per course. The main feature of the training area is the 3D representation of a multi-user virtual classroom. This virtual classroom is the central place for realizing the learning process. The participants in the virtual classroom could have two different roles: tutor (only one participant) and students, according to the privileges in the EVE Community.

The users who participate in the virtual classroom are represented by avatars. The users' avatars are able to make various types of gestures: expressing opinions (e.g., agree, disagree), expressing feelings, mimics (e.g., happy, sad), as well as showing actions (e.g., move learning content, select learning content). The virtual classroom is supported by audio collaboration and text chat functionality. Also, it provides the users with the ability to upload their content and show it to other participants in the course. This ability is realized through a 3D presentation table. Moreover, this table offers further functionality, such as shared whiteboard or simulation of a brainstorming board. The user interface of the training area is depicted in Figure 4. More information about the functionality supported by the Training area is available in Bouras and Tsiatsos (in press).

Figure 4. User interface of the training area

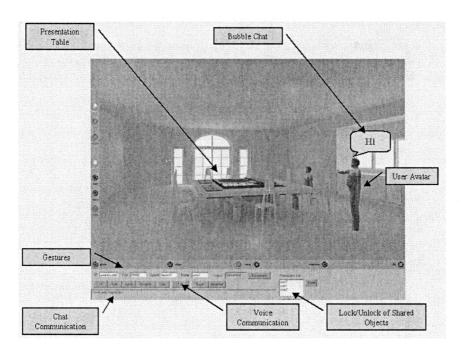

Learning Content Management Element

In this section, the design of the LCME element is presented; an LCME is a tool for the development and asynchronous delivery of high-quality learning objects and courses through the Web. Asynchronous content delivery allows for "any time" and "any place" learning and, thus, implies increased flexibility. Moreover, the functionality that the system offers to its end-users in accordance to their role (Student, Tutor, Course Manager) in the Courseware area is presented. The Web-based tool provides a comprehensible user interface and facilitates individuals with no specific computer science or e-learning skills to easily use the provided functionality (Bouras & Nani, 2004).

Design Characteristics

The tool presented in this chapter for building and accessing learning objects and online courses applies to individuals who are in different geographical locations and interested in a particular, often highly specialized, field. Their shared purpose is to gain knowledge of the field, while taking part in the learning process at any time and any place.

To extract the functional specifications of such a tool, we were based on, but not restricted to, the requirements that an up-to-date platform should meet concerning the content creation and access, and inspired by the current trends of the standardization efforts made on the learning technology field. The design characteristics can be summarized as follows:

- The system should support the import of a wide variety of content formats.

- The courseware elements, also called content model components, should be easily combined and aggregated to enable the creation of a learning content repository.

- The courseware should be divided into small modules.

- The content should be used and reused within different learning objects and/or courses.

- Online examinations and assessments should be available.

- The student's interactions with the content should be tracked.

- The courseware should be provided on a "distance learning" basis.

- The courseware should be designed to be platform-delivery independent.

- The system should provide the students with tutors with whom they can communicate online.

- The technology to be used should not demand any particular computer science or e-learning skills.

Accordingly to the aforementioned design characteristics, the LCME provides the means for creating and integrating courses and learning objects to the system and facilitates the students' access to the courseware. Students can conduct self-assessments, such as true/false, multiple-choice, multiple-answers, matching, fill-in-the-blank, and open short-paragraph questions, and get support by a tutor. Finally, a Course Manager assures the development and delivery of high quality content.

Functionality

The functionality that the platform provides to its end users, accordingly to their role in the Courseware Area, is now presented.

Tutor's Functionality

The main responsibilities of a tutor include the importation of raw material (assets) into the system, the creation of learning objects and assessments, the building of an asynchronous course, the enrichment of the learning resources with the appropriate metadata elements so that they can be accessible and reusable, and the editing of the metadata elements and the structure of an asynchronous course. However, any change to the learning content is not readily available, unless approved by the Course Manager. The main tutor's functionality is: courseware access; upload asset; create learning objects; create asynchronous course; edit course structure; edit metadata; manage courses; and manage students.

Student's Functionality

A student can access the courseware, search and retrieve content of his/her preference, access his/her personal and academic records, and get support from a tutor he or she has selected for the particular course. The student's main functionality is: access the asynchronous courses in browse or study mode; access information about the student-asynchronous course interactions; the learning objects, assessments, and related resources.

Course Manager Functionality

As already mentioned, the Course Manager: decides upon the assignment or not of the role of a student/tutor to a system member; approves or rejects any change to the learning content, thus, assuring the quality control of the courseware; and decides upon the expelling or not of a member from the courseware. The Course Manager functionality is: to see the number of the pending requests for the assignment or withdrawal of the student or tutor's role; to be informed about any change in the learning resources; and to access information about all the system members that have been assigned the student or tutor's role.

Future Work

In its current form, the platform manages to create and support Educational Virtual Environments, which can offer all the necessary tools for the communication, interaction between the members involved, access, creation and manipulation of the learning content, as well as the prerequisites for the simulation of a real classroom, thus providing all the "material" features that could be found in a real classroom (i.e., whiteboard, library, brainstorming, chat, etc.). However, EVE-II has the potential to be enriched with new features and tools that will exploit the capabilities of Virtual Reality's technologies and standards. Therefore, the graphical representation of the 3D virtual worlds could be enhanced in order to provide a more friendly and efficient knowledge environment. Finally, an important step for the fulfillment of this platform is its evaluation by users, which will bring to the surface any possible deficiencies that EVE-II may have. Furthermore, the integration of intelligent agents in EVE-II system will be a major enhancement of the functionality offered. Intelligent agents can support educational process and they can offer intelligent help to the users for the usage of the system. The incorporation of all these characteristics will lead to an integrated Educational Virtual Environment, from both pedagogical as well as technological aspect.

Concerning the LCME, it would be very useful to allow tutors to modify the various learning objects in addition to a course structure. Thus, tutors would have the ability to keep the content constantly updated without the need to develop it from scratch. This functionality, together with the possibility of replacing an asset in the Web server with a new version, presupposes the implementation of a version-control function. Moreover, the tutoring capabilities of the tool could be extended to allow the creation of new assessment objects. In this case, we should also examine how the users' answers could be tracked. Moreover, our next steps involve the research, design, and implementation of the way in which new user interactions with the content could be monitored. Examples of these interactions are: the time a user spends on an assessment object till he or she provides an answer; and the alternative content type the user selects to view (e.g., text or video). This information could provide useful information about the learning content usage and efficacy, as well as the user preferences.

Moreover, the integration of a Student Modeling System could add a significant value to the provided functionality. A Student Modeling System should facilitate the interactions among the users but, mainly, the user interactions with the system. By monitoring and analyzing the users' actions, the system could provide information about the system use, provide them with pedagogical advice, and encourage them to communicate with each other. Our future plans also include the design and implementation of a functionality that will allow tutors to export courses created in our system in a SCORM-conformant zip file (package). In this way, content created in our system could be imported into any SCORM-compliant system and, thus, be available to a wider audience.

Finally, after the completion of the aforementioned tasks, assiduous evaluation of the system contribution to the learning process could take place. This presupposes the systematic test of the provided functionality by the end users.

Conclusion

This chapter describes an integrated platform for Educational Virtual Environments. The platform, EVE-II, aims to provide an integrated learning environment, giving emphasis to both the pedagogical as well as the technological texture of the educational place. Therefore, the platform is constituted of three interlinked components, each of which supports certain type of services for providing the participating users with an integrated learning environment. Furthermore, this system is identified by the fact that it is comprised of well-distinguished roles and rights, which simulate the learning process in an efficient manner. The variety of learning tools, both in the asynchronous and synchronous mode, create a sense of community to the students and participants of the environment and form the basis for the realization of the online synchronous courses, which fundamentally provide all the functionalities of a real classroom. Thus, through a friendly to use and navigate environment, the members of EVE Community have the capability to maintain their personal profile in a private space with all their personal holdings and interests, have the potentiality to communicate, access asynchronous courses, interact with other members of the community, and participate in virtual courses, either as students or tutors, in order to obtain rich knowledge.

From a pedagogical scope, EVE has defined mindfully the roles and rights of the involved users, providing the capability to all of the users to become equally transmitters and receivers of knowledge. These roles and the rights that each of them implies form the basis for a learning environment that relies on the communication and interaction of its members, their mutual respect, and their active participation on the way to collaboration and knowledge.

From the technological scope, EVE manages to provide all the functionalities necessary for the asynchronous communication and support of its members and for the simulation of a real training area. Therefore, EVE-II used the technologies and standards available for the implementation and integration of the necessary 2D and 3D tools and created a platform that is characterized by operability and scalability.

The platform presented in this chapter includes many characteristics a distance learning platform should have. In particular, regarding the technological approach:

- The client can access the system through a standard Web browser without compelling the user to install additional software to his/her system.

- The system can run on a wide variety of platforms.

- The system adopts the metadata elements (all the mandatory and the majority of the optional) that are described in SCORM specification. The adopted content model is also inspired by SCORM. Its clear structure in combination with the metadata elements facilitates the easy reuse of the various learning resources for the creation of larger instructional units. Moreover, metadata facilitates the easy search and retrieval of the learning content.

Concerning the pedagogical approach, the platform tries to support collaborative e-learning and RBL services, thus:

- The platform encourages and accepts the users' autonomy and initiative. Students are able to communicate with their tutors in order to get help as well as with the other students. Moreover, all registered users can take part in the learning process through one or more different roles. This distribution of the rights and access levels the role model implies encourages the active participation of all the users involved in the learning process.

- For each action in the courseware area, the system provides the user with continuous feedback. For instance, when a user answers a self-assessment, the system inform him or her immediately about whether each answer was right, and which is the indicative answer to this particular question.

Moreover, the system offers the following services:

- Services for including and updating user profile.
- Services for creating and cataloguing courses.
- Services for creating tests.
- User tracking services.
- Services for creating, organizing, and managing learning content.
- Communication and collaboration tools.

From the above, it is clear that the proposed system presents various characteristics that an up-to-date distance learning environment should provide.

Last but not least, the platform utilizes open source technologies. Open source technologies are available free of charge; they do not depend on particular companies; they are usually reliable; and they have good quality (due to their qualitative control by many people and the primary evolution of the source code).

References

Bouras, C. & Nani M. (2004). A Web-based tool for building and accessing learning objects and online courses. In *Proceedings of the Fourth IEEE International Conference on Advanced Learning Technologies*, Joensuu, Finland, August 30-September 1 (pp. 645-647).

Bouras, C., Nani, M., & Tsiatsos, T. (2003). Building reusable and interactive e-learning content using Web. In *Proceedings of the International Conference on Web-based Learning (ICWL)*, Melbourne, Australia (pp. 497-508). Deakin University and The Hong Kong Web Society.

Bouras, C., Psaltoulis, D., Psaroudis, C., & Tsiatsos, T. (2001). Protocols for sharing educational virtual environments. In *Proceedings of 2001 International Conference on Software, Telecommunications and Computer Networks Split*, Dubrovnik (Croatia) Ancona, Bari (Italy), October 9-12 (Vol. 2, pp. 659-666).

Bouras, C. & Tsiatsos, T. (2002). Extending the limits of CVEs to support collaborative e-learning scenarios. In *Proceedings of IEEE International Conference on Advanced Learning Technologies*, Kazan, Russia, September 9-12 (pp. 420-424).

Bouras, C. & Tsiatsos, T. (2004). Distributed virtual reality: Building a multi-user layer for the EVE platform. *Journal of Network and Computer Applications*, April, *27*(2), 91-111.

Bouras, C. & Tsiatsos, T. (in press). Educational virtual environments: Design rationale and architecture. *International Journal of Multimedia Tools and Applications*.

Broll, W. (1997). Bringing people together—An infrastructure for shared virtual worlds on the Internet. In *Proceedings of the Sixth International Workshop on Enabling Technologies: Infrastructure for Collaborative Enterprises,* Cambridge, MA, June 18-20 (pp. 199-204). Las Alamitos, CA: IEEE Computer Society Press.

Broll, W. (1998). SmallTool—A toolkit for realizing shared virtual environments on the Internet. *Distributed Systems Engineering Journal*, Special Issue on Distributed Virtual Environments, *5*, 118-128.

Carlsson, C. & Hagsand, O. (1993). DIVE: a multi-user virtual reality system. In *Proceedings of IEEE 1993 Virtual Reality Annual International Symposium,* September 18-22, Seattle, WA (pp. 394-400). Piscataway, NJ: IEEE Service Center.

Ganesan, R., Edmonds, G., & Spector, M. (2002). The changing nature of instructional design for networked learning. In C. Steeples & C. Jones (Eds.), *Networked learning: Perspectives and issues* (pp. 93-109). London: Springer-Verlag.

Greenhalgh, C. (2000). Implementing multi-user virtual worlds (panel session): Ideologies and issues. In *Proceedings of the Web3D-VRML Fifth Symposium on Virtual Reality Modeling Language*, Monterey, CA, February 20-24 (pp. 149-154).

Laister, J. & Koubek, A. (2001). Third generation learning platforms requirements and motivation for collaborative learning. In *Proceedings of the Fourth International Workshop on Interactive Computer Aided Learning,* September 26-28, Villach,

Austria. Retrieved June 2005, from *http://www.eurodl.org/materials/2001/icl01/laister.htm*

Oliveira, M., Crowcroft, J., & Slater, M. (2000). Component framework infrastructure for virtual environments. In *Proceedings of the Third International Conference on Collaborative Virtual Environments 2000, ACM CVE 2000*, September 10-12, San Francisco (pp. 139-146).

Pandzic, I., Capin, T., Magnenat-Thalmann, N., & Thalmann, D. (1996). Towards natural communication in networked collaborative virtual environments. In *Proceedings of FIVE '96*, December 19-20, Pisa, Italy (pp. 37-47).

Pandzic, I., Joslin, C., & Magnenat-Thalmann, N. (2000). Trends in a collaborative virtual environment. In *Proceedings of International Conference on Software, Telecommunications and Computer Networks*, Split, Rijeka, Dubrovnik (Croatia), Trieste, Venice (Italy), October 11-14 (pp. 893-901). FESB-Split.

Pandzic, I., Magnenat-Thalmann, N., & Thalmann, D. (1998). Realistic avatars and autonomous virtual humans in VLNET networked virtual environments. In R. Earnshaw & J. Vince (Eds.), *Virtual Worlds in the Internet* (pp. 157-174). Cambridge, MA: IEEE Computer Society Press.

Chapter XVI

Intelligent and Adaptive Web-Based Instruction

Beverly Woolf
University of Massachusetts, USA

Mia Stern
IBM Rational Software, USA

Abstract

This chapter describes Web-based instructional tutors that support active and engaging learning. Towards that end, a theoretical foundation for designing such tutors is proposed and two Web-based tutors described. The tutors reason about a student's knowledge and their own teaching strategies while taking advantage of the possibilities of the Web, by being open to other resources (Web sites) and other people (online communities). One tutor, Rashi, provides problem-based activities and tracks a student's critical thinking in biology and geology, and the second, iMANIC, uses hypermedia to customize online lectures for individual students based on learning need. This work provides promising data points for the development of authentic and effective learning that can take advantage of the possibilities of the Web, without being rooted in extensions of what already exists in the classroom, such as lectures or bulletin boards.

Introduction

The educational potential of the Web is apparently limitless, supplying asynchronous education for millions of students who have only an Internet connection and a computer. The potential benefits outweigh anything provided by a classroom or teacher—courses installed and supported in one place, available anytime, anywhere, using multiple media, individualized for the student and targeted at all learning levels.

However, issues of style, technology, and pedagogy challenge achievement of quality Web instruction. The quality of such instruction is of critical concern because enabling full access to *poor* or *non-existing* online resources does not provide good education. Currently, no gatekeeper, for example, "Amazon.com for education," exists to evaluate instructional resources or record the opinion of students and teachers about their effectiveness. Other distance learning issues focus on isolation felt by students while working with online teaching and teachers unable to locate resources for a specific domain and student. Although schools enjoy greater connectivity and teachers use the Web more (Tech-Ed, 2000), grade school teachers do not utilize the Web for student instruction (Cuban, Kirkpatrick, & Peek, 2001).

Students are frustrated and increasingly dissatisfied by the digital disconnect they are experiencing at school. They cannot conceive of doing schoolwork without Web access and yet they are not being given many opportunities in school to take advantage of the Web. (Levin & Arafeh, 2002, p. v)

Middle and high school students want to be assigned activities "that are relevant to their daily lives" and to have Internet access beyond that available in computer labs.

Current Web instruction is not typically personalized for an individual student. Authors tend to prepare material appropriate for a fixed and undifferentiated body of students, each student receiving the same material presented in the same way. For example, a request for information about a topic on the Web typically elicits tens of thousands of responses geared to providing unstructured and non-prioritized material, including slides, class notes, glossaries, and the like, presented in a static and non-personalized manner.

The potential exists to tailor Web material to individual students, where material is customized for a student's learning level and style. Thus, a query from a grade-school child about "thyroid" might elicit a definition and simple graphic. A visually handicapped student would receive a spoken discussion and a pre-medical student, a formal description, lists of signs and symptoms within a case study, a quizzing module and perhaps real-time experimental data. Providing the same amount of customization in a classroom or non-computer environment is nearly impossible.

Issues of pedagogy and style need to be addressed before widespread customizable Web education becomes available on a global scale. The next section provides a theoretical basis for designing customized and adaptive Web education. Then, two intelligent and adaptive Web tutors are described: the first tutor helped students use critical thinking while proposing hypotheses, and the second tutor generated new content and new pages for each student based on learning needs. The future of Web-enabled instruction is discussed in the next to last section and then the founding principles of the Internet and their impact on education are discussed in the last section.

Theoretical Background

Educators from pre-school to graduate school are rethinking the very nature of teaching, learning, and schooling, based on opportunities provided by the Web (Owston, 1997). In order to fully realize this educational potential, a new theoretical framework needs to be developed that focuses on what instruction is wanted and needed on the Web, and how to build such instruction. Any such framework should begin with the premise that students need to be involved, engaged, and active in authentic and challenging work. Like all other learning environments, the Web is only useful if the learner is motivated and wants to learn. It is well known that page turning or browsing does not ensure effective learning. Flashy graphics and simulations are not enough; the experience must be authentic and relevant to the learner's life (Schank, 1994). A theoretical model for Web instruction is needed that moves beyond the "Tyranny of the Button" (Woolf & Hall, 1995) and includes use of intelligent simulation, dynamic links (online generation of links based on a student's behavior), and multimedia composition and creation.

This section proposes a theoretical framework, modeled on a foundation suggested by Bransford (2004), and based on ideas expressed in a National Academy of Sciences (NAS) report, *How People Learn* (Bransford, Brown, & Cocking, 1999). The framework suggests that active student learning requires instruction to be *knowledge-, student-, assessment-* and *community-centered*.

Knowledge-centered means that teaching is based on an analysis of a student's needs and what she will be able to do when finished with the materials. Classrooms obviously cannot adapt teaching material to an analysis of what each student will need to do with the material when finished, as students have distinct goals and learn in different ways and at different rates.

On the other hand, vast repositories of knowledge on the Web provide the potential to address alternative student goals. Instructional Web resources are not automatically *knowledge-centered*; Web pages and portals often provide linear selections of topics, mimicking classroom slides or notes, which are difficult for students to absorb. Important content opportunities should be designed by working back from how students will function and what they will need to know and do at the end of their interaction with the system. Additionally, the lack of good Web access methods, beyond search engines, often confuses and disorients students (and adults), creating a serious barrier to learning.

Learner-centered instruction means that a learner's preconceptions, strengths, and interests are considered. Students should not be treated as blank slates with respect to goals, opinions, knowledge, and time. Certainly, large lecture-style classrooms fall short on this principle. Similarly, many Web resources do not satisfy this criterion. Pages of slides, text, virtual laboratories, and simulations are not *learner-centered* if they present the same material to all students, not tracking the student's actions, goals, or knowledge. Some Web-based instruction systems, especially intelligent resources, do honor a student's preconceptions and cultural values with customized links and problems, reasoning about individual learning need and individualized responses, as described in the next section.

Assessment-centered instruction means that a student's thinking and progress is made visible, providing the student with multiple chances to review her learning. Assessment also involves providing data to teachers so they can assess the effectiveness of their teaching materials and possibly modify teaching strategies based on input about student knowledge. Most classrooms and learning environments are devoid of this feature, primarily because individual assessment requires significant effort and time from a teacher.

However, some Web homework systems do provide individualized feedback and help students revise their thinking based on feedback appropriate to the problem facing them. Several homework systems have resulted in significant increases in class grades, for example, OWL (Dufresne, Mestre, Hart, & Rath, 2002; IMMEX, 2003; Stevens & Nadjafi, 1997) and Diagnoser (Hunt & Minstrell, 1994). These homework programs assess individual student activities, broken down by problem, section, topic, or student. A student's thinking can be made visible inside laboratory and simulation materials when such environments correctly indicate accomplished procedures. Intelligent Web instruction models a student's learning, tracks student behavior, provides individual assessment through feedback, and allows learners to revise their thinking.

Community-centered instruction means that students are encouraged to collaborate, ask questions, and receive help. Only the best classrooms provide such communities. Many classrooms follow the student norm of "don't participate" and "don't get caught not

Figure 1. Biology Interview Tool. In the Biology Inquiry tutor, students interviewed the patient though free text by typing a question into the tool. The patient answered by audio, video, and transcript.

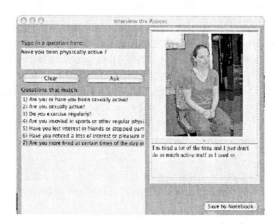

Figure 2. Patient Examination Tool. Students measured weight, pulse, and blood pressure. In this example, the student selected the neck and was given the choice of exam results for thyroid, heart, lymph, or mouth.

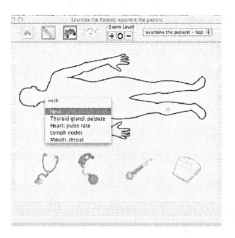

knowing something." However, as more people participate and communicate with others on the Web and distance education, *community-centered* Web environments become more likely. Online communities support students and teachers around homework help. For example, Math Forum is one of the largest teacher and student communities (over a million individuals) and most popular instructional digital libraries in existence (see http://mathforum.org). The extensive Web site indexes over 1.2 million learning resources, Frequently Asked Questions (FAQs), mathematics problems and tools, and manages a community of over 2,500,000 visitors a month. Ask Dr. Math (http://mathforum.org/dr.math/) provides both human and computer support for solving math problems. Other features include a searchable archive for mathematics problems, available by level and topic, FAQs, and a human tutor, for more detailed interaction.

The Web has enormous potential to support world-wide communities. Obviously, the quality and nature of each community, whether students feel supported or not, and the policy of each facility need to be carefully designed. A *chat* facility can be linked to any learning material so that class members can discuss concepts and learning while pursuing possibly static pages. Distance education courses often require students to participate in chat sessions and community building efforts. "People knowledge" is important in defining such online communities, as participants often want to know others at a personal level before becoming comfortable sharing their own thoughts. They also need to decide about the specification of their contributions; for example, Can I suggest outrageous ideas? Do I need to stick to the guidelines in my responses? As in any physical community, trust is important to an online community.

Two Intelligent Web-Enabled Tutors

We suggest that the Web is especially poised to realize the instructional principles listed above. This section describes two examples of intelligent and adaptive Web tutors that address many of these principles. The first tutor supported students to think critically and suggest hypotheses, observations, and data while solving a case. The second tutor customized Web content based on student learning needs. These two tutors, and many like them, provide data points to suggest that Web resources can maintain active and authentic student learning.

An Inquiry Web Tutor

The first intelligent Web tutor asked students to gather data to support or refute their hypotheses about the causes of a situation (Bruno, 2000; Bruno & Jarvis, 2001; Murray, Woolf, & Marshall, 2004; Woolf et al., 2002; Woolf et al., 2003). Students were immersed in a case, asked to observe a phenomenon, reason about it, posit theories to explain their observations, and recognize when data did or did not support a hypothesis. This tutor was *knowledge-centered* in that it represented the domain knowledge and tracked a student's mastery of that knowledge. It was *learner-* and *assessment-centered* in that it responded in the context of the student's reasoning and indicated if student reasoning was not consistent with that of the expert. It was also *community-centered* in that people at remote sites used it collaboratively to solve a single case.

Supporting inquiry learning in a classroom is difficult because faculty may not know how to encourage students to articulate new questions, to scaffold them to refine existing hypotheses, and to move students to gather new evidence and make further predictions (Bruno, 2000; Bruno & Jarvis, 2001). Teachers in traditional classrooms have difficulty tracking students' progress in articulating questions and developing hypotheses. Typically, teachers ask 95% of the questions, most of which require short answers (Graesser & Person, 1994; Hmelo-Silver, 2002). This pushes students away from inquiry-oriented instruction. Unfortunately, many computer-assisted teaching systems also deliver concepts, facts, and findings, thus directing students to a single correct answer.

Inquiry software, on the other hand, scaffolds students to synthesize observations, to confirm or refute their own hypotheses, and to learn to assess and trust the validity of their own hypotheses. Many instructional software systems present inquiry cases (Aleven & Ashley, 1997; Alloway et al., 1996; Krajcik, Blumenfeld, Marx, & Soloway, 2000; Suthers, Toth, & Weiner, 1997; White, Shimoda, & Frederiksen, 1999). These projects provided tools for gathering and organizing information during inquiry, but rarely tracked a student's argument.

The Inquiry Tutor infrastructure, called Rashi[1] supported critical thinking in multiple domains including biology, geology, and forestry. Its primary focus and contribution to the field was to directly support and scaffold a student's inquiry processes by tracking student observations, hypothesis formation, data collection, analysis, and argumentation.

Figure 3. Patient Laboratory Results. The student requested a laboratory test for the patient and was required, in some cases, to explain why a particular test was necessary.

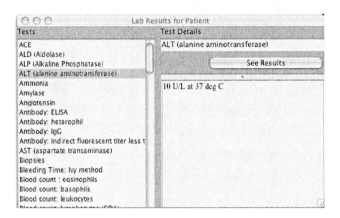

Biology Inquiry Tutor

In the biology domain, Rashi supported students as they evaluated a patient with an unknown illness. The software was used with students enrolled in introductory biology courses, who were not necessarily biology or pre-medical majors. Patient complaints formed an initial set of data from which students began the diagnostic process. They "interviewed" the patient about symptoms and examined her (Figures 1-3). Some data was made visible by student action, for example, asking for chest x-rays, prescribing a certain drug, or using a measurement tool. Some data was interpreted for the student (e.g., "x-ray normal"); other data provided raw material and the student interpreted it and drew her own conclusions.

Rashi did not enforce any order of student activity. Students moved opportunistically from one phase to a non-adjacent phase. They listened to the case description, situations, and goals, extracted pertinent information, and tried to diagnose the cause of the patient's symptoms.

Working in groups, students brainstormed a list of predictions that might resolve the problem and typed in possible causes for the observed phenomena. In this sense, the tutor was *community-centered*. Students gathered data to confirm or refute each hypothesis and resolve open questions. For example, students interviewed the patient about her symptoms and requested specific physiological signs, medical history, lab tests, or patient examinations. They used the *Inquiry Notebook* to sort, filter, and categorize data, record open questions and hypotheses, and to identify data that might reveal flaws in a hypothesis (Figure 4). They identified data that either supported or weakened each hypothesis using the *Argument Editor* (Figure 5), using a "drag and drop" feature to move data from the *Inquiry Notebook* to the *Argument Editor*.

The *Coach* provided on-demand help, hints, and feedback by comparing the knowledge base of inferences supplied by the teacher with information submitted by the student in

Figure 4. Inquiry Notebook *in Biology. Student observations from the physical exam, lab tests, and interview were automatically recorded in the* Inquiry Notebook. *Students indicated the type of proposition entered (e.g., observations, inferences and hypothesis), the importance of each observation and their confidence in the observations.*

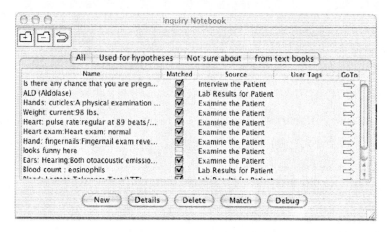

either the *Inquiry Notebook* or *Hypothesis Editor*. In this sense, the tutor was *assessment-centered*. Coaching was based on a number of rules that looked for certain conditions in the student's work and provided hints if those rules were not met. The *Coach* might state:

- "You argue that high TSH supports a diagnosis of mononucleosis. I suggest you reconsider this argument."

- "There is important data for this case that you have not found nor recorded in your notebook. See the student's prior history."

- "You have several hypotheses that have no supporting arguments."

- "You have a circular argument associated with hypothesis 3."

At some point, each student made a final electronic report that involved designating and supporting one hypothesis as the "best." This submission, sent electronically to the teacher, used data, inferences, hypotheses, justifications, competing hypotheses, and arguments from the *Inquiry Notebook* and *Argument Editor*.

Client-server software supported storing data about students. A simple database housed the text entered by students as well as the *Inquiry Notebook* and *Argument Editor* objects. Intelligence was distributed between server and client, and Java was used to implement visual activities, graphical user interfaces, and for reasoning about the student. Java handled the analysis to match student text entries against the database

Figure 5. Argument Editor in Biology. Students indicated supporting and refuting evidence for each hypothesis. The student suggested that the hypothesis "Patient has Mono" was supported by evidence, including "she seems very tired" and "TSH levels are higher than the normal range" (not shown). Evidence was dragged from the Inquiry Notebook, *Figure 4, into the* Argument Editor.

object and analysis of *Inquiry Notebook*. The server communicated the results back to the client running in a browser. The object database and all the algorithms for doing the analysis resided in the application and the server was only contacted to store student data.

Geology Inquiry Tutor

The Rashi inquiry infrastructure, described above, was also used in geology, where students explored a geologic phenomenon and tried to predict future events. The target students were enrolled in undergraduate introductory geology courses. This section describes the Fault Recognition Module in which students predicted where the next earthquake might occur. The module opened with compelling footage of a series of large and recurring earthquakes in the San Andreas area of California, USA. (Figures 6 and 7). A "click" on a highlighted spot took students to the main task, the relocation of a road destroyed by an earthquake (Figure 8). Three possible routes for a replacement road were suggested, all of which passed through combinations of four suspicious areas. As project geologists, students evaluated the area, made observations about the four

Figure 6. Fault Recognition Module. Students reviewed footage of the San Andreas fault area and then investigated hotspots.

Figure 7. Geology Tutor Observation. Each view of a significant observation provided data enabling students to identify features such as offset amount, direction sense, or orientation of a fault.

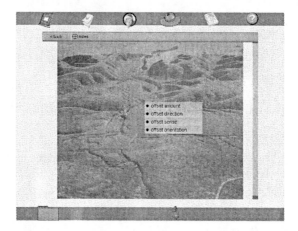

suspicious areas and inferences about their observations, and used those inferences to prepare an engineer's report containing their route recommendations.

Clicking on suspicious area #1 (Figure 9) revealed a large linear feature crossing the proposed route and extending for many miles. The student might have recognized that the feature was probably a transform fault. Other hotspots led to a slicken site (Figure 10) or sheared roots (Figure 11), where students located data about the sense, direction, and amount of the offset. As they identified these features, students noted observations

Figure 8. Proposed highway routes. Students hypothesized which of three proposed routes was least likely to experience an earthquake in the next 40 years.

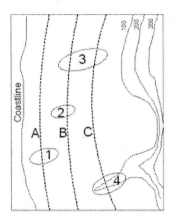

Figure 9. Linear feature. One hotspot from Figure 8 led to an aerial view of this large linear feature crossing the proposed route. Additional hotspots provided detailed data of other areas.

Figure 10. Evidence of a slicken site. Students identified data on the offset-slickenline including orientation, sense, direction, and amount.

Figure 11. Sheared roots. Students recorded data on the size and offset of sheared roots.

Figure 12. Inquiry Notebook *in Geology. Students described observations, inferences and hypotheses in the* Inquiry Notebook.

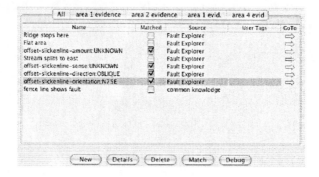

in the *Inquiry Notebook* (Figure 12), and the *Argument Editor* (Figure 13). Hotspots on additional images provided information, such as:

- A line of springs parallel to the lineament;

- A fence broken and offset 1.3 meters;

- A data set showed that the area was seismographically active; and

- A long-term data set showed that major seismographic events have occurred here about every 22 years and showed the recurrence interval for Parkfield quakes.

Figure 13. Argument Editor *in Geology. Students used the* Argument Editor *to indicate which observations supported or refuted which hypotheses.*

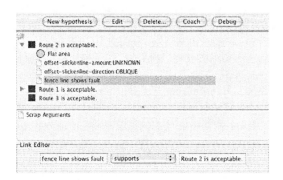

How Does the Inquiry Tutor Work?

Rashi allowed learners to differentiate various steps of the inquiry cycle. At each decision point, the tutor compared a student's observations and inferences to a database of expert cases prepared by the teacher. The *Coach* prompted students to reexamine their work if their observations or hypotheses veered off course. Thus, Rashi provided *knowledge-, student-,* and *assessment*-centered instruction.

Dialogue between Student and Tutor

Coaching feedback was enabled by a database of expert rules that established the relationship between observations and inferences. These rules formed the basis of evaluation of the students' inferences and hypotheses (e.g., the recommendations for relocating a road in the above scenario). In turn, the rules provided the basis of the dialog that guided students toward better solutions.

Student Input

After the student observed an image or an activity, she chose a feature (e.g., lineament or slickenlines in geology) to describe, and entered it into the *Inquiry Notebook* (Figure 12). Elsewhere in the notebook students entered inferences (interpretations) of observations along with supporting reasoning. For example, s/he may have inferred that a lineament was an active fault and supported that inference with multiple evidential citations. Finally, the student made a recommendation (conclusion) of the best hypothesis supported by observations and inferences.

Tutor Input

For each potential observation (e.g., lineament, seismic record, microstratigraphy, in geology), the database contained the following information: (1) description of feature, (2) list of possible student inferences (interpretations), and (3) ranking of interpretations (ranging from strongly supportive, to irrelevant, to strongly unsupportive). The expert rules of the domain provided the basis of the database. The tutor generated a new table for each student session that compared a student's responses with expert rules. If this comparison revealed student weakness or error, the tutor guided the student by either directing him/her to reexamine the data or to seek other observations. The tutor did not interpret natural language input. Instead, the student crafted his/her observations and inferences from pull-down menus that contained more items than needed, as well as distracter items.

Rashi supported teachers to develop new modules for their own needs or based on their own photo collections (Murray, Woolf, & Marshall, 2004). *Authoring tools* enabled subject matter experts to specify content (images, text, numeric values, etc.) that populated the various data gathering tools and data source lists. To support coaching, authors also specified evidential relationships (supports, refutes, etc.) between potential hypotheses and data and indicated which hypotheses were reasonable conclusions for each case.

Evaluation of the Inquiry Tutor

Students have used the inquiry tutors at three universities: the University of Massachusetts Amherst, the University of Rhode Island, and Hampshire College. Detailed interviews, surveys, essay questions, group discussions, and pre- and post-essay activities have shown that participants were enthusiastic and impressed with the potential of Rashi. Students were comfortable using the system, although numerous specific technical issues were present. Interactivity was seen as a very positive attribute, with the interactive body diagram in biology cited as one of the better components. Most aspects of the tutor were rated positively by roughly half of the users. Students' perception of learning the inquiry process was favorable (Table 1). Half the students felt the experience had taught them how to better approach a comparable inquiry problem. College faculty demonstrated that they could use the authoring tools to develop new modules in weeks instead of months.

A prototype essay question examined students' scientific reasoning skills on a novel problem unrelated to what they were studying in class. In scoring the essays about solving the novel problem, students were given points for: making observations; designing a problem statement and hypotheses; identifying the information needed to be tested, data to be collected and measurements to be made; and describing how data would be evaluated to test the hypotheses. This essay was administered in two classes; students were presented with the question shortly before using Rashi and a couple of weeks after the assignment was completed.

Table 1. Student reaction to the Human Biology Tutor, Fall '03

Please rate how well you were able to:	%Well/ Very Well
Create hypotheses	53%
Become comfortable with the tutor	53%
Learn the content material	47%
Find needed information	47%
Understand the rules for using it	47%
Use the notebook to organize	47%
Perform tests	40%
Find the process enjoyable	40%

A teacher development course at the University of Rhode Island provided the most complete evaluation of the Fault Recognition module. Junior and senior high school teachers enthusiastically endorsed this approach with their students. Many suggestions were offered, in particular to make the module more accessible to younger users. In summary, students enjoyed the modules, the approach to teaching, and specifically lauded the interactive components and engaging nature of the cases. The Rashi approach appears to have the potential to benefit a wide audience ranging from junior high school to college-aged students with minimal alteration.

An Adaptive Web Tutor

The second example of an intelligent and adaptive Web tutor was iMANIC, which customized audio-taped lectures and slides for an individual student (Stern, 2001; Stern & Woolf, 2000). iMANIC used an overlay student model to record student ability and preferences and then used adaptive technology to customize Web-enabled material based on each student's learning needs. This tutor was *knowledge-* and *learner-centered* in that it modeled domain knowledge (teaching computer networking), tracked a student's mastery, and then customized subsequent pages based on student need. iMANIC was also *assessment-centered* in that it provided frequent quizzes to help both the tutor and the student understand what has been learned. It was not *community-centered*, though that was possible.

Traditional Multimedia Asynchronous Networked Individualized Courseware (MANIC) develops effective Web-based stored materials and presentation paradigms[2]. It delivers audio and HTML versions of lecture slides over the Web (Stern, Steinberg, Lee, Padhye, & Kurose, 1997; Stern, Woolf, & Kurose, 1997). Even non-intelligent Web-enabled courses can be considerably more interactive than traditional computer-mediated courses,

Figure 14. The iMANIC Tutor Interface. iMANIC slides were customized for students based on their learning. Students selected a definition, explanation or example.

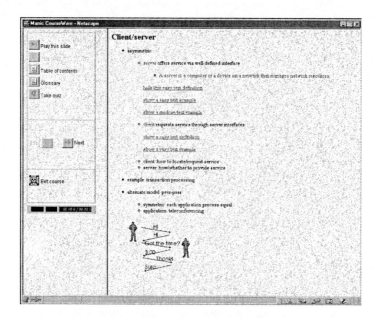

allowing students to take more control over their learning. For example, in traditional MANIC, students have several options for viewing course material by controlling the speed, direction, and linearity of slides and audio playback. Students can play the audio from the beginning to the end, stop and start the audio and slides, or "randomly" traverse the material using the table of contents provided as a guide.

The intelligent Web-enabled delivery of MANIC (iMANIC) was designed to give students a more active role in their learning. Although the audio and slides were taken from existing video-taped courses, iMANIC's courses were not simple direct translations of those courses. By examining which slides were seen and which quizzes taken, the student model determined a student's learning and guided the student through the material, dynamically generating course content and adaptive quizzes at the appropriate level of difficulty. Generated course content was accomplished by using adaptive hypemedia techniques including *adaptive navigation* and *adaptive content*.

Students traversed the course by using either the "next" and "previous" buttons (Figure 14) or the table of contents to randomly jump to another point in the course. Since the topic structure was not linear, *adaptive navigation* was used to choose the next topic, and *stretchtext* was used to allow the student to see more detailed information associated with that text.

iMANIC was *knowledge-centered* in that it stored domain topics in a simple semantic network, with links indicating the relationship between a topic and its pre-topics (pre-topics preceded the topic in the semantic net), co-requisite, and related topics. Subtopics allowed the tutor to reason at a finer level about the student's knowledge. When a topic was displayed, a static set of material, consisting of a linear ordering of pieces of text or graphics called content objects, was presented to every student. As the topic was presented, it was broken into pages, or "slides," containing these content objects.

In addition, there were also keywords, or concepts, that were part of the domain. As the tutor presented the topics and a concept word appeared, the tutor dynamically chose additional content, for example, extra examples, graphics, or explanations, to teach that concept. Each piece of additional content had a level of difficulty assigned by a domain expert, indicating the level of knowledge needed to understand that information.

The tutor was *student-centered* in that it reasoned about an individual student's learning needs and where to put page breaks, based on how much additional content should be presented. When displaying a slide, only one screen's worth of material was presented at a time to prevent making the student scroll. However, before slides were displayed to the student, the tutor did not know how much supplementary information it would choose to show. Therefore, as the tutor presented a topic, it dynamically decided where to put page breaks after deciding how much supplementary material to give each student.

In Web-based non-linear domains, students might find themselves "lost in hyperspace" (Brusilovsky, Schwarz, & Weber, 1996). An intelligent guide such as iMANIC avoided this problem by selecting relevant topics on the basis of the current student model and helped sequence the curriculum topics based on modeling the student and understanding the topics. It was assumed that a student was "ready to learn" a topic only if she performed sufficiently well on its pre-topics. The problem thus decomposed into determining: (1) how well the student performed on topics in the course, called the "learned" score; and (2) how to combine the ratings for all the pre-topics, as well as the rating for the current topic, called the "ready" score.

How Well was a Topic Learned?

In open environments like the Web, information beyond quizzes is needed to judge how well a topic is learned, because students are free to explore without being required to take tests. The student's access pattern for viewing the course material, for example, time spent studying a topic and whether topics were reviewed multiple times, contribute to knowledge about how well a topic is being learned. Three factors were important in iMANIC to grade a student's knowledge of a topic: how well the student performed on quizzes, how well the topic was studied, and how much the topic was reviewed. These three pieces of evidence were combined to determine how well a topic was "learned."

Quizzes were dynamically constructed from a question database and covered topics most recently completed, as well as topics that should be reviewed. Because quizzes provided such concrete evidence of a student's knowledge, students were required to take quizzes on all topics in the domain. Each question had a level of difficulty as determined by the course instructor (Boyle & Encarnacion, 1994; Brusilovsky & Pesin, 1994; Brusilovsky, Schwarz, & Weber, 1996), indicating the level of mastery a student should have to answer the question correctly. This level of difficulty was used to update the student model after the student answered the questions posed. Clearly, correctly answering a harder question demonstrated a higher ability than correctly answering an easier one. Similarly, failing at a harder question was not as damaging as failing at an easier one.

Students using iMANIC spent most of their time reading and listening to course material. Therefore, some judgment was made about the comprehension a student gained through these activities. The problem of determining if a student understood the material became one of judging how sufficiently each content object in the topic was studied. The premise was that students who did not spend enough time studying were not learning the material well and students spending too much time were having difficulty understanding the material. In order to assess the time spent on a content object, the tutor plotted the amount of time spent studying the object using a normal curve, with the mean and standard deviation determined by the course instructor before the course was presented to students. Once the content objects were plotted for a student and the new scores obtained, they were averaged over all content objects in the topic. This became the studied score for the topic.

Selecting the Next Topic

Once each topic's "learned" score was calculated, a "ready" score for other topics was determined. This score determined which topic the student should study next, based on how well the pre-topics were learned. Rules that adjusted the pre-topics' learned scores took into consideration the link types between a topic and its pre-topics in the semantic network. Each link type had a threshold, indicating the minimum score for mastery of the pre-topic. The weights were adjusted based on how close the learned score was to the threshold. Scaling rules were used to give more weight to different kinds of relationships. Once the weights of links were determined, the ranking on the topic was computed by averaging the adjusted link weights of the pre-topics of the topic in question.

When the student linearly progressed through a topic and came to the end of that topic, s/he had the option of letting iMANIC choose the next topic. When a student did not learn a topic sufficiently, that topic had a higher priority over new topics to study. Thus, among topics to be repeated, the one with the lowest "learned" value was chosen as the next topic to study.

If no topics needed to be repeated, the tutor's goal became guiding the student forward through the curriculum. To fulfill this goal, the "next" topics from the current topic were evaluated to see if they were "ready." If one or more topics had "ready" values, the one with the highest value was taught. If no such next topic existed, then the semantic net was recursively searched backwards from these next topics, looking for a previous topic with the highest "ready" value. This policy ensured that topics that could help the student move on to new topics would be taught next and, thus, momentum through the curriculum preserved.

Adaptive Content

The goal of *adaptive content* in iMANIC was to provide a presentation that was not too hard or too easy, while taking into account a student's learning style preferences. For example, one student might have preferred pictures to textual explanations, while another preferred definitions at first but examples later on. A two-pass method was used to determine which supplemental information should be given to each student. The first determined which content objects from the concepts were at the correct level of difficulty, taking into consideration how much a student knew about the concept. The second determined student preference and took into consideration how the student preferred to learn.

A machine learning algorithm was used to decide which additional objects to present to the student. The tutor chose objects that matched the student's preferences—as he demonstrated on previous pages—from among those objects at the correct level of difficulty. Each content object had a set of abilities, including instructional type (e.g., definition, explanation, example), media type (e.g., picture, text), place in concept (e.g., beginning, end), and wanted (e.g., yes, no). The tutor deduced which abilities the student liked to see and which he did not, by analyzing which objects the student had elected to view or hide in previous browsing activities. Those objects comprised the Naïve Bayes Classifier's example space. When a concept was to be presented, the tutor examined the content objects at the right level of difficulty and used the Naïve Bayes Classifier to predict if the object would be wanted or not. If the classifier returned a "yes" answer, the object was shown; otherwise, it was not. It should be noted that if an object was shown, the student was given the option to hide the object. Similarly, hidden objects had an option that allowed them to be shown.

iMANIC Tutor Architecture

The iMANIC architecture consisted of four main parts: the client, the HTTP server, the port server, and the student model servers (Figure 15). The client consisted of a Web browser and a control applet that allowed the student to traverse the course material. The applet contained buttons such as "next page" and "glossary." Also, the RealAudio© plug-in was embedded in the applet. The HTTP server used Common Gateway Interface (CGI) scripts to interact with the port server and with the student model servers. The port server controlled the creation of the student model servers; one server was created for each student using the system.

The main communication link in the architecture was between the HTTP server and a student model server. The HTTP server used "cookies" to maintain state with a given client and thus knew which student model server to contact for each interaction. Cookies stored the student's name, the server's IP address, and the port on which the student's server was listening. Once the HTTP server contacted a student model server, it simply waited for the student model server to send back a reply, which was in the form of HTML code. The HTTP server then sent the information received from the student model server directly to the Web browser. Thus, the HTTP server contained no intelligence at all.

Figure 15. The iMANIC Tutor Architecture. CGI scripts interacted with the port server and student model server. HTTP servers contacted the student model server through "cookies."

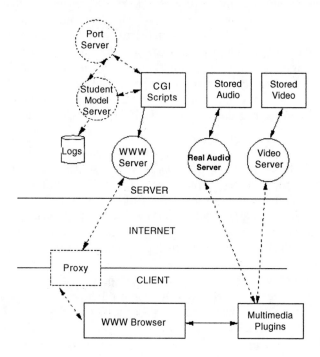

Student model servers were the elements of the system that performed all the "reasoning" and dynamic construction of course content. Each time the student made an action, his student model server was connected both to log that action and to generate the content as a consequence of the action. The student saw an HTML page generated dynamically by the student model server.

Evaluation of iMANIC

iManic was tested over the Web with students who had no training in the tutor and no access to a teacher. One objective was to see if students enjoyed the experience more and learned more when the tutor predicted their behavior, specifically the next page, media type, and preferred topic. This objective was not achievable due to the fact that so few students actually finished the entire course. Thus, the evaluation focused on the predictive power of the tutor.

Table 2. Accuracy of Naïve Bayes Classifier. The prediction of the tutor about media or instructional type.

Student	Accuracy
1	84.11
2	74.16
3	60.06
4	76.97
5	84.71
6	59.50
7	84.62
8	90.53

Students used the tutor on the Web at remote locations and had the aid of the student model during half of their time, thus material was presented in a way that the tutor thought was preferred. During the rest of the time, students did not have a student model, thus *adaptive presentation* was disabled and content was not dynamically changed. Students were surveyed to determine the impact of the student model. The items that were dynamically adjusted by the tutor included media type (graphic, text), instructional type (explanation, example, definition), and whether the topic was wanted or not.

The accuracy of the Naïve Bayes Classifier was determined by measuring each object the classifier was asked to classify (Table 2). When a slide was first displayed, predictions were made about what was wanted, and when the student left a slide displayed, those prediction were checked for accuracy in terms of how many objects the student used, changed, or asked for. The number of objects predicted varied with the experience of the student and the way the student progressed through the tutor. For one student, the tutor made a decision about 1374 objects; for another student, only 65 objects. Some students elected to follow the table of contents and others were evenly split between choosing topics on their own and letting the tutor choose the topic. Students used both *direct guidance* and *annotations* extensively.

Results showed that students responded best to a variety of teaching policies. Some students needed more time to read and understand, while others needed less time. Learning was correlated with time spent learning but the direction of that correlation was not consistent. For half the students, there was a significant positive correlation between time studied and quiz performance (the more time studying, the better the performance on a quiz); for other students there was a negative correlation (the less time studied, the higher the quiz grade).

The final conclusion is that a tutor can learn which teaching policy to use on a per student basis. Specifically, the student model was able to learn, within just a few slides, how to classify the student to achieve the best accuracy. Since students responded to individual teaching policies, a tutor must have multiple teaching policies that are appropriate for different kinds of users. Furthermore, the tutor must be able to learn which policy to use for which student and must be able to continue to adapt and learn since the best policies for a given student may change.

Future Trends

By providing abundant and freely available educational resources, the Web has already had a great impact on education. This effect has been most strongly felt by higher educational institutions, whose existing organizations have long enjoyed a monopoly over education. Due to constraints of geography and time and the monopoly on certification through awarding degrees, higher education has maintained a cottage industry in which individual courses are handcrafted and made-to-order by each faulty member (Dunderstadt, 1998). Faculty members develop original courses and handcraft slides for a specific audience fixed in time and space. In an effort to gain revenue through distance education projects, many universities sell their courses on the Web based primarily on the power of the instructor's slides.

In contrast, the Massachusetts Institute of Technology, in Cambridge, Massachusetts, freely distributes slides for all its courses through its open Web educational resource, OpenCourseWare (http://ocw.mit.edu/OcwWeb/index.htm). This supports MIT's mission to advance knowledge and education in the 21st Century. Clearly, teaching at MIT involves more than transmitting hand-crafted slides; "intellectual property" includes, in addition to slides, motivating students, engaging in research, and managing active learning. Faculty, students, and self-learners around the world do share in each MIT professors' slides, and yet students at MIT still profit from the institutes extraordinary research environment.

Like other "deregulated" industries, for example, healthcare or communications, education is evolving. The evolution of education into an open learning industry is both evident and irresistible (Dunderstadt, 1998). Students now take classes with global experts and the classroom experience is "commodity" driven, provided to anyone, anywhere. Education has spawned new players such as virtual universities and for-profit organizations who now take advantage of the market interest. As the global society becomes ever more dependent upon new knowledge, educated people, and knowledge workers, the global knowledge business must be viewed as one of the most active growth industries of our times. This industry has a combination of large size (approximately the same size as health care), disgruntled users, lower utilization of technology currently, and possibly the highest strategic importance of any activity in which global countries engage.

Conclusion and Discussion

The Web provides abundant and freely available educational technology and has captured the imagination and interest of educators at all levels. Now we need to question the very nature and content of that instruction. This chapter provided a theoretical framework for exploring issues about Web instruction, suggesting that instructional resources should be *knowledge-, student-, assessment-,* and *community-centered.* If the Web is to be worthy of the large investment of time and resources required to impact education, it must be flexible and powerful enough to respond to the challenges provided by such a theoretical framework and others provided elsewhere.

This chapter examined two intelligent and adaptive Web tutors: Rashi, an inquiry tutor that tracked a student's critical thinking in biology and geology, and iMANIC, a tutor that customized lectures for individual students using adaptive technology. These tutors and many others provide promising data points for the existence of authentic and effective Web learning based on satisfying some of the four theoretical desiderata. Neither tutor was rooted in extensions of what already exists in education, such as lectures or bulletin boards; traditional classrooms are often deficient in addressing these four principles. Although many technological and social barriers still need to be addressed, these examples indicate how we might begin to design and implement Web instruction to revitalize and enhance education through the Web.

As a communication device, the Web has two primary advantages. The first and more obvious one is that it provides a (theoretically) platform-independent, richly featured, easy way to deliver multimedia to users, including text, linked text, graphics, simulation, and animations. Most educational software has utilized only this first and simpler advantage.

A second and more powerful communication role of the Web has only become evident recently. This role is providing a general standardized framework for lightweight network communication. This role of the Web provides a powerful framework for building intelligence and adaptivity into Web learning. Existing ready-to-use Web servers or Web server extensions can handle questions of user management and scaling. Therefore, authors, for example, ought to be able to simply choose an existing architecture that best serves their needs and spend time implementing tutors rather than writing support structures for low-level networking tasks. This, of course, assumes that other authors have developed extensible, self-contained adaptive and intelligent modules using Web programming standards and that these modules and tools are made widely available.

The existence of a network does not provide a well-sorted repository of information, just as the existence of paper does not provide a library (Berners-Lee, 1996). Similarly for education, the existence of endless instructional material does not itself establish effective education. For example, the fact that a hypertext link can point to anything is both powerful and risky; the material might be fallacious, irrelevant, misleading, or non-existent. Educators, who revel in the opportunity provided by the Web, must also be diligent in chasing down and verifying the integrity of Web material.

The original dream behind the Web was of a common information space in which humans would communicate by sharing information. The same dream applies to education; the Web enables stakeholders (students, teachers, parents, and industries) to communicate and develop community. There was a second part of the Web dream, too, dependent on the Web being so generally used that it became a realistic mirror (or in fact the primary embodiment) of the ways in which we work and play and socialize (Berners-Lee, 1996). This dream can also be applied to education. Once sufficient intelligent and adaptive teaching material is available on the Web, education will become universal, a realistic mirror of anytime and anyplace instruction. When this becomes a reality, the Web will provide support for individual students, empowering each with relevant and student-centered material. Then the Web will become, as was its original intent, a primary source and environment for education.

Acknowledgments

Research on Rashi was funded in part by the U.S. Department of Education, " Expanding a General Model of Inquiry Learning," Fund for the Improvement of Post Secondary Education, Comprehensive Program, #P116B010483, B. Woolf, P.I., and by the National Science Foundation under Grant DUE-0127183, "Inquiry Tools for Case-based Courses in Human Biology," M. Bruno, P.I. and B. Woolf, Co-P.I., NSF-DUE 0341197, "Engaging Undergraduates in Online Inquiry Learning: A Case-Based Cyber Library in Human Biology," M. Bruno, P.I. and B. Woolf and NSF-DUE 0340864, "Online Inquiry Learning in Geology," D. Murray, P.I. and B. Woolf, Co-P.I.

Any opinions, findings, and conclusions or recommendations expressed in this material are those of the authors and do not necessarily reflect the views of the funding agencies.

The authors sincerely thank the designers and developers of the Rashi tutor: Dave Marshall, Tom Murray, and Matthew Mattingly, University of Massachusetts, Amherst; Dan Murray and Jim Sammons, University of Rhode Island; and Merle Bruno, Hampshire College.

References

Aleven, V. & Ashley, K. D. (1997). Teaching case-based argumentation through a model and examples: Empirical evaluation of an intelligent learning environment. In B. du Boulay & R. Mizoguchi (Eds.), *Artificial intelligence in education, Proceedings of AI-ED 97 World Conference* (pp. 87-94). Amsterdam: IOS Press.

Alloway, G., Bos, N., Hamel, K., Hammerman, T., Klann, E., Krakcik, J., Lyons, D., Madden, T., Margerum-Leys, J., Reed, J., Scala, N., Soloway, E., Vekiri, I., & Wallace, R. (1996). Creating an inquiry-learning environment using the World Wide Web. In *Proceedings of the International Conference of Learning Sciences*. Evanston, IL: Northwestern University.

Berners-Lee, T. (1996) The World Wide Web: Past, present and future. *IEEE Computer, 29*(10), 69-77. Retrieved from *http://www.w3.org/People/Berners-Lee/1996/ppf.html*

Boyle, C. & Encarnacion, A.O. (1994). MetaDoc: An adaptive hypertext reading system. *User Modeling and User-Adapted Interaction, 4*, 1-19.

Bransford, J.D. (2004) Toward the development of a stronger community of educators: New opportunities made possible by integrating the learning sciences and technology. Retrieved June 28, 2005, from *http://www.pt3.org/VQ/html/bransford.html*, *Vision Quest, Preparing Tomorrow's Teachers to Use Technology.*

Bransford, J. D., Brown, A.L., & Cocking, R. R. (Eds.) (1999). *How people learn: Brain, mind, experience, and school.* Committee on Developments in the Science of Learning, Commission on Behavioral and Social Sciences and Education, (CBASSE), National Research Council. Washington, DC: National Academy Press.

Bruno, M. (2000). Student-active learning in a large classroom. Presented at Project Kaleidoscope 2000 Summer Institute. Keystone, Colorado. Retrieved June 28, 2005, from *http://carbon.hampshire.edu~mbruno/PKAL2000.html*

Bruno, M.S. & Jarvis, C. D. (2001). It's fun, but is it science? Goals and strategies in a problem-based learning course. *The Journal of Mathematics and Science: Collaborative Explorations, 4*(1), 25-42.

Brusilovsky, P. & Pesin, L. (1994). An intelligent learning environment for CDS/ISIS users. In J. J. Levonen & M. T. Tukianinen (Eds.), *Proceedings of the interdisciplinary workshop on complex learning in computer environments (CLCE94)* (pp. 29-33). Joensuu, Finland: EIC. Retrieved from *http://cs.joensuu.fi/~mtuki/www_clce.270296/Brusilov.html*

Brusilovsky, P., Schwarz, E., & Weber, G. (1996). ELM-ART: An intelligent tutoring system on World Wide Web. In C. Frasson, G. Gauthier, & A. Lesgold (Eds.), *Intelligent tutoring systems* (Lecture Notes in Computer Science) (Vol. 1086, pp. 261-269). Berlin: Springer-Verlag.

Cuban, L., Kirkpatrick, H., & Peck, C. (2001). High access and low use of technology in high school classrooms: Explaining an apparent paradox. *American Educational Research Journal, 38*(4), 813-834.

Dufresne, R., Mestre, J., Hart, D., & Rath, K. (2002). The effect of Web-based homework on test performance in large introductory physics classes. *Journal of Computers in Mathematics and Science Teaching, 21*(3), 229-251.

Dunderstadt, J. (1998). Transforming the university to serve the digital age. *Cause/Effect* 20(4), 21-32.

Graesser, A.C. & Person, N. (1994). Question asking during tutoring. *American Educational Research Journal, 31*, 104-137.

Hmelo-Silver, C. (2002). Collaborative ways of knowing: Issues in facilitation. In G. Stahl (Ed.), *Proceedings of the Conference on Computer Support for Collaborative Learning* (pp. 217-226). Hillsdale, NJ: Erlbaum.

Hunt, E. & Minstrell, J. (1994). A cognitive approach to the teaching of physics. In K. McGilly (Ed.), *Classroom lessons: Integrating cognitive theory and classroom practice* (pp. 51-74). Cambridge, MA: MIT Press.

IMMEX. (2003). IMMEX on the Web. UCLA. Culver City, CA. Retrieved from *http://www.immex.ucla.edu/ContactMainFrame.htm*

Krajcik, J., Blumenfeld, P., Marx, R., & Soloway, E. (2000). Instructional, curricular, and technological supports for inquiry in science classrooms. In J. Minstrell & E. H. van

Zee (Eds.), *Inquiring into inquiry: Science learning and teaching* (pp. 283-315). Washington, DC: American Association for the Advancement of Science Press.

Levin, D. & Arafeh, S. (2002). The digital disconnect: The widening gap between Internet-savvy students and their schools. Pew Internet and American Life Project. Retrieved June 28, 2005, from *http://www.pewinternet.org/pdfs/PIP_Schools_Internet_Report.pdf*

Murray, T., Woolf, B., & Marshall, D. (2004). Lessons learned from authoring for inquiry learning: A tale of three authoring tools. In *Proceedings of the Seventh International Conference ITS 2004,* Maceio, Brazil, August-September (pp. 197-206). Springer.

Owston, R. (1997). The World Wide Web: A technology to enhance teaching and learning? *Educational Researcher, 28*(2), 27-33.

Schank, R. (1994). Active learning through multimedia. *IEEE MultiMedia, 1*(1), 69-78.

Steinsaltz, A. (1976). *The essential Talmud.* New York: Perseus Books, Basic Books.

Stern, M. (2001). *Using adaptive hypermedia and machine learning to create intelligent Web-based courses.* PhD thesis, Department of Computer Science, University of Massachusetts, Amherst.

Stern, M., Steinberg, J., Lee, H.I., Padhye, J., & Kurose, J. (1997b). MANIC: Multimedia asynchronous networked individualized courseware. In *Proceedings of Educational Media and Hypermedia.*

Stern, M., Woolf, B.P., & Kurose, J. F. (1997a). Intelligence on the Web? In *Proceedings of World Conference on Artificial Intelligence in Education* (pp. 490-497). Amsterdam: IOS Press.

Stern, M. K. & Woolf, B. P. (2000). Adaptive content in an online lecture system. In *Proceedings of Adaptive Hypermedia and Adaptive Web-Based Systems,* Lecture Notes in Computer Science 1892 (pp. 227-238). Trento, Italy; Berlin: Springer-Verlag.

Stevens, R. & Nadjafi, K. (1997). Artificial neural networks as adjuncts for assessing medical students: Problem solving performances on computer-based simulations. *Computers and Biomedical Research, 26,* 172-187.

Suthers, D., Toth, E., & Weiner, A. (1997). An integrated approach to implementing collaborative inquiry in the classroom. In *Proceedings of the Second International Conference on Computer Supported Collaborative Learning '97,* December 10-14, Toronto (pp. 272-279).

Technology in Education (2000). QED's Internet Usage in Public Schools 2000, 5th Market Data Retrieval, Shelton, CT. Retrieved June 28, 2005, from *http://www.infotoday.com/MMSchools/jan01/net0101.htm*

White, B., Shimoda, T., & Frederiksen, J. (1999). Enabling students to construct theories of collaborative inquiry and reflective learning:Computer support for metacognitive development. *International Journal of Artificial Intelligence in Education, 10,* 151-182.

Woolf, B. & Hall, W. (1995). Multimedia pedagogues: Interactive systems for teaching and learning. *IEEE Computer, 28*(5), 74-80.

Woolf, B. P., Marshall, D., Mattingly, M., Lewis, J., Wright, S., Jellison, M., & Murray, T. (2003). Tracking student propositions in an inquiry system. In U. Hoppe, F. Berdeho, & J. Kay (Eds.), *Artificial intelligence and education* (pp. 21-28). The Netherlands: IOS Press.

Woolf, B. P., Reid, J., Stillings, N., Bruno, M., Murray, D., Reese, P., Peterfreund, A., & Rath, K. (2002) A general platform for inquiry learning. In *Proceedings of the Sixth International Conference on Intelligent Tutoring Systems*, Lecture Notes in Computer Science 2363 (pp. 681-697). France; Berlin: Springer-Verlag.

Endnotes

[1]   Rashi was a biblical scholar who introduced inquiry methods in the 11th Century. He wrote extensive commentaries, produced queries, explanations, interpretations, and discussions of each phrase and verse of the Bible. Today, these and other commentaries, assembled in the Talmud, have been extended to nearly 40 volumes and continue as a source of biblical law (Steinsaltz, 1976).

[2]   MANIC (renamed RIPPLES) is further described at http://manic.cs.umass.edu/about.html

Chapter XVII

A Special Purpose E-Learning Environment:
Background, Design and Evaluation

Maria Kordaki, University of Patras, Greece

Abstract

This study presents the concept of Special Purpose E-Learning Environments (SPELEs). The main aim of these environments is to meet the learners' individual learning differences related to a specific learning subject. An architecture of the design of SPELEs is presented. The background of this design, which is based on interpretations of modern constructivist and social views of learning in the Internet context, is also presented. Based on this architecture a specific SPELE, designed for the learning of concepts related to Files and Peripheral Storage Devices (FPSD.), is demonstrated and its pilot evaluation study with real students is reported. The analysis of the data verifies the theoretical design of SPELEs, which consists of five parts: (a) organization of the content of a specific learning subject, (b) learning activities (c) learner activity space (d) learner assessment, and (e) learner communication. The analysis of the data also gives evidence for future improvements of the specific SPELE mentioned above.

Introduction

General Purpose E-Learning Environments (GPELEs) are designed to support the learning of all learning subjects. Some well-known examples of GPELEs are: WebCT (www.webct.com), Learning Space (www.lotus.com/ home.nsf/welcome/learspace) and CENTRA-Symposium (www.Centra.com/products/ symposium), and the like. A number of studies have shown the positive learning results achieved by learners in the context of these environments. Despite this fact, these environments do not provide the learners with opportunities to use specific tools and representation systems to support active and constructive participation for the learning of each specific subject. Moreover, GPELEs do not provide tools and representation systems that take into account specific research studies illuminating the learners' individual differences regarding a specific subject. As a result, in the context of GPELEs, the learners' individual learning differences are not fully treated.

It is worth mentioning that the learning process is closely related to each learning subject as well as to learners' individual learning differences. These differences are also firmly dependent on each learning subject, as it has been reported by the relevant scientific communities. Based on the above, the value of Special Purpose E-Learning Environments (SPELEs) designed for the learning of a specific group of concepts within a specific knowledge domain is obvious. Furthermore, the concept of SPELEs is well situated in the context of modern constructivist and social theories of learning, where the learning process is viewed as an active, subjective, and constructive activity in a context rich in computer tools (Noss & Hoyles, 1996; von Glasersfeld, 1987; Vygotsky, 1978).

In the context of these theories, a new general architecture for the design of SPELEs has been constructed. This architecture emphasizes learning in a context supporting: (a) the learning of essential aspects of each learning subject (von Glasersfeld, 1987), (b) open real-life learning activities (CTGV, 1992; Jonassen, 1991, 2000; Liu & Hsiao, 2002), (c) the learners' individual differences as they emerged from relevant research studies (Kordaki & Potari, 2002), (d) content presentation in multiple hyperlinked representation systems organized by using the learning activity as the basic structure-unit (Jonassen, 2000), (e) active learning using a variety of representation systems and computer tools (Kaput, 1994), as well as experimentation with representations and tools handling primary sources of data and using hands-on experience (NCREL, 2005), (f) multiple ways of assessment (von Glasersfeld, 1987), including the participation in appropriately designed games, (g) appropriate intrinsic and extrinsic feedback for self correction (Papert, 1980), (h) multiple ways of communication (Harasim, Hiltz, Teles, & Turoff, 1995), and (i) real-life operations and objects used as metaphor-representation systems of computer operations and objects acknowledged. It is worth mentioning that SPELEs based on such an architecture have yet not been reported.

The proposed architecture was used for the design of a SPELE for the learning of concepts related to Files and Peripheral Storage Devices (FPSD) for secondary-level education students. These concepts are viewed as essential for elementary computer learning. Such an e-learning environment for the concepts mentioned above has also not yet been reported.

The chapter is organized as follows: the background of SPELEs is presented in the following section. Next, the proposed architecture for the general design of SPELEs is demonstrated. Then, the design and the pilot evaluation of the FPSD e-learning environment using real students are reported. Finally, the empirical results from this study are discussed in relation to the specifications of the proposed architecture for the general design of SPELEs. The chapter ends with the conclusions.

Background

The Internet has been recognized by a number of researchers as a medium that gives opportunities for the design of learning environments based on modern constructivist and social theories regarding knowledge construction (Dillenbourg, Schneider, & Synteta, 2002; Harasim, 1989; Hofstetter, 1998; James, 2000; Jonassen, Carr, & Yueh, 1998; Tam, 2000). Moreover, the fact that the Internet gives learners the chance to learn in their own time and place contributes towards equal learning opportunities. In addition, the Internet provides schools with opportunities to exchange learning experiences, so they can acquire a new perspective and broaden their world to society (Harasim et al., 1995). At the same time, the communication capabilities (Computer-Mediated Communication) provided by computer networks and especially by the Internet expand and alter the learners' communication abilities (Harasim, 1990; Harasim et al., 1995; Miranda & Pinto, 1996; Tam, 2000).

E-learning environments can be mainly identified by the following features (Dillenbourg et al., 2002):

- A designed information space;

- A social space for educational interactions;

- An explicit representation of the information/social space (this representation can vary from text to 3D immersive worlds);

- A possibility for the learners to be not only active, but also actors—they co-construct the virtual space;

- An integration of heterogeneous technologies and multiple pedagogical approaches; and

- Representation of physical environments.

In the design of Internet-based learning environments, the selection of appropriate learning theories has a potential impact. In fact, courseware effectiveness is bound to the pedagogical context of use: the pedagogical scenario in which the courseware is integrated, the degree of teacher involvement, the time frame, the technical infrastructure, and so forth (Dillenbourg et al., 2002). Certain technological scenarios might lead to more centralised control or to higher shares of individualised learning as opposed to partner work. Such potential changes originating from the inherent logic of the technology without a clear pedagogical justification should not be accepted. The design of educational scenarios should first be based on pedagogical premises and objectives (Hoppe, 2002).

Traditional "behaviorist" learning theories (Skinner, 1968) are usually implied in those e-learning environments that are dedicated to the learning of all learning subjects. These environments can be characterized as General Purpose E-Learning Environments (GPELEs). The design of such environments mainly emphasizes the eye-catching presentation of the learning content in a variety of forms. Multimedia, hypermedia, sounds, animations graphics, and bright colors are used. Usually, the content is organized sequentially, starting from the simplest topics of the learning subject and gradually moving to the more advanced ones. Furthermore, the proposed learning content usually does not stress the essential and basic concepts of a specific domain of knowledge but covers all its concepts irrespectively. The proposed learning activities are mainly in the form of "drill and practice," that is, school-book like activities, while the motives given for learning are external and concern mainly the passing of tests.

High-level critical thinking is not cultivated by these kinds of activities whose solutions are usually standardized. Using such activities, the evaluation of learning is easy as it can be automatically performed by the computer. As a consequence, the learners' assessment is mainly based on the results they produce when performing the given tasks. The use of communication is usually limited to explanations given to the learners by their teachers.

In the case of the Internet, it is mainly used for giving out the learning matter in the students' own place, and no emphasis is given on ensuring rich communication between those involved in the learning process. Moreover, the learners' individual learning differences are not respected, as it is the authority of both the content and the teacher that is acknowledged. In the context of these environments, the learners usually accept a passive role, as they have to spend much of their learning time focusing on reading the provided book-like learning materials. On the whole, the learners' interaction within such environments is limited to searching for information through the provided learning materials and trying to perform recall-based learning activities.

Constructivist and social theories of learning are more suitable for the design of SPELEs. Designers of computer-based learning environments are influenced by these theories (CTGV, 1991; Duffy, Lowyck, & Jonassen, 1993; Laborde & Strasser, 1990; Noss & Hoyles, 1996; Papert, 1980). Constructivist learning theories emphasize the active, subjective, and constructive character of knowledge, placing the learners at the centre of the learning process (von Glasersfeld, 1990). In addition, social theories of learning stress the importance of computer tools and, more specifically, the significance of computer-based learning environments in the learning process (Crawford, 1996a, 1996b; Noss & Hoyles, 1996). In contrast to traditional theories, modern theories of learning put emphasis on the essential and fundamental concepts that structure a specific domain of knowledge. Furthermore, modern constructivist and social theories of learning emphasize the role of a context, rich in appropriately designed tools, aiming for the performance of holistic, real-life, problem-solving learning activities. These types of activities enable learners to develop a strong motivation so that they can be actively involved in their learning processes. Moreover, the performance of these activities puts the learners in the problem-solvers' position by requiring a high level of critical thinking. In addition, these activities are designed to be solved in many ways, so that the learners' individual differences are acknowledged. In enabling learners' to express their individual differences regarding each specific learning subject, the role of multiple and linked representation systems are necessary (Dyfour-Janvier, Bednarz, & Belanger, 1987; Kaput, 1994; Kordaki & Potari, 2002). Learners can construct their own solution strategies in handling the given tasks by selecting those most appropriate for their own cognitive development from the provided representation systems.

A number of representation systems can be used in the context of the Web, such as tables, graphs, diagrams, and so forth (Kaput, 1994). New representation systems have to be invented in order to meet the learners' individual needs. Among representation systems, the simulations of real-life situations can be effectively used as metaphors to help learners in their understanding of learning subjects. By the use of multiple representation systems (MRS), it is possible for learners to make a smooth transition from the real world—with objects and activities of everyday life—to the computer world—with computational objects and operations. Moreover, the use of multiple representations of variable cognitive transparency in the design of computer learning environments has been recognized as significant in the process of learning abstract concepts (Dyfour-Janvier, Bednarz, & Belanger, 1987; Kordaki & Potari, 2002; Sutherland, 1995) and, more specifically, in the process of learning concepts of Computer Science (Vlachogiannis et al., 2001).

A number of e-learning environments designed to take into account modern theories of learning have been reported by the literature. Some of them emphasize the presentation of the learning content using Multiple Representation Systems (MRS) (Tretiakov, Hong, Kinshuk, & Patel, 2003). MRS are proposed in contrast to the content creation tools included in commercial GPELEs such as WebCT and LearningSpace that offer specialized WYSIWYG interfaces for educational content creation. Layered presentation of the learning content is also proposed as helpful for learners of different learning styles (e.g., INSPIRE: Papanikolaou, Grigoriadou, Magoulas, & Kornilakis, 2002). Real-life activities are also proposed as essential for the design of e-learning environments (Dillenbourg et al., 2002; Tretiakov, Kinshuk, & Tretiakov, 2003; Zikouli & Kordaki, 2004). Tools for forming concept maps as well as for forming flow-charts in student collaboration within e-learning settings are also proposed (e.g., SCALE: Grigoriadou, Gogoulou, Gouli, & Samarakou, 2004; SYNERGO: Voyatzaki, Christakoudis, Margaritis, & Avouris, 2004). In addition, simulation programs are integrated into computer learning environments to support learners in actively exploring the learning concepts in focus (Grigoriadou & Kanidis, 2003). Microworlds, including a number of appropriately designed tools to support learners in actively constructing solutions to the tasks given, are also reported (e.g., Cabri-Geometry II, for the learning of the Euclidean Geometry, Laborde & Strasser, 1990). Moreover, tools that help students' active experimentation in MRS have been also used in the design of computer based learning environments (e.g., LECGO, a computer environment for the learning of Programming and C, Zikouli, Kordaki, & Houstis, 2003).

Finally, an interesting trend in the development of learning environments is the linking of digital texts and exploratory and simulation educational software (e.g., Absorb Mathematics, http://www.crocodile~clips.com/absorb/math).

A General Architecture for the Design of SPELEs

In this section, an architecture of a typical representative of SPELEs is presented. The construction of this architecture was based on modern constructivist and social theories as mentioned in the previous section. An attempt also was made to exploit the advantages of the reported experience regarding the design of specific computer-based/Internet-based learning environments and to integrate this experience in the design of the architecture proposed. On the grounds of modern theories of knowledge construction, a number of specifications were formulated and were used for the construction of the architecture. The proposed architecture consists of five parts: (a) organization of the learning content, (b) learning activities, (c) learner activity space, (d) learner assessment, and (e) learner communication. The description of the design of each of these parts follows.

Part A: Organization of the Content

This part of the design of SPELEs includes specifications related to the design of the content of a specific learning subject. The content is organized into four hyperlinked layers. In each layer, different forms of the content are presented. The forms of the content in each layer follow.

- **First layer:** The basic structural element of the content is the learning activity. Therefore, the content is organized as a group of fundamental, appropriate, efficient learning activities that are adequate for the learning of each specific learning subject. The selection of activities is crucial in order to focus on the basic concepts of each learning subject and to avoid those of minor importance. For the design of these activities the context of modern theories of learning is appropriate. The design specifications for such activities will be presented in the next section (Part B). The representation of each activity in multiple representation systems is also important for the design of an attractive content that will satisfy different learning needs. A variety of representation systems can be used, such as animations, full text, transparencies, hypertext, multimedia, diagrams, tables, graphs, and so forth.

- **Second layer:** The content is organized as a glossary consisting of a brief presentation of each learning concept.

- **Third layer:** The content is organized as an encyclopaedia of the learning concepts. Here, these concepts are presented in details.

- **Fourth layer:** The content is presented in reference to a wider context consisting of a variety of resources such as: URLs, books, and references.

The selected activities presented in the first layer are hyperlinked with the associated concepts, formulas, and other learning elements that are implied in their performance. In fact, the four layers of the content mentioned above are hyperlinked. In this way, the learners have the opportunity to access learning information in a form that is more appropriate to their cognitive needs.

Part B: Learning Activities

Learners can take significant advantages in their learning process when they are engaged in appropriate learning activities. Modern constructivist and social views of learning constitute a fruitful theoretical framework for the design of appropriate learning activities. This part of the design of SPELEs includes basic specifications related to the design of constructivist learning activities suitable in a computer context. In terms of design specifications, these activities:

a. **Focus on both:**
   - (i)   the fundamental aspects of the learning subject, and
   - (ii)   the specific learning points where the learners illuminate difficulties.

b. **Create interest:** Thus, they enable strong motivation for the learners. Such activities are situated in the context of the learners' every-day life.

c. **Stimulate the learners' higher mental functions:** Problem-solving activities are appropriate as they enable analytical and synthetical thinking skills as well as critical thinking.

d. **Are open:** This means that these activities allow the learners to:
   - (i)   perform them in many ways. Thus, learners have the opportunity to construct their own solution strategies and to express their inter- and intra-individual differences.
   - (ii)   construct solution strategies in different representation systems.
   - (iii) have control over their learning. This means that the activities can be solved using such representation systems that provide appropriate feedback (intrinsic visual and/or explicit numerical). Learners can reflect on the feedback of their actions and then have the opportunity to correct their solution strategies.
   - (iv)   express different kinds of knowledge such as previous knowledge, school knowledge, intuitive knowledge, real-life knowledge, visual knowledge, and so on.

(v)   reflect on flexible feedback. That means that the provided feedback is designed in correspondence to the different kinds of knowledge that the learners can express. Therefore, they can reflect on the provided feedback and can correct their solution strategies.

e.   Encourage the learners to experiment by handling primary sources of data while at the same time acquiring hands-on experience.

f.   Do not demand of the learners extra complicated knowledge from other disciplines.

Part C: Learner Activity Space

This part of the design of SPELEs includes specifications for the design of *learner activity space*. Learner activity space is a virtual place where the learners can actively construct their own knowledge by performing the selected group of learning activities, using a variety of specifically designed tools. The design of the provided tools within a learner activity space is strongly related to the specific learning subject. The definition of both the basic concepts that structure a specific domain of knowledge and the most representative and essential activities for the learning of its concepts is crucial for the design of the tools included in the learner activity space. A successful design has to avoid allowing a superabundance of tools while, at the same time, focusing on the construction of a limited number of tools that can successfully help the learners perform the basic learning activities mentioned previously. The main objectives of the design of the provided tools are to provide the learners with opportunities to:

a.   perform different solution strategies to the selected essential learning activities, thereby expressing their individual learning differences;

b.   perform the same solution strategy using different representation systems;

c.   solve different classes of essential activities for the learning of each specific learning subject; and

d.   overcome basic difficulties regarding each specific learning subject.

The differentiation of representation systems and their associated tools is closely related to the differentiation of their cognitive transparency. Some representation systems and tools can help learners handle primary sources of data while simultaneously acquiring hands-on experience. Other systems and tools can help learners to manipulate more sophisticated types of data using different types of data-manipulation tools, such as tables, graphs, equations, and so forth. Other systems and tools, for example, real-life simulations, can help learners to construct knowledge by exploring dynamic representations of the learning concepts.

Learners can take advantage of the variety of the provided tools in their attempts to construct different solution strategies for the given tasks. To design tools that support the construction of different problem-solving strategies, the research on how the learners cope with each specific learning subject is crucial. By exploiting the results of such studies in the design of the provided tools, the designers can safely claim that such tools are reliable as learning tools and can successfully support a variety of learners.

Part D: Learner Assessment

This part of the SPELEs design includes specifications related to the design of assessment activities. From the constructivist perspective, assessment can become a valuable tool for learning. From this perspective, the emphasis of assessment is placed on each individual's learning processes and not exclusively on her/his learning outcomes. Holistic real-life activities can be used as a basic structural element of the learners' assessment. So, a combination of methods can be used, such as:

- self-assessment by reflecting on appropriately designed intrinsic and/or extrinsic feedback;
- self-assessment by answering multiple choice questions, automatically corrected by the system;
- longitudinal assessment by the teacher by providing the learners' with opportunities to add in electronic portfolios posting their work over an extended period;
- assessment by both the teacher and the learner based on project work; and
- assessment by participating in appropriately designed educational games. Games are powerful tools for assessment, as they motivate the learners to be actively involved in their learning.

Part E: Learner Communication

This part of the design of SPELEs includes specifications related to the design of communication activities. The role of holistic real-life activities is central in the communication process. Learners communicate in a variety of group settings in order to perform the given activities. They can learn by collaborating their knowledge with the knowledge of their colleagues, including their teachers, using synchronous and asynchronous communication and combinations of both. To support learners in performing all these communications, the system can support a large number of asynchronous conferences.

The Proposed Design Methodology for SPELEs

The design methodology for SPELEs to meet the specifications described above consisted of seven basic steps. These steps are:

Step1.   Defining the basic concepts of the specific learning subject. At this point it is crucial to emphasize the basic concepts that structure the specific domain of knowledge.

Step 2.   Defining the appropriate, essential learning activities for the learning of the concepts defined in the Step 1.

Step 3.   Investigating how the learners perform the essential activities selected for the learning of each specific subject. At this point, the role of field studies is crucial to the establishment of both: (a) the learners' possible paths towards the performance of the given tasks, including their mistakes, and (b) the learners' main difficulties.

Step 4.   Defining the appropriate representation systems to appropriately meet the learners individual learning differences as they emerged from the field studies performed using real students.

Step 5.   Designing the appropriate tools included in the learner activity space. This step consists of the design of the appropriate tools that learners can use to perform the activities selected in Step 2 using the representation systems defined in the Step 4.

Step 6.   Designing the tools for assessment, so that the learning based in the performance of the activities selected in Step 2 using the representation systems and tools (defined in Steps 4 and 5) can be evaluated.

Step 7.   Designing the facilities to provide for communication in order to give the learners the opportunity to communicate in multiple ways to perform the activities selected in Step 2 using the representation systems and tools defined in Steps 4 and 5.

The Design of the FPSD E-Learning Environment: A Case Study

In this section, the design of a SPELE using the proposed architecture is presented. This environment is designed for the learning of the concepts of Files and of Peripheral Storage Devices. Part of the design of this software is reported in Venakis, Giannakopoulos, Pirli, and Kordaki (2002). The technical issues regarding the implementation of FPSD are also presented.

Files are basic information storage units and the need to organize them so the user can access them quickly and easily is primal and fundamental. In addition, peripheral storage media are a substantial and necessary part of computer systems. Despite this fact, the concept of files and their management and the concept of peripheral storage media are not cognitively transparent for primary- and secondary-level education learners (Kordaki, 2004). In order to give high school students the chance to understand in an active way the previously mentioned concepts, an Internet-based, multiple representations learning environment was created. The environment's design was based on the framework of the proposed architecture described in the previous section. The design and the implementation of such an environment for the learning of these specific concepts have not yet been mentioned in the literature. The basic steps of the design methodology of this software as well as the presentation of its functions follow.

Step 1 and Step 2 involve defining the basic aspects of files and of peripheral storage media for secondary level education students. The main aspects of the previously mentioned subjects and the selected appropriate learning activities are:

- **Recognising different types of files:** Such as system files, specific programs, and files created by the user. Providing the learners with a variety of files of different types and asking for recognition is a useful activity.

- **Managing files:** Here, the finding of a criterion by which to sort files into classes and then store them in folders is important. So, providing the learners with a number of different files and asking for sorting is an appropriate activity.

- **Orientation in a file microworld:** Here, as well, the searching for a specific file is an important activity.

- **Recognising the limited capacity of a storage medium:** At this point, the task of storing a variety of files in a simulation of a storage medium, such as a hard disk, a CD-ROM, or a floppy disk—each with given capacity (small, in the case of a hard disk), can give the learners a sense of their respective limited storage capacities.

- **Disk formatting:** Here, as well, the use of a visual simulation of the disk formatting operation is important in providing the learners with a visible meaning to such an invisible operation.

- **Basic operations** that can be performed on the content of a file. Such operations include paste, cut, copy, delete, and so on. Activities that provide the learners with opportunities to edit different types of files can be helpful for them.

Step 3 is the investigation of how the learners learn the specific learning subject. To clarify the ways and the difficulties of secondary-level students concerning the concepts of files and peripheral storage media as mentioned above, a field study was conducted, as there were no references on this topic in the literature. The main results of this study (Kordaki, 2004) show that students found it difficult to:

- recognise various types of files with the exception of text documents, sound files, and bitmap files;

- find a criterion and use it to sort files in folders;

- find a specific file classified in a folder;

- resolve the different operations that can be performed on the content of a file, such as paste, cut, copy, delete, copy and paste, cut and paste, and so on;

- recognise Read Only files;

- recognise that a storage medium and, in particular, a hard disk have limited capacity; and

- understand the disk formatting operation.

Based on both the work described above and the general specifications for the design of SPELEs, the anatomy of FPSD involved the design and the implementation of the following five parts:

Part A: Organization of the Content

The content is organized into four layers:

- **First layer:** In this layer, the basic structural element of the content takes the form of learning activities. Here, two types of activities are used: (i) simulations of real-life activities where operations and objects were used as metaphors of computer-based operations and objects related to the specific learning concepts, and (ii) computer activities using computer-based operations and objects related to these concepts.

The presentation of real-life activities is done with the use of multimedia and moving image techniques. More specifically, as far as peripheral storage media are concerned, a hard disk is compared to a wardrobe, a CD-ROM is compared to a rucksack, and a floppy disk is compared to a handbag. Real-life objects of different size and nature act as data and are stored in the aforementioned storage media. Files are compared to jars where the inserted data is coffee or jam. Folders are compared to shelves where the jars are classified. The jars are classified according to their content. The concept of disk formatting is presented through a real-life metaphor-activity—the clearance of a field by a bulldozer in order for the field to become suitable for sowing seed (Figure 1a).

The selected metaphors of real-life activities are situated in the context of young students' everyday lives and are easily understandable. The moving, colorful presentation of the associated images can create an internal motivation for the students as well. These metaphor activities can act as scaffolding activities for the students' learning of the analogous activities performed using computer files, folders, and peripheral storage media (Figure2b). These last types of activities are also demonstrated to the students, again using moving image techniques.

More specifically, the activities of sorting files and of classifying them in folders in the context of a typical computer environment were presented to the students, using the previously mentioned techniques. Moreover, activities of storing files and folders on a real hard disk and on real CD-ROM, as well as on a real floppy disk were demonstrated. Furthermore, the process of formatting a real disk is displayed (Figure 1b).

- **Second layer:** In this layer, the main points of the learning concepts are presented in brief in the form of written text.

- **Third layer:** In this layer, an analytical description of the learning concepts in the form of text is presented. In addition, the learner can proceed from a brief presentation of the main points to a detailed presentation via hyperlinks.

- **Fourth layer:** In this layer, hyperlinks to Web sites with content relevant to the learning concepts described above are available to the learners so that they can further expand their knowledge.

Part B: Learning Activities

The design of learning activities took into account the students' difficulties regarding their understanding of Files and Peripheral Storage Devices as they emerged from the information collected from the field study mentioned in Step 3 in the previous section. The categories of learning activities that have been formed are:

- *1st Category of Activities: Exploring a file microworld.* Here, a variety of files are presented to the learners who are asked to recognize the various types by their name or icon. If this is impossible, students can search for extra information by double clicking on each file.

- *2nd Category of Activities: Management and orientation in a simulation of a real-life microworld.* Learners are provided with a number of real-life objects so that it will be impossible for them to remember each one and are then asked to store these objects in a variety of storage media. Next, they are asked to find a specific object. This type of activity enables the students to develop their cognitive skills regarding classification and orientation in a context consisting of simulations of real-life objects and operations.

Figure 1. Disk formatting

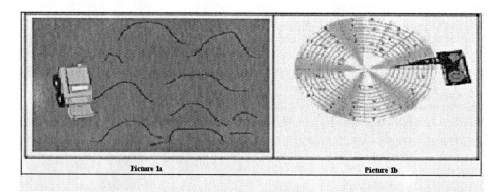

Picture 1a   Picture 1b

- *3rd Category of Activities: Management and orientation within file and peripheral storage media microworld.* Learners are provided with a number of computer files so that it will be impossible for them to remember each one, and then are asked for classification in computer folders. Next, they are asked to store the folders in a variety of peripheral storage media such as a hard disk, a CD-ROM, and a floppy disk. Finally, they are asked to find a specific file. This category of activity enables the students to develop their cognitive skills regarding classification and orientation in a microworld consisting of computer files and operations.

- *4th Category of Activities*: *Transformations in a file microworld.* Learners are provided with various files, for example, document files or image files, and then are asked to select parts of them in order to produce new files using basic file operations such as cut and paste, delete, copy, and so forth. This category of activity enables the students to develop their cognitive skills regarding analysis and synthesis in a microworld consisting of computer files containing different kinds of data. This category of activity also enables the students to develop their technical skills regarding basic file operations mentioned above.

Part C: Learner Activity Space

Representations and tools for the active performance of the selected categories of activities relating to the concepts of files and of peripheral storage media were designed; a description of each follows.

Real-Life Representation Systems

A variety of real-life objects are provided to the students. Students can drag and drop these objects using the mouse in order to store them in storage places. More specifically, here the student is asked to sort some real-life objects in a kitchen cupboard, moving them with the mouse. These objects metaphorically represent files, whereas the cupboard shelves metaphorically represent folders (Figure 2a). These objects are different from those used in the respective content presentation activities (Part A, previous section), in order to compel the students to think and act, thus preventing them from reproducing their previous experience (Figure 2b). In the context of these representation systems students can perform activities of the 2nd Category (Part B, previous section).

Representations of Files Used in Actual Computer Interfaces

A variety of different types of computer files are presented to the students. Actual computer folders are also provided (Figure 3a). In this context, *actual file-sorting activities* can be performed. Two types of these activities can be performed. The one type involves the student sorting various files in folders in the way she/he prefers. More specifically, the student is given three computer folders called "Courses," "Music," and

Figure 2. Everyday life representation systems

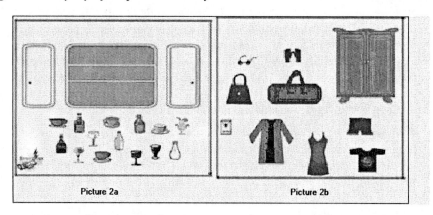

Picture 2a   Picture 2b

"Pictures." A number of various file icons are provided for sorting into folders. These files represent photograph files, music files, and files relevant to school courses. The student is asked to store the files in the folders in any way she/he likes. After the sorting is finished, the student is asked to find certain files (different ones in each execution of the program), so that she/he will realize why it is useful to sort files in folders correctly. The other type of sorting activity is almost identical to that previously mentioned, differing only in the fact that the program does not allow the student to sort a file in a folder where it does not match. This was decided in order to give the learner the opportunity of realizing how files can be correctly sorted in folders (Figure 3a). In these representation systems, students can perform activities of the 1st and 3rd categories (Part B, previous section).

Representations of Actual Computer-based Storage Media

Moreover, simulations of peripheral storage media with a certain capacity are provided, such as a hard disk, a CD-ROM, and a floppy disk (Figure 3b). Students can also drag and drop the folders and the files using the mouse in order to store them in these peripheral storage media. Each file has a set size that is inscribed on it, while the total size of all the files together exceeds the capacity of the hard disk. In this activity, the student is asked to store some computer files in a storage medium of a certain capacity. This was considered necessary in order for the student to realise that a storage medium and especially a hard disk has finite capacity. In these systems, activities of the 3rd category (Part B, previous section) can be performed.

Games as Representation Systems

A labyrinth game was designed to support students learning of basic file operations such as copy, paste, delete, cut, and so on (The game is under implementation). In the context of this game, each student can visit the different rooms of the labyrinth, but she/he cannot go out until correctly performing some specific basic file operations. In some rooms, new computer files are presented to the visitor to manipulate. In other rooms, the visitor is asked to perform specific basic file operations. Learners are asked to perform two types of activities regarding file transformation: (a) to use different files and perform the necessary transformations in order to produce a predefined file (by the teacher), and (b) to use different files and perform transformations in order to produce their own files. The game was designed to assess automatically the first type of activity. The game is also designed to provide the learners with various files, for example, document files, image files, and so forth, as well as the basic file operations such as cut and paste, delete, copy, and so on. In the context of these representation systems students can perform activities of the 4th Category (Part B, previous section).

(Part C is referred to Step 4 and Step 5 of the proposed design methodology, previous section)

Part D: Learner Assessment

Assessment by the Teacher

On entering the software environment, the learner is asked to give a login name and a password. For new users, there is a link for registration. The system asks for the user's personal data in order to create a log file of her/his actions that can be used as a source of information for further study, research, and assessment by the teacher and the researcher.

Figure 3. Representation systems used in actual computer interfaces

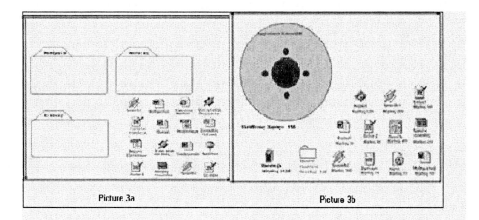

Self-Assessment

The software enables the learner to evaluate him/herself through a game in the form of a quiz. Young learners are interested in quizzes and use them to amuse themselves in their everyday lives. The questions aim to investigate and illuminate the learners' difficulties regarding the learning concepts. In each step, the learner has to choose between similar answers to the question posed. If she/he chooses the most correct answer, the quiz proceeds to a question on another point; otherwise, it poses a new question on the same point. The answers are constructed in such a way as to enable the student to realize where she/he made a mistake. The same process goes on for four questions concerning the same subconcept. The learners' answers are not labeled by the system as right or wrong. At the end of the game, each learner gets a score, which is the total sum of the scores that she/he got by answering the questions throughout the test. The winner of the game is the learner who gets the lowest score and higher points are assessed for incorrect answers.

Longitudinal Assessment

In this context, electronic portfolios can be created for each student where she/he can post her/his work. In addition, project-based assessment can be performed by dividing the students into groups and assigning a specific project to each group.

(Part D is referred to Step 6 of the proposed design methodology, previous section)

Part E: Learner Communication

The software environment enables the students to communicate with one another and with their teacher, asynchronously, using e-mail, text-chat, forum, teleconferencing, and Web boards where every group of users can post a message.

(Part E is referred to Step 7 of the proposed design methodology, previous section)

The Software's Technical Characteristics

For the software's implementation, the Macromedia Flash 4 and 5, Javascript, and PHP v. 4.0.6 technologies were used, as well as the database MySQL v. 3.23.31. Minimum system requirements are Pentium II, 300MHz, memory 64MB, Hard Disk space 2MB, and Internet Explorer Version 6.0 or higher.

The Pilot Evaluation Study of FPSD

The Context of the Pilot Study

The environment's pilot evaluation study was conducted under the constructivist perspective emphasizing the student's evolution during her/his interaction within a learning environment (von Glasersfeld, 1990). In terms of methodology, this research is a qualitative study (Cohen & Manion, 1989). The main objectives of this study were to investigate: (a) the students' prior knowledge of the concepts in question, (b) how the students' knowledge progressed during their interaction within the context of the FPSD learning environment, and (c) the functionality and the usability of the software.

The study was conducted in the 3rd High School of Egion with the participation of 10 students of the 2nd grade (14-15-years-old) and lasted two hours. The students worked on computers in pairs, exchanging places so that everyone could interact with the software. Initially, the students were asked to fill in an answer sheet, which served to determine their prior knowledge regarding the specific learning concepts. The same answer sheet was given to them at the end of the pilot phase in order to investigate the evolution of their comprehension. The researchers' part in the study was mainly as observers, intervening only when it was necessary so as not to influence the students' actions, but to record anything they said or did during their interaction with the system. The data sources of the study were the aforementioned notes and the log files that were created. The communication forum was not used during the software's evaluation. This was done mainly due to lack of time, since the asynchronous nature of this type of communication requires long-term involvement of the students with the software.

Analysis and Interpretation of the Pilot Phase Results

The Student's Prior Knowledge

Even though the students participating in the pilot study had been taught this specific subject recently, their answers to the answer sheet questions showed that almost all of them had failed to understand the concept of file, and they were confused about folders and file sorting. Few students (two students) seemed to understand the importance of the existence of different storage media, and nobody seemed to know anything about magnetic medium formatting. No student had ever used the Internet, and only one had a personal computer.

The Students' Interaction with the Software Environment

a.   Introducing the FPSD environment. All students needed help in order to complete the "new user insertion form," since this was the first time they had come into contact with an Internet application, especially with an environment that required new user registration.

b.   The role of the home page. All students expressed their admiration for the introductory bright animations presented in the home page of FPSD All of them devoted an amount of their time to enjoying these images.

c.   The role of the game. It is noteworthy that the students' first choice was the "Quiz," presumably because they were more familiar with this word than with other activities. However, most of the students spent only a few minutes on it because, at this point, they could not meet its requirements.

d.   The role of real-life activities in the content presentation. The next choice for most students (eight students) was the presentation of the learning content through real-life activities, presented by using moving images. The students' answers to the researchers' questions showed that most of them understood the analogy of real-life objects and activities with the activities of sorting and storing using actual computer operations and objects for peripheral storage media, files, and file sorting. There were three students who could not understand the above analogy and the meaning of the presented activities, so they had to review the content a few times. The point that was completely opaque for the students had to do with the magnetic medium formatting presentations. The concept of "disk formatting" was new to all students.

e.   Student interactions within the learner activity space. All students visited the learner activity space. The students performed the activities in the order that they were presented on the interface. Most of them dedicated a lot of time to the real-life activities and all completed them successfully. However, many students (eight students) performed the "sorting files in folders" activities in a random and incorrect way, and when they were asked to retrieve certain files from the folders, they had difficulty in doing so. After several attempts, they performed the activity of file sorting correctly. It is worth mentioning that there were some students (two students) who sorted the files correctly from the beginning. In the specific activity where the student is asked to store files of a set size in a hard disk of finite capacity, few students (two students) understood why they couldn't store all the files on the disk. One asked, "Why can't this file go into the disk?" The researchers replied that a hard disk has finite capacity.

f.   Self-assessment in a game's context. Next, the students tried the quiz. Initially, they all said they would prefer a system that informed them whether their answers were right or not. However, because they didn't know if they had answered correctly and where they had made mistakes, when they saw that other students achieved better scores they continued to play again and again. In the end, they admitted that it was better this way because they found most correct answers on their own.

g.   Students' navigation through the text-based presentations of the learning content. It is worth noting that the students spent very little time reading the main points concerning the learning concepts, which was presented in the form of written text, and hardly any time reading the detailed descriptions of the subject. The majority resorted to the brief description after the researchers' urging so they could get information about disk formatting. Others resorted to it in order to fill in the final answer sheet.

Finally, the analysis of the students' answers to the answer sheet given after their interaction with the software showed that this software helped them to a certain degree in understanding the concepts of files and folders and less in understanding peripheral storage media and disk formatting.

Discussion and Future Trends

The concept of Special Purpose E-Learning Environments (SPELEs) was presented in this study. In contrast to the concept of General Purpose E-Learning Environments (GPELEs), which incompletely support the learning of any learning subject, SPELEs are designed to support more efficiently the learning of a specific subject matter. A typical architecture for the design of SPELEs was proposed. This architecture was based on interpretations of constructivist and social views of learning in the Internet context.

More specifically, the proposed architecture supports the design of such e-learning environments where learning is realized in a context consisting of: (a) content presentation using as a basic structural element the learning activity performed in multiple hyperlinked representation systems, (b) constructivist, open real-life learning activities, (c) active learning using multiple representation systems and tools designed by taking into account specific research studies investigating how the learners cope with the concepts of the specific learning subject, (d) tools that assist experimentation using primary sources of data while at the same time providing opportunities for hands-on experience, (e) representation systems that can act as metaphors of real-life activities, (f) multiple ways of assessment emphasizing the learning process and not only the learning outcomes, (g) multiple ways of communication emphasizing combinations of both group and whole class conferences, using synchronous and asynchronous modes.

The proposed architecture consisted of five parts: (a) organization of the content of a specific learning subject, (b) learning activities, (c) learner activity space, (d) learner assessment, and (e) learner communication.

A 7-step methodology was formed for the construction of the architecture above:

Step 1. Defining the basic concepts of the specific learning subject.

Step 2. Defining constructivist, essential learning activities for the learning of the defined concepts.

Step 3. Investigating how the learners perform the essential activities selected for the learning of each specific subject through field studies using real students.

Step 4. Defining the appropriate representation systems to meet the learners' individual learning differences.

Step 5. Designing the appropriate tools included in the learner activity space.

Step 6. Designing the tools for assessment.

Step 7. Designing the facilities provided for communication.

In the framework of this architecture, a SPELE was constructed for the learning of the concepts of Files and Peripheral Storage Devices (FPSD). The FPSD was evaluated in a pilot study using real students. Here, the parts of the proposed architecture are discussed in relation to the data that emerged from this pilot study.

Part A: Organization of the Content

The content was organized in four hyperlinked layers. In the first layer, the content was organized as a group of two types of activities: (i) simulations of real-life activities where operations and objects were used as metaphors of computer-based operations and objects related to the learning concepts in question, and (ii) computer activities using computer-based operations and objects related to these concepts. The necessary concepts related to the performance of these activities were hidden and illuminated according to the needs of each individual learner via hyperlinks. These concepts were presented in brief (in the second layer), in detail (in the third layer), and in a wider context including a variety of resources such as URLs, electronic books, and so forth (in the fourth layer).

As shown by the results of the pilot evaluation study of FPSD, the students mainly paid attention to the two different types of learning activities used for the presentation of the learning content. It is worth noting that the students were attracted by the real-life activities that were used as metaphors for the activities using computer operations and objects. Even though the activities were hyperlinked with brief and analytical descriptions of the necessary knowledge for their performance, a small number of students accessed the brief descriptions while no one tried the analytical ones.

Part B: Learning Activities

The categories of the learning activities were designed by examining: (a) the basic concepts that constitute the learning of files and peripheral storage media for secondary-level education students, and (b) the students' approaches and cognitive difficulties in their learning of the concepts in question. These approaches and difficulties had been investigated by performing field studies using real students. The basic aspects and skills regarding the concepts above were: (a) the recognition of various types of files, (b) file management, (c) orientation in a file microworld, (d) basic operations that can be performed on the content of a file, (e) the recognition of the limited capacity of a storage medium, and (f) disk formatting operations. The investigated students' difficulties related to all these aspects.

As a result, four categories of learning activities were designed:

1. Exploring a file microworld, for the understanding of (a) above,
2. Management and orientation in a simulation of a real life microworld, for the understanding of (b, c, e and f) above,
3. Management and orientation within file and peripheral storage media microworld, for the understanding of (b, c, e and f) above, and
4. transformations in a file microworld, for the understanding of (d) above.

The designed activities are well situated in the context of modern learning theories as they were: a) open, enabling the learners to perform them in alternative ways as well as to express different kinds of knowledge such as school knowledge, intuitive knowledge, real-life knowledge, and visual knowledge, b) interesting, as they were situated within the students' world, c) appropriate for the learning of the basic aspects of the subject matter, d) cognitively challenging since they focused on management and orientation of files, e) self-explanatory in that they provided the students with appropriate feedback for making corrections in their sorting and storing attempts, f) practical, enabling the learners to experiment by handling primary sources of data while at the same time acquiring hands-on experience, and g) not demanding, as the learners were not expected to have extra complicated knowledge from other disciplines.

As the results of the pilot study show, the designed activities occupied the attention of all students as well as their active participation in the pilot evaluation experiment. More specifically, the use of real-world activities, objects, and operations as metaphors for the activities performed in the computer word using its functions and objects greatly helped in the understanding of the aforementioned concepts. Moreover, students were helped by the activities that led them to a cognitive conflict, such as the demand to find certain files stored in folders and the storing of files of total size greater than the capacity of the available hard disk.

Part C: Learner Activity Space

The design of the representation systems and their associated tools provided to the students for active learning, within the context of learner activity space, was based on the proposed methodology for the general design of SPELEs. So multiple representation systems and their associated tools were designed and implemented. There were:

a. Real life representation systems. These systems were used to support the performance of activities included in the 2nd category (Part B, previous section).
b. Representations of files used in actual computer interfaces. In these representation systems, students can perform 1st and 3rd category activities (Part B, previous section).

c.   Representations of actual computer-based storage media. These systems were used to support the performance of activities included in the 3rd category (Part B, previous section).

d.   Games used as representation systems to support the performance of activities included in the 4th category (Part B, previous section).

The analysis of the data that emerged from the pilot evaluation study of FPSD shows that all the provided tools were used by all the students who participated in this experiment. Moreover, this study shows that the previously mentioned systems and tools helped the students' performance of the designed categories of learning activities and supported them in expressing different kind of knowledge regarding the learning concepts, such as school knowledge, intuitive knowledge, real-life knowledge, and visual knowledge.

Part D: Learner Assessment

FPSD supports a variety of ways for assessment:

a.   assessment by the teacher, by studying the log files automatically created by the software. These files were also used to evaluate this experiment,

b.   Longitudinal assessment, by using electronic portfolios, and

c.   Self-assessment by participating in a specifically designed game.

Despite the fact that the FPSD supports a variety of ways for assessment, the short duration of the experiment limited the students to trying self-assessment by participating in the provided game in the form of a quiz. This quiz does not provide explicit feedback in the form of messages that inform the user of the correctness of her/his answers to the questions provided. The questions are organized in such a way so that in the case of a wrong answer another similar but easier question is posed for the learner to answer. A group of four similar questions are available with which the learner can experiment. As demonstrated by the data that emerged from the pilot evaluation study of FPSD, students enthusiastically and tirelessly played the game more than once until they gained good results!

Part E: Learner Communication

The limited time dedicated to this pilot evaluation study does not provide us with data for the communication that could be performed within the context of FPSD. More time is needed to gather data regarding effective communication using the related facilities of FPSD.

Future Trends

As far as magnetic medium formatting goes, it is obvious that the software should be modified in order to allow the student a deeper observation of this procedure. The design of the interface could also be changed so that the objects it contains will be more interesting for the students. Further study with a greater sample of students, as well as testing the communication facilities and the game designed for experimentation with basic file operations (which is under final testing) could bring to light more interesting issues regarding the software and its influence on the students' learning processes.

Finally, the core of all specifications described for the design of a SPELE was taken into account for the design of the FPSD. Even though improvements and developments for the FPSD e-learning environment can be proposed, it is worth mentioning that a sense of security came as a result of its pilot evaluation experiment. This sense was grounded both in the results based on the answer sheet completed by the students after their interaction within the context of FPSD and on their enthusiastic participation in this experiment.

Conclusion

This study demonstrated the background, the implementation, and the pilot evaluation of a Special Purpose E-Learning Environment (SPELE) for the learning of concepts of Files and Peripheral Storage Media. This environment was pilot tested in the field with real students. The analysis of the data that emerged from this experiment verifies the methodology used and the core specifications of the proposed architecture for an effective design of a SPELE. More specifically, the design of this environment was based on constructivist and social theories of learning that were interpreted in the Internet context, thus forming a general architecture for SPELEs. This architecture consisted of five parts: (a) organization of the content of a specific learning subject, (b) learning activities, (c) learner activity space, (d) learner assessment, and (e) learner communication.

The main points of the proposed architecture that were addressed by the experimental evaluation study emphasize: (a) activity based presentation of the content, (b) multiple representation systems and tools assisting both the presentation of the activities that compose the content and the performance of learning activities so as to support various learners in expressing their individual learning differences, (c) essential, problem-solving, open, holistic, real-life activities, (d) real-life operations and objects used as metaphors of computer operations and objects, (e) games as a motivating way for self-assessment, (f) appropriate feedback to lead the students firstly to a cognitive conflict and next to self correction. More research is needed to extend the constructed prototype for the learning of other related concepts as well as for the evaluation of the provided communication facilities.

Acknowledgments

Many thanks to Sally McKevitt for proof reading and assisting with the English.

References

Bishop, A. J. (1988). *Mathematical enculturation*. Dordrecht: Kluwer Academic Publishers.

Cognition and Technology Group at Vanderbilt (CTGV). (1991). Some thoughts about constructivism and instructional design. *Educational Technology*, 16-17.

Cognition and Technology Group at Vanderbilt (CTGV). (1992). Emerging technologies, ISD, and learning environments: Critical perspectives. *Educational Technology Research and Development, 40*(1), 65-80.

Cohen, L. & Manion, L. (1989). *Research methods in education*. London: Routledge.

Crawford, K. (1996a). Vygotskian approaches in human development in the information era. *Educational Studies in Mathematics, 31*, 43-62.

Crawford, K. (1996b). Distributed cognition, technology and change. In A. Gutierrez (Ed.), *Proceedings of the 20th Conference of PME,* July 8-12, Valencia, Spain (Vol. 1, pp. 81-112).

Dillenbourg, P., Schneider, D., & Synteta, P. (2002). Virtual learning environments. In A. Dimitrakopoulou (Ed.), *Proceedings of 3rd Pan-Hellenic Conference:* "*ICT in Education,*" Rhodes, Greece, September 26-29 (pp. 3-18).

Duffy, M.T., Lowyck, J., & Jonassen, H. D. (1993). *Designing environments for constructive learning*. Berlin: Springer-Verlag.

Dyfour-Janvier, B., Bednarz, N., & Belanger, M. (1987). Pedagogical considerations concerning the problem of representation. In C. Janvier (Ed.), *Problems of representation in teaching and learning of mathematics* (pp. 109-122). London: Lawrence Erlbaum Associates.

Grigoriadou, M., Gogoulou, A., Gouli, E., & Samarakou, M. (2004). Activity as a structural element of learning and co-operation in SCALE. In M. Gregoriadou, A. Raptis, S. Vosniadou, & C. Kynigos (Eds.), *Proceedings of 4th Pan-Hellenic Conference: "ICT in Education"* Athens, Greece, September 29-October 3 (pp. 525-534).

Grigoriadou, M. & Kanidis, E. (2003). Design and evaluation of a cache memory simulation program. In V. Devedzik, J. M. Spector, D. G. Sampson, & Kinshuk (Eds.), *Proceedings of 3rd International Conference on Advanced Learning Technologies 2003*, Athens, Greece, July 8-9 (pp. 170-174).

Harasim, L. (1989). Online education: A new domain. In R. Mason & A. Kaye (Eds.), *Mindwave: Communication, computers & distance education* (pp. 50-69). Oxford: Pergamon Press.

Harasim, L. (1990). *Online Education: Perspectives on a new environment*. New York: Praeger.

Harasim, L., Hiltz, S.R., Teles, L., & Turoff, M. (1995). *Learning networks: A field guide to teaching and learning online*. Cambridge, MA: MIT Press.

Hofstetter, F. (1998). Cognitive versus behavioral psychology. Retrieved June 23, 2005, from *http://www.udel.edu/fth/pbs/ webmodel.htm*

Hoppe, H.U. (2002). Computers in the classroom—A disappearing phenomenon? In A. Dimitrakopoulou (Ed.), *Proceedings of 3rd Pan-Hellenic Conference: "ICT in Education"*, Rhodes, Greece, September 26-29 (pp. 19-30).

James, G. (2000). *Advantages and disadvantages of online learning*. Allen Communications White Paper. Retrieved May 12, 2000, from *http://www.allencomm.com*

Jonassen, H. D. (1991). Objectivism versus constructivism: Do we need a new philosophical paradigm? *Journal of Educational Research, 39*(3), 5-14.

Jonassen, H. D., Carr, C., & Yueh, H-P. (1998). Computers as mindtools for engaging learners in critical thinking. *Tech Trends, 43*(2), 24-32.

Jonassen, H.D. (2000). Revisiting activity theory as a framework for designing student-centered learning environments. In D.H. Jonassen & S.M. Land (Eds.), *Theoretical foundations of learning environments* (pp. 89-121). London: Lawrence Erlbaum Associates.

Kaput, J.J. (1994). The representational roles of technology in connecting mathematics with authentic experience. In R. Biehler, R. W. Scholz, R. Strasser, & B. Winkelman (Eds.), *Didactics of mathematics as a scientific discipline: The state of the art* (pp. 379-397). Dordrecht: Kluwer Academic Publishers.

Kordaki, M. & Potari, D. (2002). The effect of area measurement tools on children's strategies: The role of a computer microworld. *International Journal of Computers in Mathematical Learning, 7*(1), 1-36.

Kordaki, M. (2005, in preparation). Students' conceptions of files and of peripheral storage media.

Laborde, J.-M. & Strasser, R. (1990). Cabri-Geometre: A microworld of geometry for guided discovery learning. *ZDM, 5*, 171-177.

Liu, M. & Hsiao, Y.-P. (2002). Middle school students as multimedia designers: A project-based learning approach. *Journal of Interactive Learning Research, 13*(4), 311-337.

Miranda, J.E.P. & Pinto, J.S. (1996). Using Internet technology for course support. *WWW Special Issue of SIGCSE Bulletin, 28*, 96-100.

North Central Regional Educational Laboratory (NCREL) (2005). Critical issue: Providing hands-on, minds-on, and authentic learning experiences in science. Retrieved April 29, 2005, from *www.ncrel.org/sdrs/areas/issues/content/cntareas/science/sc500.htm*

Noss, R. & Hoyles, C. (1996). *Windows on mathematical meanings: Learning cultures and computers*. Dordrecht: Kluwer Academic Publishers.

Papanikolaou, K., Grigoriadou, M., Magoulas, G., & Kornilakis, H. (2002). Towards new forms of knowledge communication: The adaptive dimension of a Web-based learning environment. *Computers and Education, 39*(4), 333-360.

Papert, S. (1980). *Mindstorms: Pupils, computers, and powerful ideas.* New York: Basic Books.

Skinner, B.F. (1968). *The technology of teaching.* New York: Appleton.

Sutherland, R. (1995). Mediating mathematical action. In R. Sutherland & J. Mason (Eds.), *Exploiting mental imagery with computers in mathematics education* (pp. 71-81). Berlin: Springer-Verlag.

Tam, M. (2000). Constructivism, instructional design, and technology: Implications for transforming distance learning. *Educational Technology & Society, 3*(2), 50-60.

Tretiakov, A., Hong, H., Kinshuk, & Patel, A. (2003). Adding value to educational content by applying MRA filtering. In V. Devedzik, J.M. Spector, D.G. Sampson, & Kinshuk (Eds.), *Proceedings of 3rd International Conference on Advanced Learning Technologies 2003*, Athens, Greece, July 8-9 (pp. 27-31).

Tretiakov, A., Kinshuk, & Tretiakov, T. (2003). Designing multimedia support for situated learning. In V. Devedzik, J.M. Spector, D.G. Sampson, & Kinshuk (Eds.), *Proceedings of 3rd International Conference on Advanced Learning Technologies 2003*, Athens, Greece, July 8-9 (pp. 32-36).

Venakis, P., Giannakopoulos, Y., Pirli, M., & Kordaki, M. (2002). A Web-based multi-representational environment for the learning of files and of peripheral storage devices. In A. Dimitrakopoulou (Ed.), *Proceedings of Panhellenic conference with international participation "Informatics in Education,"* Rhodos, Greece, September 26-29 (pp. 624-631).

Vlachogiannis, G., Kekatos, V., Miatides, M., Misedakis, J., Kordaki, M., & Houstis, E. (2001). A multiple-representations environment for the learning of the bubble sort algorithm. I V. Makrakis (Ed.), *Proceedings of Pan-Hellenic Conference "New Technologies in Education and in Distance Education,"* Rethymnon, Greece, June 8-10 (pp. 481-495).

von Glasersfeld, E. (1987), Learning as a constructive activity. In C. Janvier (Ed.), *Problems of representation in teaching and learning of mathematics* (pp. 3-18). London: Lawrence Erlbaum Associates.

von Glasersfeld, E. (1990). An exposition of constructivism: Why some like it radical. In R. B. Davis, C. A. Maher, & N. Noddings (Eds.), *Constructivist views on the teaching and learning of mathematics* (pp. 1-3). Reston, VA: N.C.T.M.

Voyatzaki, E., Christakoudis, C., Margaritis, M., & Avouris, N. (2004). Teaching algorithms in secondary education: A collaborative approach. In *Proceedings of ED-MEDIA 2004,* Lugano, Switzerland, June 21-25 (pp. 2781-2789). Norfolk, VA: AACE Publications.

Vygotsky, L. (1978). *Mind in society.* Cambridge, MA: Harvard University Press.

Zikouli, K. & Kordaki, M. (2004). A framework for the evaluation of students' learning regarding basic aspects of programming and C. In M. Gregoriadou, A. Raptis, S.

Vosniadou, & C. Kynigos (Eds.), *Proceedings of 3rd Pan-Hellenic Conference: "ICT in Education"*, Athens, Greece, September 29-October 3 (pp. 598-606).

Zikouli, K., Kordaki, M., & Houstis, E. (2003). A multi-representational environment for the learning of programming and C. In V. Devedzik, J.M. Spector, D.G. Sampson, & Kinshuk (Eds.), *Proceedings of 3rd International Conference on Advanced Learning Technologies 2003*, Athens, Greece, July 8-9 (p. 459).

About the Authors

Zongmin Ma received a PhD from the City University of Hong Kong in 2001 and is currently a full professor in the College of Information Science and Engineering at Northeastern University, China. His current research interests include intelligent database systems, knowledge management, Semantic Web and XML, life science data management, e-learning systems, intelligent planning and scheduling, decision making, engineering database modeling, and enterprise information systems. Dr. Ma has published more than 40 papers in international journals, conferences, edited books, and encyclopedias in these areas since 1998. He also edited and authored several scholarly books published by Idea Group Publishing and Springer-Verlag.

* * *

Kimberly Addicott is a graduate student working toward a master's degree in education at North Dakota State University, USA. She is currently working with a cross-departmental research team that investigates the use of virtual environments in the teaching of science. Her primary focus involves creating curriculum materials, facilitating assessment of student learning in virtual environments, and assisting with the implementation and assessment of virtual worlds for learning in secondary classrooms. In addition to her work with virtual environments, Kimberly teaches ninth grade US history.

Naomi Augar completed her Bachelor of Computing (applied computing) with Honors in 2002 at Deakin University, Melbourne, Australia. Presently, she is a PhD candidate in the School of Information Technology at Deakin University. Her PhD research focuses on virtual learning communities. Her research interests include issues relating to constructing an online identity, virtual communication, and e-learning.

Christos Bouras earned his diploma and PhD from the Department of Computer Engineering and Informatics of Patras University, Greece. He is currently an associate professor in the same department. He is also a scientific advisor of Research Unit 6 in Research Academic Computer Technology Institute (CTI), Patras, Greece. His research interests include analysis of performance of networking and computer systems, computer networks and protocols, telematics and new services, QoS and pricing for networks and services, e-learning networked virtual environments, and WWW issues. He has published 200 papers in various well-known refereed conferences and journals. He is a co-author of seven books in Greek. He has been a PC member and referee in various international journals and conferences. He has participated in R&D projects and is a member of experts in the Greek Research and Technology Network (GRNET), Advisory Committee Member to the W3C, Member of WG3.3 and WG6.4 of IFIP, Task Force for Broadband Access in Greece, ACM, IEEE, EDEN, AACE, and New York Academy of Sciences.

Manuel Ortega Cantero earned his MSc in science and his doctorate in science at the Universidad Autónoma de Barcelona, Spain. He is a full professor of computer languages and systems at the Escuela Superior de Informática de Ciudad Real, Universidad de Castilla-La Mancha, Spain. His research focuses on artificial neural networks, computers in education, collaborative systems, and ubiquitous computing. He is the secretary of the Asociación para el Desarrollo de la Informática Educativa (ADIE) in Spain, the coordinator in Spain of the Red Iberoamericana de Informática Educativa (RIBIE), and the director of the Computer-Human Interaction and Collaboration (CHICO) Research Group.

Antonella Carbonaro (carbonar@csr.unibo.it) received a degree in computer science from the University of Bologna, Italy (1992). In 1997, she finished her PhD studies on artificial intelligent system, in particular, working on machine learning techniques. From 1997 to 1999, in addition to serving on the Faculty of Computer Science of the University of Bologna, she received a research fellowship with the theme of search "artificial intelligence." Now she is an assistant professor in the Department of Computer Science of the University of Bologna. Her current research interests concern information filtering, evolutionary algorithms, and personalized learning environment.

Alexandra I. Cristea received her doctorate in IS and worked at the University of Electro-Communications, Tokyo, Japan. She is presently an assistant professor at the IS Group, Faculty of Mathematics & Computer Science, Eindhoven, University of Technology, The Netherlands. Her research interests include AEH and adaptive hypermedia authoring, UM, Semantic Web, AI, neural networks, adaptive systems, concept mapping, ITS, and Web-based educational environments. She authored and co-authored more than 100 research papers and course booklets. She is a member of IEEE, was a program committee member of Hypertext, AH, ICCE, ICAI, IKE (a.o.) and was a reviewer or session chair for many conferences; she is executive peer reviewer of the *ET&S Journal*.

Lisa M. Daniels is an assistant professor in the School of Education at North Dakota State University, USA. Dr. Daniels is a member of a cross-departmental research team that investigates the use of virtual environments in the teaching of science. Other research projects include working with regional science teachers to design lesson plans and assessments effective for diverse learners, evaluating the effect of dispositions on teaching, and determining the effectiveness of federal education reforms. She teaches courses in educational foundations, and the societal implications of and on schools. Daniels serves as an affiliate of the Center for Science and Math Education at NDSU.

Elena García-Barriocanal obtained a university degree in computer science from the Pontifical University of Salamanca in Madrid (1998) and a PhD from the Computer Science Department of the University of Alcalá. From September 1998 to February 1999, she worked as a lecturer in the Computer Languages and Information Systems Department of the Pontifical University, and in 1999, she joined the Computer Science Department of University of Alcalá as an assistant professor. Since 2001, she has been associate professor with the Computer Science Department of the university of Alcalá and a member of the Information Engineering Research Group of this University. Her research interests mainly focus on topics related to the role of knowledge representation in fields, like human-computer interaction and e-learning; concretely, she actively works on ontological aspects both in learning technologies and in usability and accessibility. She supervises several PhD works in those areas.

Eleftheria Giannaka obtained her diploma from the Informatics Department of the Aristotelian University of Thessaloniki, Greece, and her master's degree from the Computer Engineering and Informatics Department of Patras University. She is currently a PhD candidate in the Department of Computer Engineer and Informatics of Patras University. Furthermore, she is working as an R&D computer engineer at the Research Unit 6 of the Computer Technology Institute in Patra, Greece. Her interests include computer networks, virtual networks, system architecture, Internet applications, electronic commerce, database implementation and administration, virtual reality applications, performance evaluation, and programming. She is currently involved with the project VirRad.

Ioannis Hatzilygeroudis is currently a lecturer at the Department of Computer Engineering & Informatics, University of Patras, Greece. Dr. Hatzilygeroudis is member of the editorial boards of the *International Journal of Artificial Intelligence Tools (IJAIT)*, the *International Journal of Web-Based Communities (IJWBC)* and the *International Journal of Computational Intelligence (IJCI)*. He has also been member of the PCs of several AI related conferences (e.g., IEEE ICTAI, FLAIRS) and organized a number of special/invited sessions. He is the guest editor of a special issue of *IJAIT* on "AI Techniques in Web-Based Educational Systems." He has published more than 50 papers in international journals, and edited volumes and proceedings of conferences and workshops. His main research interests are knowledge representation, expert systems, and intelligent educational systems.

Patrícia Augustin Jaques earned a PhD in computer science from the Federal University of Rio Grande do Sul, Brazil, in 2004. During her PhD studies, she spent one year researching at the Leibniz Laboratory in France. Currently, she is a researcher and assistant professor of Computer Science at Federal University of Rio Grande do Sul. Her research interests are intelligent tutoring systems, multi-agent systems, and affective computing.

Pythagoras Karampiperis holds a diploma and MSc in electronics and computer engineering from Technical University of Crete (2000 and 2002, respectively). He also holds an MSc in operational research from the Technical University of Crete (2002). Currently, he is a PhD candidate at the Department of Technology Education and Digital Systems of the University of Piraeus, Greece, and member of the Advanced eServices for the Knowledge Society Research Unit (ASK) at the Informatics and Telematics Institute (ITI) of the Center of Research and Technology Hellas (CERTH). He is a member of the Technical Chamber of Greece and a student member of IEEE.

Kinshuk is an associate professor at the Massey University, New Zealand. He is also director of Advanced Learning Technology Research. He has been involved in large-scale research projects for exploration-based adaptive educational environments and has published over 115 research papers in international refereed journals, conferences, and book chapters. He is currently chairing the IEEE Technical Committee on Learning Technology, New Zealand Chapter of ACM SIGCHI, and the International Forum of Educational Technology & Society. He is also editor of the SSCI indexed *Journal of Educational Technology & Society* (ISSN 1436-4522) and *Learning Technology Newsletter* (ISSN 1438-0625). He is editorial board member of more than a dozen journals and programme committee member of several conferences in educational technology every year.

Maria Kordaki holds a bachelor's degree in mathematics, an MSc in education, and a PhD in educational technology. She is an advisor of high-school mathematics teachers and adjunct professor in the Department of Computer Engineering and Informatics, University of Patras, Greece. Her research interests include design, implementation and evaluation of paper and pencil, computer-based and e-learning environments, using modern theories of learning. She is publishing in international journals as well as in local and international conferences. She has designed and tested in the field using real students with positive results a number of open, constructivist, computer environments for the learning of concepts referred to mathematics and computer science by primary and secondary-level education students.

Elicia Lanham received her BComputing (information management) and BComputing (Honours) degrees from Deakin University, Melbourne, Australia (2001 and 2002, respectively), and a Certificate II in small business management from the Vocational and Educational Training Accreditation Board (VETAB), Australia (2000). She is currently a PhD candidate in the School of Information Technology, Deakin University, Melbourne,

Australia. Her research interests include practical and cultural issues of Internet education, cross-cultural learning styles, and e-learning.

Taiyu Lin is a postgraduate researcher at Massey University, New Zealand. He finished his master's of Information Science in 2003 and is currently working toward his PhD. He is currently working on the research of cognitive trait model, which attempts to build a cognitive profile of the learner, for adaptive virtual learning environments. His research interest includes also student modelling, authoring tool for virtual learning environments, mobile learning, and adaptive learning environments. He is an assistant editor of *Educational Technology & Society* journal (ISSN 1436-4522).

Alke Martens is Dr-Ing of computer science. She received her PhD in the area of formal methods for intelligent tutoring systems. Her research areas are modeling and simulation, teaching and training systems, and a combination thereof under the perspective of cognitive sciences. Current application domains of her research are medicine, education of students in the area of medicine, and education of computer science students in the area of modeling and simulation. She is currently a research scientist at the Modeling and Simulation Group at the University of Rostock, Germany.

Phillip McClean is a professor of plant sciences at North Dakota State University, USA, with teaching responsibilities in genetics (http://www.ndsu.nodak.edu/instruct/mcclean/plsc431), and plant molecular genetics (http://www.ndsu.nodak.edu/instruct/mcclean/plsc731/index.htm). Dr. McClean received the Excellence in Teaching-Early Career from the NDSU College of Agriculture in 1994, the Excellence in Teaching-Senior Career from the NDSU College of Agriculture in 2000, and the Peltier Award for Innovation in Teaching from NDSU in 1998. Dr. McClean was also honored in 1999 with an Innovative Excellence in Teaching, Learning and Technology Award at the 10th International Conference on College Teaching, Learning and Technology. Dr. McClean's current research focus is the development software and analytical tools for gene-by-gene cloning in orphan crops.

Paul McNab has a bachelor's degree in human resource management from Massey University with a strong emphasis on training and development through computer-mediated learning. Paul has more than 14 years experience in training, instructional design, human resource development, and staff management. He has more than five years experience in designing, building, and project managing ICT and e-learning applications. Paul specialises in learning systems architecture by combining his practical experience in technology, education, and human resource management. Paul is the founder and managing director of Online Learning Systems, Ltd., New Zealand. Through Paul's leadership, the company has completed several major e-learning projects.

Tom Murray is a research scientist working at the University of Massachusetts and Hampshire College, USA. He has been researching and publishing in field of advanced and adaptive learning environments since 1984. Project areas include adaptive hyperbooks

(MetaLinks), coached inquiry environments (Rashi), authoring tools (Eon), glass box simulation-based inquiry learning (SimForest), and collaboration tools supporting perspective and integrity (Perspegrity) (all described at http://www.tommurray.us). In addition to research activities, Murray teaches graduate and undergraduate courses at Hampshire College and the University of Massachusetts.

Maria Nani obtained her diploma and her master's degree from the Computer Engineering and Informatics Department of Patras University, Greece. She has worked as an R&D computer engineer at the Research Unit 6 of the Computer Technology Institute in Patras, Greece, for three years.

Claus Pahl is a graduate from the Technical University of Braunschweig. He holds a PhD from the University of Dortmund. After academic positions at universities in Germany, Denmark, and Ireland, he lectures at Dublin City University, Ireland. Dr. Pahl has published more than 80 papers in journals and conferences—including *Computers & Education* and the *International Journal of E-Learning*. His main research interests are in Web technologies, in particular for teaching and learning. He currently leads two research projects in educational technologies—the INVITE project on e-learning infra-structures and the OntoGoLe project focusing on knowledge-based learning technology systems.

Alexandros Panagopoulos obtained his diploma from the Computer Engineering and Informatics Department of Patras University, Greece. In 2000, he became a member of Research Unit 6 of the Computer Technology Institute (CTI). He is also attending his first year of postgraduate studies on "Computer Science and Technology" of the Computer Engineering and Informatics Department of Patras University, Greece. His interests include computer networks, multi-user virtual environments, telematics, and C/C++ and Java programming.

Jim Prentzas received his PhD from the Department of Computer Engineering & Informatics, University of Patras, Greece (2002). His PhD thesis was on "Intelligent Hybrid Modular Systems." He is currently a member of the teaching staff at the Department of Informatics & Computer Technology, Technological Educational Insti-tute of Lamia, Greece. He has been member of the PC of FLAIRS conferences for some years. He has participated in a number of National and European research projects. He has published over 30 papers in international journals, edited volumes, and proceedings of conferences and workshops. His main research interests are artificial intelligence, intelligent tutoring systems, Web applications, and geographical information systems.

Juha Puustjärvi obtained his BSc and MSc in computer science (1985 and 1990, respectively), and his PhD in computer science (1999), all from the University of Helsinki, Finland. Currently, he is a professor of information society technologies at the Technical University of Lappeenranta. He is also a docent of eBusiness technologies at the

Technical University of Helsinki, and a docent of computer science at the University of Helsinki. His research interests include e-learning, e-business, knowledge management, Semantic Web, and databases.

Ruth Raitman received her BSc (mathematics) and BComputing (Honours) degrees from Deakin University, Australia (2000 and 2001, respectively), and is currently a PhD candidate in the same university, intending to complete all requirements by the end of 2005. She is the HDR representative of the Faculty of Science and Technology School of Information Technology School Board at Deakin and also acts as an online facilitator and tutor for several units. Her research interests include e-learning, online collaboration, and the employment of wikis in the virtual environment.

Bernhardt Saini-Eidukat is a petrologist, mineralogist, and economic geologist who is currently working in two research areas: the tectonomagmatic evolution of the Somoncura area of northern Patagonia, Argentina, using radiogenic isotope methods, and inquiry into how active learning of geologic concepts can be promoted by using role-playing software. An associate professor and chair of the Department of Geosciences at North Dakota State University, USA, Dr. Saini-Eidukat teaches a variety of courses including physical geology, mineralogy, petrology, geochemistry, hydrogeology, environmental geology, and field courses.

Demetrios Sampson holds a diploma in electrical engineering (1989) from Demokritus University of Thrace and a PhD in multimedia communications (1995) from University of Essex, UK. He is the head of the Advanced eServices for the Knowledge Society Research Unit (ASK) at the Informatics and Telematics Institute (ITI) of the Center of Research and Technology Hellas (CERTH) and an assistant professor on e-learning at the Department of Technology Education and Digital Systems of the University of Piraeus, Greece. He is also the vice chairman of the IEEE Computer Society Technical Committee on Learning Technology. His main scientific interests are in the areas of technology enhanced learning. He is the co-author of more than 135 publications in scientific books, journals, and conferences, with at least 110 citations. He received the Best Paper Award at the IEEE International Conference on Advanced Learning Technologies ICALT01, Madison, WI, USA (August 2001) and at the IEEE International Conference on Advanced Learning Technologies ICALT04, Joensuu, Finland (August 2004). He is a Senior Member of IEEE, Co-Editor-in-Chief of the *Educational Technology and Society Journal* and Member of the editorial boards of six international journals (including the *AACE Journal of Interactive Learning Research* and the *International Journal on E-Learning*).

Salvador Sánchez-Alonso obtained a university degree in computer science from the Pontifical University of Salamanca, Madrid, Spain (1997). He worked as an assistant professor at that university (1997 to 2000), and later as a software engineer at a software solutions company (2000 and 2001). Again, in 2002, he worked as a professor at the Pontifical University of Salamanca in Madrid. In February 2005, he moved to the

University of Alcalá. His research interests include learning objects reusability, metadata, Web engineering and object-oriented technologies, and he is currently finishing his PhD thesis on the design and use of contract-based learning objects.

Donald P. Schwert is a surficial geologist, with a research specialty in ice age environments. Schwert is director of NDSU's Center for Science & Mathematics Education, and he serves as program coordinator for a major NIH-funded initiative to enhance undergraduate science education.

Miguel-Ángel Sicilia obtained a university degree in computer science from the Pontifical University of Salamanca in Madrid, Spain (1996) and a PhD from Carlos III University in Madrid, Spain (2002). In 1997, he joined an object-technology consulting firm, after enjoying a research grant at the Instituto de Automática Industrial (Spanish Research Council). From 1997 to 1999, he worked as assistant professor at the Pontifical University, after which he joined the Computer Science Department of the Carlos III University in Madrid as a lecturer, working simultaneously as a software architect in ecommerce consulting firms, and as a member of the development team of a personalization engine. From 2002 to October 2003, he worked as a full-time lecturer at Carlos III University, working actively in the area of adaptive hypermedia. Currently, he works as a full-time professor at the Computer Science Department, University of Alcalá, Madrid, Spain. He is a member of the Information Engineering Research Group and his research interests are primarily adaptive hypermedia, learning technology, and human-computer interaction, with special focus on the role of uncertainty and imprecision handling techniques on those fields.

Brian M. Slator is a professor of computer science at North Dakota State University, USA. His research interests are artificial intelligence and intelligent educational media. Dr. Slator is currently involved in several research projects in the area of immersive, multi-user, virtual environments. He is also involved in research for developing software tools for constructing virtual worlds, and innovative methods for assessing learning in virtual environments.

Mia Stern's research interests are in the areas of user modeling and adaptive and intelligent user interfaces. She holds a BA in cognitive science and mathematics: computer science from the University of Rochester. She received both her MS and PhD in computer science from the University of Massachusetts at Amherst. She is currently a GUI software engineer at Rational Software, part of IBM Software Group, USA.

Craig Stewart is a research student in the School of Computer Science and Information Technology at the University of Nottingham, UK, and a member of the Web Technologies Research Group. His research subjects include e-learning, adaptive hypermedia, and internationalization of educational materials and contexts. He has published 12 papers and been a reviewer for three international conferences.

Jeff Terpstra is an associate professor of statistics at North Dakota State University, USA. His educational interests include distance education, technology-enhanced learning, and statistical methods for educational research. In regards to statistical research, Dr. Terpstra has published several scientific papers in peer-reviewed journals in the areas of robust time-series analysis, ranked-set sampling, and inference for ordered alternatives. Dr. Terpstra is a member of the American Statistical Association and has served as an elected officer for the Section on Nonparametric Statistics.

Thrasyvoulos Tsiatsos obtained his diploma, his master's degree, and his PhD from the Computer Engineering and Informatics Department of Patras University, Greece. He is currently an R&D computer engineer at the Research Unit 6 of Computer Technology Institute, Patras, Greece. His research interests include computer networks, telematics, distributed systems, networked virtual environments, multimedia and hypermedia. More particularly, he is engaged in distant education with the use of computer networks, Real-Time protocols, and networked virtual environments. He has published nine papers in journals and 30 papers in well-known refereed conferences. He has participated in R&D projects such as OSYDD, RTS-GUNET, ODL-UP, VES, ODL-OTE, INVITE, and EdComNet, and he is currently involved in the project VirRAD.

Rosa Maria Viccari received her PhD in electrical engineering and computers from the University of Coimbra (1990). Currently, she is an associate professor of the Federal University of the Rio Grande do Sul, Brazil. She published 20 articles in specialized journals, 159 works in events, 10 chapters of books, and seven published books. She also supervised 24 master's works and 10 PhD theses in the area of computer science. Her research interests are: intelligent tutoring systems, multi-agent systems, distance education, and affective computing.

Pedro Pablo Sánchez-Villalón got his MA in English language philology at the Universidad Complutense de Madrid, Spain, in 1980. He is preparing his doctoral thesis on e-Learning. He is professor of English language at the Escuela Oficial de Idiomas in Ciudad Real. He belongs to the CHICO Research Group at the Universidad de Casilla La Mancha. His research focuses on computers in education, e-learning, ubiquitous computing, and Web applications. He also trains university teachers and lecturers to write their research papers in English and to use the information and communication technologies in education.

Alan R. White is a professor in the Department of Biological Sciences and dean of the College of Science and Mathematics at North Dakota State University, USA. Dr. White's plant cell biology research interests include the structure of plant cell walls, the synthesis of cell wall polysaccharides, and the structure and functional organization of Golgi membranes in plant cells. His interests in cell biology are also channeled into the development of the Virtual Cell, a virtual environment for teaching cell biology.

Beverly Woolf is an associate research professor in computer science at the University of Massachusetts, USA. She has a PhD in computer science and a doctorate in education and is a leader in the area of intelligent multimedia tutoring systems, collaborating on multidisciplinary research projects to model, individualize, and improve learning. Multimedia and knowledge about the user, domain, and dialogue are used to produce real-time performance support and on-demand advice. The systems have been deployed and evaluated in academic and industrial environments, and demonstrated at more than 50 sites and 11 foreign countries. Dr. Woolf is a fellow of the American Association of Artificial Intelligence.

Wanlei Zhou received BEng and MEng degrees from Harbin Institute of Technology, Harbin, China (1982 and 1984, respectively), and his PhD from The Australian National University, Canberra, Australia (1991). He is currently the chair professor of IT and the head in School of Information Technology, Deakin University, Melbourne, Australia. Before joining Deakin University, Professor Zhou had been a programmer in Apollo/HP in Massachusetts, USA, a chief software engineer in HighTech Computers in Sydney, Australia, a lecturer in National University of Singapore, Singapore, and a lecturer at Monash University, Melbourne, Australia. His research interests include theory and practical issues of building distributed systems, Internet computing and security, and e-learning. Professor Zhou is a member of the IEEE and IEEE Computer Society.

Index

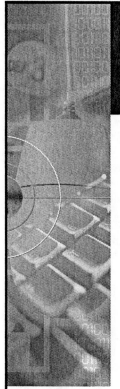